Information and
Communication in Economics

Recent Economic Thought Series

Editor:

Warren J. Samuels; Michigan State University; East Lansing, Michigan, U.S.A.

Other books in the series:

Feiwel, G., *Samuelson and Neoclassical Economics*
Wade, L., *Political Economy: Modern Views*
Jarsulic, M., *Money and Macro Policy*
Samuelson, L., *Microeconomic Theory*
Mirowski, P., *The Reconstruction of Economic Theory*
Lowry, Todd, *Pre-classical Political Economy*
Officer, L., *International Economics*
Asimakopulos, A., *Theories of Income Distribution*
Earl, P., *Psychological Economics; Development, Tensions, Prospects*
Thweatt, W., *Classical Political Economy*
Peterson, W., *Market Power and the Economy*
DeGregori, T., *Development Economics*
Nowotny, K., *Public Utility Regulation*
Horowitz, I., *Organization and Decision Theory*
Hennings, K. and Samuels, W., *Neoclassical Economic Theory, 1870 to 1930*
Samuels, W., *Economics as Discourse*
Lutz, M., *Social Economics*
Weimer, D., *Policy Analysis and Economics*
Bromley, D. and Segerson, K., *The Social Response to Environmental Risk*
Roberts, B. and Feiner, S., *Radical Economics*
Mercuro, N., *Taking Property and Just Compensation*
de Marchi, N., *Post-popperian Methodology of Economics*
Gapinski, J., *The Economics of Saving*
Darity, W., *Labor Economics: Problems in Analyzing Labor Markets*
Caldwell, B. and Boehm, S., *Austrian Economics: Tensions and Directions*
Tool, Marc R., *Institutional Economics: Theory, Method, Policy*

Information and Communication in Economics

edited by

Robert E. Babe
University of Ottawa

Kluwer Academic Publishers
Boston/Dordrecht/London

Distributors for North America:
Kluwer Academic Publishers
101 Philip Drive
Assinippi Park
Norwell, Massachusetts 02061 USA

Distributors for all other countries:
Kluwer Academic Publishers Group
Distribution Centre
Post Office Box 322
3300 AH Dordrecht, THE NETHERLANDS

Library of Congress Cataloging-in-Publication Data

Information and communication in economics / edited by Robert E. Babe.
    p. cm.—(Recent economic thought series)
  Includes bibliographical references and index.
  ISBN 0-7923-9358-9
  1. Information technology—Economic aspects.
  2. Communication.
I. Babe, Robert E. II. Series.
HC79.I55515357 1993
330'.041—dc20   93-13259
                                                                    CIP

Copyright © 1994 by Kluwer Academic Publishers

All rights reserved. No part of this publication may be reproduced, stored in a retrieval system or transmitted in any form or by any means, mechanical, photo-copying, recording, or otherwise, without the prior written permission of the publisher, Kluwer Academic Publishers, 101 Philip Drive, Assinippi Park, Norwell, Massachusetts 02061

Printed on acid-free paper.

Printed in the United States of America

Contents

Preface ix
Robert E. Babe

1
The Information Economy Revisited 1
D. McL. Lamberton

Commentary by Gilles Paquet 34

2
The Place of Information in Economics 41
Robert E. Babe

3
Commodities as Sign-systems 69
Ian Parker

Commentary by Sandra Braman 92

4
The Political Economy of Communication: Lessons from the Founders 105
Vincent Mosco

5
Economic Theory: Rhetoric, Reality, Rationalization 125
Walter Adams/James W. Brock

Commentary by Herbert I. Schiller 138

6
The Political Economy of Communications Research 147
William J. Buxton

7
All the Editorials Fit to Print: The Politics of "Newsworthiness" — 177
Edward S. Herman

Commentary by Gertrude J. Robinson — 200
Reply by Edward S. Herman — 208

8
The Information Economy in a Spatial Context: City-states in a Global Village — 211
Mark Hepworth

Commentary by Nicholas Garnham — 229

9
The Emerging Mass Media Environment — 233
Barry R. Litman/Scott Sochay

Commentary by Gilles Paquet — 269
Commentary by Nicholas Garnham — 274

10
Application of Neoclassical Economics to African Development: a Curse in Disguise — 281
Bernard Z. Dasah

11
Communication, Information, and Transnational Enterprise — 293
Jill Hills

12
Communications and Economics — 321
James W. Carey

Index — 337

Contributing Authors

Walter Adams
Department of Economics
Michigan State University
East Lansing, Michigan
48824 U.S.A.

Robert E. Babe
Department of Communication
University of Ottawa
Ottawa, Ontario
K1N 6N5 Canada

Sandra Braman
Institute of Communications
 Research
College of Communications
University of Illinois at Urbana-
 Champaign
Champaign, Illinois
61820 U.S.A.

James W. Brock
Department of Economics
Miami University
Oxford, Ohio
45056 U.S.A.

William J. Buxton
Department of Communication
 Studies
Concordia University
7141 Sherbrooke Street West
Montreal, Quebec
H4B 1R6 Canada

James W. Carey
College of Communications
University of Illinois at Urbana-
 Champaign
Champaign, Illinois
61820 U.S.A.

Bernard Z. Dasah
Graduate Program in
 Communications
McGill University
3465 Peel Street
Montreal, Quebec
H3A 1W7 Canada

Nicholas Garnham
Centre for Communication and
   Information Studies
University of Westminster
235 High Holborn Street
London
WC1V 7DN U.K.

Mark Hepworth
Public Policy Research Unit
Department of Political Studies
University of London
London
E1 4NS U.K.

Edward S. Herman
Finance Department
Wharton School
University of Pennsylvania
Philadelphia, Pennsylvania
19104-6367 U.S.A.

Jill Hills
Department of Social Sciences
City University
Northampton Square
London
EC1V OHB U.K.

Donald Lamberton
Urban Research Program
Research School of Social
   Sciences and Pacific Studies
The Australian National University
GPO Box 4
Canberra, ACT
2601 Australia

Barry R. Litman
Department of Telecommunication
Michigan State University
East Lansing, Michigan
48824 U.S.A.

Vincent Mosco
School of Journalism and Mass
   Communication
Carleton University
Ottawa, Ontario
K1S 5B6 Canada

Gilles Paquet
Faculty of Administration
University of Ottawa
Ottawa, Ontario
K1N 6N5 Canada

Ian Parker
Department of Economics
Scarborough Campus
University of Toronto
1265 Military Trail
Scarborough, Ontario
M1C 1A4 Canada

Gertrude J. Robinson
Graduate Program in
   Communications
McGill University
3465 Peel Street
Montreal, Quebec
H3A 1W7

Herbert I. Schiller
Department of Communication
University of California, San Diego
La Jolla, California
92093 U.S.A.

Scott Sochay
Department of Telecommunication
Michigan State University
East Lansing, Michigan
48824 U.S.A.

Preface
Robert E. Babe

Information and communication have long been recognized as central to economic processes. Until recent decades, however, neoclassical economics had all but avoided studying information and communication, assuming rather the existence of perfect knowledge. F. A. Hayek, for instance, explained that prices are "quantitative indices (or 'values')" which summarize the significance of each scarce resource or commodity relative to all others. Confronted with an array of market prices, he continued, autonomous agents adjust strategies to maximize wealth, profit or utility "without having to solve the whole puzzle *ab initio*" (Hayek, 1945, p. 525).

Since particularly the 1960's, however, mainstream economics has paid increasing, albeit circumscribed, attention to information. As detailed in chapter 2, three main lines of inquiry are evident: 1) Stigler (1961) and Marshak (1968) pioneered analyses of information as the lessening of market uncertainty, a theme continued and expanded upon by others, indeed to such an extent that Kenneth Arrow in no uncertain terms once declared: "The meaning of information is precisely a reduction in uncertainty" (Arrow, 1979, p. 307). Related studies emphasized the coordination function of information, whether in the economy at large or within firms and organizations. 2) At the macroscopic level Machlup (1962) and Porat (1977) constructed time series measuring the size and relative importance of an information-related sector of the U.S. economy since the turn of the century, contending that there had been remarkable relative as well as absolute growth in the information sector (See D. McL. Lamberton's chapter in this volume.) 3) In yet other instances neoclassical economists have down played any particular uniqueness to the information sector (Globerman, 1983), satisfied that externalities and the public good aspect of information are not of sufficient importance to cause "market failure," meaning that information can be treated by economists as any other commodity, and that traditional analytical methods can be applied with equanimity to firms and industries producing information for sale.

This book, in part, disputes what may be seen as a highly reductionist stance toward information/communication on the part of neoclassicism: Why is information only a *lessening* of uncertainty? Surely news of a hurricane *increases* uncertainty in the larger sense than merely answering "Will it be rainy tomorrow?" Nor do discoveries, inventions, public relations, propaganda, advertising, music and the arts or language itself fit well the neoclassical paradigm. Sandra Braman (1989) has postulated four hierarchic conceptualizations of information, only one of which (information as commodity) aligns with the neoclassical approach, and of which the highest (information as constitutive force in society) would encompass even neoclassical economics as part of the knowledge/ideological/cultural system within which markets for commodities take on shape and slope. (See herein the Adams/Brock chapter and commentary by Herbert Schiller.)

By contrast, institutional economists—prototypically Thorstein Veblen, Harold Innis and Kenneth Boulding—have adopted more expansive conceptions of information and communication. Veblen (1909) perceived institutions as "habits of thought"; for him changes in "habits of thought" or institutions are intrinsic to social/economic/cultural change since successive generations of individuals differ little in intellectual capacity or in instinctual propensity, whereas ways of seeing, or habits of thought, can and do undergo cumulative change. Through his definition of institution, then, Veblen interleaved the symbolic, the economic and the communicatory. Likewise in *The Theory of the Leisure Class* he pioneered an embryonic analysis of the symbolic or communicatory properties of consumer goods, a topic increasingly of interest to cultural anthropologists as well as to institutional economists, but seldom tackled by mainstream economists, quite possibly because of the threat such analyses pose for neoclassicism. (See Ian Parker's chapter in this volume.)

Harold Adams Innis, a Canadian economic historian, addressed information/communication directly in his final two books, *The Bias of Communication* (1951) and *Empire and Communications* (1950). There he contended that media are central to the economic/cultural life and development of every society. He maintained that each mode of communication is "biased," in terms either of time or space, thereby helping extend power and control either through time (traditional cultures), or over geographic expanse (modern cultures). Media that are recalcitrant to work with (for example, stone or clay tablets), those that have low storage capacity, and those that are durable and difficult to transport, Innis termed "time-binding," and are characteristically employed by cultures more intent on conserving stocks of knowledge (due to limited capacity for storage) than on developing new knowledge. Lighter, less recalcitrant and less durable media (for example paper and radio), he termed "space-biased"; they are ideally suited to administering empires over space. Consequently, they are also erosive of local cultures. Space-bound cultures, dependent upon and devolving from space-binding media, are oriented toward change rather than continuity, toward regional and global interactions as opposed to local ones; toward secular institutions instead of the sacred; and to technical, instrumental knowledge as opposed to humanities and mystical knowledge. Several chapters in this volume deal with aspects of the internationalization of cultures and economies as enabled by new media. (See particularly those by Vincent Mosco, Mark Hepworth, Barry Litman/Scott Sochay, Bernard Dasah and Jill Hills.) Innis believed, however that stable society is possible only when space and time-biased media balance one another so as to ensure also a balance between secular and moral authority. To both Mosco and Dasah, as well as James W. Carey, all in this volume, neoclassical economics itself is an amoral, space-binding "medium" of communication; hence these authors make a 'plea for time."

A third institutionalist, Kenneth Boulding, has probably done more than any other to expound upon the dynamic interrelations between information/knowledge on the one hand and society/economy on the other. By substituting the triad know-how, energy and matter for the traditional land, labor, capital as basic factors of production, Boulding contends that similarities become evident in developmental processes of biological, societal and physical systems. He writes:

> Production, whether of the chicken from the egg or a house from a blueprint, involves three essential factors: know-how, energy, and materials. Genetic structure or *know-how*, whether this is coded in DNA patterns of the biological genes or in human knowledge and the blueprints of the production of human artifacts, must be able to direct *energy*, to sustain appropriate temperatures, and to transport and transform selected *materials* into the improbable structures of the phenotype (the chicken or the automobile). (Boulding, 1978, p. 12).

For Boulding, only "know-how" or its equivalent in the form of improbable structures, grows or evolves, making therefore knowledge crucial for evolutionary theory and economic dynamics. Whereas matter and energy are subject to the law of conservation (neither can be created or destroyed) and to the law of entropy (continued degradation from useable to nonuseable or less complex forms), information and knowledge, alone of the basic factors of production as set forth by Boulding, can increase and be negentropic. Boulding writes: "It is a powerful and accurate metaphor to see the whole evolutionary process from the beginning of the universe as process in the increase of knowledge or the information structure" (Boulding, 1978, p. 33).

For political economists, positing information/knowledge at the very center of the evolutionary process raises questions concerning the distribution of this knowledge, of this power to direct societal development. Indeed, institutionalists such as Horace Gray and J. K. Galbraith view institutions as centers of power, as opposed to mere economizers of informational/transactions costs, as neoclassicists contend (Coase, 1937; Arrow, 1974). Informational institutions, then, in the institutionalist view, do not merely produce informational commodities; they also produce consciousness, society-wide modes of perception, and cultures. (See chapters by Edward S. Herman and William Buxton in this volume.) Far from adopting the neoclassicists' reductionist conceptualization of information/communication, institutionalists/political economists then adopt a more comprehensive conceptualization. Whereas neoclassicists treat information as mere commodity (either satisfying preexisting wants, or reducing uncertainty in the sale or acquisition or production of other commodities), institutionalists/political economists perceive information's commodity aspect to be merely the tip of the iceberg; information for them lies at the very heart of social, cultural, political and economic change.

The fundamental question addressed by this book, then, may be stated as follows:

> What difference does an expansive, as opposed to reductionist, definition or conception of information make in terms of both economic analysis and public policy?

In this context a number of subsidiary objectives are addressed, including:

- The integration of economic analysis and communication studies through expansive conceptualizations of information/communications (i.e. institutionalist analysis or political economy).
- Application of an expansive conception of information to sectors producing, diffusing and storing information.

- Demonstration of endemic limitations of neoclassicism in its treatment of information/communication, having the effect of favoring the powerful (i.e. those with economic and communicatory power).
- Demonstration of the importance of the configuration of telecommunications systems in distributing economic/political power, both domestically and internationally.

This volume draws on a range of scholarship: from "radical" to liberal antitrust; from theoretical to concrete; from impassioned to dispassionate; from scholars working within economics departments to political economists and cultural theorists placed in communication departments. It is hoped that this range of scholarship, while doctrinally diverse in important respects, will as a whole make the case for an expansive as opposed to reductionist conceptualization of information/communication for economic analyses in the future.

In this volume's introductory chapter, D. McL. Lamberton, an early pioneer in the field of information economics, surveys the historical development and present status of orthodox economics' treatments of information/communication. While Professor Lamberton, as evidenced by his proposed research agenda, remains optimistic that traditional economic theory and orthodox empirical studies can incorporate information/communication in consistent and useful ways, less sanguine are authors of ensuing chapters.

In chapters 2 and 3 for instance, Robert Babe and Ian Parker respectively argue that neoclassicism has reached an impasse on account of its commodity—only treatment of information. Both argue that the time has come to explore much more deeply than hitherto implications for economic theory and analysis of incorporating broader conceptualizations of information, and of acknowledging the message/communicatory properties of traditional commodities, quite reversing neoclassical practice. Since communicatory interaction, by definition, entails influence by message senders on recipients, these proposals entail in essence also the supercession of mere economics by political economy.

In chapter 4 Vincent Mosco also, albeit on other grounds, argues for the restoration to predominance of political economy, claiming informational/communicatory processes raise profound questions of moral philosophy, considerations incorporated fully in by gone years by the discipline's founders (Adam Smith, David Ricardo, Thomas Malthus, Karl Marx and others), but since the turn of the century at least broadly ignored by mainstream economics.

Authors of chapters 5 through 7 next provide diverse political economy treatments of informational/communicatory phenomena. The Adams/ Brock chapter (chapter 6) is noteworthy for exposing rhetorical, even apologetic characteristics of neoclassicism. Through careful selection of topics and through circular logic, neoclassicism affects popular and academic perceptions regarding the nature of economic activity, and does this in a way so as to benefit the richest and most powerful. Neoclassicism itself, then, as communicatory discourse, is a topic for political economy analyses, an immensely important idea pursued yet further by Herbert Schiller in commentary.

In chapter 6 William Buxton documents the influence in the 1930s of one rich and powerful interest, the Rockefeller Foundation, in limiting the range of discourse for a then-emerging discipline, namely communication studies, a discipline it may be added that has profound policy (and hence political economy) implications.

In chapter 7 Edward S. Herman explores dimensions of the propaganda model whereby mass media of communication are held to be instruments of domination and control, particularly in "democratic" societies where physical coercion is not the norm. By comparing recent U.S. press coverage on El Salvador with that on Cuba, Herman provides empirical support for the propaganda model.

The next four chapters each touch on international implications of the "information revolution." Mark Hepworth in chapter 8 notes heightened importance for metropolitan areas coupled with reduced sovereignty for nation states, both trends resulting from the proliferation of information and communication technologies. He maintains that "city states" increasingly vie with one another to host transnational business but concludes that this intense competition is not entirely benign.

Barry Litman/Scott Sochay (chapter 9) describe and evaluate globalization as it impacts on corporate media structures, particularly conglomeration and transnationalization, while in chapter 10 Bernard Dasah asserts that neoclassicism is granted too much credence by international agencies such as the World Bank and the International Monetary fund, whose "structural adjustment" programs imposed on Third World countries disregard important indigenous cultural (communicatory) aspects of economic interchange, needlessly thereby imposing disruption and hardship.

In chapter 11 Jill Hills addresses transnational control aspects of communication technologies, again in the context of globalization, remarking also on national governments' role in augmenting transnational corporate power through deregulatory and privatization schemes. She notes these trends, both domestically and internationally, also accentuate the precedence afforded corporate information flows and private communication networks at the expense of public communications—trends she has termed "the real politique of the New World Order."

The evocative concluding essay by James W. Carey, was undertaken initially as commentary for chapters 10 and 11, but developed into a chapter in its own right. Perceiving an "urgency of the inquiry into economics and communications," Professor Carey nonetheless concludes that integration by single, consistent framework of these two disciplines and modes of human interaction is impossible. Rather, he advises, the framework we should seek is one of difference, of countervailing power whereby "the phenomena of communications contain and control economics in the name of public life and discourse, and, on the contrary, economics permits a sphere of private life and action."

Appreciation is extended to Warren J. Samuels, general editor of Kluwer's series on Recent Economic Thought, for inviting a book proposal on information and communication in economics, and to Zachary Rolnik, general editor at Kluwer, for seeing that the proposal was accepted. In addition to the chapter authors listed above I would also like to extend my appreciation to the book's commentators—Gilles Paquet, Sandra Braman, Herbert Schiller, Gertrude Robinson and Nicholas Garnham.

References

Arrow, K. (1974). *The Limits of Organization*. New York: Norton.
Arrow, K. (1979). "The Economics of Information." In Michael Dertuouzos and Joël Moses (eds.). *The Computer Age: A Twenty-Year View*. Cambridge, Mass.: MIT Press. pp. 306–317.
Braman, S. (1989). "Defining Information: An Approach for Policymakers." *Telecommunications Policy*, September, pp. 233–242.
Boulding, K. E. (1978). *Ecodynamics: A New Theory of Societal Evolution*. Beverly Hills, CA: Sage Publications.
Coase, R. (1937). "The Nature of the Firm." *Economica* 4:386–405.
Globerman, S. (1983). *Cultural Regulation in Canada*. Montreal: Institute for Research on Public Policy.
Hayek, F. A. (1945). "The Use of Knowledge in Society." *The American Economic Review* 35(4):519–530.
Innis, H. A. (1950). *Empire and Communications*. Toronto: University of Toronto Press.
Innis, H. A. (1951). *The Bias of Communication*. Toronto: University of Toronto Press.

Machlup, F. (1962). *The Production and Distribution of Knowledge in the United States*. Princeton, N.J.: Princeton University Press.

Marshak, J. (1968). "Economics of Inquiring, Communicating, Deciding." *American Economic Review* 58(2):1–18.

Porat, M. (1977). *The Information Economy*. Washington, D.C.: U.S. Government Printing Office.

Stigler, G. (1961). "The Economics of Information." *Journal of Political Economy* 69(3):213–225.

Veblen, T. (1909). "The Limitations of Marginal Utility." *Journal of Political Economy* 17(9):620–636.

Veblen, T. (1899). *The Theory of the Leisure Class*. N.Y.: Macillan.

Information and
Communication in Economics

1 THE INFORMATION ECONOMY REVISITED

D. McL. Lamberton

Introduction

Attempts to characterize our contemporary world have yielded both complex concepts like post-industrial society and the information economy, and attributions of a dominant role to specific change agents, for example, the clock, the telephone and, more recently, information technology (OECD, 1992). The complexity of reality is acknowledged in this modelling. Rosegger, for example, wrote:

> Even a careful reader has difficulty synthesizing some common elements from the many facets proposed for post-industrial society, but I take it that they include at the least the following: the accumulation of knowledge in place of the accumulation of physical capital; innovations that improve the "quality of life" rather than innovations that further increase real output; the growth of services, especially in the communications and leisure-time industries, in place of growth in manufacturing and related activities; the development of technological and administrative fixes for social problems; and an attenuation of the work ethic and other bourgeois values (1990, p. 31).

And with a sharper sense of immediacy, *The New York Times* asked on December 31, 1989 which strand from the 1980s was dominant. Was it the Age of Revolution reflecting the thunderous transformation of Eastern Europe; or the Age of Greed with US society condoning the rise of great fortunes and the homeless sleeping in doorways. They settled for the 1980s as the Age of Speed: When Information Accelerated, marvelling at the fax machine, VCRs and MTV:

> The 1980's now bequeath to the 1990's their exhilaration and their acceleration—and, lest anyone forget, their relentless miseries. The poor. The addicted. The uneducated. As this decade was shaped by decades past, so will it shape the next (p. 10 E).

How does such thinking relate to modelling of the economy? First and foremost we must accept that economic activity is a process, its participants having both histories and contexts. The actors on the economic stage have limited information, facing uncertainty "about which pregiven state will obtain, but also about which states are possible" (Langlois, 1986, p. 228). Progress lies in learning, storing information and using it selectively and effectively. As Lionel Robbins observed:

> In the last analysis the difference between the economic potential of the Stone Age and the twentieth century is a difference of range of relevant technique and information (1968, p. 83).

From this perspective we can view economic development as the increasing complexity of economic systems, "the costs of processing, transmitting and storing information have by now taken over the role ... that transportation costs played for so long" (Leijonhufvud, p. 165). Even such a basic notion as comparative advantage has had to be updated. It no longer resides in natural resources, climate, location, nearness to raw materials and markets. Now that information costs account for the greater part of resource use in the economy, comparative advantage has become a matter of labour skills, technology and management, with the latter increasingly concerned with control, coordination and innovation.

But here too we must not overlook equity considerations. Those who argue the importance of IT imperatives should ask whether information justice is achievable while, more than a century after Alexander Graham Bell received his telephone patent—considered the most valuable patent ever issued in the United States—and almost a half century after Arthur Clarke's seminal paper on satellite communication, half the world's population is said by the UN telecommunications organization, the International Telecommunication Union, to be more than two hours walking distance from the nearest telephone (Butler, 1988, p. 1).

Information Economy and Economic Thought

From Neglect to Centre Stage

The neglect of information and knowledge in the history of economic thought is generally accepted. According to Robbins, Edwin Cannan attributed neglect "partly to a shrinking from platitude, partly to a certain peculiarity in the treatment of the subject by Adam Smith [He subsumed it under a general view of the advantages of the division of labour] . . . and partly to the fact that knowledge is often a free good and [in Cannan's words] 'economists have generally been inclined to neglect things of no value, however important they may be'" (p. 83). Robbins went on to assert that

> It is just not true that the economic thought of the past was unaware of the relevance to development of technical or other forms of knowledge or that there is lacking in the literature conspicuous emphasis on its importance (p. 83).

He makes a good case by examining the work of a number of contributors starting with Bacon and including Babbage, Rae, Charles Knight, McCulloch and Senior. Quite clearly they were aware of the importance of knowledge to the processes of economic development. What he failed to do was to attempt to make a case for knowledge production, its diffusion and utilization being endogenous, as an integral part of the economic system. Perhaps an economics of a less mechanistic kind might have emerged had its practitioners recognized the limited capabilities of individuals for observing, recording, processing and analyzing information and tried to grapple with the intricacies of human communication.

As early as 1921 Frank Knight wrote about "the most thoroughgoing methods of dealing with uncertainty, i.e., by securing better knowledge of and control over the future" (p. 260). Control of the future and increased power of prediction were, he believed, "closely interrelated, since the chief practical significance of knowledge is control, and both are closely identified with the general progress of civilization, the improvement of technology and the increase of knowledge" (p. 239). "Information" he saw as "one of the principal commodities" supplied by economic organization (p. 261). He observed an information industry including market associations, trade journals, statistical bureaus, advertising and a "veritable swarming of experts and consultants in nearly every department of industrial life" (p. 262). Curiously, he then dismissed what he had observed as "merely the objective of all rational conduct" (p. 260), without exploring the cost and resource allocation implications.

At the present time we can find some (e.g., Shin) deploring, not the banishing of information to the world of footnotes as Knight effectively did, but the occupying of centre stage by information issues. To the extent that this is true, there is an excessively sharp focus on the economics of asymmetric information; a focus so sharp that it is often equated with information economics.

There are, fortunately, signs of change. Cremer and Khalil (1992) investigate information gathering before signing a contract. Their central proposition is that "the fundamental asymmetry lies in the ability to acquire information" (p. 566). This leads them to draw the distinction between asymmetry of information and asymmetry in the ability to gather information. This is a move in the right direction, but it must be taken much further. What of asymmetry in the ability to use information? We will suggest later that a capability concept is needed, that it links with organizational aspects and has implications for growth.

The growth of the influence of rational expectations theory, which I have called the economics of limited foresight (Lamberton, 1992a) has further restricted the analytical treatment of the role of information. The actors on the economic stage are said to form their expectations rationally, i.e., they make the most of the information that is available to them. "But cognition, computation, and information have costs; they do not just subsist in some immaterial effluvium. We are, after all, only human" (Cherniak, p. 3). These activities are part of the economic process; the availability of information *now* is a consequence of earlier investment decisions and decisions might be delayed while further investment in information is undertaken. Likewise, the capability of using the information depends upon prior learning and organizational capital. Perhaps these inadequacies will in time lead to less aggregative, less ambitious theory that absorbs some of what information economics has to offer.

Perusal of the latest issue of the *Journal of Economic Literature* does not really support the centre stage claim. Amongst the articles, the economics of managing of necessity treats the decentralization of information processing and the decentralization of information (pp. 1382–1415). Information asymmetries are essential to the Schumpeterian process of innovation (p. 1420). Informational or organizational imperfections as part of the structure of the labour market help produce unemployment (p. 1480).

In the book reviews there is an echo of G. B. Richardson's neglected book, *Information and Investment* (1960 but recently reissued) in a conclusion that "the assumption that firms can buy information in increments of any size and that they will do so at the moment when its value exceeds its theoretical cost is appealing but may not reflect the unfolding dynamics of information acquisition and its use within firms" (Yates).

The Annotated Listing of New Books under Information and Uncertainty has four items focussing on decision theory and there is a similar emphasis in the coverage of the Subject Index of Articles in Current Periodicals with Selected Abstracts (pp. 178-4). Classification systems do, however, conceal what we are seeking. Many of the other categories, e.g., Industrial Organization; Economic Development, Technological Change, and Growth, have items contributing to or bearing upon the role of information in the economy. Nevertheless, a literature search for contributions on "the information economy" would produce little or nothing.

The Emergence of Information Economics

Elsewhere (Lamberton, 1978, 1984) I have traced the emergence of information economics, attributing it to a combination of circumstances: recognition of the deficiencies of economic theory that rested on unrealistic assumptions about the richness and sureness of the information available to decision-makers, reactions to failures of government and business policies, and the spectacular advent of intelligent electronics with its greatly enhanced capacities for communication, computation and control.

There is always room for disagreement about which are the important contributions in the emergence of a new sub-discipline and, in any case, it is difficult to separate those that provoked the new developments by overzealous statements of the old theories, by asking questions or by making suggestive comments, from those who contributed directly to the new statements. All these were participants in the process which I must view in terms of my own learning experience. With hindsight, the most important names in the emergence phase are Knight, Hayek, Boulding, Marschak, Shackle, Machlup, Simon, and Arrow. Their work spans the half century from 1921 until 1971 when the first anthology on information economics (Lamberton, 1971) was published.

The contributions of Marschak and Machlup complemented each other and set the stage for much of the theoretical and empirical work that followed. Each sought answers to questions that were to become central concerns in information economics. Building on his interest in and earlier work on expected utility theory, statistical decision theory, and subjective probability theory, Marschak probed the importance for economic behaviour of anticipating information. From this beginning, he wrote his

"Towards an Economic Theory of Organization and Information" (1954), "Remarks on the Economics of Information" (1959) and "Economics of Inquiring, Communicating, Deciding" (1968). These papers are available in Marschak (1974).

The notion of optimality was central to his thinking, the value of information depending upon the benefits that would flow from its use. But the unbundling process was now underway: the component activities of inquiring, communicating and deciding were distinguished as were the limitations on the transmission of information. Henceforth, information had to be regarded as costly.

Machlup's research had studied separate components of the economic information system: markets, the patent system, education, and policy. Seeing both the common element of the role of information and the interdependence between components, he developed the notion of the knowledge industry. Its role was so pervasive that it could be analyzed only within the framework of national accounting but the conventional national accounting did not meet his needs. From this came his pioneering work, *The Production and Distribution of Knowledge in the United States* in 1962. Marschak had speculated that the cost of thinking was formidable; Machlup told us that it was 29 percent of GNP. His later work (e.g., Machlup, 1980, 1982, 1984) provided a rich statistical account of information activities and (with Machlup and Mansfield, 1983) profound insight into the methodological and philosophical implications. Together these contributions inspired a series of comparative studies (e.g., OECD, 1981; Jussawalla, Lamberton and Karunaratne, 1988; Lee and Gomez, 1992).

The National Accounting Initiative

The national accounting initiative had as its original objective the assessment of the importance of information and information activities in the economy, or in Machlup's terminology the role of the knowledge industry. While a summary statistic like 29 percent of GNP had a certain shock value, when set against mainstream theory with its assumption of perfect knowledge which, strictly interpreted, led to the conclusion that such information activities were zero percent, the opportunity to use the rearranged national accounting data to study structural relationships and the process of growth was created.

National accounting data were rearranged to provide the first of two basic measures of information activity in the economy: the primary infor-

Table 1−1. Primary Information Sectors % GDP (Factor Cost)

	1970s
Australia	36
United States	24
Singapore	24
United Kingdom	22
France	19
Japan	19
New Zealand	19
Sweden	17
Malaysia	16
Fiji	15
Philippines	13
Papua New Guinea	11
Venezuela	10
Thailand	10

* Data do not relate to the same year so furnish only a broad comparison.
Source: OECD, 1986; Jussawalla *et al*.; Lamberton, 1987; M. Rubin (Personal communication).

mation sector, i.e., traded information goods and services, contribution to gross domestic product. The underlying idea is that the goods or services included must intrinsically convey information, or be directly useful in producing, processing or distributing information (OECD, 1986, p. 25). Table 1–1 shows the contribution to GDP for a number of countries. The diversity is apparent and raises questions of both methodology and interpretation.

The definition left room for considerable argument and there are many measurement problems. Wellenius (1988) made some cogent remarks. The accounting categories are highly aggregate, with a category like transport and communication lumping together all forms of transport, telecommunications, postal services, media and even publishing. Disaggregation is possible but costly. A second problem arises from the recorded diversity. Table 1–1 indicates that the primary sector contribution is greater in industrial and newly industrializing countries but it also poses some puzzles about the extent to which some countries are information-intensive. Is Australia twice as information-intensive as Sweden? And is Sweden comparable to Malaysia? There are also some important theoretical aspects to be considered. Assume that the information sector exhibits larger than average scale economies—a matter we shall return to when we consider growth theory—and it would appear that a high contribution to GDP would point to a small economy rather than an advanced one. In general, this measure may not be related to either efficiency or modernization. Wellenius concluded with a plea for better measurement, adding that

> a better defined sector concept will help reduce confusion in information economics between information as commodity, resource, and relationship, between information and telecommunication, and between telecommunication services and specific technologies used to realize them (p. xii).

Misinterpretation has reflected some of these issues and at times amounted to a rerun of the misuse of national R&D statistics. Vested interests had been able to misuse the R&D statistic as a means of pleading their case for more funds, usually from government. Now it was the turn of the vested interests of the information sector—the new name for Machlup's knowledge industry—to plead for expansion of their sector as a means to general economic growth. In doing so they ignored the extent to which information activity, like R&D, was a consequence rather than a cause of growth; and they mostly pleaded their cases in terms of their own component parts of the information sector.

This facilitated "technology push." Information technology and especially telecommunications is perhaps the best known modern case and it was aided and abetted by the willingness of governments to use the mere creation of technology as evidence of the beneficial use of information. Evidence of "technology push" is of many kinds; first, there is investment expenditures. The American story is that information processing equipment as a percentage of all the durable equipment bought by private enterprise (excluding farms) increased from 11 percent in 1970 to 51 percent in 1989. Reporting this change, *The Economist* commented that corporate America "gorged itself on information technology.... Employees and information technology are companies' two biggest single expenditures. But the marriage of the two has proved most unproductive" (1991, p. 30).

Consider too a recent occasion: the Geneva 1991 World Telecommunication Exhibition and Forum, the latest in a 20-year series reflecting the growth of the telecommunications industry. The organizers judged it a great success, their criteria being the number of visitors, total expenditure of more than $US0.5 billion, the presence of the "stars of the industry"—ministers, chairmen and other top officials—and the writing of business "at a dizzying pace." But even the *Telecom 91 Daily* could see a down side: "inattention to the needs of developing countries," the absence of a "clear theme" and the 'technical pornography" (pp. 1, 70).

We find much the same mix of "technology push" and neglect of equity considerations if we look to the future with the cyberspace experts. The world they contemplate and seek, the ultimate human-computer interface, is to give access to "vast data bases that constitute the culture's deposited wealth, every document is available, every recording is playable, and every picture is viewable" (Benedikt, 1991, dust jacket). There are no economic resource constraints; corporate power is enhanced; sweatshops can exist in the man-made information jungle; and unlimited information access brings the Orwellian threat of total organization.

In an interesting way these future projections reflect some important features of the information economy that now exists. The underlying economic characteristics of information and the organizations that are created to use information, the combination of uncertainty, indivisibility and capital intensity, place limits on both markets and on organizations (Arrow, 1974). Because information can be a commodity to only a limited extent and because there are inherent economies of scale in its use (Arrow, 1984, p. 142), growth of the information-intensive economy has witnessed internalization of information activities. Simon (1991) argues that what goes on inside organizations is more important than what happens in markets.

While there is room for difference of opinion, it seems clear that any overall assessment of the importance of information activities and analysis of structural relationships must take these in-house activities into account. This has been done through the concept of the secondary information sector, to complement the primary information sector. It records the value added of information activities (employee compensation of information workers and capital consumption allowances of information equipment) used in producing non-information goods and services (OECD, 1986, p. 26).

Here again there are conceptual and measurement difficulties. In particular, the failure to exclude the non-information activities of the producers of information goods and services led to an element of overstatement. And in any case data for the secondary sector estimates were hard to come by and they required not only definition of "information goods and services" but also definition of "information workers." To these were added the familiar problems of capital consumption measurement, with added doubts about what constituted capital in these new information industries, which were themselves information-intensive, used machines

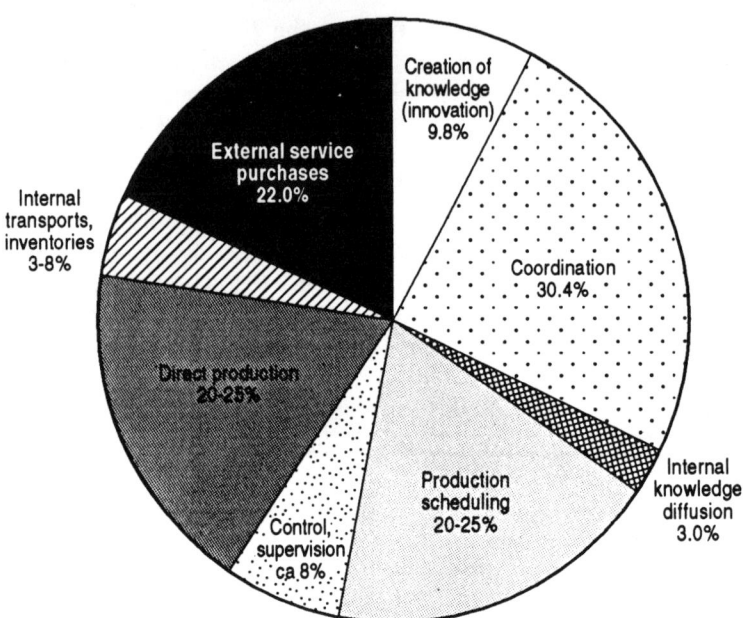

Figure 1. Distribution of Labor Costs on Functions
Large Swedish Manufacturing Firms—International Operations
Source: Eliasson et al., p. 68. External services purchases of 22 percent have been included, raising the total to 122 percent.

that became obsolete quickly, and needed software and organizational arrangements that did not fit easily with either business practice or taxation systems, let alone with the methods of economic researchers.

US data (OECD, 1986, pp. 18, 29) suggested the primary information sector accounted for almost a quarter of GDP at factor cost, which was very close to the overstated estimates for the secondary information sector. With the rough adjustment to make these additive, we might conclude that the aggregate measure was rather more than 40 percent. In appreciating the significance of this statistic, it is helpful to look at more micro data for a sample of large Swedish manufacturing firms (Eliasson et al. 1990). Figure 1 shows the distribution of labour costs on various functions for the 1986 worldwide operations of manufacturing firms with more than 200 employees. Note that the inclusion of external purchase of services raises the total to 122 percent.

This analysis by The Industrial Institute for Economic and Social Research, Stockholm, when expressed as percentages of total labour

Table 1-2. Typology of Information Occupations

INFORMATION PRODUCERS
  Scientific and technical workers
  Market search and co-ordination specialists
  Information gatherers
INFORMATION PROCESSORS
  Administrative and mangerial
  Process control and supervisory
  Clerical and related (components)
INFORMATION DISTRIBUTORS
  Educators
  Communication workers
INFORMATION INFRASTRUCTURE OCCUPATIONS
  Information machine workers
  Postal and telecommunications workers

costs, indicates the following: creation of new knowledge, 8 percent; coordination, 25 percent; internal knowledge transfer, 3 percent; external purchase of services, 18 percent; and goods manufacturing, 46 percent.

Employment Measures

The national accounting approach has been supplemented by and, as we noted above, has required statistics of the information workforce. These were created by defining information occupations as those primarily concerned with the creation and handling of information *per se* (OECD, 1986, p. 8). Table 1-2 shows the basic typology of occupations that has come into use. This approach has yielded the now-familiar graphs of the information economy employment, with all countries for which data have become available showing the upward trend indicative of increased information-intensity. There are many problems in such a statistical exercise so users must be tolerant; although they should note the implications of "primarily concerned" in the definition, as this means that changed degrees of specialization associated structural change as well as increased information-intensity is captured in this measurement.

It is difficult at times to reconcile the story in employment terms with the national accounting data. For example, in the Australian case 41.5 percent of the economically active workforce are officially reported to be in information occupations—although a careful analysis by Engelbrecht

(1985, p. 379) lowers this by almost 4 percentage points to allow for non-information workers in the primary information sector. The primary sector employs 43.5 percent of all information workers and accounts for 36 percent of GDP. The secondary sector employs the remaining 56.5 percent of information workers. There would seem to be scope for research into productivity patterns. Perhaps a recent report on "futzing," i.e., unproductive time spent tinkering with computer software, whether trying to get it to work, just playing, or wasting time at the computer, which was estimated to cost nearly 2 percent of GDP holds a clue! (*The Australian*, 1992, p. 34).

Information and Organization

Information Systems and Networks

The focus of much effort in information economics until the 1970s was market efficiency, and the central idea relating to information was that it improved market performance. It reduced uncertainty for the firm and for the consumer, both of whom could therefore make better decisions. This was basically the information-as-oil viewpoint. As lubricant, information was a minor albeit important aspect of the system. Its cost was not great and once a routine servicing arrangement had been set in place, little more thought had to be given to the matter. It had, of course, policy implications as we will see later on: the provision of information could be a form of policy intervention.

The measurement and analysis of the secondary information sector concerned the in-house provision of information services and the utilization of information. Here theoretical and managerial concerns appeared to converge. Following on from Marschak's 1954 paper, team theory attempted to address the role of organization—a team being an organization whose members have the same interests and beliefs but have different information. The issues are posed once we accept that there are gains from specialization by members, costs of communication, and potential economies of scale, scope and networking associated with at least some of the information activities involved.

This is not the place to review the extensive team theory literature that developed from the initial contributions. Instead I take the opportunity to suggest a shift of perspective on the interests-beliefs-information nexus. While it is always desirable to make simplifying assumptions for analytical purposes, we must be careful that in doing so we do not exclude the important relationships. In studying the processes of information activities, it is important to admit the possibilities that there are divergent interests and beliefs, flowing, for example, from different property rights, different histories, different experiences, and that these divergencies imply differences in information and differences in capabilities of using information.

Why is it important that we investigate these aspects of the information system? First, as mentioned earlier what goes on in organizations is important, in a quantitative sense, and this has very serious implications for economics:

> In sum, an organizational economy poses the questions of why the larger part of a modern economy's business is done by organizations, what role markets play in connecting these organizations with each other, and what role markets play in connecting organizations with consumers. Moreover, the boundary between markets and organizations varies greatly from one society to another and from one time to another. What mechanism maintains the highly fluid equilibrium between them? Until these questions are answered, it will be difficult to draw conclusions about the relative efficiencies of different forms of ownership and control of organizations, or the relative efficiency of markets versus central planning (Simon, 1991, p. 29).

Secondly, as the Swedish research findings made clear, even in manufacturing firms, information activities dominate the cost scene. To this we must add the destination of the output of information goods and services. This calls for a careful rearrangement of information sector accounts on a two-sector basis, i.e., production and information sectors, separating physical production or material processing operations from information handling and processing.

Jonscher's US data are summarized in Figure 2, which highlights some central features of the information sector. The most important of these features for our purposes here is that the bulk of the goods and services produced in the information sector are used in production activities rather than being consumed by households. It should be noted also that the information sector grew much more rapidly than the production sector; and that the most rapid growth rate recorded was that of the production sector's supply of goods and services to the information sector.

All this is consistent with Roach's historical sketch (1986) depicted in Figure 3 which points to the significant crossover when investment per worker in high-tech industries first exceeded that in basic industrial industries. It suggests that the firm's information activities need to be brought into sharp focus. In terms of theory the need is, as Arrow has pointed out, to change the assumptions made about the firm: it cannot

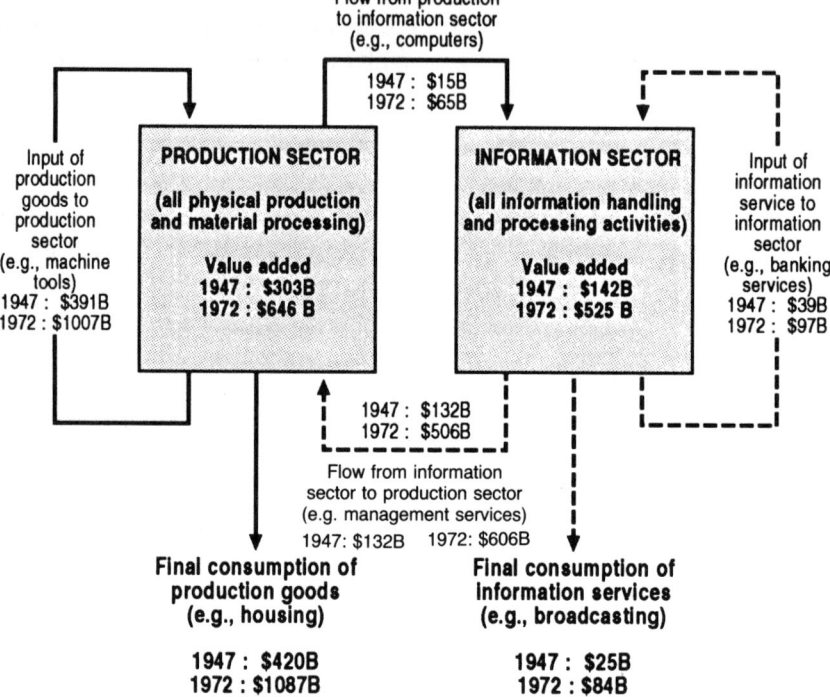

Figure 2. Two-Sector Model of the US Economy
Source: Jonscher, p. 17.

any longer be a point; it must be "an incompletely connected network of information flows" (1984, p. 147). And this network concept must be applied to the members of the team, the component participants in activities within the firm.

A necessary first step here is to replace the R&D concept with a much wider notion of exploratory activity (Lamberton, 1992b). A neglected contributor, E. R. Walker (1942, p. 94), noted that "A great proportion of actual behaviour in the real world, if businessmen are 'on the job,' must be experimental." We can identify many forms of exploratory behaviour with associated expenditures: e.g., organizational change, marketing, industrial intelligence, computing, employee training, risk assessment, competition and cooperation with other firms, and efforts to reduce the margins of error in regularly used sources of information. Much of this behaviour can be brought under the general heading of

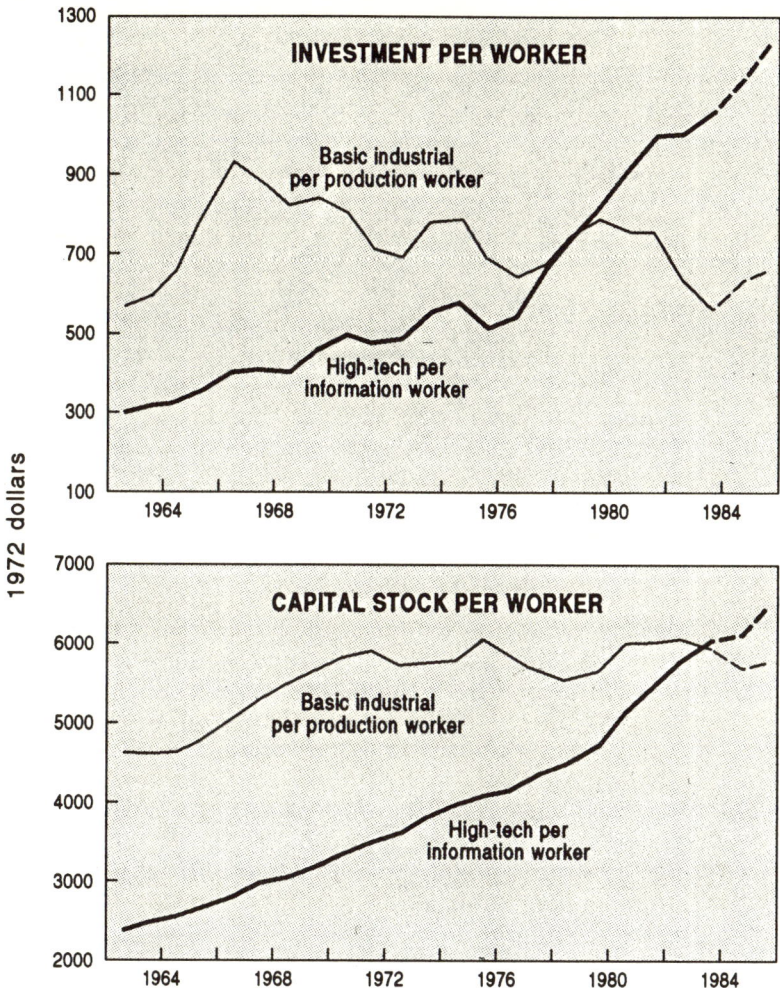

Figure 3. US Investment and Capital Stock per Worker
Source: Roach, p. 99.

business intelligence, which has been defined as the ability to acquire new information and knowledge, make judgements, adapt to the environment, develop new concepts and new strategies and act in a rational and effective way (Dedijer and Jéquier, 1987).

Information and Learning Systems

Recognizing that information is costly can be the starting point for the economics of internal organization or the economics of managing (Radner, 1992). Not only are networks to be seen as ways of handling the combination of specialization in monitoring the environment and collecting information with the distribution of information to the appropriate decision-makers through a communication system; they have also to take account of the limits to appropriability that are involved.

Success in business competition calls for the protecting and enhancing of firm-specific information. Rosegger (1991) distinguishes four major determinants of the rate at which a firm acquires technical knowledge:

1. The rate at which the firm produces new knowledge internally.
2. The rate at which the firm acquires public-goods type knowledge from its environment.
3. The rate at which the firm acquires other firms' proprietary knowledge.
4. The rate at which the firm generates new technical knowledge jointly with other firms.

But production and acquisition of information do not ensure effective utilization. They need to be complemented by learning processes. Here again a wider view is called for, wider than that provided by the "learning by doing" ideas that have slowly penetrated economics. A recent typology set out by Melerba (1992) holds promise:

1. Learning by doing, internal to the firm and related to production activity.
2. Learning by using, internal to the firm and related to the use of products, machinery and inputs.
3. Learning from advances in science and technology, external to the firm and related to the absorption of new developments in science and technology.
4. Learning from interindustry spillovers, external to the firm and related to what competitors and other firms in the industry are doing.
5. Learning by interacting, external to the firm and related either to the interaction with upstream or downstream sources of knowledge such as suppliers or users or to the cooperation with other firms in the industry.
6. Learning by searching, internal to the firm and related (mainly) to formalised activities (such as R&D) aimed at generating new knowledge (1992, p. 848).

The categories used by Malerba can be fitted together with those of Rosegger, but the Malerba contribution lies in the emphasis on learning and the diverse processes that may be involved.

Information acquisition goes on both internally and from external sources. It must be complemented by learning processes. It must be evaluated in terms of cost and appropriability. There is still a missing element: the essence of management which lies in corordination and control and here it seems useful to think, not of the learning firm or the learning organization, as so much management and organization studies literature has been doing, but rather of the learning manager. I recall the important notion that Shackle introduced to the discussion of decision theory, that of seriability (Lamberton, 1965, pp. 69, 191). It might help to treat the learning manager as the embodiment of a form of organizational capital, i.e., a capability of minimizing the seeming uniqueness of the events about which major decisions are being made.

At this point it might be helpful to remind the reader of the earlier comments on asymmetry. There I suggested that it was a step forward to split the assumption of asymmetry of information into asymmetry of information and asymmetry in the ability to gather information. Marschak saw the decision process and its information components dividing into inquiring, communicating, deciding. Once we have introduced the capability asymmetry, we should consider other components: inquiring, gathering, processing, computing, communicating, deciding. Such unbundling certainly makes the analysis more realistic and more complicated. Just as Marschak acknowledged trade-off possibilities between inquiring, communicating and deciding, so we must allow for such possibilities over this wider range of component activities. In other words, the unbundling has led into the full study of organization.

An important input to the development of theory and the conduct of empirical research has been largely neglected. In a pioneering effort, Kornai (1971) examined the flows between organizations and units in the economic system. He distinguished two kinds of flows: product flows and information flows. He acknowledged the advance made in the Leontief tradition but added: "Less satisfactory are the results in the description and analysis of information flows" (p. 58). We might claim that the information sector statistical compilations and research has made some progress but that effort has not addressed the information flow *per se*.

As early as 1972 Arrow, interviewed on the occasion of his Nobel Prize award, suggested that comparative study—as of traditional departmental structure and a profit centre form of organization—called for study of the pattern of message flows:

What I would like to do is analyze what kinds of messages flow in the two kinds of situations, what instructions are given, maybe just count the number of words that get transmitted, or the amount of time spent in record-keeping—to see if there are economies in going from one system to another (p. F5).

Message flows can be recorded and analyzed and can contribute to our understanding of economic activity (Lamberton, 1976). Progress in this respect has been made since the days when Boulding could suggest a *wit* as a possible unit of information. For example, Griliches (1990) has argued that patent statistics are interesting despite all the difficulties that arise in their use and interpretation and Oniki (1992) has paid much more attention to information flow in his masterly synthesis of intellectual property thought.

There are even attempts to deal with the unit problem that may have some bearing on these economists' difficulties. Devlin (1991), a specialist in mathematical logic, asserts the importance of information, believes we can side-step the question "What is information," and focusses on "the nature of information flow and the mechanisms that give rise to such a flow" (p. 2). Two distinctive features of his effort are the concepts of an *infon* and of a *situation*. "An 'infon' may be thought of as a discrete item of information and the word 'situation' may be understood in its normal, everyday sense, to refer to some part of the activity of the world..." (p. 11). *Constraints* such as natural laws, conventions, analytical rules, linguistic rules, empirical, lawlike correspondences, make the information flow possible, their role being conveyed by the word *means*.

Devlin builds on Dretske's ideas (1981) about analog-digital conversion, distinguishing two stages in the extraction of information from the environment: perception and cognition. His concern lies with the conceptual information of the cognition stage, the agent being assumed to have the capacity of cognition. So here again we have met the need to develop some concept of capability as we did earlier in discussing asymmetry.

Capability is a difficult word and we can gain some help from an insightful comment by Nussbaum:

"Capability"—by now a standard term in the literature of economics and development—in intended to be the modern equivalent of the Aristotelian term *dunamis*, meaning, very generally, that condition in virtue of which one is *able* to do something. Some capabilities are internal "capacities" but many include states of the world external to the person's own condition. For example, the capability of voting includes but is not identical to the internal capacity for making political choices: for it also includes being given the rights and privileges of a citizen (1992, p. 47).

Dretske, Devlin and like-minded workers have not solved these problems but economists need to pay heed to their writings. They point to the woeful inadequacy of the very logic we use when we address these informational problems. I turn now to the growth context.

The New Organization and Economic Growth

There would appear to be a consensus that the "New Organization" is emerging in this Information Age; or, more correctly that new forms of organization are emerging. While this supports the contention that analytically we should treat the organization as a variable (Lamberton, 1984), it is clear that there are conflicting views about the nature of the new organization (Lamberton, 1992b). While the organizational behaviour approach suggests withering hierarchy and flat structures, events in the real world leave some doubt: organizational inflexibilities show promise of replacing the physical capital inflexibilities of earlier days.

This has a bearing on economic growth. A "new" school of thought, e.g., Romer (1990), argues that neoclassical theory needs revision, another factor of production—knowledge—being added to capital and labour. It is said that this modelling gives more plausible conclusions. It raises the return on investment but is costly. However, from its productivity comes the funding of further investment in knowledge with further gains in productivity, i.e., the positive sum strategy.

Is it permissible to add a further factor, be it knowledge or information? One response would be to say the answer "turns upon the empirical question of whether increasing marginal productivity does or does not apply to the intangible asset knowledge" (Shaw, 1992, p. 616). However, we must be careful about the definition of knowledge and the changes in the mix of resource inputs that are being contemplated.

The knowledge must be operative; there must be a capability of using the knowledge to achieve identified ends (Lamberton, 1992c). There have always been large, complex systems for organizing societies and economies and they have made heavy calls on resources. The information economy is no different in this respect but it calls for the design of organizations to become a deliberate process, an analytical task that has barely begun (Arrow, 1979, p. 312).

If we extend the Romer reasoning to the addition of two new factors: knowledge and organization we may be getting closer to a satisfactory modelling. It has been part of the economist's liking for optimal rather than non-optimal outcomes that has led to the "black box" mentality and unwillingness to become involved in the study of either technology or internal organization. Eminently sensible conclusions about the investment problems of developing countries that turn on complementarities between physical investment and human and social capital and suggest "that backward infrastructure and low levels of education and training substantially reduce rates of return to physical investment" (Dowrick, 1992, p. 610), point in this direction—provided infrastructure includes organization as well as roads, dams, power lines and telecommunications.

The creation and strengthening of endogenous technological capability in developing countries has featured prominently in United Nations efforts. Enos (1991) offers a systematic framework in which evolution of this capacity can be analyzed. He begins his study by noting that the "appropriate technology" phase failed because those technologies demanded as much scarce resources as the advanced technologies would have done; and the kind of products sought, which ranged from high-yielding seeds to consumer durables and armaments, needed advanced technologies. Furthermore, the introduction of the advanced technologies was more in line with national aspirations. So the new approach became the creation of technological capability.

Enos distinguishes three fundamental components of this capability, explaining them as follows:

> The first of these components probably gives rise to the least disagreement; technological capability resides in individuals with the inclination, training and experience which enable them to cope with certain portions of the overall body of useful knowledge that we call technology. The second fundamental component of technological capability is the institution within which individuals with different talents and know-how are assembled. Operating singly in a technologically complex environment, individuals can produce little, regardless of their ambition and enterprise. In order to absorb or advance a technique, they need to be brought together within an institution. The integrating institution may be a capitalist firm, a family enterprise, a co-operative, a commune or a state-owned company or agency: whatever its legal form, it exists to mass the resources, distribute the risks and provide the continuity that no individual can. So the second of the three components is the umbrella under whose protective ribs the skilled and experienced individuals shelter.
> The third component is arguably the most vital, but unarguably the most ambiguous: it is a common purpose . . . [I]t is only when they are co-operating, with some objective in sight, that their talents are fully exploited (p. 2–3).

Much detailed discussion follows on the creation of technological capability in the primary, secondary and tertiary sectors. This is seen very largely as an exercise in the development of skills in the proportions needed but a sense of disappointment develops quickly, not from the analysis but because of the limited knowledge base. The tertiary sector must play a crucial role in the process of creating the technological capability, yet we are told that the concept of "Technological capability in the tertiary sector, since it has so little relation to the physical environment, is amorphous . . . not only local but immeasurable" (pp. 109–110). Turning from the evidence on the existence of technological capability in the tertiary sector, to the creation of that capability, we read that "it is almost impossible to summarise the evidence, meagre and diverse as it is. The technologies are not physically determined and transferable between countries, but are politically and socially determined and unique to each developing country" (pp. 116–117).

The story does not change much when we turn to the "most vital" component: the instilling of purpose and co-ordination. It is in the discussion of policy towards co-ordination that we find explicit mention of information flow. Free flow is advocated but pessimism dominates: "the requisite amount of information is seldom available to those carrying out research and development and training, or to those co-ordinating their efforts" (p. 164). A useful recommendation is made: training should be conducted in the national language, but while artificial barriers to information flow are acknowledged, no solutions can be offered beyond the fostering of the will to develop. Presumably such informational deficiencies will somehow be banished with the better climate of opinion that it generated.

This is a disappointing state of affairs. It could be much more helpful to view the informational efficiency question as one common to developed and developing countries. We noted earlier Robbins' comment about "a difference of range of relevant technique and information". The role of information may exhibit some unchanging characteristics through the continuum of development.

Should we not be asking more about asymmetry in the developing country context, both in information and in the capability of using information? Does such asymmetry confer power on "the embezzlers of knowledge" and stifle development? Are there possibilities in programs that invest in the advanced technologies of telecommunications and other information technology and, *at the same time*, ensure accompanying development of the capability of using information? This would require looking into the political and social determination of forms of organization with a view to assessing their comparative informational efficiency. This search for common ground gains some support from the heavy emphasis that some scholars place on the combined organizational and informational aspects of the growth of modern industrial enterprise (e.g., Chandler).

Information Policy

Technology policy has loomed large in the debate about the causes of success amongst the developing countries, e.g., the dynamic Asian economies. What special features explain, for example, South Korean development? Westphal (1990) contends that success was achieved not by reducing the domestic market's insulation from import competition so much as by insulating export activity from adverse influences. He found extensive externalities related to technological development. Intervention, the achievement of both economies of scope and network economies, and the stretching of capacity can be very important; but for policy success, "information relevant to judging potential comparative advantage must be sought continuously from every possible source" (Westphal, 1990, p. 57).

If the exploitation of technological capability calls for the use of information "from every possible source," information policy must be all-embracing. It relates to decisions by all those involved concerning the allocation of resources to the acquisition, production and distribution of information (Hayes, 1985, p. 17). In Dunn's words, information policy extends to

> [w]hat we know as a people, what we are doing to learn more, and the tools that we use to conduct individual transactions and to communicate on a person-to-person basis... There is value in bringing together the ideas and issues in this set of national activities, because doing so calls to our attention the interrelatedness and importance in our lives. There are opportunities for improving the operation of the systems that provide information services. Many of these opportunities will be enhanced by taking an integrated view of this area (1982, p. 38).

There have always been rival views as to the scope of information policy, with changes of focus dictated by the economic climate (Lamberton, 1976). Information requirements were held to be so great as to prevent the working of a central planning agency. Some focussed on the role of science in development, while others stressed the provision of information services, e.g., libraries, and the availability of communications technology.

Given the national accounting contributions to the study of the information economy, it is convenient to say that information policy is concerned with policy issues lying in the primary (market) and secondary (in-house) information sectors. Three cautions are needed. First, neither the sector analysis nor the policy concept stems from the need to reflect the impact of the very latest in information technology (Lamberton, 1991a), as a firm basis for such an approach had already been laid by Machlup (1962). Second, and closely linked to the first caution, it is all too easy to overemphasize the convergence theme, e.g., the convergence of computer and telecommunications technologies. Despite all that has been written about convergence, the nature of the process, its manifestations in backward and forward linkages, still lack precision. And third, the buzzword, global has likewise been more misleading than helpful (Lamberton, 1991b). Global means pertaining to or embracing the totality of a group of items, categories, or the like. It would seem to imply, at a miniimum, the involvement of all economies. Does it extend to complete economic integration as in global village thinking?

In one of the few theoretical papers that explore the workings of a *global* economy, Holland notes important features: there are many dispersed units acting in parallel; there are rarely any global controls; the economy has many levels of organization and interaction; systems adapt in a climate of perpetual novelty; and the economy operates far from an optimum. In such circumstances, there will be an important role for accumulated experience, affecting both new technology and the interactions between units. In other words, culture must find a place in this analytical framework, as would a theory of learning.

These policy considerations can be illustrated by asking what role manufacturing has in a modern economy. Manufacturing matters so long as we recognize that its productivity, trade performance and profitability revolve around information, its management and exploitation. This has been obscured by the spurious separation of manufacturing from services, brought about by the difficulties of definition, the associated lack of good statistics, and our preoccupation with real assets as opposed to intangibles like patents and business intelligence.

The information model of the economy enables us to draw aside this veil of ignorance and to portray the complementary relationships between manufacturing and services, between tangible and intangible assets (Lamberton, 1991c). This exercise can be quite revealing and leads to reinterpretation of the decline of manufacturing. Perhaps deindustrialization was more a shift of producer (information) services out of recorded manufacturing activity than a real decline.

To provide these producer services, the information sector has increasingly used the new communication and information technologies.

The advent of intelligent electronics has combined with other broad changes, e.g., lowering of the rate of economic growth, fluctuating interest rates, and flexible exchange rates, to bring about increased specialization in many of these producer services. Out-sourcing is the new jargon for what used to be discussed under the old heading of Make or Buy? While the new technologies held promise of cost reductions as activities were hived-off, costs of communication and co-ordination tended to increase, offsetting the gains. These consequences of the process tend to go unquestioned because the rise in these costs is less visible and less a cause for anyone's concern than the prospective cost savings believed to be derivable from the new technologies—or said, in "technology push" circumstances, to be derivable from those technologies.

An information economy perspective presses us to abandon conventional thinking about industrial policy. The choice posed is no longer that of picking winners, of choosing between Industry A with its product(s) and Industry B with its rival product(s). The choice has now to be made between such direct industry investment and spreading available funds over factories *and* the provision of an informationally efficient infrastructure.

Much policy discussion acknowledges the role of infrastructure but fails to get down to specifics. The need to do so was highlighted by a "bottom-up" study of U.S. industrial performance—from factory floor to the boardroom—by a distinguished group of MIT experts, which revealed systematic weaknesses hampering US industry's ability to adapt to a changing international environment (Berger *et al.*, 1989). These were

- Outdated strategies
- Neglect of human resources
- Failures of co-operation
- Technological weaknesses in development and production
- Government and industry working at cross-purposes
- Short time horizons

For our purposes here, the interesting feature of this list is that it does not relate to natural resource and the capital stock but to information and decision processes, attitudes and expectations, and an overriding need for co-ordination. Does the market fail in these respects? The answer appears to be yes; institutions and policies do matter and attention must turn to efforts to design alternatives.

In doing so close attention must be given to the basic economic characteristics of information. The progress of information economics has furnished a list of these characteristics:

- Information handling (in all its forms) is a basic form of the modern division of labour.
- Information is costly, even in this supposed Age of Information plenty.
- Information is indivisible in use and difficult to appropriate.
- The cost of producing information is independent of the scale on which it is used, so there are inherent economies of scale.
- Cost of production may be only a small part of total cost, with a major part being met by the user.
- Information can be absorbed slowly.
- There are always significant asymmetries, at each stage of the information-handling process.
- Information and information-handling organizations have the characteristics of capital.
- The output of information goods and services is mainly used by industry, commerce and government rather than households.
- The demand for information technology is a derived demand.

Against this background, the theorist might well say to those discovering the inadequacy of the market mechanism, I could have told you so. Information can be a commodity but only to a limited extent. Those who prattle about global information markets reveal their ignorance about those characteristics, as they are talking about information services rather than information itself.

All this suggests old-fashioned industrial policy must give way to information policy. This is readily apparent in trade matters where the essence of comparative advantage is to be found in R&D activity, technology transfer, the management of information in the innovation process, joint ventures, networks, business intelligence, language capabilities, TRIPS (trade-related intellectual property rights), and the like.

The organizational capability that must accompany technological capability is not only a matter of governmental policy and participation. There is an important complementarity between the government and industry components of organizational capital. Exposing industry to the full blast of international competition, if neither their firms nor the infrastructure are informationally efficient can have only a predictable outcome: business failure. The alternative suggested by strategic trade theory is not to be interpreted as a return to old-fashioned protection; rather it is to seek to be well-informed (because the notion of optimality that would identify perfect knowledge has no meaning in an uncertain world). This is the best interpretation of "an appropriate climate" for business open to us, and one that even Adam Smith might have endorsed.

The Failure of the Information Society Approach

Ideas about the information economy have been difficult to keep separate from images of the information society; and there are, of course, contexts in which they should not be separated. For example, the instilling of purpose for development purposes; or the shaping of those imprecise but significant long-run expectations that somehow seem to eventually be translated into reality. Have those images been misleading ones?

> What ever happened to the Information Society? Where is the Information Age? What, indeed, happened to the so-called workerless factory, paperless office, and cashless society? Why aren't we all living in the "electronic cottage," playing our part in the push-button "teledemocracy," or simply relaxing in the leisure society, while machines exhibiting artificial intelligence do all the work? (Forester, 1992, p. 133).

The story that has unfolded reflects both the weaknesses of forecasting and the unintended consequences of the introduction of the new technologies and reactions to them. Forester can argue that "We are still awaiting the workerless, unmanned, or fully automated factory" (p. 135) but can it be that the major error has been in the estimate of the speed of change, rapid though it has been? Manning of ships has been reduced dramatically and there has been a considerable growth in the use of robots. Many traditional jobs have disappeared; clerical occupations have expanded, as have legal and lobbying activities. Such changes are understandable as a part consequence of the pressures towards increased information-intensity of the economy, with its need for more observation and more recording of those observations; more conflict and more need to resolve conflict.

That the changes have not been as rapid as predicted no doubt has many contributing factors. First and foremost, I suggest that the neglect of organizational change highlighted by the view that the gains on the factory floor have been frittered away in the office is a significant matter. The persistence of the notion of information "overload" over generations is indicative of the long-run nature of the kind of imbalance that can occur: the more rapid reduction in the costs of transmitting information than in the costs of thinking and understanding—an imbalance that has not been the focus of policy and has not been perceived as a major profit-making opportunity.

The fundamental limit may lie in the individual human's capabilities, which can be extended, but only extended, by inventiveness and capital formation. If that is not the case, then the failure might be thought to lie in the approach to education. This could be a relatively simple matter of co-ordination failure, based on faulty manpower prediction. It could also follow from a lack of understanding of the kinds of training and education that are needed—or from what is essentially an extension of this point, training and education that emphasizes individualism so accentuating the costs of co-ordination and of reaching agreement. This line of reasoning takes us into unexplored territory of the culture of the information society.

Similarly, we can provide simplistic explanations of the other failures Forester catalogs in entertaining fashion, or we can probe for deeper understanding, through interdisciplinary efforts. For example, Arrow has presented the theme

> that the combination of uncertainty, indivisibility, and capital intensity associated with information channels and their use imply (a) that the actual structure and behavior of an organization may depend heavily upon random events, in other words on history, and (b) the very pursuit of efficiency may lead to rigidity and unresponsiveness to further change (1974, p. 49).

This is an economist's explanation for the "blinkers" we all wear and that lead down the path to obsolescence of both our information capital and the capital of the organization(s) to which we belong. It might be regarded as an economist's version of the psychologist's cognitive dissonance. It can be invoked in respect of performance in work contexts, ranging from the factory bench to leadership roles in "schools of thought" in academic disciplines. Essentially, it involves being locked into information assets in much the same way as into physical assets.

Arrow's theme is an important one. However, there is an aspect that has not received adequate attention and that is his reference to history. The process view of economic activity can readily accomodate the role of history but in organizational terms there is a tension between the pressures created by the random events and those associated with the pursuit of efficiency. How are these reconciled within the organization? The first category would seem to be more allied with the initiatives that created the organization and would, if the random events come frequently enough, continue to shape the design of the organization. This suggests a possible counterforce opposing organizational scelerosis, with possible lessons for management education.

This theme does provide one answer to Forester's question why predictions go wrong; the blinkers lead us to look in the wrong place, to model the process in a misleading way, and to overestimate or underestimate various factors. It may also be that we simply do not probe deeply enough. There is a slowly growing recognition of the profound complexity of the inter-relationships between economic, organizational and psychological factors that is not reflected in the allocation of research funds. Quite generally, predictions of the consequences of technological change are simplistic and do not incorporate detailed specification of the technologies, the processes of change, and the policy elements.

Another critique addresses the notion of a service-based, post-industrial economy as the natural successor to an industry-based economy. Cohen and Zysman (1987) rightly reject the notion that such a service economy represents a natural evolution and a solution to the US difficulties in trade competition. Their argument turns on "direct linkage": a very substantial part of service employment, especially, as we have noted earlier, in information activities, is directly linked to manufacturing. Such services are complements to manufacturing.

Are there any reasons why manufacturing activities should not move off-shore, leaving behind a service economy? Given the structural link between services and manufacturing, this would imply trade in services. Such trade has expanded, with the aid of many information and communications technology developments. The crucial issue is whether the networks that have been a necessary part of the domestic "direct linkage" can operate as effectively across national borders and on a broad international scale. We can attempt to measure economies of scale with econometric technique but evaluation of potential benefits of network arrangements in the international setting is fraught with difficulties. The problems are much the same as those involved in the process of creating technological capability, where the emphasis is on the political and cultural aspects.

Conclusion

The doubts admitted, the questions raised, and the missing data in these pages catalog lengthy research agenda. Is it possible to highlight some priorities? The major deficiency would appear to be in relation to the demand for information, and in order to analyze demand we need to know more about the use of information. This suggests that the role of information through the successive phases of the decision-process is a starting point. Here ideas about substitutability are in need of revision. We can readily understand that an industrial plant in a developing country may make more use of trade publication sources than of scientific abstracts; but substitutability has to comprehend the substitution of "follow-a-leader" behaviour instead of seeking and using information.

Bikhchandani et al (1992) have sought to generalize such behaviour with their theory of fads, fashion, custom, and cultural change as informational cascades.

More knowledge of the successive phases of the decision-process is clearly needed. As we noted the small step taken by Cremer and Khalil points the way for a new range of asymmetry studies. The results can clarify the value of information—after all we have few studies of even a conventional kind of the demand for information. Such efforts could make use, from an economic perspective, of Dretske's notion of "nested" information (1981, p. 71).

The role of computing as an important element in information-handling needs to be elaborated, but done in the consciousness that the decline in computing costs relative to the other component activities may have led to distortion similar to that involved in the case of information overload.

The contrast between individual and group use of information needs to be developed. Traditional approaches have emphasized the individual but the informational cascades notion may have much wider application than has been suggested.

In nominating these priorities, I do not wish to play down the need for continued work on many existing fronts. There may be good payoff from further work in national accounting approaches—especially at a local level—and cost analysis. However, each needs to be complemented by attention to the actual information flows.

Because of trade interests, the international dimension of the information economy will no doubt continue to attract funding. This can be beneficial provided the customary focus on R&D is widened to embrace all kinds of exploratory behavior.

Information justice should retain a place. Our discussion has suggested many ways in which access proves to be at best a beginning rather than an end of the information use process. "The poor. The addicted. The uneducated" remain with us, even when they are within two hours walking distance of a telephone.

Policy debate has been primarily concerned with access, new technology, and the investment that technology requires; and with regulation and deregulation. More attention should be given to the informational components of regulatory policy (Besanko and Sappington, 1987; Magat and Viscusi, 1992).

References

Arrow, K. J. (1972). "Interview: Nobel Winner Engrossed by Balancing Act," *New York Times*, November 26, p. F5.
Arrow, K. J. (1974). *The Limits of Organization.* New York: Norton.
Arrow, K. J. (1979). "The Economics of Information." In M. L. Dertouzos, and Joel Moses (eds.), *The Computer Age: A Twenty-Year View.* Cambridge, Mass.: MIT Press.
Arrow, K. J. (1984). *Collected Papers of Kenneth J. Arrow*, Vol. 4: *The Economics of Information.* Oxford: Blackwell.
Australian, The. (1992). "'Futzing' Costs US $139 bn a Year." October 13, p. 34.
Benedikt, Michael, ed. (1991). *Cyberspace: First Steps.* Cambridge, Mass.: MIT Press.
Berger, S., M. I. Dertouzos, R. K. Lester, R. M. Solow, and L. C. Thurow. (1989). "Toward a New Industrial America." *Scientific American*, 260(6): 39–47.
Besanko, David, and D. E. M. Sappington. (1987). *Designing Regulatory Policy with Limited Information.* New York: Harwood Academic Publishers.
Bikhchandani, S., D. Hirshleifer, and I. Welch. (1992). "A Theory of Fads, Fashion, Custom, and Cultural Change as Informational Cascades." *Journal of Political Economy* 100(5):992–1026.
Butler, R. E. (1988). "Deregulation in the 1990s." *International Telecommunications Union*, March 8.
Chandler, A. D. (1992). "Organizational Capabilities and the Economic History of the Industrial Enterprise." *Journal of Economic Perspectives* 6(3):79–100.
Cherniak, Christopher. (1986). *Minimal Rationality.* Cambridge, MA: MIT Press.
Clarke, Arthur C. (1945). "Extra-Terrestrial Relays: Can Rocket Stations Give World-wide Radio Coverage?" *Wireless World*, LI (October):305–308.
Cohen, Stephen S., and John Zysman. (1987). *Manufacturing Matters: The Myth of the Post-Industrial Economy.* New York: Basic Books.
Cremer, Jacques, and Fahad Khalil. (1992). "Gathering Information Before Signing a Contract." *American Economic Review* 82(3):566–578.
Dedijer, S., and N. Jéquier. (1987). *Intelligence for Economic Development. An Inquiry into the Role of the Knowledge Industry.* Oxford: Berg.
Devlin, Keith. (1991). *Logic and Information.* New York: Cambridge University Press.
Dretske, F. (1981). *Knowledge and the Flow of Information.* Cambridge, MA: MIT Press.
Dowrick, S. (1992). "Technological Catch Up and Diverging Incomes: Patterns of Economic Growth 1960–88." *Economic Journal* 102(412):600–610.
Dunn, D. A. (1982). "Developing Information Policy." *Telecommunications Policy* 6(1):21–38.
Economist, The. (1991). August 24, p. 30.
Eliasson, G., S. Fölster, T. Lindberg, T. Pousette, and E. Taymaz. (1990). *The*

Knowledge Based Information Economy. Stockholm: Industrial Institute for Economic and Social Research.
Engelbrecht, H.-J. (1985). "An Exposition of the Information Sector Approach with Special Reference to Australia." *Prometheus* 3(2):370–386.
Enos, J. L. (1991). *The Creation of Technological Capability in Developing Countries.* London: Pinter Publishers.
Forester, Tom. (1992). "Megatrends or Megamistakes? What Ever Happened to the Information Society?" *The Information Society* 8:133–146.
Griliches, Zvi. (1990). "Patent Statistics as Economic Indicators: A Survey." *Journal of Economic Literature* 28(4):1661–1707.
Hayes, R. M., ed. (1985). *Libraries and the Information Economy of California.* Los Angeles: GSLIS/University of California Los Angeles.
Holland, J. H. (1988). "The Global Economy as an Adaptive Process." In P. W. Anderson, K. J. Arrow, and David Pines (eds.), *The Economy as an Evolving Complex System.* Menlo Park, California: Addison-Wesley, pp. 117–124.
Jonscher, Charles. (1983). "Information Resources and Economic Productivity." *Information Economics and Policy* 1(1):13–35.
Journal of Economic Literature. (1992). 30(3).
Jussawalla, Meheroo, D. M. Lamberton, and N. D. Karunaratne, eds. (1988). *The Cost of Thinking: Information Economies of Ten Pacific Countries.* Norwood, New Jersey: Ablex.
Knight, F. H. (1921). *Risk, Uncertainty and Profit.* Boston: Houghton Mifflin.
Kornai, J. (1971). *Anti-Equilibrium On Economic Systems Theory and the Tasks of Research.* Amsterdam: North-Holland.
Lamberton, D. M. (1965). *The Theory of Profit.* Oxford: Blackwell.
Lamberton, D. M., ed. (1971). *Economics of Information and Knowledge.* Harmondsworth, UK: Penguin Books.
Lamberton, D. M. (1976). "National Policy for Economic Information." *International Social Science Journal* 28(3):449–65.
Lamberton, D. M. (1978). "The Economics of Communication." In S. A. Rahim, D. M. Lamberton, D. Wedemeyer, J. Holmstrom, J. Middleton, and B. Hudson, *Planning Methods, Models, and Organization: A Review Study for Communication Policy Making and Planning.* Honolulu: East-West Center.
Lamberton, D. M. (1984). "The Economics of Information and Organization." In M. E. Williams (ed.), *Annual Review of Information Science and Technology (ARIST)* (19):3–30.
Lamberton, D. M. (1987). "The Australian Information Economy: A Sectoral Analysis." In Trevor Barr (ed.), *Challenges and Change: Australia's Information Society.* Melbourne: Oxford University Press.
Lamberton, D. M. (1991a) "Review of Miles, *Mapping and Measuring the Information Economy.*" *Prometheus* 9(2):405–406.
Lamberton, D. M. (1991b). "The Information and Communication Industries' Globalization and Regionalization: The Current Trends and Future Prospects." *Proceedings of the KISDI International Conference: Globalization, Regional-*

ization and Informatization, Korea Information Society Development Institute, Seoul.
Lamberton, D. M. (1991c). "Information Policy: A National Imperative?" In M. Costa, and M. Easson (eds.) *Australian Industry: What Policy?* Sydney: Pluto Press, pp. 207–218.
Lamberton, D. M. (1992a). "Information Economics: 'Threatened Wreckage' or New Paradigm?" In Ulf Himmelstrand (ed.), *Interfaces in Economic & Social Analysis*. London: Routledge, pp. 113–123.
Lamberton, D. M. (1992b). "Information, Exploratory Behaviour and the Design of Organizations." *Human Systems Management* 11(2):61–65.
Lamberton, D. M. (1992c). "Guest Editor's Preface: The New Organization." *Human Systems Management* 11(2):51–52.
Langlois, Richard N., ed. (1986). *Economics as a Process: Essays in the New Institutional Economics*. Cambridge: Cambridge University Press.
Leijonhufvud, Axel. (1989). "Information Costs and the Division of Labour." *International Social Science Journal* 120 (May):165–176.
Lee, Chang Seek, and Ely D. Gomez. (1992). "The Contribution of the Information Sector to the Industrial Growth of Korea." *Media Asia* 19(3):156–164.
Machlup, Fritz. (1962). *The Production and Distribution of Knowledge*. Princeton, New Jersey: Princeton University Press.
Machlup, Fritz. (1980, 1982, 1984). *Knowledge: Its Creation, Distribution, and Economic Significance*, vol. I, 1980. *Knowledge and Knowledge Production*, vol. II, 1982. *The Branches of Learning*, vol. III, 1984. *The Economics of Information and Human Capital*, Princeton, New Jersey: Princeton University Press.
Machlup, Fritz, and Una Mansfield, eds. (1983). *The Study of Information: Interdisciplinary Messages*. New York: John Wiley.
Magat, Wesley A., and W. Kip Viscusi. (1992). *Informational Approaches to Regulation*. Cambridge, Mass.: MIT Press.
Marschak, Jacob. (1974). *Economic Information, Decision and Prediction Selected Essays*: vol. II. Boston: Reidel.
Malerba, Franco. (1992). "Learning by Firms and Incremental Technical Change." *Economic Journal* 102 (July):845–859.
New York Times. (1989). December 31, p. 10.
Nussbaum, Martha. (1992). "Justice for Women!" *The New York Review of Books* 39(16):43–48.
OECD. (1981). *Information Activities, Electronics and Telecommunications Technologies: Impact on Employment, Growth and Trade*, vol. I. Paris: OECD.
OECD. (1986). *Trends in the Information Economy*. Paris: OECD.
OECD. (1992). *Information Networks and New Technologies: Opportunities and Policy Implications for the 1990s*. Paris: OECD.
Oniki, Hajime. (1992). "Mathematical Appendix." In Meheroo Jussawalla (ed.), *The Economics of Intellectual Property in a World Without Frontiers: A Study of Computer Software*. New York: Greenwood Press, pp. 115–135.

Radner, Roy. (1992). "Hierarchy: The Economics of Managing." *Journal of Economic Literature* 30(3):1382–1415.

Richardson, G. B. (1960). *Information and Investment: A Study in the Working of the Competitive Economy*. Oxford: Oxford University Press.

Roach, S. S. (1986). "Macrorealities of the Information Economy." In R. Landau, and N. Rosenberg (eds.), *The Positive Sum Strategy: Harnessing Technology for Economic Growth*. Washington, DC: National Academy Press.

Robbins, Lord. (1968). *The Theory of Economic Development in the History of Economic Thought*. London: Macmillan.

Romer, P. M. (1990). "Are Nonconvexities Important for Understanding Growth." *American Economic Review* 80(2):97–103.

Rosegger, Gerhard. (1990). "Aspects of the Life Cycle in Industry and Trade." In T. Vasko *et al*. (eds.), *Life Cycles and Long Waves*. Springer-Verlag, pp. 19–34.

Rosegger, Gerhard. (1991). "Advances in Information Technology and the Innovative Strategies of Firms." *Prometheus* 9(1):5–20.

Shaw, G. K. (1992). "Policy Implications of Endogenous Growth Theory." *Economic Journal* 102(412):611–621.

Shin, Hyun Song. (1989). "Review of Rasmussen, *Games and Information: An Introduction to Games Theory*." *Economic Journal* (99):864–865.

Simon, Herbert A. (1991). "Organizations and Markets." *Journal of Economic Perspectives* 5(2):25–44.

Telecom 91 Daily. (1991). October 15, pp. 1, 70.

Wellenius, Bjorn. (1988). "Concepts and Issues on Information Sector Measurement." In Jussawalla, Lamberton, and Karunaratne (eds.), *op cit.*, pp. vii–xii.

Walker, E. Ronald. (1942). *From Economic Theory to Policy*. Chicago: University of Chicago Press.

Westphal, Larry E. (1990). "Industrial Policy in an Export-Propelled Economy: Lessons from South Korea's Experience." *Journal of Economic Perspectives* 4(3):41–59.

Yates, JoAnne. (1992). In Peter Temin (ed.), *Inside the Business Enterprise*. Chicago: University of Chicago Press. p. 152 as quoted by William Lazonick, *Journal of Economic Literature*, 30 (September 1992):1532.

Commentary by Gilles Paquet

From the Information Economy to Evolutionary Cognitive Economics

The true power of any paper is not gauged so much by the temporarily-definitive answers it purports to provide us with as by the heuristics it triggers. By that standard, Lamberton's paper deserves praise, for it is bound to serve both as a very effective springboard for many readers (as it did for this one), and as a sound basis to test the real promises of alternative approaches.

The Lamberton paper on the information economy bears all the characteristics of our climacteric age. It surveys effectively a diverse and dispersed literature pertaining to the *information economy*—a concept Lamberton himself has done so much to drill into our consciousness. Yet this revisiting of the land that Lamberton has tilled for more than twenty years ultimately leaves one with a feeling that the literature on the information economy is at an impasse.

Our comment provides firstly a guided tour through the paper, secondly a very summary evaluation of Lamberton's neo-classically-bent review of the literature, and thirdly some suggestions to refocus the debate on the information economy.

The Thrust of Lamberton's Paper

The paper contains two major sections standing between a general introduction and a concluding section sketching a research agenda. The first major section is a thorough review of the literature on the different ways in which economists have handled the information economy from Adam Smith to the present OECD employment measures; the second is an analysis of the complex relationship between information and organization.

The paper has an encyclopedic thrust. As an introductory chapter, it is extremely informative and should enable readers not familiar with the literature on the information economy to gain a sense of what has been going on, and of what critical issues are currently being debated. The paper is conservative in its approach: the author makes a determined effort to search for convergences in all this variegated mass of writings, and this leads him to be somewhat selective in his overview and less radical in his evaluation of the neo-classical paradigm than many authors in this volume.

The paper clearly announces (in the first couple of pages) that "economic activity is a *process*, its participants having both *histories* and *contexts*," and that "progress lies in *learning*" (our emphasis). Yet Lamberton does not feel bound by these limiting premises in the rest of the paper: instead of focusing on the analysis of these dimensions (which are not permeating all the literature) Lamberton allows himself to be dragged onto the terrain of the different authors.

Since he lends an attentive and generous ear to all, he does not have time and space to go beyond some bemoaning that the more fundamental dimensions have not been satisfactorily explored. Yet, as we suggest later, some other emergent fields in economics would appear to be able to contribute to enriching the analysis of those dimensions.

Finally, the synthetic effort of the first main section of the paper has a somewhat amphibological quality. Lamberton documents well the failures of traditional economics in its efforts to analyze the information economy (and even underlines the high degree of cognitive dissonance that mars that literature) but he also appears to remain undeterred by these inadequacies and confident that the confluence of new works in those diverse traditions will lead to a "less aggregative, less ambitious theory" that will prove both insightful and operational.

In the second main section, Lamberton cobbles together some of the elements that should (in his view) be at the center of the new synthesis. This work is presented explicitly as a preliminary collage of taxonomies and not as an alternative paradigm. In this carpentering, Lamberton has chosen a deliberate strategy: to retain as the most effective/helpful language, the "language of problem solution" in good currency in neo-classical economics. This is a self-imposed constraint that endows the paper with some useful role as a bridge between mainstream economists and "information economists," but it also limits considerably the scope of analysis to the extent that Lamberton operates strictly within a paradigm that, by his own admission, would appear to be less than perfectly suited for the task at hand.

Even though Lamberton does not say so explicitly, he would appear to feel that the time is not yet ripe for a new synthesis, and to suggest that, when a new synthesis crystallizes, the Marschak-Arrow scheme might be a plausible anchor. On that, Lamberton would appear to stand at odds with many of his colleagues who feel that the time for reframing is now, and that such a reframing is unlikely to have a strong Marschak-Arrow flavour.

The Neoclassical Approach to the Information Economy: a Dollar Short and a Day Late

Sometimes directly and sometimes obliquely, Lamberton reasserts a basic gamble on continuity in economic thought. It is most certainly understandable on the part of an author who has spent much of the last twenty years trying to persuade mainstream neoclassical economists that in order to analyze the information economy properly, some retooling is necessary. His paper documents the extent to which progress has been slower than anticipated. One of the main reasons would appear to be that the original texture of communication links, and the process of learning it underpins, have often been swept aside as a result of the efforts to capture in a commodity form the central features of information and knowledge-based economy.

In the neoclassical framework, information (à la Frank Knight) remains one of the principal *commodities* supplied by economic organization; information is costly and is the result of earlier investment in search. Lamberton acknowledges that much of information and knowledge is "a commodity to only a limited extent" but he would appear to agree (reluctantly) that it is a commodity nonetheless. Markets, firms, hierarchies and organizations in general are the most efficient contraptions to process such information-commodity. Neo-classical analysis therefore appears salvageable.

Markets handle commodities well; but they do not process noncommodities as effectively. The neoclassical urge to focus on information as a commodity is therefore much like the normal reflex of the drunkard who, having lost his watch in the back alley, searches for it under the lamp post because there is light there. The reductionist process was therefore both foreseeable and natural for it is not unlike what has been perpetrated when uncertainty has been domesticated in the Arrow-Debreu world. By enumerating all the contingent states of nature and allowing for trade-offs between them to be established, one abolishes uncertainty, but does not provide any meaningful basis for taking uncertainty into account in management strategy.

The cost of this reductionism appears to many as much too high. Reducing the communication process to "information bits" is a double denial of its very nature, i.e., of *communication* as relation, and of *process* as an on-going concern. Yet this is exactly the artificial condition neoclassical economics imposes. Communication and learning cannot be reduced to information and knowledge bits. This is why it may be said that neoclassical economics remains a dollar short (despite Lamberton's generosity).

As to the possibility that a new framework capable of reintegrating the full life of communication and learning into the analyses of the information economy might emerge through the convergence of the different research programs referred to in Lamberton's survey, it would appear to be low. The current exploration of the interfaces between management strategy and economics has shown that the latter is more likely to cannibalize the former without producing much help for those interested in practical knowledge. A true convergence may exist, but it has not been shown to exist; and, if it ever materializes, it might turn out to be more than a day late.

Toward an Evolutionary Cognitive Framework

Even though Lamberton evokes context and history, and emphasizes learning and process, his reliance on the notion of information as *commodity to some extent* leads him into swampy territory. Information costs or knowledge costs are mechanically incorporated into production functions, and informational resources allocated like physical resources. The organization form (market, firm, hierarchy, etc.) becomes little more than an organizational dual of the minimum-cost allocation of informational resources. While there are references made to the difficulties of mixing knowledge with other physical inputs, these difficulties are not examined in great depth. Learning is brought into the picture, but it goes scarcely beyond a scanning of the production possibility block; and interaction is fiercely limited to a variety of forms of externalities: it lends little reality to the overbearing dimensions of history and context.

Information and knowledge cannot be reduced to the level of physical inputs any more than management or entrepreneurship can be regarded as just another input. In both cases, we are referring to *enabling resources* that inform and shape and catalyze other resources. Lamberton is clearly aware of this, and yet he deals with the central problems of perception and cognition only in passing as he makes reference to the work of Dreske and Devlin. He neither feels the urge to pursue these side avenues in his already fairly long survey paper nor indicates the special asymmetric design character of these processes on the whole production process. This would have required some additional forays into new emerging fields in economics: *cognitive economics* and *evolutionary economics* (McCain, 1992; Nelson/Winter, 1984).

The processes of perception and cognition, and the polymorphous process of evolutionary learning and change are central to any understanding of the information economy, and would appear to hold promises of both underpinning a richer notion of information and knowledge and of refocusing on the discussion on the very dimensions Lamberton has identified right from the start as central.

Cognitive economics examines the process of extraction of information from the environment through perception, and the development of knowledge through communication. In this framework, information exists to the extent that it becomes embodied in the brain as pattern or in an artifact (capital) designed to act as a surrogate for the brain. Instead of focusing on the allocation of existing informational resources, cognitive economics focuses on the production of new knowledge.

To the extent that cognition is conditioned and restricted by the mechanism of brain and mind, it is all but impossible to understand how information and communication matter without a fair idea of the way in which people gain knowledge. This is the main reason for cognitive economics to focus on the protocols leading to cognition.

The brain registers sensory inputs. These inputs are information extracted by perceptual systems. In the beginning is the percept. The perceptual systems search the environment for behaviorally relevant change and extract information patterns from the invariants in the environment. This information is then registered in the brain in the form of neuronal nets (i.e., of interactive assemblages of neurons in patterns). A new experience creates a pattern recognition cascade often built from existing patterns plus a small set of new patterns generated as new neurons fire in response to input. A nontrivial message therefore triggers a modification, a reframing or reconfiguration of existing patterns through the firing of new neurons (Paquet, 1989; Coward, 1990).

Cognitive economics focuses on the cognition process *per se* which is a much more limited area than what is labelled "the information economy." Cognition is the source of meaningful, i.e., behaviorally-relevant information, and cognitive economics aims at developing a higher ratio of meaningful information to noise through an improvement of the various information/communication enhancement mechanisms: more effective skills at extracting patterns, easier transformation of frames of reference, reduction of cognitive dissonance, etc.

But cognition does not occur only at the individual level. Creative individuals can rarely reach their goals in isolation. They operate in the context of organizations embodying a communication network. Organizations learn from experience. It is interesting to learn from experience with real-world groups (Hutchins, 1991) that change in informational environment as a result of new circumstances or breakdown/loss of perceptual equipment generates new stable work configuration that is not unlike a modified neuronal network. Evolutionary economics might prove useful to the extent that it studies the processes of organizational learning in context.

Evolutionary economics is based on the principle of ecological interaction. It focuses explicitly on communication relationships. This requires that history and context be reimported into the representation of the *communication process*, for transformation is at the core of evolution and evolves largely from history and context.

Toulmin has sorted out change mechanisms into four categories (Toulmin, 1981). Calculative change is triggered by rational choice as employed by mainstream economic theory; homeostatic change occurs in response to stimuli in accordance to fixed rules as in single-loop learning in an organization (finding new means); development change is typified by life-cycle theories and might correspond to instances of double-loop learning (learning new goals), i.e., to the restructuring of the selecting unit, its goals or mission; finally populational change is triggered by changes in the environment and in the adoption of selective units (i.e., a change in its probability of being adopted and nurtured by the environment)—natural selection.

An adaptation-adoption model entirely built on the sole calculative and populational forces of change is somewhat simplistic. Individuals more or less deliberately create institutions and organizations that evolve, and inject homeostatic and development changes. The nature of organizations and the modification of their rules of functioning may affect dramatically the direction and speed of the learning process: new information may either feed or inhibit evolution, and the cognition process may accelerate or decelerate the process of change. Evolution is not unbounded, but evolutionary epistemology is already a blossomming field capable of clarifying these boundaries (Hahlweg/Hooker, 1989).

* * *

Whether or not this cognitive/evolutionary twist will penetrate the core of the new synthesis about information economies is not necessarily ordained. It would appear likely however that these three parallel emerging strands in economics (information economics, cognitive economics, and evolutionary economics) will be led to tap this source of synergy. On the one hand, since both cognitive economics and evolutionary economics are searching for appropriate laboratories, informational economies may provide exactly what is needed. On the other hand, information economics is in need of some conceptual refurbishment, and cognitive and evolutionary economics might help reframe the current debate over the information economy.

This is only one of the many avenues worth exploring that are hinted at in Lamberton's paper. Many others will also be sketched in the rest of this volume—more radical and more vehemently anti-neoclassical economics, but these may turn out to be too radical to develop roots instantly. In that context, the great merit of Lamberton's paper is its modest provocation coefficient. His paper ends up performing three separate jobs rather well: 1) it provides a handy list of issues that require urgent attention from those interested in information economics, 2) it shows how ineffective the neoclassical apparatus has proved in tackling these issues and challenges the reader to open new trails and search for new mental tools, and 3) it serves as a testing ground to ensure that new approaches promising to deliver new vistas are forced to face some reasonable test of reality. This is quite an accomplishment for the lead chapter of a book.

References

Coward, L. A. (1990). *Pattern Thinking*. New York: Praeger.
Hahlweg, K., and C. A. Hooker, eds. (1989). *Issues in Evolutionary Epistemology*. Albany: State University of New York Press.
Hutchins, E. (1991). "Organizing Work by Adaptation." *Organization Science* 2(1): pp. 14–39.
McCain, R. A. (1992). *A Framework for Cognitive Economics*. New York: Praeger.
Nelson, R. R., and S. G. Winter. (1984). *An Evolutionary Theory of Economic Change*. Cambridge, Mass.: Harvard University Press.
Paquet, G. (1989). "Liberal Education as Synecdoche." In C. Andrew, and S. B. Esbensen (eds.), *Who's Afraid of Liberal Education?* pp. 1–20. University of Ottawa Press.
Toulmin, S. (1981). "Human Adaptation." In U. Jensen, and R. Harre (eds.), *The Philosophy of Evolution*. Havester.

2 THE PLACE OF INFORMATION IN ECONOMICS
Robert E. Babe

> *There is no more important prerequisite to clear thinking in regard to economics itself than is recognition of its limited place among human interests at large.*
>
> —Frank Knight (1951)[1]

> *The very concept of a knowledge industry contains enough dynamite to blast traditional economics into orbit.*
>
> —Kenneth E. Boulding (1963)

Introduction

In recent decades theorists such as George Stigler, Gary Becker and Richard Posner have endeavored to extend the applications of neoclassical theory into areas as diverse as family planning, racial discrimination, crime, marriage, divorce, drug addiction, politics, suicide. Indeed, for such "economic imperialists," (Stigler, 1988, pp. 191–205), "*all* behavior involving scarce resources" can be illuminated by neoclassical price theory (Adams and Brock, 1991, p. 6).

This chapter takes exception to that position. Focusing on information/communication, the chapter proposes instead that neoclassical economics be taken captive, contending that neoclassicists' notions of "market," "price," "value," "commodity," "demand," "supply," and "exchange" are but specialized instances of broader communicatory phenomena. Recognition and acceptance of this position have far-reaching implications for such basic economic concepts as efficiency, comparative advantage, optimality, equilibrium and as well for such standard neoclassical policy prescriptions as deregulation, privatization, free trade, and down-sizing the public sector. Information/communication poses severe challenges indeed to the neoclassical paradigm.

Two main parts follow this Introduction. The first addresses treatments of information/communication by three principal approaches within the mainstream discipline: first, the macroeconomic or sectoral approach; second the applied microeconomic or industry studies approach, known also as industrial organization; and third, the theoretical microeconomic approach, often called "information economics" when focusing on information/communication. While differences in treatment afforded information/communication among these three approaches are readily evident, of far greater importance are the similarities. In particular, the three approaches are of one accord in treating, or in endeavoring to treat, information as commodity.

The main thrust of the argument in the following part is as follows: Mainstream economics, premised as it is on the ubiquity of commodity exchange, needs to treat information as commodity in order to account for information within the mainstream or orthodox paradigm. Information, however, does not fulfil the definitional or conceptual requirements of commodity, thereby placing the discipline in a crisis concerning its own internal validity. Moreover, insisting that information is commodity obscures many essential properties of information, as well as consequences of informational exchange, creating thereby also a crisis of external validity.

The concluding part of this chapter reverses the Becker/Stigler/Posner analysis by exploring possibilities for "economic colonialism," contending that economics' crises can be resolved only if the discipline is viewed more modestly as but one means of investigating communicatory interaction. However, despite internal inconsistencies and incongruity with external phenomena, mainstream economics remains remarkably influential. To understand the source of this unwarranted influence requires acknowledgement of the broader political economy which shapes mainstream analysis. There is wealth, status and other emoluments to be had from "proper" economics, since economics as discourse confers advantages to some. Put more positively, recognition of the limitations of mainstream economics, and positioning it within a broader communicatory context, offers the prospect of a more sustainable and equitable future.

Information and Communication as Economic Phenomena

Three Mainstream Treatments of Information

1. Information Economy Treatment. Fritz Machlup's 1962 book, *The Production and Distribution of Knowledge in the United States* was seminal in conceiving information and/or knowledge production, processing and distribution as important economic activities. Prior to publication of Machlup's work macroeconomic or aggregate analyses typically countenanced but a threefold division for the economy, distinguishing agricultural, manufacturing and service sectors. By calculating, however, that nearly 29 percent of U.S. output and 32 percent of the U.S. employment in 1958 were accounted for by "knowledge industries" whose annual growth averaged between 8 and nearly 11 percent, Machlup justified constituting a fourth sector, one based on informational and communicatory activities and products.

Subsequently Marc Porat (1977) took up and extended Machlup's work, pronouncing that the United States had become an "Information Economy." Porat estimated that by 1967 the information sector accounted for about 46 percent of U.S. GNP.

In principle macroeconomic or sectoral studies such as Machlup's and Porat's, by proposing a distinct informational sector, would seem to indicate that "economic activities associated with processing information have unique attributes, and deserve to be studied separately from other activities in the national economy" (Rubin, 1983, p. 1). To a limited extent this has been true; some economists believe, for instance, that information/communication will continue to outpace manufacturing and agricultural sectors in the most developed economies, a perception that has led the U.S. in particular to adopt aggressive "free trade" stances respecting informational products and services in GATT (Braman, 1990) and in bilateral negotiations (Parker, 1988).

Despite such caveats, it also remains true in a broader sense that aggregate or sectoral analyses proposing a distinct, even predominant, informational sector imply that informational/communicatory activities are equivalent to other transactional activity, and can with equanimity be studied in money terms. Which is to say these analyses imply that informational/communicatory processes can and should be treated as subsets of broader processes of economic (commodity) exchange.

There are problems with this approach, however, as hinted at by Marc Porat himself when he declared: "Information is by nature, a heterogeneous commodity . . ." (Porat, 1977/1983, p. 16); and: "There is no single definition of information that embraces all aspects of the primary sector" (1977/83, p. 16); and further: "Information cannot be collapsed into one sector—like mining—but rather the production, processing, and distribution of information goods and services should be thought of as an *activity*" (1977/83, p. 18; emphasis in original).[2]

In the same vein economist Beth Allen (1990, p. 269) writes:

> The preceding argument that various types of information may be available in the economy suggests immediately that we should treat information as a differentiated commodity.

The very notion of commodity requires, however, that replicas of the good in question be "physically identical," even though available "in different places and at different times" (Ingrao and Israel, 1990, p. 5). Such standardization permits counting. Indeed *measurement* according to Abraham Kaplan (1964, pp. 173, 182), "in a word, is a device *for standardizaton*, by which we are assured equivalences among objects of diverse origin. . . . When we count, we are always determining how many things there are of a certain *kind*" (emphasis in original). This is precisely what Porat and Allen declare that informational commodities and activities lack—a standard with which to measure and compare.

Porat tried to resolve or rather avoid the measurement problem respecting information by turning *from* "heterogenous" informational commodities *to* information *markets* and information *activities*, measuring such markets and activities in two ways: by employment, and by value added. Defining a "primary information market" as one which is established when a technology of information production and distribution is organized by firms, and an exchange price is established," Porat combined such diverse "markets" and "activities" as education, banking, office furniture, mass media, telecommunications, advertising, insurance, finance, and the post office.

Labor content or labor intensity, does not, of course distinguish informational activities and commodities from other activities and commodities. Indeed there are huge disparities in "labor-intensity" within Porat's information sector. While some activities may be highly labor-intensive (live theatre, authorship), others are highly capital-intensive. Joseph Pelton (1983, p. 59) reports, for instance that much of the information "generated and transmitted through the global telenet is processed and analyzed by machines, not people."

Note also that sectoral analysis restricts communicational activities to those "organized by firms" and for which "an exchange price is established" (Porat, 1977/83, p. 17). In other words, much if not most of our communication is excluded from the sectoral approach simply because it does not pass through markets and therefore does not command a price or "value".[3]

The complex interrelationship among money, price, and informational "quantity" is addressed below. Briefly, money price states how much exchange value an informational commodity "contains," but is silent regarding its quantity of information.

2. Information Industry Studies. The area within mainstream economics known as "applied microeconomics" ("industrial organization") investigates the structure and behavior of industries in an economy (Stigler, 1968, p. 1). Shepherd (1975, p. 11) has remarked on characteristics of mainstream economic industry studies in general: 1) "Each market is regarded as a distinct entity, in line with Marshallian partial analysis"; 2) "The context of the market is considered to be extraneous" ... 3) "Behavior is normally perceived, primarily as matters of pricing and interfirm strategies"; 4) "Performance criteria are matters of minimizing costs and prices; there is usually little attention to content or equity."

Whatever the implications of these aspects may be for "normal" industries, they are particularly disconcerting for economic studies of information industries. Consider the following points in turn:

1. Information pervades economies, and among other things helps co-ordinate through prices activities of disparate economic agents (see section on "information economics" below). Therefore, it may well be unduly partial to apply "Marshallian partial analysis" to information industries.
2. Since information is cumulative, or is at least dependent upon existing knowledge, and since symbols need to be comprehended in order for them to constitute information, it is a great and possibly improper simplification to consider the context of an information market as "extraneous." Information "markets" both derive from the cultural/economic setting, and in turn impinge upon it.
3. Behavior in information industries entails more than mere pricing,

since informational artifacts are unique creations which may, however, have many copies. Litman (1990, p. 193), for example, pointed to the uniqueness of informational products in motion picture production:

> [A motion picture studio] is unlike a modern industrial enterprise, where automobiles or steel are turned out in large quantities over long manufacturing runs; rather, each film is hand-crafted with a very short product life and only occasional opportunities for reuse of the creative input.

4. Content and equity, many would argue, are of the essence for informational activity. For purposes of analysis economists, and others, however, tend to ignore content and depict output in terms of the "hardware," or "containers." "Containers" include paper, videotape, compact discs, column inches, feature films as generic artifacts, books as generic artifacts, minutes of television broadcasting, and so on. Increasingly firms charge per call, per view, per bit, and per screenful of information (Mosco, 1989, p. 27). In *this* sense there is indeed an increasing commoditization of symbolic artifacts, but none of the quantitative measures devised for pricing or for analytical purposes touch directly upon the informational content; all relate rather to capacity for storing or transmitting content. Ignoring the informational content is a serious omission since it is the content that gives the "hardware" its value. The conclusion from this is that most mainstream economic analyses of information industries are fundamentally flawed.

3. Information Economics Treatment

Information and the Price System. For years microeconomic theorists paid scant attention to information. On the one hand, enraptured by the purely competitive model which assumes perfect knowledge, and on the other convinced that price theory provides abundant insight into real world phenomena, neoclassicists by and large rested content in the assumption that the price system generates and processes automatically information sufficient to ensure economic efficiency. Economies, neoclassicists assumed, are constrained by limited capacities for obtaining and processing materials, not by similar limitations concerning the information needed to organize and coordinate production and distribution (Jonscher, 1982, pp. 62–63).

The great Marshall, for example (1890/1934) introduced his classic treatise extolling money as the means whereby even inward "desires, aspirations and other affections of human nature" become measurable once expressed outwardly in market activity (pp. 14–15). Marshall declared economics the most exact of the social sciences on account of the market's capacity to quantify.

Hayek (1945) too lauded the informational properties of the price system, viewing prices as "quantitative indices (or 'values')" (p. 525). Each index or price Hayek contended should be understood as *concentrated information* reflecting the significance of any particular scarce resource relative to all others. The index or price borne by each commodity, Hayek enthused, permits autonomous economic agents to adjust their strategies "without having to solve the whole puzzle [input-output matrix] *ab initio*" (p. 525).

Prices, then, for Hayek as for modern information economists, *are* information. Note, for instance, Arrow's more recent formulation of the idea:

> The competitive system can be viewed as an information and decision structure. Initially, each agent in the economy has a very limited perspective. The household knows only its initial holdings of goods (including labor power) and the satisfactions it could derive from different combinations of goods acquired and consumed. The firm knows only the technological alternatives for transforming inputs into outputs. The "communication" takes the form of prices. If the correct (equilibrium) prices are announced, then the individual agents can determine their purchases and sales so as to maximize profits or satisfactions. The prices are then, according to the pure theory, the only communication that needs to be made in addition to the information held initially by the agents. This makes the market system appear to be very efficient indeed; not only does it achieve as good an allocation as an omniscient planner could, but it clearly minimizes the amount of communication needed (Arrow, 1979, pp. 313–314).

One begins to see, in this context, the reasoning behind Kenneth Boulding's remarks quoted at the start of this chapter, for as extracts from Marshall, Hayek and Arrow indicate, "informational considerations [are], in fact, central to the analysis of a wide variety of phenomena [and constitute] a central part of the Foundations of Economic Analysis" (Stiglitz, 1985, p. 21). But with up to 50 percent of the labor force engaged in informational activities, questions arise regarding the presumed capacity of markets to spontaneously generate information sufficient to ensure economic efficiency.[4] Indeed, long before Machlup published his seminal work, intimations of doubt were being expressed in the mainstream economics literature.

Precursors of Information Economics

One influential pioneer was Ronald Coase (1937) who defined the firm as an organization purposefully bypassing or suppressing the price mechanism. Firms according to Coase consciously or deliberatively administer internal flows of resources, instead of relying on markets to accomplish this. Coase then questioned why firms, or "islands of conscious power," as he called them, arise at all given the purported efficacy of the price system. His response: "There is cost of using the price mechanism."
He continued:

> The most obvious cost of "organizing" production through the price mechanism is that of *discovering what the relevant prices are*. This cost may be reduced but it will never be eliminated by the emergence of specialists who *will sell* this information. The costs of negotiating and concluding a separate contract for each exchange transaction which takes place in a market must also be taken into account (p. 326; emphasis added).

A second notable precursor was Frank Knight (1921/1946) who constructed a theory of risk, uncertainty and profit. True profit, Knight wrote, stems from uncertainty since with perfect knowledge, markets discount future shortages, obviating the possibility of economic profit. Profit he defined as the reward over and above a "normal" return. Profit, for Knight then, is a measure of market imperfection attributable to imperfect knowledge (that is, to uncertainty). Profit for Knight is the entrepreneur's reward for engaging in activities whose outcomes are uncertain even in the probabilistic or actuarial sense, making them uninsurable.

Knight has had his critics. As Seligman (1962, pp. 663–664) notes his concept of profit, bereft of monopoly considerations, was a "panegyric to the entrepreneurs". Nonetheless, as was true with Coase, Knight addressed relationships among imperfect knowledge, information and money, anticipating thereby today's "information economists" who define information as reduction in uncertainty and perceive it as commodity. According to Kenneth Arrow (1979, p. 307), for instance, "The meaning of information is precisely a reduction in uncertainty." Likewise, information economist Charles Jonscher writes:

> Demand for information arises because of the presence of uncertainty; without uncertainty there is no need for information (Jonscher, 1982, p. 63).

"Information economists" undoubtedly adopt a much narrower conception of information than do either the macroeconomic analysts (Machlup/Porat), or the information industries analysts. By defining "information" as "reduction in uncertainty," information economists endeavor to resolve the definitional problem besetting the other approaches. While their conception initially appears to be more precise (no talk here of information being a "heterogeneous" or "differentiated" commodity, for instance), in fact information still remains ill-defined, as we will see shortly. Moreover, for information to be incorporated as commodity (as opposed to residual) into the neoclassical model, information must itself be quantified and treated on "a par with . . . a 'regular' (noninformation) economic commodity, such as iron ore" (Jonscher, 1982, pp. 67–68). This has proved impossible. While individual "packets" of information can indeed be assigned value, there is no means of quantifying "information" as such. Nor does information exhibit properties of tangible goods. We turn now to how neoclassicists have struggled with this conundrum.

The Modern Era

Despite implied or muted warnings by Coase, Knight and others, analyses of information and implications for economic theory of imperfect knowledge languished in mainstream economics into the 1950's,[5] causing George Stigler in 1961 to remark: "[Information] occupies a slum dwelling in the town of economics" (Stigler, 1961/1968, p. 171).

Proposing to begin remedying this neglect, Stigler applied "standard economic theory of utility-maximizing behavior" (Stigler, 1983, p. 539) to one important problem of information—the ascertainment of market price" (Stigler, 1961/68, p. 171). Since prices are continually in flux, Stigler advised, there must exist at any given time and place ignorance as to what prices are. Buyers confronted with an array of prices for even homogeneous goods must "search" in order to find the lowest price. A search will entail a cost, but also will produce a benefit. The "value of information" in the face of this uncertainty, Stigler wrote, is "the amount by which the information reduces the expected cost to the buyer of his [sic] purchases" (pp. 183–184). Stigler concluded that the "optimal amount of search" would be found "if the cost of search is equated to its expected marginal return" (p. 175).

More generally, given each economic agent's "subjective probability distributions over the possible states of the world," the value of information can be defined as "the increase in the expected value of the outcome resulting from a choice made after, as compared with before, the information becomes available" (Jonscher, 1982, p. 66).

It is to be noted that the approach suggested by Stigler and amplified by Jonscher seems to preserve the purported automaticity and effectiveness of the price mechanism, by turning prices ("information") into a commodity. Ascertainment of knowledge respecting prices itself commands a price. The implication is that information required for markets to function effectively will be generated automatically in optimal quantities through the incentive system.

But Stigler's "solution" to the problem of uncertainty was more apparent than real, since he was unable to arrive at a general measure whereby information could be quantified, a requirement for supply and demand schedules to exist. Stigler assumed "the cost of search for a consumer may be taken as approximately proportional to the number of (identified) sellers approached" (Stigler, 1961/68, p. 175). Each "approach" then yields one seller's price. But not all prices are equally informative: being apprised of one price is more informative if only two sellers exist than if there are ten. As an aside it may be noted that some information economists conclude that markets with few selllers are more "competitive" than those with many: the higher information content of each price in markets with few sellers induces purchasers in these markets to search prices more extensively than in markets with many sellers, thereby increasing (relatively) price elasticity of demand (Dasah, 1992).

Returning to the main point, Stigler himself remarked in somewhat the same vein: "The expected saving from given search will be greater, the greater the dispersion of prices" (Stigler, 1961/68, p. 175).

What this latter statement essentially means is that the informational content of each given price varies according to the dispersion in prices. If all prices are (known to be) the same, no information results from inquiring the price of any given seller; if prices are (known to be) almost the same, little information is attained from inquiry. But if the dispersion is large, each price ascertained can be highly informative. Rothschild (1974) demonstrated that price searches can inform searchers of the probability distribution of prices in addition to the price charged by individual sellers.

More generally stated, information does not exist objectively in and of itself so as to be countable. It exists only in particular contexts; changing contexts changes (the quantity of) the information.

These arguments and observations indicate, then, that there is no one-to-one relationship between the commodity acquired (here a price), and its information content.

Shortly after completing his seminal article on uncertainty concerning commodity prices, Stigler prepared a second, addressing uncertainty over wages in the labor market (1962/1968). Stigler's work has proved to be influential, stimulating an evolving literature on the theory of price search (see *inter alia* Nelson, 1970; Telser, 1973; Rothschild, 1974; Diamond, 1978).

Meanwhile, others such as Debreu (1959/89), and Radner (1968/89) endeavored to incorporate uncertainty within general equilibrium models, attempts that were not entirely successful (Grossman and Stiglitz 1980; Akerlof, 1970; Rothchild and Stiglitz 1976; and Pauly, 1974). Surveying the literature, Spence (1974) for instance, concluded that "in general the recent work reported here demonstrates that informational problems cause market failures of various kinds" (p. 57), while Stiglitz (1985) concluded:

> We have learned that much of what we believed before is of only limited validity; that the traditional competitive equilibrium analysis, though having the superficial appearance of generality—in terms of superscripts and subscripts—is indeed not very general; the theory is not robust to slight alteration in the informational assumptions. It is but a special—and not very plausible—"example" among the possible set of informational assumptions which can be employed to characterize an economy (p. 21).

Two of the informational problems that have beset information economics over the years are "moral hazard" and "adverse selection." The former can result when a purchaser's behavior (unknown to the supplier) affects the cost of providing a commodity. For example, as noted by Arrow (1962/1971), a fire insurance policy "changes the incentives of the insured . . . creating an incentive for arson or at the very least, carelessness" (p. 87). "Adverse selection" occurs when imperfect information causes different commodities or people to be grouped together and to be treated as if they were the same. Akerlof, for example, showed that trade could cease if potential car sellers know the qualities of particular cars they are trying to sell while buyers are aware only of average qualities. Akerlof turned then to describing institutions that might alleviate such market breakdowns, demonstrating that there are means other than prices whereby information can be conveyed in economic systems.

Why do some commentators feel that information and uncertainty undermine the neoclassical edifice? Why are they unconvinced by the Stigler/Jonscher approach, whereby commoditized information is seen to resuscitate neoclassicism? One answer relates to information's problematic status as commodity.

Impossibility of the Information "Commodity"

To be sure, information economists have noted that the "information commodity" possesses some unique characteristics: Allen (1990, pp. 269, 270) for instance, remarks that "satiation occurs at one unit of information *of any given type* [since] identical copies of the same information [the normal requirement for "commodity"] are worthless unless the duplicates can be sold."

Stiglitz has pointed to another peculiarity of the information "commodity." How, he asks, is an individual to resolve the infinite regress of whether it is worthwhile to obtain information concerning whether it is worthwhile to obtain information . . . (Stiglitz, 1985, p. 23). Arrow posed a different formulation of the same dilemma in 1962:

> [Information's] value for the purchaser is not known until he [sic] has the information, but then he has, in effect, acquired it without cost (1962/1971, p. 148).

Other problems with information as commodity have been identified as well. For example, information is "indivisible," which means that partial information can be useless. Either one is informed of a price, or one is not informed (Allen, 1990, p. 270). Moreover, according to Arrow, since information can be reproduced at little or no cost while "the cost of transmitting a given body of information is frequently very low" (Arrow, 1962/1971, p. 147), information can be difficult to appropriate; but capacity to be appropriated is a condition for commoditization. Market exchange entails, after all, the transmittal of property rights.

Difficulties of appropriation aside, it is not clear that ownership would be desirable in any event. Information is a "public good" in the sense that many can "possess" the same information at the same time, and possession by one does not detract from the ability of others to be apprised. To restrict access to those able and willing to pay is "inefficient," even in neoclassicists' terms, since there is no additional cost entailed in allowing greater access to information already produced. While some argue that markets for information are needed to induce production (Ploman and Hamilton, 1980), the economic case for intellectual or symbolic artifacts as commodity is certainly not clearcut.

Apart from the foregoing, however, the main problem as far as "information economics" is concerned, is the absence of a measuring standard. Spence (1974) alluded briefly to this in writing:

> Economic agents have different "amounts" of information. Speaking about amounts of information suggests that we have an economically relevant measure of the quantity or value of information. This is not in fact the case.

Unfortunately, Spence quickly drew away from pursuing the implications of his insight by remarking:

> However, in the special case in which one person knows everything that another knows and more, we can say the former has more information. That suffices for my discussions of asymmetrically located information (1974, p. 58).

Mention must be made of the one means so far devised to quantify "information." Ascribed to Claude Shannon and Warren Weaver (1949) this "mathematical theory of communication" has been immensely useful in fields as diverse as engineering, physics, biology, cybernetics (Ritchie, 1991, pp. 7–8; Rifkin, 1989, pp. 208–218). Shannon and Weaver defined information in the context of selecting choices from an array of predetermined and known possibilities, lending at first blush a correspondence to the "information economists'" definition of information as uncertainty reduction (Jenner, 1966/1971).

According to Shannon and Weaver the quantity of information in the simplest cases is the logarithm to base 2 of the number of available choices (p. 9). If there are only two choices, a sender can inform a receiver of the selection of one of them with a single burst of signal (or "bit")—an "on" or a "one" instead of an "off" or a "zero." Likewise, if there exist 16 alternatives, four "bits" (or binary digits) are sufficient to signal any given selection ($16 = 2^4$; i.e. $\log_2 16 = 4$). In this latter instance Shannon and Weaver measure the "quantity" of information transmitted as 4 units or 4 bits since every one of the 16 choices can be uniquely identified by sequences of four binary digits.

Unfortunately for "information economics" Shannon and Weaver's method quantifies something other than what is meant by "information" in the economists' sense. As Weaver explains, "information must not be confused with meaning" (p. 8).[7]

To understand the divergence between Shannon and Weaver's definition and method of measuring "information" and the neoclassicists' use of the term, it is useful to conflate these two systems. According to Shannon and Weaver's method, a buyer confronting two possible and equally probable prices for a commodity receives one unit of information when informed of a seller's price, whereas in facing 16 possible and equally probable prices receives four units of information when made aware of a seller's price. According to information economics, however, the "amount" of information imparted depends not at all on how many options a single seller has to select from in isolation, but rather on the number of sellers and the dispersion in *their* prices. For information economics the buyer in being apprised of one price receives more information in confronting two sellers than in confronting sixteen.

Implications

Frustration is evident in the ranks of information economists. Upon reviewing the uncertainty literature, Spence sighs, "There is no sweeping conclusion to be drawn from this survey . . ." (1974, p. 58), while in like manner Stiglitz remarks:

> There seems to be a myriad of special cases and few general principles (Stiglitz, 1985, p. 21).

One reason for these conclusions is the fact that economists have not and cannot quantify information. Each case becomes then a "special case", since "information" means something different in each instance. "Information" in information economics is akin to an error term or residual which restores tautologies: If uncertainty exists over prices, then a unique parcel of "information" with "value" may restore equilibrium, but its "value" cannot be disassembled into price and quantity components, or alternatively quantity is always 1 for each unique informational "packet"; information is, as Arrow noted, "indivisible." The inability to devise a measure for information means, ultimately, that information stands out-side or beyond neoclassical treatment.

Since information on the one hand constitutes "a central part of the foundations of economic analysis," yet on the other, stands outside neoclassical modelling, a fundamental inconsistency becomes apparent. A more promising approach would be to stop "force-fitting" information into the commodity mode and indeed to reverse the process, treating commodity as but one form or function information can take (see Parker's chapter *infra*). Market exchange then is to be viewed as a particular generic instance of broader communicatory interaction. The concluding part to this chapter pursues facets of this approach.

The Question of External Validity

In defining information as commodity, and indeed in the case of "information economics" confining it to uncertainty reduction, economists render invisible many important consequences, economic and otherwise, of informational interchange and transfer. To illustrate:

On 30 October 1938, Orson Welles's science-fiction broadcast, *War of the Worlds*, was heard by at least six million radio listeners. Of those, at least one million panicked or were seriously frightened, believing that Martians had indeed landed. According to Lowery and de Fleur (1988, pp. 61–62): "Terrified people all over America prayed and tried frantically in one way or another to escape death from the Martians. . . . Hundreds of people fled their homes. Bus terminals were crowded. . . . [In Pittsburg] a man came home in the middle of the broadcast and found his wife in the bathroom with a bottle of poison in her hand and screaming, 'I'd rather die this way than that.' "

Looking beyond the pale of information-as-commodity and information-as-reduction-in-uncertainty, new analytical possibilities open up, concerning not only this particular broadcast, but more importantly concerning communicatory activity more generally. Consider the following:

First, the capacity to communicate, to package and diffuse information, means power. It is not simply the case, as mainstream economists contend, that buyers survey an array of informational commodities and purchase the one or ones that seem most in tune with the buyers' needs, given prices and income constraints. Albeit unintentionally, Orson Welles drove hundreds, perhaps thousands, from their homes. He affected, however briefly, the thoughts and emotions of six million or more people, many of whom took action based on these mental states. More generally, broadcast media give programmers, including *inter alia* advertisers, politicians, public relations firms, news agencies and "entertainers," "access to the thoughts and emotions of people in the audience" (Vogel, 1989, pp. 155–156). Communication *means* influence and a capacity to exert influence over perhaps millions means power. Power, however, is not a primary concern for most mainstream economists (Adams and Brock, 1986, chpt. 2), certainly not for neoclassicists; and commoditization/reduction-in-uncertainty treatments afforded information indeed enable mainstream analysts to skirt considerations of power. Stated another way, less restrictive conceptions of information restore considerations of power to economic analyses and so entail the replacement or supercession of "economics" by "political economy" (Babe, 1993).

Second, Welles's broadcast shows that information is not enveloped or contained in a single place or time, as are "normal" commodities, but permeates time and space (Innis, 1950/1972). Moreover, information generates or spawns more information, as *inter alia* press reports on Welles's broadcast, an ensuing study by the Office of Radio Research of Princeton University, policy statements from the Federal Communications Commission, Lowery and de Fleur's chapter, and indeed this very page indicate. Societal evolution, as Veblen (1909) and more recently Boulding (1978; 1981) have understood, is in the first instance informational.

Third, information constitutes a shared "space," a symbolic environment, a communications ecology (Nevitt, 1982), in which people live.

Our physical environment is experienced or perceived in large part symbolically, and our symbolic constructs in turn influence actions upon the material environment. I return to this at the close of the chapter.

Economics as Communication

Two Models

To restore internal and external validity to economics, this concluding part suggests that economic processes be viewed as but special instances of more general communicatory processes. It makes a big difference whether human interaction is interpreted in terms of the market paradigm, or in terms of a more general communication system model.

At the outset it is to be noted that a superficial similarity exists between the economists' "market" and the communicologists' "communication system" (Babe, 1993). Both entail circular flows. In the former instance, a seller transmits property rights in and perhaps physical possession of a "commodity" to a buyer and in return receives money, the amount being determined "impersonally" through supply and demand. In the latter instance, a sender transmits a message (heretofore termed "information") by means of some medium of transmission (air, paper, radio, etc.), to a receiver, who decodes or interprets the message and responds in some way ("feedback").

The similarities mask profound differences, however. In the economics model buyer and seller exert no influence on one another. They are assumed to be autonomous "others," rationally engaging in activities to maximize their individual welfare. By contrast, the communication system posits selves in dialogue, interpenetrating and transforming one another through "mutual semiosis"[8] (Perinbanyagam, 1991, p. 31).

Which of these two models is most apt in any given circumstance hinges on whether it is a "commodity" or "information" that is exchanged. If that which is exchanged is "inert," exerting no effect or influence upon the perceptions, values or cognitive patterns of the receiver, and if monetary payment is made in exchange, then truly the economists' "market" is operative. Communication scholars question, however, whether it is possible to participate in any exchange and remain unchanged.

What Then Is Information?

Physicist Carl Friedrich von Weizsäcker (1980) takes "information" to be rooted in "form," or "pattern," or "structure." He writes:

> This "form" can refer to the form of all kinds of objects or events perceptible to the senses and capable of being shaped by man: the form of the printer's ink or ink on paper, of chalk on the blackboard, of sound waves in air, of current flow in a wire, etc. (pp. 38–39).

Matter and form, von Weizsäcker continues, are conceptual complements: "In the realm of the concrete, no form exists without matter; nor can there be matter without form" (p. 275). He continues:

> A cupboard, a tree are made of wood. Wood is their "matter"... But the cupboard isn't simply wood, it is a wooden cupboard. "Cupboard" is what it is intrinsically; cupboard is its *eidos*, its essence, its form. But a cupboard must be made of something; a cupboard without matter is a mere thought abstracted from reality (p. 274).

Energy too, as with the telegraph, can be ordered or formed or organized so as to be capable of being understood.

Information then, may be termed epiphenomenal in the sense that "it derives from the *organization* of the material world on which it is wholly dependent for its existence"[9] (Beniger, 1986, p. 9). It is this epiphenomenal quality of information that makes it so difficult to appropriate. Different substances, and even human memories, can easily be shaped or formed to convey or hold the "same" information.

The mere existence of form, however, is not sufficient to constitute information; it is also required that meaning be conveyed. In addition to matter (or energy) and to form there must be language, that is a code or codes assigning pre-arranged meanings to these "forms." As well, the receiver must be cognizant of a code that incorporates the forms (or "signs") in question (von Weiszäcker, p. 39).

In this conception information defies measurement, and for a number of reasons. First, information is immaterial; information relates to the form matter takes, but is not the matter itself.

Second, forms have no meaning, or rather as symbols have no meaning, in and of themselves,[10] but rather take on meaning because a code or language exists which imputes or ascribes meaning to them. This is probably what Lee Thayer meant in writing: "To be human is to be denied life in a world of things; it is to be given life in a world of the *meaning* of things" (Thayer, 1987, p. x; emphasis in original). In this view, meaning (information) does not exist objectively so as to be countable, but exists only in subjectivity, that is in interpretation. For example, different languages or codes may ascribe different meanings to the "same" form, and different "readers," therefore, bringing different codes to the "same" forms may derive or impute markedly different meanings. According to Gregory Bateson, "nothing has meaning except it be seen in some context" (Bateson, 1979, p. 14). Here, the context is the code or language brought by the "reader," but equally any given form, or component of a message, exists only in the context of the whole message where components modify one another syntagmatically. The whole message thereby takes on much greater meaning than can be ascribed to individual components considered separately. Likewise, the meaning imputed to each form depends also on the "paradigm" from which it was selected, and indeed the "reader's" knowledge of the elements of the paradigm (Webster, pp. 166–204; Solomon, 1988; Bonney and Wilson, 1990).

It is evident that we have ventured into the field of semiotics, which aspires to answer how forms take on meaning. Without dwelling here, there is an added point that deserves emphasis. Languages, or codes, that enable us to decode or impute meanings relate to and are derived from cultures and subcultures. (Fiske, 1982; Hall, 1982). We learn languages and codes from our communities. To quote Thayer once more, "To be human is to be *in* communication in *some* human culture and to be *in* some human culture is to see and know the world—to communicate—in a way which daily recreates that particular culture" (Thayer, 1987, p. 45). James Carey likewise defines communication as "a symbolic process whereby reality is produced, maintained, repaired and transformed" (Carey, 1989, p. 23). (See also Berger and Luckman, 1966; and Kuhn (1970).)

It follows, therefore, that information and communication should engage the analyst in a social or methodologically collectivist discourse (as opposed to the methodologically individualist discourse of the economist), for at least two reasons: First, messages frequently radiate into and permeate many minds, often simultaneously, producing, maintaining, and transforming societies and the individuals comprising them. Second, any individual's "reading" of forms (signs, text, or information) comes not only from his/her unique life experiences, but also (and more importantly) from the shared languages or codes of the culture(s) and subculture(s). As expressed by Mikhail Bakhtin, "Language enters life through concrete utterances (which manifest language) and life enters language through concrete utterances as well" (quoted in Perinbanayagam, 1991, front page).

The Political Economy of the Information Commodity

It may seem that we have strayed far from mainstream economics and the methodologically individualist analysis of commodity exchange, but not as far as might at first appear. Following Carey we can interpret mainstream economics, and particularly neoclassicism, as but a particular symbolic or "informational" system producing, maintaining, repairing and transforming economic reality. Even the physical sciences, as Boulding notes, do not merely investigate the world, but as well create the world they are investigating (Boulding, 1969/1971, p. 451). It was indeed in full realization that the economics discipline acts upon and transforms the economic world that the "economics as discourse" and "economics as rhetoric" literatures arose (Samuels, 1990; Klamer, McCloskey and Solow, 1988), from whence it is but a short further step to address the power, money and control lying behind and motivating mainstream economic analyses—the political economy of mainstream economics. (See Adams and Brock's chapter, and commentary by Schiller.)

Consider the following example, highly pertinent to the subject matter of this chapter, as illustrative of how mainstream economics channels thought so as to advantage some and disadvantage others, thereby endowing mainstream economics itself with "exchange value." The issue is the international economic impact of information's status as "commodity."

By insisting within GATT and in bilateral trade negotiations that information be treated as commodity and that there be a dismantling of informational trade barriers and beefed-up copyright, the United States, which domiciles the world's largest information companies, positions itself to increase exports of informational products in exchange for energy, resources, foreign currencies and labor intensive manufactured goods. The United States, or rather corporations located principally in the U.S.A. currently hold a competitive advantage in the mass production of informational "commodities."

Virtually all of the mainstream economics literature—from the sectoral analyses of Machlup/Porat, to the information industries studies, to the field of "information economics"—can be invoked in support of information's commodity status, despite as we have seen, critical problems concerning economics' internal and external validity arising from commodity treatment of information.

If communication, on the other hand were to be defined as, say, the mutual engagement of dialogic partners (Perinbanayagam, 1991), or as a basic human right as was attempted in UNESCO's call for a New International Information and Communication Order (Preston, Herman and

Schiller, 1989), then America's trading partners could rightly insist on a free and *balanced* flow of information: "communication" would no longer be a "one-way street."

But dialogic interaction interferes with the commodity status of information, since receivers are no longer perceived and treated as mere "consumers." And communication as a basic human right is much less beneficial to the export trade of transnational "communication industries."

Economics, Communication, and the Ecosystem

Consider a further instance where resisting economic imperialism can have salutary effects—preservation of the ecosystem.

In mainstream economics, nothing has intrinsic value. Nothing has a right to exist simply because it is. Value (in exchange) derives solely from human preferences and from the scarcity of items to satisfy human desires. Indeed the foundational assumption of mainstream economics is that dogged pursuit by individuals of their desires and wants, in aggregate, determines production, distribution, price and value. The economists' conception of value, in a word, is anthropocentric (Rowe, 1989). And for mainstream economists, "land"[11] is merely another type of commodity, one among many, and its worth is the price it commands in market exchange.

Value was not and is not always perceived in these terms. In other traditions, as noted by Daly and Cobb, "existence in general, and especially life, are to be affirmed in themselves, not merely in relation to ends that transcend them; the goodness of the world in general cannot be understood simply as its value for human beings"[12] (1989, p. 104).

The ecological crisis, however, confronts the economists' anthropocentric perception of value, demolishing "the fiction of human self-sufficiency" (Rowe, 1989). Now, even economists must begin to perceive the whole globe as an "ecological entity... of which people as individuals and as communal groups in their built environments are parts" (Rowe, 1989). As Daly and Cobb (1989, p. 109) express it: "There seems no way to take the evidence of science and of universal experience seriously without affirming the reality of the natural world and the place of the human being as part of it."

Among more progressive mainstream economic theorists the "solution" to the environmental crisis is, in principle at least, simple: prices should be altered through taxation or subsidy so as to equal "social marginal cost" (Mishan, 1969, p. 83). As Mishan admits, however, while "the principle is straightforward enough, estimates of damage (and benefits) can pose considerable practical difficulties" (Mishan, 1969, p. 83).

It is here contended, however, that measurement is not the major issue. Rather, "the principle" itself is misguided. Communicologists understand that "naming is always classifying" (Bateson, 1979, p. 30). And naming the world as a monetary phenomenon *means* that all things so named are to be taken as commodities, available for sale and purchase and disposal as one pleases (Dyer, 1989, p. 508). Adjusting prices to better reflect "social costs" and "social benefits," as recommended by Mishan, does nothing to counter the individualism, avarice and anthropocentrism inherent in the price system. Rather it continues the practice of representing nature or proprietary segments of it as but containers of exchange value that can be compared to and exchanged for all other objects and experiences. Naming "land" in terms of price symbolically transforms it into commodity and this naming mediates or impacts upon our very understanding of the ecosystem (Dyer, 1989, p. 508).

The transition to sustainable development (WCED, 1987)[13] in part requires, then, resolving a huge problem in symbolization. It means rejecting current practices of naming or symbolizing the ecosystem and portions thereof in money terms as commodity, and instead "knowing it as a gift" (Dyer, 1989, p. 509). Dyer continues:

> Briefly, this means symbolically representing the environment so that it embodies specific obligations and responsibilities to the community. Thus, naming the environment as a gift rather than as a commodity would encourage social bonding through means other than the search for private profits. (Dyer, 1989, p. 509).

Dyer's challenge of renaming the ecosystem as gift rather than as commodity[14] is quite probably the most important communication/ economic problem humankind faces. Indeed, "It's a matter of survival" (Gordon and Suzuki, 1990).

Notes

1. As quoted in Lutz and Lux (1988, p. 179).
2. Porat continues: "An information market enables the consumer to know something that was not known beforehand: to exchange a symbolic experience; to learn or relearn something; to change perception or cognition; to reduce uncertainty; to expand one's range of options; to exercise rational choice; to evaluate decisions; to control a process; to communicate an idea, a fact, or an opinion. An information market may sell topical

knowledge with a very short, useful life; it may exchange long-lasting knowledge. It may involve a completely specialized or unique configuration of knowledge, useful only to one person in one situation, or it may be public knowledge available to all simultaneously and generally useful in many contexts..." (Porat (1977/83), p. 16).

3. Below distinctions will be made among "value-in-exchange" (the only "value" recognized by mainstream economics), "value-in-use," and "intrinsic value."

4. Moreover informational activity challenges the static analysis characteristic of so much of the mainstream method. Information implies change—in wants and preferences, in production techniques, in produced commodities, in markets. In such a dynamic world, basic economic concepts, like efficiency, optimality and equilibrium are in danger of being rendered meaningless.

5. Joseph Schumpeter declared that theoretical work on uncertainty peaked with Dobb and Knight in the 1920's, thereafter to "peter out," while "factual work in this field... did not get beyond beginnings." (1954, pp. 894–895).

6. Serious also are the contentions that the introduction of uncertainty into the neoclassical model undermines standard neoclassical assumptions of nondiscontinuities, convexities, and reversible change (i.e., nonunidirectional time). See Stiglitz, 1985; and Rothschild and Stiglitz, 1976).

7. Weaver continues: "Two messages, one of which is heavily loaded with meaning and the other of which is pure nonsense, can be exactly equivalent, from the present point of view, as regards information.... Information is a measure of one's freedom of choice when one selects a message.... The two messages betwen which one must choose, in such a selection, can be anything one likes. One might be the text of the King James Version of the Bible, and the other might be 'Yes'" (pp. 8–9).

8. Following semiologist C. S. Peirce, Perinbanayagam (1991, p. 31) defines semiosis as "an action or influence which is, or involves, a co-operation of *three* subjects, such as a sign, its object, and its interpretant, this tri-relative influence not being resolvable into action between two pairs." Tri-relative influence implies that initiator and respondent may have quite different interpretations ("interpretants") for a given message or "sign," if and when their experiences with the external world ("object") differ. Symbolic exchange can *create* uncertainty, launching dialogic partners onto paths that take unforeseeable twists and turns (Babe, forthcoming).

9. But then, equally, the material world can be deemed "epiphenomenal" inasmuch as matter cannot exist without assuming form, while forms can "exist" without matter as pure thought.

10. The word choice is extremely important here, bearing on the question of whether forms (or objects—or subjects) have or can have meaning (value) in and of themselves (intrinsic meaning or value) or whether meaning/value exist only in relation to other objects. Communication studies and economics appear to be alike in contending that forms or objects have meaning/value only in relation to other forms or objects. Communication studies terms the relationship "symbolic meaning," whereas economics calls it "exchange value."

11. "Land," economists' usual term for nature, resources, ecosystem, etc., is held to be one of the three main "factors of production," the others being "labor" and "capital."

12. As Daly and Cobb rightly point out at the conclusion of their study, to affirm life (for example) as valuable in and of itself is also, fundamentally, to affirm a divine order. In that sense even "intrinsic value" is extrinsic to Being.

13. For critique and extension of WCED's proposals for sustainable developmental, see Goodland, Daly and Serafy (eds.) (1992).

14. For an extended comparison of gift and commodity, see Hyde (1979).

References

Adams, Walter, and James W. Brock. (1986). *The Bigness Complex*. New York: Pantheon.
Adams, Walter, and James W. Brock. (1991). *Antitrust Economics on Trial: A Dialogue on the New Laissez-Faire*. Princeton, N.J.: Princeton University Press.
Akerlof, George A. (1970). "The Market for 'Lemons': Quality Uncertainty and the Market Mechanism." *Quarterly Journal of Economics* 84(3):488–500.
Allen, Beth. (1990). "Information as an Economic Commodity." *American Economic Review* 80(2):268–273.
Arrow, Kenneth J. (1962). "Economic Welfare and the Allocation of Resources for Invention." In *The Rate and Direction of Inventive Activity: Economic and Social Factors*. Princeton, N.J.: National Bureau of Economic Research, pp. 609–26; reprinted in D. M. Lamberton (ed.), 1971. *Economics of Information and Knowledge*. Harmondsworth: Penguin, pp. 141–159.
Arrow, Kenneth J. (1979). "The Economics of Information." In Michael L. Dertouzos, and Joel Moses (eds.), *The Computer Age: A Twenty-Year View*. Cambridge, Mass.: MIT Press, pp. 306–317.
Babe, Robert E. (1993). "Communication: Blindspot of Western Economics." In Manjanuth Pendakur *et al.* (eds.), *Illuminating the Blindspots*. Norwood, N.J.: Ablex.
Babe, Robert E. (forthcoming). "Communication and Economics." *Research in the History of Economic Thought and Methodology*. Greenwich, Connecticut: JAI Press.
Bateson, Gregory. (1979). *Mind and Nature: A Necessary Unity*. New York: E.P. Dutton.
Beniger, James R. (1986). *The Control Revolution: Technological and Economic Origins of the Information Society*. Cambridge: Mass.: Harvard University Press.
Berger, Peter, and Thomas Luckman. (1966). *The Social Construction of Reality: A Treatise in the Sociology of Knowledge*. Harmondsworth: Penguin.
Bonney, Bill, and Wilson, Helen. (1990). "Advertising and the Manufacture of Difference." In Manuel Alvarado, and John O. Thompson (eds.), *The Media Reader*. London: British Film Institute.
Boulding, Kenneth E. (1963). "The Knowledge Industry." *Challenge* May, pp. 36–38.
Boulding, Kenneth E. (1969). "Economics as a Moral Science." *American Economic Review* 59:1–12. Reprinted in Kenneth E. Boulding. (1971). *Collected Papers, Vol. 2: Economics*. Boulder, Colorado: Colorado Associated University Press, pp. 449–460.
Boulding, Kenneth E. (1978). *Ecodynamics: A New Theory of Societal Evolution*. Beverly Hills: Sage.
Boulding, Kenneth E. (1981). *Evolutionary Economics*. Beverly Hills: Sage.
Braman, Sandra. (1990). "Trade and Information Policy." *Media, Culture and Society*, Vol. 12. London: Sage, pp. 361–385.

Carey, James W. (1989). *Communication As Culture: Essays on Media and Society*. Winchester, MA: Unwin Hyman.

Coase, Ronald. (1952). "The Nature of the Firm." *Economica* Vol. 4, pp. 386–405. Reprinted in George J. Stigler and Kenneth E. Boulding (eds.) *Readings in Price Theory*. Homewood: Irwin, pp. 331–351.

Daly, Herman, and John Cobb. (1989). *For The Common Good: Redirecting the Economy Toward Community, the Environment, and a Sustainable Future*. Boston: Beacon Press.

Dasah, Bernard Z. (1992). "The Treatment of Information/Communication by Neoclassical Economics." Unpublished paper.

Debreu, G. (1959). *Theory of Value*. New York: Wiley; excerpted in Peter Diamond and Michael Rothschild (eds.), 1989. *Uncertainty in Economics: Readings and Exercises*, revised. San Diego, CA: Academic Press, pp. 163–173.

Diamond, P. A. (1978). "Welfare Analysis of Imperfect Information Equilibrium." *Bell Journal of Economics* 9(1):82–105.

Dyer, Alan W. (1989). "Making Semiotic Sense of Money as a Medium of Exchange." *Journal of Economic Issues* 23(2):503–510.

Fiske, John. (1982). *Introduction to Communication Studies*. New York: Methuen.

Goodland, Robert, Herman E. Daly, and Salah El Serafy, eds. (1992). *Population, Technology and Lifestyle: The Transition to Sustainability*. Washington, D.C.: Island Press.

Gordon, Anita, and David Suzuki. (1990). *It's A Matter of Survival*. Cambridge, Mass.: Harvard University Press.

Grossman, Sanford J., and Joseph E. Stiglitz. (1980). "On the Impossibility of Informationally Efficient Markets." *American Economic Review* June, 393–402.

Hall, Stuart. (1982). "The Rediscovery of 'Ideology': Return of the Repressed in Media Studies." In Michael Gurevitch *et al.* (eds.), *Culture, Society and the Media*. New York: Methuen.

Hayek, F. A. (1945). "The Use of Knowledge in Society." *American Economic Review* 35(4):519–530.

Hyde, Lewis. (1979). *The Gift: Imagination and the Erotic Life of Property*. New York: Vintage Books.

Ingrau, Bruna, and Giorgio Israel. (1990). *The Invisible Hand: Economic Equilibrium in the History of Science*. Cambridge, Mass.: MIT Press.

Innis, Harold. (1972). *Empire and Communications*. Toronto: University of Toronto Press.

Jenner, R. A. (1966). "An Information Version of Pure Competition." *Economic Journal* 76:786–805. Reprinted in D. M. Lamberton (ed.), 1971. *Economics of Information and Knowledge*, 83–108.

Jonscher, Charles. (1982). "Notes on Communication and Economic Theory." In Meheroo Jussawalla, and D. M. Lamberton (eds.), *Communication Economics and Development*. Elmsford, N.Y.: Pergamon Press, pp. 60–69.

Kaplan, Abraham. (1964). *The Conduct of Inquiry: Methodology for Behavioral Science*. New York: Harper and Row.

Klamer, Arjo, Donald M. McCloskey, and Robert M. Solow, eds. (1988). *The Consequences of Economic Rhetoric*. New York: Cambridge University Press.

Knight, Frank. (1946). *Risk, Uncertainty and Profit*. Boston: Houghton Mifflin Company.

Kuhn, Thomas S. (1970). *The Structure of Scientific Revolutions*, 2nd edition. Chicago: University of Chicago Press.

Litman, Barry R. (1990). "The Motion Picture Entertainment Industry." In Walter Adams (ed.), *The Structure of American Industry*, 8th edition. New York: Macmillan, pp. 183–216.

Lowery, Shearon A., and Melvin L. DeFleur. (1988). *Milestones in Mass Communication Research*, 2nd edition. New York: Longman.

Lutz, Mark A., and Kenneth Lux. (1988). *Humanistic Economics: The New Challenge*. New York: The Bootstrap Press.

Machlup, Fritz. (1962). *The Production and Distribution of Knowledge in the United States*. Princeton, N.J.: Princeton University Press.

Machlup, Fritz. (1980). *Knowledge and Knowledge Production*, Vol. 1 of *Knowledge: Its Creation, Distribution, and Economic Significance*. Princeton, N.J.: Princeton University Press.

Marshall, Alfred. (1938). *Principles of Economics: An Introductory Volume*, 8th Edition. London: Macmillan.

Mishan, E. J. (1969). *The Costs of Economic Growth*. Harmondsworth: Pelican.

Mosco, Vincent. (1989). *The Pay-Per Society: Computers and Communications in the Information Age*. Toronto: Garamond Press.

Nelson, P. (1970). "Information and Consumer Behavior." *Journal of Political Economy* 78(2):311–329.

Nevitt, Barrington. (1982). *The Communication Ecology: Re-presentation versus Replica*. Toronto: Butterworths.

Parker, Ian. (1988). "The Free Trade Challenge." *Canadian Forum* (March): 29–35.

Pauly, Mark V. (1974). "Overinsurance and Public Provision of Insurance: The Roles of Moral Hazard and Adverse Selection." *Quarterly Journal of Economics* (88):44–54.

Pelton, Joseph. (1983). "Life in the Information Society." In Jerry L. Salvaggio (ed.) *Telecommunications: Issues and Choices for Society*. New York: Longman, pp. 51–58.

Perinbanayagam, R. S. (1991). *Discursive Acts*. New York: Aldine de Gruyter.

Ploman, Edward, and L. Clark Hamilton. (1980). *Copyright Intellectual Property in the Information Age*. London: Routledge and Kegan Paul.

Porat, Marc U. (1977). *Definition and Measurement*, Vol. 1 of *The Information Economy*. Washington, D.C.: U.S. Government Printing Office. Excerpted in Michael Rogers Rubin (1983), pp. 16–25.

Preston, William Jr., Edward S. Herman, and Herbert I. Schiller. (1989). *Hope and Folly: The United States and UNESCO 1945–1985*. Minneapolis: University of Minnesota Press.

Radner, Roy. (1968). "Competitive Equilibrium Under Uncertainty." *Econo-

metrica (56):31–58. Reprinted in Peter Diamond and Michael Rothschild, eds. (1989). *Uncertainty in Economics: Readings and Exercises*. San Diego, CA: Academic Press, pp. 177–204.

Rifkin, Jeremy. (1987). *Time Wars*. New York: Simon and Schuster.

Ritchie, L. David. (1991). *Information*. Newbury Park, CA: Sage.

Rothschild, Michael. (1974). "Searching for the Lowest Price When the Distribution of Prices is Unknown." *Journal of Political Economy* 82(4):589–711.

Rothschild, Michael, and Joseph Stiglitz. (1976). "Equilibrium in Competitive Insurance Markets: An Essay on the Economics of Imperfect Information." *Quarterly Journal of Economics* (90):629–650.

Rowe, J. Stan. (1989). "What on Earth is Environment?" *The Trumpeter, Journal of Ecosophy* (Autumn).

Rubin, Michael Rogers. (1983). *Information Economics and Policy in the United States*. Littleton, Colorado: Libraries Unlimited.

Samuels, Warren J., ed. (1990). *Economics As Discourse: An Analysis of the Language of Economists*. Boston: Kluwer Academic Publishers.

Schumpeter, Joseph A. (1954). *History of Economic Analysis*. New York: Oxford University Press.

Seligman, Ben B. (1962). *Main Currents in Modern Economics*. New York: Free Press of Glencoe.

Shannon, Claude E., and Warren Weaver. (1949). *The Mathematical Theory of Communication*. Urbana, Illinois: University of Illinois Press.

Shepherd, William G. (1975). *The Treatment of Market Power: Antitrust, Regulation and Public Enterprise*. New York: Columbia University Press.

Solomon, Jack. (1988). *The Signs of Our Time: The Secret Meanings of Everyday Life*. New York: Harper and Row.

Spence, A. Michael. (1974). "An Economist's View of Information." In Carlos A. Canadia, Ann W. Luke, and Jessica L. Harris (eds.), *Annual Review of Information Science and Technology*, Vol. 9. Washington, D.C.: American Society for Information Sciences, pp. 57–78.

Stigler, George J. (1968). "The Economics of Information." *Journal of Political Economy*, 69(3). Reprinted in *The Organization of Industry*. Homewood, Illinois: Irwin, pp. 171–190.

Stigler, George J. (1968). "Information in the Labor Market." *Journal of Political Economy*. 70(5). Reprinted in *The Organization of Industry*. Homewood, Illinois: Irwin, pp. 191–207.

Stigler, George J. (1983). "Nobel Lecture: The Process and Progress of Economics." *Journal of Political Economy* 91(4):529–545.

Stigler, George J. (1988). *Memoirs of an Unregulated Economist*. New York: Basic Books.

Stiglitz, Joseph. (1985). "Information and Economic Analysis: A Perspective." *Economic Journal* (95):21–41.

Telser, Lester G. (1973). "Searching for the Lowest Price." *American Economic Review* 63(2):40–49.

Thayer, Lee. (1987). *On Communication: Essays in Understanding*. Norwood, N.J.: Ablex.

Veblen, Thorstein. (1909). "The Limitations of Marginal Utility." *Journal of Political Economy*. Reprinted in Thorstein Veblen. (1990). *The Place of Science in Modern Civilization*. New Brunswick, N.J.: Transaction Publishers.

Vogel, Harold L. (1990). *Entertainment Industry Economics: A Guide For Financial Analysis*, 2nd edition. Cambridge: Cambridge University Press.

Von Weizsäcker, Carl Friedrich. (1980). *The Unity of Nature*. New York: Farrar, Straus, and Giroux.

Webster, Frank. (1980). *The New Photography*. London: J. Calder.

World Commission on Environment and Development (WCED). (1987). *Our Common Future*. New York: Oxford University Press.

3 COMMODITIES AS SIGN-SYSTEMS
Ian Parker

[A] commodity is a good or a service completely specified physically, temporally, and spatially. It is assumed that there is only a finite number l of distinguishable commodities; these are indicated by an index h running from 1 to l. It is also assumed that the quantity of any one of them can be any real number.... The space R^l will be called the commodity space.... [An] action [by an economic agent] is ... represented by a point a of R^l.

—Gerard Debreu (1959)

The hedonistic conception of man is that of a lightning calculator of pleasures and pains, who oscillates like a homogeneous globule of desire of happiness under the impulse of stimuli that shift him about the area, but leave him intact.... According to [the later psychology], ... [a person] is not simply a bundle of desires that are to be saturated by being placed in the path of the forces of the environment, but rather a coherent structure of propensities and habits which seeks realisation and expression in an unfolding activity.

—Thorstein Veblen (1919)

> Gold... *[Much]* of this will make black white,
> foul fair,
> Wrong right, base noble, old young, coward valiant. ...
> This yellow slave
> Will knit and break religions, bless the accursed. ...
> Thou visible God.
> That solder'st close impossibilities,
> And mak'st them kiss! That speak'st with every tongue,
> To every purpose!
>
> —William Shakespeare, *Timon of Athens*, Act 4, Scene 3

> *A commodity appears, at first sight, a very trivial thing, and easily understood. Its analysis shows that it is, in reality, a very queer thing, abounding in metaphysical subtleties and theological niceties.*
>
> —Karl Marx (1965)

Introduction

The above passages indicate some of the principal themes of this chapter. The notion of a commodity, as a good or service that can be owned and consumed (either as an input within a process of production or as an article of final consumption) and which is or can be exchanged for other commodities (including money), is at the core of conventional or mainstream, price-system-based, economic theory. A commodity, in classical, Austrian, and modern neoclassical economic theory, is said to possess or embody two types or forms of "value": "*use*-value," or "utility," or usefulness for various purposes; and "*exchange*-value," which is a relative measure, indicating the quantity of other commodities (including money, as the universal equivalent form of exchange-value) for which the commodity could be exchanged. This quantity (viewed as an exchange-equivalent) constitutes a measure of the exchange-value of a given commodity in terms of these other commodities.

In basic modern neoclassical economic theory, it is typically assumed that *all* combinations or bundles of commodities potentially available for final consumption by every individual economic agent can be instantaneously and costlessly ranked by each agent within the economic system in his or her capacity as a direct consumer, regardless of whether each agent has actually experienced the consumption of each bundle of commodities beforehand. Formally, for each consumer it is assumed that there exists a complete preference preordering. The ranking procedure is fairly straightforward: of any two bundles (or vectors) of commodities, x_1 and x_2, it is assumed that x_1 is preferred by the consumer to x_2, or that the consumer is indifferent between x_1 and x_2, or that x_2 is preferred by the consumer to x_1.[1]

It is possible, within the neoclassical paradigm, mathematically to generalize this logic to situations of *risk* (sometimes, misleadingly, called "uncertainty"), where the state of the world in which a given commodity-bundle occurs may condition its ranking relative to other commodity-bundles that could occur in this state of the world. If all agents have identical prior well-defined cardinal probability estimates regarding the likelihood of occurrence of all conceivable states of the world, and well-defined attitudes toward risk, it is possible (with several ancillary assumptions) to guarantee that a general economic equilibrium can exist. There is (as a general rule), however, no reason to believe that a "general economic equilibrium," involving the exchange at "equilibrium" prices of "equivalent" amounts of the set of commodities among all agents, will *necessarily* exist.[2]

The "free-market solution" to the problem of "allocating scarce resources among alternative and competing ends,"[3] in short, requires some highly unrealistic assumptions as a basis for its results. As Arrow and Hahn (1971: vi–vii) correctly observed in their pioneering canvass and extension of neoclassical-economic general equilibrium theory:

> [A number of economists] have sought to show that a decentralized economy motivated by self-interest and guided by price signals would be compatible with a coherent disposition of economic resources that could be regarded, in a well-defined sense, as superior to a large class of possible alternative dispositions. . . . The proposition having been put forward and very seriously entertained, it is important to know not only whether it *is* true, but also whether it *could* be true.

It is for this reason that Veblen's critique of the neoclassical hedonistic image of economic agents as frozen, utilitarian optimizers, or "homogeneous globules of desire," still retains much of its force today, although his remarks were first published in 1897. Veblen was concerned with the fact that economics was not an "evolutionary science," at least by his criteria. Veblen's principal concern, as is suggested by the passage quoted at the outset of this chapter, was that the neoclassical or "hedonistic" representation of the economic agent was highly restricted. Neoclassical economics did not adequately reflect the active, realization-seeking and expressive character of the economic agent, nor the agent's possession of "propensities and habits."

Insofar as the economic agent's involvement with commodities is concerned, one of Veblen's major reservations regarding the hedonistic calculus implicit in neoclassical, equilibrium-based economic theory was that it did not adequately allow for the role of information and knowledge in human existence, and more particularly for the active *desire* for knowledge and social self-realization on the part of the individual economic agent, in the achievement of which knowledge and self-realization, the consumption of commodities by the agent played a directly productive role. What Veblen's analysis suggests, both here and elsewhere in his writings (Veblen, 1899; 1919; 1932), is that commodities are not merely elements or "arguments" in each economic agent's preordained utility function, but are rather, both in and of themselves and in their semiotic, symbolic and informational aspects, integral components of each individual agent's social-economic self-definition, status, knowledge, and behavior.

Shakespeare's commentary on gold, in its capacity as the universal equivalent or monetary form of commodities, represents a still more radical aspect of the semiotics of commodities, inasmuch as Shakespeare (in passages quoted repeatedly by Marx in his analysis of commodity-money) treats gold in its commodity-money role as a *transformer* of meaning. Monetary gold, for Shakespeare, at a crucial historical nexus in the transition from feudalism to capitalism, was both a "slave" and a "God," a servant and a director of human desire, a means of transfiguring the significations of the world.

Shakespeare's recognition of the radical transformative semiotic capacity of commodities, as epitomized most strikingly in the case of the universal equivalent commodity, monetary gold, constitutes (along with the *Herrschaft-Knechtschaft* analysis of Hegel's *Phenomenology of Mind*) one of the primary bases of Marx's complex analysis of "commodity fetishism." This phenomenon is associated by Marx with the widespread penetration of the price system and the generalized production of commodities for exchange in society. With this development, according to Marx, a fundamental inversion, a form of "fetishism" (the attribution of human or superhuman powers to inanimate objects) occurs: "[the] relation of the producers to the sum total of their own labor is presented to them as a social relation, existing not between themselves, but between the products of their labor" (Marx, 1965: 71, 132; Parker, 1983: 163–72).

For Marx, the development of a *system* based on commodity exchange leads to a profound semiotic reversal. In this reversal or *Aufhebung*, material goods and services, as commodities, appear to take on an autonomous life of their own within a significative economy in which the modes of social cooperation among human producers recede into the epistemic background. Marx's thesis is that the rise of a world of commodities, in and of itself, has its own *systematic* message, over and above the semiotic content of each individual commodity.

A world of commodities is simultaneously a referential system in which commodities, taken collectively, constitute the significance of the *system*, over and above the significative and/or "utilitarian" weight of each individual commodity, taken either in and of itself or in its one-to-one relationships with each and every other element in the set of commodities. The transition from a world based primarily on household, subsistence-based, production for *use* to a world based primarily on production for *exchange*, as a result of the penetrative powers of the price system (Innis, 1956: 252–272), creates a radically transformed political-economic *and* semiotic field for the social distribution of use-values. At the outset of the latter third of the nineteenth century, Marx, with considerable prescience, had recognized the critical significance of Shakespeare's even more prescient animadversions on the semiotic consequences of the social-economic hegemony of the price system. The perspective developed by Shakespeare in the early seventeenth century and refined by Marx in the nineteenth century requires further articulation, however, if it is to cope with the semiotics of commodities in the twenty-first century.

Commodities in the Late Twentieth and Twenty-first Centuries

In the above context, the purpose of this chapter is to explore the implications of the significatory, semiotic, informational and communicative functions of commodities for contemporary economic theory. This exploration, however, is not intended to be solely abstruse or narrowly academic in character. The fact of the matter is that the twentieth century has witnessed a number of major transformations in the global economy, particularly in the advanced capitalist nations, virtually all of which transformations have increased the practical urgency of systematically integrating a recognition of commodities as sign-systems into the core of economic theory. If anything, the pace of these transformations has accelerated since the Second World War, and it is probable (notwithstanding the global economic slowdown of the early 1990s) that the transformations will continue unabated into the twenty-first century.

The major contours of change are familiar to almost everyone, although their full implications have not always been absorbed, notably within mainstream economic theory itself. In the 1870s, in North America, about 70 percent of Gross Domestic Product (GDP) was based on material commodity production, with commoditized services constituting about 30 percent of GDP. By the early 1990s, these percentages had been almost exactly reversed, with commoditized services constituting close to 70 percent of recorded GDP. The rise of the service sector, and its obverse side, the relative decline of primary material commodity production, have been two of the most fundamental sectoral shifts in North American capitalism, and particularly since 1945 similar patterns have emerged in virtually all of the advanced-capitalist OECD (Organization for Economic Cooperation and Development) nations.

This shift can be accounted for in part in terms of the rising importance of the capitalist state over the course of the twentieth century, as a result of demands for the coordination of an increasingly integrated and complex global economic system. Yet for the past three decades, in most OECD nations, the average share of real government expenditures in real GDP has been roughly on a plateau. The continued relative growth of the service sector over these decades has been due primarily to two main factors: first, the commoditization of activities or services formerly provided within the household, as, for example, with the rise of fast-food outlets and the expansion of day-care services (both of which are significantly related, on both demand and supply sides, to the rapidly increasing participation of women in the wage-labor market since 1945); and second, the rapid growth of the informational economy, involving the production and distribution of commoditized knowledge, which was first systematically analyzed in Machlup's (1962) pioneering work.

Since Machlup's initial study appeared in 1962, technological and organizational changes have increased the economic importance of commoditized knowledge in the advanced capitalist nations and in the global economy. The period since 1962 has witnessed the emergence or widespread diffusion of color television, cable television, new generations of mainframe computers, the explosion of personal computers, telesatellites, personal satellite dishes, telefacsimile (FAX) services, videocassette player-recorders, MODEMs, CD-ROMs, audio compact-discs, and a host of other actually or potentially synergistic media. The capacities enabled by these technological developments have contributed to the acceleration of trends towards the globalization of capital, including the increasing integration of global financial markets; the expansion and increase in scale of transnational corporations; the growing pattern of systematic collaboration (as well as of competition) between and among transnational corporations; the significant geographical shift in the international division of labor whereby hardware design and software-creation activities are carried out principally in a small handful of advanced-capitalist environments, while an increasing share of material commodity production occurs in less developed Pacific Rim and other countries; the increased preoccupation of the major capitalist states (particularly those of the U.S., Japan and Germany) with extending the GATT (General Agreement on Tariffs and Trade) accords to remove barriers to global free trade in information and services as well as goods; and the growing pressure, particularly by the United States, to provide for increased international protection of private property rights in information (in the form of copyright, patent and related restrictions) and increased rates of remuneration to those holding such property rights.

The above developments in the global economy have been associated with an increased centralization of control over information, and the growth of what Harold Innis (1964; 1972) referred to as "monopolies of knowledge." To the extent that this centralization of control of information has occurred, the latter decades of the twentieth century have involved a widening gap between informational haves and have-nots, both between the advanced capitalist nations and less developed countries and within the advanced capitalist nations themselves. At the same time, particularly in the advanced capitalist countries, the degree of access to general information has sharply increased, particularly as a result of the development of television and other mass media as augmented by the effects of cable and direct broadcast satellite (DBS) systems and digitalized signals.

As a result, we are confronted with the seemingly paradoxical phenomenon of a rapid and significant increase in the *absolute general-*informational density of advanced capitalist economies, combined with an increase in the *relative* concentration, or monopolization, of *specialized* knowledge. (Parker *et al.*, 1988: 240–243) This seeming paradox, however, is more apparent than real. Both trends are quite compatible: indeed, they are mutually reinforcing. Statistically speaking, most of the *general-*informational signals received via television and other mass media by the average household are received in the form of entertainment or that hybrid product, "infotainment"; most of them belong in the "bread and circuses" category, albeit on occasion with somewhat more intellectual content. In contrast, the use and effective deployment of most *specialized* knowledge typically requires significantly larger fixed expenditures on developing an appropriate system of information-retrieval and organization; possession of or access to adequate databases; analytical and interpretative (and possibly advertising or propaganda) skills; and the resources to implement strategies based on the new knowledge produced. Adequately informed wealth can, within this analytical framework, generate or purchase productive commoditized information that can augment its accumulative capacity, and in the process (given restricted disclosure of its accumulated knowledge) increase the potency and spatial-temporal range of its monopoly of knowledge.

Prolegomena to an Analysis of Commodities as Sign Systems

The foregoing global economic developments have all increased the theoretical and practical importance of viewing commodities as signsystems. In the first place, theoretically speaking, once commodities can no longer be viewed as simple and straightforward arguments in fixed, frozen and predetermined individual utility functions, but instead must be viewed as both use-values *and* information-transmitters, a significant proportion of standard neoclassical economic theory is called into question. Specifically, if the production, consumption, distribution or exchange of a commodity generates *new* information in *any* form, then the assumptions of perfect information, perfect certainty (or cardinally determinate risk), unchanging tastes, and constant technology (or cardinally probabilistically foreseeable technical change) that undergird the standard general-equilibrium results of conventional mainstream economics obviously no longer hold.[4] More radically, utility functions themselves can no longer be treated as invariable *or* predictable. This problem is likely at least as theoretically profound and intractable as the more familiar catalogue of problems posed for conventional general economic equilibrium theory by such interrelated phenomena as imperfect competition, "public goods," "externalities," indivisibilities, increasing returns to scale, and transactions and transportation costs.[5] Moreover, it goes without saying that all of *these* problems have *also* been exacerbated by increases in the semiotic or informational content of commodities, in the form that these increases have taken.

A second factor increasing the importance of conceptualizing commodities as sign-systems has been the secular increase in *per capita* income, over much of the globe (especially in the advanced capitalist countries), since the Industrial Revolution. At low (or *"basic* subsistence") levels of income, in societies characterized by high levels of decentralized, largely self-sufficient subsistence production, "production for use" rather than "production for exchange" tends to be of relatively greater importance; and much of aggregate productive effort is hence devoted to production of *goods* (or "*use*-values") rather than of *commodities* (or "*exchange*-values"). The types of staple goods produced in the former situation (such as rice, millet, sorghum, wheat, maize, bananas, yams, fish, milk and meat; basic shelter using indigenous materials; and basic clothing, often largely household-produced) tend to be locally restricted in number and relatively undifferentiated among households, thereby reducing the opportunities for market-extension and increased specialization and division of labor.

The *basic*-subsistence character of goods production, which still characterizes much of the Third World, by no means eliminates the economic-semiotic dimension of production, consumption, distribution and exchange in such societies, as anthropologists like Douglas (1970), Turner (1967), Lévi-Strauss (1966; 1969) and students of the North American west-coast Amerindian potlatch have argued, and as anyone from a technically advanced country who has had the privilege of having a meal as a guest of a subsistence-production-based family will testify. The substantial place of rituals and traditions in the normal acts of everyday life in continuously reproducing the social-economic and informational foundations of a given political-economic system is often more transparent to the guest, or outsider, in subsistence-based communities than in more technologically complex societies, even when much of the internal historical logic of these traditions is at best obscure.[6]

Yet with the extension of market exchange, the "commoditization" of previously nonmarketed goods, the growth of specialization and the division of labor, the development of new forms of "cooperation" (Marx, 1965: Ch. 13), and the increase in productivity and *per capita* real income, there are several significant senses in which the importance of the informational aspect of goods (or more properly, at this stage of development, of exchange-based commodities) rises. First, at the level of *production*, production itself tends to become more technically sophisticated; technical and organizational change becomes more prevalent, rapid, and continuous; and the monopolization of knowledge and information, wealth, and power by those who control the means and processes of production typically tends to become more institutionalized and pronounced, particularly as the creation and establishment of new technological equipment and organizational patterns become increasingly separated from the productive workers themselves.[7]

The message of a commoditized capitalist economy, at the level of production, is typically a significant eventual structural shift in the distribution of access to information and control regarding production from the immediate producers to those who own and/or direct the production process.

At the level of *exchange*, commoditization of an economic system typically implies the rise of specialized traders, spatially and temporally extended marketing networks and institutions, an increased distance between initial producer-suppliers and final end-users (or consumers), and hence a further potential for the development of exchange-based specialization and monopolies of knowledge. While in principle the processes of market competition should over time reduce the effects of exchange-based monopolies of knowledge, in practice factors such as spatial isolation, imperfect knowledge, insider information, patent and copyright systems, and other barriers to entry often limit the degree to which exchange-systems approximate the perfectly competitive model for extended periods of time, as Adam Smith (1904), the inventor of the "invisible hand," was one of the first economists to recognize. In short, the tendency towards separation in exchange between direct producers and direct consumers entailed by the shift to a system of commodity exchange also has informational consequences, insofar as this separation implies an increased potential for monopolization of knowledge by the middleman, with consumer surveys, advertising, promotions, and more general forms of monopoly as the long-term, information-intensive, historically and economically intelligible outcome.

Developments in both of the foregoing spheres (production and exchange) also have informational-economic implications for the *distributional* sphere. The distributional function of all economic systems involves what Joan Robinson called the *cui bono* question: Who gets the swag? There are many different potential systems of income and wealth distribution, and neoclassical economics rests on a theoretical version of *one* of them, the marginal-productivity theory of income-distribution in a world of commodity-production (a theory which, in its basic form, implicitly requires a staggering amount of *costless* information about the capacities of available potential "factors of production," and in its more advanced and complex forms, as for example in the "search," "screening," and "training and education" literature, provides no distribution mechanisms that are strictly consistent in terms of their informational assumptions with pure general-equilibrium economic theory). What is of importance for the neoclassical theory of income distribution, in a system founded on private property rights in the means of production, is that (in a world of constant returns to scale) the "marginal value product" (the net addition to total revenue produced by the *last* unit of *each*, homogeneous, factor of production purchased or hired by any given firm) precisely equals (at no informational cost to the firm) the "marginal factor cost" (the additional cost to the firm occasioned by purchasing the last unit of that factor), for *all* firms in an economy.

The practical informational requirements to perform this hypothetical exercise in neoclassical economic distribution theory have to date never been realized empirically, and hence it could in principle be argued that the *theory* is essentially correct, but that, in its purest form, its *empirical* preconditions have not *yet* been fulfilled. At issue then is whether the types of information necessary to legitimize the *pure* neoclassical economic theory of income-distribution could in principle be *costlessly* obtained, or whether (as is argued below), given uncertain costs and benefits of information-gathering regarding the *potential* marginal value-productivity of *possibly* homogeneous (*but untested*) factors of production, purchase of these factors will not necessarily generate a perfect, Pareto-efficient, general free-market equilibrium, with equitable rewards to *all* of the factors of production.

The bottom-line answer to the second part of the question, when it costs real resources to come up with the answer to a seriously *under-determined* question regarding future performance, which *cannot* in principle, in and of itself, be answered without actually utilizing the potentially purchasable resources, training, adapting, or preparing them as appropriate, and inserting them into the production process, to determine their (pre-preparation or post-preparation) *actual* level of estimated-MRP performance with a given combination of other resources, is "No." In *any* realistic or practical situation requiring *costless prior* assumptions of homogeneity among factors and/or some fixed training costs, prior estimates of Marginal Revenue Product are essentially meaningless. Hence, whenever genuine uncertainty and informational considerations seriously enter the distributional realm of commodity production, the neoclassical economic concept of the Marginal Revenue Product of *any* factor becomes untenable, and with it so does the neoclassical economic theory of income (and *a fortiori*, *wealth*) distribution.

With the rise in *per capita* incomes, the expansion of the service sector, and the associated growth in lability of consumer preferences and hence producers' market uncertainty, the problem becomes more acute. The outputs of the service and informational sectors are typically more difficult to measure than the outputs of the material-commodity sector: a ton of steel of given specifications is easier to measure than a ton of haircuts, and much easier than a ton of information. The greater the semiotic content of a commodity , the more (typically) is being paid for that content, and since the exchange-value of that semiotic content is inherently much more indeterminate and volatile than that of a standardized material commodity, the more indeterminate is the exchange-value of the commodity, and hence of the Marginal Revenue Product of those "factors" or commodity inputs used to produce it.

"Sell the sizzle, not the steak," goes the old advertising slogan. Yet the units in which sizzle is measured are not well defined: sizzle is essentially a subjective notion. In order to develop a *theory* of the demand for sizzle, we would require an epistemologically much more sophisticated theory of the social-psychological semiotic economy, at an *individual* level, than social psychology itself, and *a fortiori* mainstream economic theory, can currently provide. If the determinants of the demand for sizzle are not rigorously definable, and the units in which sizzle is measured are not readily determined, then the entire Marginal Revenue Product edifice effectively collapses as the basis of a rigorous theory of the distribution of income and wealth.[8]

Much of the foregoing analysis of production, exchange, and distribution is also directly relevant to the sphere of *consumption* in a commodity-based economic system. Consumption is viewed in neoclassical economic theory as the ultimate *end* of economic activity. In a number of respects, however, despite the intuitive appeal of this approach, commodity consumption is in practice considerably more complex than the basic neoclassical view suggests.

In the first place, to begin with one of the most apparently straightforward conceptual issues, the mainstream economic measure of commodity consumption (as calculated in standard national income accounts) allows only for the consumption of *commoditized* or marketed goods and services: hence the familiar paradox (or, more appropriately, "accounting convention") whereby the executive who marries her chauffeur thereby lowers national income. This problem, however, is relatively straightforward to handle, at least in principle, and in fact empirical estimates have been made of the value of non-exchanged household production of goods and services, both in advanced capitalist countries and in less developed countries. The basic method employed in such estimates involves the establishment of equivalences between the value of nonmarketed goods and services produced within the household and that of similar marketed commodities. The method is rough-hewn and, practically, inaccurate, but it is at least apparently reasonable.

Unfortunately, even this elementary, first-order, apparently reasonable method of assessing the value of the host of social-economic consumption activities not directly included within the compass of the price-system, viewed as a semiotic institution, raises major theoretical problems. The method presupposes that non-marketed, household-produced goods and services can be valued simply by analogy with those related commodities that pass through the price system. The prime fallacy in such "shadow-price" calculations is that they privilege commoditized modes of valuation in their valuation of nonmarketed activities. Many heterosexual couples, for instance, might regard as demeaning the equation of their lovemaking with acts of prostitution, for purposes of social valuation. Moreover, the question as to whether he was to receive imputed gigolo's wages or she was to receive imputed call-girl's wages, or whether both were to be credited with their "fair share," or alternatively split the difference in order to avoid double-counting, would need to be scientifically assessed. The interested reader can explore the accounting issues at his or her leisure.

The preceding parodic sketch of "scientific" social accounting carried to *reductio ad absurdum* lengths should suggest not only some of the biases and limits of price-system-based measures of the value of primary social activities, but also the qualitatively different semiotic content of the consumption of the commoditized services of a professional provider of immediate sexual gratification, as contrasted with the noncommoditized, sustained mutual gratification and gift-giving of lovemaking with one's chosen long-term life-partner, regardless of whether the temporal, spatial and physical characteristics of the two acts of consumption (Debreu, 1959) are identical. In his imaginative and detailed empirical analysis of the gift relationship, using alternative blood-donor systems as a case study, Titmuss (1972) documented convincingly that the growth of commercially based blood-donor systems in the United States, relative to the voluntary systems in place elsewhere (which emphasized blood donations as an individual's social responsibility of providing the "gift of life"), did *not* result in a significant increase in the supply of blood, and moreover was associated with a decline in the average *quality* of blood provided, as drug addicts and others came to use the sale of their blood as a form of primary or supplementary income, and were hence tempted to lie about their exposure to hepatitis and other blood-transmitted diseases, in order to make the sale.

The sphere of consumption also raises further, equally theoretically intractable issues. Conventional general-equilibrium economics rests on the assumption that it is possible to separate sharply the spheres of production and consumption, and indeed the "separating-hyperplane" theorems used by Debreu and others to establish the existence of general economic equilibrium depend critically on this assumption. Yet in more than a metaphoric sense, production processes necessarily entail consumption, or destruction, or the transformation of inputs into outputs, and equally, so-called final consumption processes necessarily imply the production or reproduction of the economic agents who comprise the system. Descartes' "I think, therefore I am," however profound, requires supplementation by the principle: "I eat, therefore I am, therefore I think." In the pure neoclassical world, there is in fact no guarantee that the equilibrium set of prices will guarantee the *survival* of all relevant economic agents over the relevant period. This theoretical embarrassment can be dealt with by various *ad hoc* theoretical assumptions (Koopmans, 1957), but such ad-hocus-pocus is not the firmest of foundations for a supposedly general theory. In practice, in most historical social-economic systems, there tends to be a presumption that the starvation of "unsuccessful" economic agents is not to be encouraged, but this presumption (with its semiotic weight) is not *intrinsic* to conventional economic theory, in its purest forms.

The difficulty of separating commodity consumption from production and reproduction is intensified when we shift from a focus on the minimum material prerequisites of biological subsistence to a consideration of forms of consumption in which there is a more clearly apparent informational and semiotic component. In virtually all acts of communication, the artificial separation of production and consumption becomes more obviously arbitrary. James Joyce's query in *Ulysses* ("My consumers, are they not my producers?") points to the dialectical relationship between writer and reader in the production of the meanings of a text: in a very real sense, the act of "consumption" of a work of art is an act of *production* of the meaning of that work by the reader.

The economics of education (particularly in its human-capital forms) is constantly forced to deal with the issue of whether education is a consumption-good or an investment-good. While for purposes of calculating the returns to education (notwithstanding the serious theoretical inadequacies of most existing models in the field) this issue appears important, in practice, the neophyte's response ("Well, if you feel moved to pose the issue in that way, surely the answer is 'Both'!") is almost certainly correct. Moreover, the theoretical separation between production and consumption cannot be seriously sustained without a much more profound understanding of the production function for knowledge than even the most ardent exponent of human capital theory would currently pretend to possess. Not only is it extraordinarily difficult to measure precisely *what* it is that education produces (and so-called objective tests merely underline the extent of our current ignorance), but the production process *itself*, and the respective roles of educator and educatee within the educational dialectic, are still far from being adequately understood. At a more radical level, it is distinctly possible that if (as Penrose, 1990, has suggested) there is a necessarily non-algorithmic aspect to the creative process, then a determinate production function for knowledge is *in principle* unattainable. Finally, insofar as information-*consumption* is simultaneously information-*production*, and insofar as the consumption of new information involves not merely *additive* supplements to one's existing stock of knowledge, but rather the potential for a complex process of qualitative reconfiguration and revaluation of the constituents of one's preexisting stock of knowledge, the consumption of new knowledge (regardless of the above-mentioned limits of the consumption metaphor) raises basic and intractable difficulties for economic theories where *additivity* of commodities is assumed, including mainstream economic theory.

The sphere of commodity consumption, viewed from a semiotic standpoint, raises still further difficulties for conventional general-equilibrium theory. That theory (necessarily, from a mathematical standpoint) requires what has been described as a methodological-individualist assumption. The import of this assumption is that every consuming agent's level of utility depends exclusively on the set of commodities he or she consumes, and is entirely independent of the levels of consumption of all other individuals within the economic system. It might be supposed that the net effect of this assumption is to *strengthen* the conclusions one can draw regarding the Pareto-efficiency of the competitive market system: "*Even* if every individual economic agent acts *solely* to maximize his or her economic welfare, *without* regard for the welfare of others, the competitive market (under certain assumptions) can generate a general economic equilibrium, sustained by a set or vector of prices in which no agent can be made better off without making at least one other agent worse off." The fact of the matter, however, is that this supposition is false.

If one relaxes the methodological-individualist assumption of completely *independent* utilities, and instead allows for the possibility of *interdependent utilities* (so that the welfare of any agent in an economic system is conditioned by either the level of consumption *or* the level of utility achieved by any other agent within the system), then in general the competitive price-system will be unable to generate a sustainable, Pareto-efficient, general competitive equilibrium. While the mathematical aspects of this *negative* theorem are (or can be) fairly abstruse, the economic intuition undergirding it is fairly straightforward. The *only* permissible act between or among agents in a perfectly competitive, price-system-based economy of the standard form is an act of *exchange*, at the equilibrium set of commodity prices. Nonmarket transactions, such as unilateral gifts, armed robbery, government redistribution, and so on, may improve one's welfare but are excluded by the rules of the free-market game.

Hence, for instance, even if A were unconditionally to give B a quantity of commodity X, and this act increased both A's and B's level of utility (since for A the loss of utility attendant upon A's loss of some X was more than compensated for by the satisfaction experienced by A as a result of the net increase in B's utility level, while for B the loss of utility associated with any odium of being the beneficiary of a unilateral act of *caritas*, or charity, from A was more than compensated for by B's enjoyment of the additional X), such a transaction would violate the *quid pro quo* (or "equals exchange equals for equals with equals," at equilibrium prices) assumption of the core model. In particular, A's gift would violate the assumption that *only one price rules* in the competitive market for X, since A's gift of X to B essentially implies that (for *this* transaction) the effective price of X is *zero*. Other examples could be developed, but the basic point would only be reinforced: in *any* social-economic system in which individual utility levels are interpersonally interdependent, the competitive exchange economy as conventionally modeled is necessarily incapable on its own of generating Pareto-efficient patterns of distribution and consumption. In such cases, the free-market myth is economically and semiotically bankrupt.

Thorstein Veblen (1899) was one of the theoretical pioneers in the study of interdependent utilities, with his analysis of conspicuous leisure and conspicuous consumption, as means of invidious distinction. Duesenberry (1967) relied in part on Veblen's inspiration in his post-Keynesian analysis of the determinants of the Keynesian consumption function, which introduced keeping up with the Joneses into mainstream macroeconomic literature. Liebenstein (1950) analyzed the conditions under which Veblen effects could result in upward-sloping commodity demand curves, where (over some price-range, in a partial-equilibrium setting), *ceteris paribus*, an increase in the relative price of a commodity could be associated with a *higher* quantity demanded, because the purchase of a more highly-priced commodity confers greater social status on the purchaser. Veblen's influence also penetrates Galbraith's (1963) less technical analysis of the political and cultural economy of the affluent society. Baudrillard's (1972) early work may be regarded as a derivative but creative amalgam of the insights of Veblen and McLuhan, in which the perceptions of these North American thinkers regarding the semiology of commodities were replayed to North America with a Gallic, post-structuralist twist, much as the Beatles, the Rolling Stones, and other groups constituted the basis of a British invasion of the North American music market based substantially on a reworking of delta blues, Chuck Berry, the Everly Brothers, Buddy Holly and other influential American sources. The work of all these theorists underlines the practical untenability of ignoring the interdependence of individuals' utility functions, yet such ignorance or disregard is mathematically essential to the validity of neoclassical general economic equilibrium theorems.

The foregoing sketch of the genuine problems posed for conventional economic theory by the presence of interdependent utilities at best scratches the surface of the more radical set of implications of which these problems are symptomatic. What is required is not only an economics of envy, an economics of philanthropy, an economics of beholdenness, an economics of social myth, ritual and custom, and an economics of hope and fear, but also an acknowledgment that the set of social relations and semiotic processes that *practically* sustain actual historical social-economic systems is much richer, more complex and variegated, *and* much more susceptible to economic-historical study, than the reductionistic, methodologically individualist, exchange-biased image present in the hegemonic vision of neoclassical economics is currently capable of delineating.

A related consideration, in assessing the semiotic component of the sphere of consumption, concerns the question of the *origin* of the tastes, preferences, habits, myths, rituals, concepts, and socially prescribed, permitted and proscribed patterns of acceptable consumption behavior that determine, to a significant extent, the *actual* consumption patterns of individuals, viewed as commodity consumers. Neoclassical economic theory typically evades this issue, either through the *assumption* that at any time all individuals in an economy, as consumers, have costlessly given complete preference preorderings over the entire nonnegative orthant of the commodity-space; *or* by assuming that the determination of tastes, preferences and so on is a matter beyond the scope of economics, to be dealt with by the sociologist, anthropologist, psychologist or semiotician (whose scientific results can in turn be used, or consumed, by the economist as input *data*).

The first solution is a purely formal one, since it effectively assumes away the question. The second solution is in a sense more ideological, in that it apparently acknowledges the importance of having an empirical basis for the analysis of the origins of these forms of knowledge and desire, but leaves the actual tasks to others who are supposedly more qualified by virtue of their specialized positions within the disciplinary division of intellectual labor to provide the answers.

There are three difficulties, however, with this second solution. The first concerns Thomas Schelling's parable of the fictitious colleague: when the problem is handed over to the colleague, the colleague isn't there, or else is more interested in his or her own research agenda than in the economist's. In addition, the solution assumes that the colleague is *capable* of providing the answer, and that the answer will be welcomed with open arms by economists, thereby neglecting the role of *hubris*, mystery, and pecking orders in the maintenance of priesthoods and other hierarchical disciplinary monopolies of knowledge. Finally, even assuming that these obstacles could be surmounted and that the fictitious colleague had properly understood the question, the solution neglects the fact that a major act of *translation* would currently be required to convert an analysis derived within another discipline into a *usable* form for mainstream economics.

Notwithstanding the genuineness of these obstacles, it does, however, seem that economics *itself*, viewed in broader terms than mainstream neoclassical economics currently tends to promote, *should* be able to contribute significantly to an understanding of these semiological-economic issues. The italicized *should* operates in at least two senses. First, insofar as economics is the study of forms and processes of production, exchange, distribution, and consumption (all of which involve *primary* activities in *all* historical social-economic systems), it has accumulated considerable empirical-historical knowledge and a wide range of potentially relevant tools, developed within a considerable number of divergent schools of economic thought (Austrian, neoclassical, Keynesian, post-Keynesian, institutionalist, Innisian, neo-Ricardian, and Marxian, to name a few), and cross-disciplinary tools from hybrid fields like economic geography and economic history. The hegemony of *neoclassical* economic theory has tended to marginalize many of these alternative economic approaches, and has resulted in serious problems of unused theoretical capacity within economic theory itself. Yet economics, or political economy, taken as a whole, has a theoretical asset-structure that is, at least potentially, significantly more productive in relation to the semiotic-economic issues sketched in this chapter than the above critical remarks regarding the capacity limits of neoclassical economic theory in this sphere might tend to suggest.

Second, if economics is to become a more practical guide to human action in the twenty-first century, when the informational-semiotic dimension of economic activities will increase in importance, and increasingly exceed the analytical capacities of current neoclassical economic theory, economics as a discipline will *have* to become more self-reflexive, more eclectic within itself, more cosmopolitan, more equipped to utilize currently marginalized capacities for economic thought, and more humble and open to the insights and methods of cognate disciplines. The requirement of self-reflexivity simply implies that economics (as a *social*-scientific discipline) should be able to account for its *own* existence *in its own terms*, since it is *itself* a product and process of social-economic activity. Increased self-reflexivity necessarily implies a *semiotic* dimension, insofar as economics, *writ large*, is itself a medium of communication, a language, a set of tools (or produced means of intellectual production) for understanding, a form and a forum for the production and distribution of (commoditized and noncommoditized) knowledge, and hence an ideal subject for the testing of the explanatory power of its own methods.

In such an enterprise, intellectual *humility* is a prime requirement. Fortunately, these days, neoclassical economics has much to be humble about. Its batting average, insofar as empirical understanding, theoretical explanation, historical predictions, and policy prescriptions are concerned, has been fairly low. This chapter has indicated that a good part of the explanation for these failures stems from the radical incapacity of neoclassical economics to address the informational-semiotic dimensions of an increasingly commoditized world in which information itself is in the process of becoming one of the predominant commodities. Mainstream neoclassical economics, particularly in its purest general-equilibrium forms, is becoming an increasingly otiose relic in the analysis of production, consumption, distribution and exchange, for the reasons outlined above, as well as others which cannot be explored here for reasons of space.

Conclusion

It would be possible to read the preceding sections of this chapter as constituting the basis for an argument that the insights of current semiotic research, if properly translated into economese and absorbed by economists, could save economics from itself, and enable a properly chastened, expanded, and reformed economics to deal adequately with the challenges posed by the semiotic dimension of commodities, as we approach the twenty-first century.

Such a conclusion would be both wide of the mark and overly sanguine. To begin with, regardless of the validity and/or truth of *all* of the criticisms of the neoclassical economic model sketched above, the fact remains that the ideological power of the core neoclassical myth is still very considerable. At a vulgar level (which is nonetheless important), it is still *believed* by many economists and economic lay people. Moreover, its free-market message (without resorting to crude formulations regarding "the hegemonic power of ruling-class ideology") happens to be extraordinarily compatible with the views of many who have both the will and the resources to extend the longevity of the myth. In addition, most practitioners of economics have themselves sunk years (often decades) into learning the core models, teaching them, and theoretically extending and/or empirically testing them. An individual economist in this situation is likely to think in terms more of Ptolemaic epicycles than of Copernican revolutions. Finally, given the extent of the society that "speaks neoclassical economics fluently," the path of least resistance in effective short-run communication is strongly biased towards reproducing the core neoclassical model with minor variations rather than towards theoretical rebellion or revolution. Cynics might describe this activity as akin to shifting the location of the deck-chairs on the *Titanic*, but it is important to appreciate that the probability of theoretical conservatism is intelligible from both economic *and* semiotic standpoints.

The second major consideration is that semiotics (or semiology) itself is scarcely a unified discipline, and moreover tends to be characterized to a much greater degree than economics by internecine struggles for power, rapid vocabulary shifts, correspondingly high proportions of idiosyncratic jargon, and a flavor-of-the-month or faddish (who's hot and who's not) theoretical aspect. These characteristics are typical of innovative and rapidly developing fields, in the absence of theoretical hegemony. Moreover, the explicit analytical thrust of the works of some major semiotic theorists, such as Derrida (1967), Lacan (1966), and Deleuze (1977), has been self-consciously, almost painfully, anti-hierarchical and/or deconstructionist in character, although the anarchic and/or nihilistic aspects of their works have not wholly relieved them of responsibility for the catachrestic contributions of some of their more ham-handed acolytes and groupies. "To the founder of a school, everything may be forgiven, except his school." (A. Guérard, quoted in Innis, 1964: 4) Finally, as Best and Kellner (1991) have carefully argued, one of the *weakest* links in the chains of thought forged by current semiotic theory concerns the material or *economic* bases of semiotic processes in society.

As we enter the twenty-first century, it is clear that the theoretical-capacity limits of current mainstream economics have been significantly exceeded by the demands posed (in intensified form) as a result of the semiotic, or meaning-bearing, character of commodities, as reinforced by the increasingly central role of commoditized information within the global political economy. A well-grounded political economy of commoditized information appears to be a *sine qua non* in enabling the development of a world in which the role of commodities as sign-systems is becoming increasingly strategic, in which commoditized information is becoming one of the primary factors of production, and in which the erstwhile bogeyman of eco-catastrophe is in the process of establishing itself as a day-to-day reality.

It should be clear, from the analysis of this chapter, that the semiotic dimension of commodities poses genuinely intractable problems for mainstream neoclassical theory, insofar as it attempts to analyze the spheres of production, exchange, distribution and consumption. Moreover, the chapter has, at best, only scratched the surface of some of the issues raised by this dimension of the world of commodities. Yet it should also have suggested that, within a *broader* definition of economics, economics itself already contains many of the tools necessary for an escape from its current impasse, and that with an appropriate degree of humility, a willingness to import theoretical software from other disciplines, and a preparedness to scrap some of its obsolescent current intellectual fixed capital, economics may yet prove to be one of the principal disciplines essential to an understanding of the twenty-first-century global political economy.

Notes

1. This axiomatic structure, in and of itself, is of course insufficient to generate a unique general-equilibrium solution, in the absence of *further* ancillary assumptions such as non-satiation, strict convexity of preferences ("diminishing marginal utility"), and so on. At this stage, the crucial point is simply that this complete preference pre-ordering is *costless* and *preordained*, and independent of the agent's past consumption experience.

2. Some cases in which general economic equilibrium cannot in general occur are considered below in this chapter.

3. This phrase is derived from Robbins (1962).

4. It might be argued that any information transmitted *via* the production, exchange, distribution, or consumption of a commodity should *already* be incorporated into the *definition* of the commodity. Yet this argument is fallacious on two counts: first, the neoclassical framework effectively presupposes that such an informational-semiotic component does *not* exist; and second, if it *did* exist, the difficulties for analysis as posed in the text would not be obviated, but would rather parallel and reinforce the concerns raised in the text.

5. Moreover, the problem is not resolved by expedients such as those adopted in the imaginative attempt at an extension of the basic neoclassical paradigm by Stigler and Becker (1977), which implicitly and explicitly relies at a number of points on a psychologically crude theory of "habituation". Neither the "costs" of changing utility functions nor the unpre-

dictable character of such changes can be adequately modeled within their heuristically interesting framework.

6. At times, the economic wisdom and the meaning of traditions is made more explicit in proverbial form: for instance, a Swahili saying from Tanzania, *Siku mbili mgeni, siku ya tatu, mpe jembe* ("For the first two days he's a guest; on the third day, give him a hoe") renders explicit the appropriate conventional limits of hospitality, on a time-frame correlated with the demands of life and production at the margin of subsistence.

7. For a perceptive, if perhaps somewhat narrow, perspective on this issue, see the valuable contribution of Braverman (1974).

8. Further limits of the neoclassical model in this sphere are underlined in the works of Robertson (1951) and Thurow (1980).

References

Arrow, K., and F. Hahn. (1971). *General Competitive Analysis*. San Francisco: Holden-Day.
Baudrillard, J. (1972). *Pour une Critique de l'Economie Politique du Signe*. Paris: Gallimard.
Best, S., and D. Kellner (1991). *Postmodern Theory*. New York: Guilford.
Braverman, H. (1974). *Labor and Monopoly Capital*. New York: Monthly Review Press.
Debreu, G. (1952). *Theory of Value*. New Haven: Yale University Press.
Deleuze, G. (1977). *Anti-Oedipus*. New York: Viking.
Derrida, J. (1967). *De la Grammatologie*. Paris: Editions de Minuit.
Douglas, M. (1970). *Natural Symbols*. New York: Pantheon.
Duesenberry, J. (1967). *Income, Saving, and the Theory of Consumer Behavior*. New York: Oxford University Press.
Galbraith, J. K. (1963). *The Affluent Society*. New York: New American Library.
Innis, H. A. (1956). *Essays in Canadian Economic History*. Toronto: University of Toronto Press.
Innis, H. A. (1964). *The Bias of Communication*. Toronto: University of Toronto Press.
Innis, H. A. (1972). *Empire and Communications*. Toronto: University of Toronto Press.
Koopmans, T. (1957). *Three Essays on the State of Economic Science*. New York: McGraw-Hill.
Lacan, J. (1966). *Ecrits*. Paris: Editions du Seuil.
Lancaster, K. (1971). *Consumer Demand: A New Approach*. New York: Columbia University Press.
Lévi-Strauss, C. (1966). *The Savage Mind*. Chicago: University of Chicago Press.
Lévi-Strauss, C. (1969). *The Raw and the Cooked*. New York: Harper & Row.
Liebenstein, H. (1950). "Bandwagon, Snob, and Veblen Effects in the Theory of Consumer's Behavior." *Quarterly Journal of Economics* (Vol. LXIV):183–207.
Machlup, F. (1962). *The Production and Distribution of Knowledge in the United States*. Princeton: Princeton University Press.

Marx, K. (1965). *Capital: Vol. I.* Moscow: Progress Publishers.
Parker, I. (1983). " 'Commodity Fetishism' and 'Vulgar Marxism': On Re-thinking Canadian Political Economy." *Studies in Political Economy* (10):143–172.
Parker, I. (1985). "Harold A. Innis: Staples, Communications, and the Economics of Capacity, Overhead Costs, Rigidity and Bias." In D. Cameron (ed.), *Explorations in Canadian Economic History.* Ottawa: University of Ottawa Press.
Parker, I., J. Hutcheson, and P. Crawley. (1988). *The Strategy of Canadian Culture in the 21st Century.* Toronto: Harold Innis Foundation.
Penrose, R. (1990). *The Emperor's New Mind.* New York: Vintage.
Robbins, L. (1962). *An Essay on The Nature and Significance of Economic Science.* London: Macmillan.
Robertson, D. (1951). "Wage Grumbles." Reprinted in American Economics Association, *Readings in the Theory of Income Distribution.* Philadelphia: Blakiston, pp. 221–236.
Smith, A. (1904). *The Wealth of Nations.* (2 vols.) London: Henry Frowde.
Stigler, G., and G. Becker. (1977). "De Gustibus Non Est Disputandum." *American Economic Review* 67 (December).
Thurow, L. (1980). *The Zero-Sum Society.* New York: Basic Books.
Titmuss, R. M. (1972). *The Gift Relationship.* New York: Vintage.
Turner, V. (1967). *The Forest of Symbols.* Ithaca: Cornell University Press.
Veblen, T. (1899). *The Theory of the Leisure Class.* New York: Macmillan.
Veblen, T. (1919). *The Place of Science in Modern Civilization.* New York: B. W. Huebisch.
Veblen, T. (1934). *Essays in Our Changing Order.* New York: Viking.

Commentary by Sandra Braman

Babe and Parker place themselves within ongoing discussions about the key features of the information economy and possible responses by economic theory to problems that have emerged from efforts to treat information creation, processing, flows and use within neoclassical terms. Here, their work will be contextualized within those discussions, followed by exploration of policy-making considerations and concluding with an appreciation of some key features in their ideas that identify a critically necessary research program.

Conceptualizations of the Information Economy

Three types of arguments have been used to characterize this period as an economic information age—this is an information economy because the proportion of economic activity generated by information as an intermediate and final product now dominates, because the economy has expanded through commodification of information and its processing, or because information flows have come to replace the market as the economy's key coordinating mechanism. Each is discussed below.

Dominance of the Economy by Information

This is fundamentally the approach taken here by Babe and Parker, who both refer to quantitative measures of the type developed by Porat (1977) as evidence of the growing importance of information to the economy, and who both argue that the problems they are discussing are exacerbated because of this trend. This is also the most widespread approach in North America, within the popular imagination as well as among scholars and analysts, partially because it underlies the widely diffused ideas of Daniel Bell, and partially because it is the most accessible notion of the three theoretically.

(Differences in the experience of the information society globally, and at different times, should receive more attention. In Japan, for example—where the concepts of the information society and informatization first emerged [Ito, 1991]—planning for the information society became central to research and development, and government policymaking in the early 1960s. In around the same period, a coup brought a government into power in Brazil that self-consciously controlled the range of information industries and ultimately led to the relatively radical policy of forbidding use of computer technologies developed outside of the country in its effort to develop an internal computer industry. In a third type of example, Germans as late as the late 1980s resisted identification cards in response to their World War II experiences: their experience of possible effects of the ownership of information was concrete. In each of these settings, individual, social, cultural, and political experience of the information society has differed significantly).

Expansion of the Economic Domain by Commodification of Information

This line of argument has been developed by political economists such as Mosco and Schiller. From this perspective, just as capital serves its need for expansion of markets through globalization, it can do so by commodifying more and more domains of human life. By now, commodification has extended even to that information which is most personal (genetic information, or the thoughts in one's head for a journalist undergoing scrutiny for actual malice in a libel suit in the U.S.), the most public (through privatization of governmental information intended to serve "the public interest"), and the most sacred or aesthetic.

Many of our philosophers of technology, going back at least to McLuhan (see McLuhan 1964; McLuhan and Nevitt, 1973; McLuhan and Powers, 1981), also take the expanding commodification of information and its flows as a working assumption. Thinkers like McLuhan and Baudrillard (1983) are most concerned about this process because of the profound ways in which it transforms the individual and society. McLuhan suggested that both the human body and the body social are numbed by the use of electronic information technologies, and thought the effects of this process were already significant by the beginning of the 20th century. Several post-structuralists take this analysis more deeply into the body. They also take it into time, arguing first that time has sped up, and then, ultimately, that it has reversed itself (Kroker, 1984, 1992). The implications of this latter point for information have not yet been worked out, though there have been suggestions: "The future has gotten tangled up in the present" (Woolf, 1992).

Replacement of the Market with Information Flows for Economic Coordination

The economic historian Alfred Chandler, Jr., first noted this process in his seminal work, *The Visible Hand* (1977). Chandler analyzed the impact of the introduction of automation into manufacturing and distribution and described, among other things, the shift of decision-making from the human to the automated procedures themselves and, concurrently and at a second-order level, the replacement of owners with managers as designers of the corporate form. From this perspective, as soon as manufacturing plants and office operations began to be automated to any degree, some functions that had previously been in the marketplace—and therefore governed by the "invisible hand"—had come to be governed by automated decision-making procedures internal to corporate organizations—the "visible hand." It is these decision-making procedures that have recently become the center of interest in terms of property rights—and ignited a new interest in studies of organizations.

Antonelli (1992), basing his ideas on years of empirical research into the transformations of transnational corporations (e.g., 1981, 1984), has pushed economic theory towards what he calls "network economics," in which the key unit of analysis is no longer the firm or the industry, but the project; network firms are understood via their interdependencies rather than their characteristics as independent units; and cooperation and coordination are as important to the functioning of the economy as competition. Antonelli takes the final step, working from within the terms of "mainstream" economic theory out, in arguing that the marketplace has been replaced with flows of information when he notes, radically, that price is no longer a signal. From this perspective, efforts to include trade in services under the General Agreements on Tariffs and Trade (GATT) (Braman, 1990a) and harmonization of production line monitoring systems and the sharing of management theory under arms control agreements (Braman, 1990b, 1991) appear as efforts in support of the harmonization of organizational forms for the purposes of increasing coordination and cooperation.

Pushed to an extreme, this perspective also winds up back in the arms of McLuhan. For Antonelli, too, what is now important is no longer the content of information flows, but their structural sheen. McLuhan said the content of any new medium is the medium which went before; Antonelli describes an organizational environment in which the new medium is the global information infrastructure, and the content of the medium flows of capital (themselves already transformed into information flows).

Information Economics

It is a great strength of the Babe and Parker chapters that they explore in detail many of the problems confronting attempts to deal with information with neoclassical economic tools. Economists have had three sets of responses to these problems: denial, rejection of neoclassical theory in favor of radically different alternatives, and attempts to work within prevailing economic terms to move theoretically forward in response to empirical research, theoretical developments internal to the field, and theoretical developments external to the field.

Denial

Some—heavily represented among working policy-makers—have responded by denying that any problems exist at all, and that information and its flows are different in any pertinent ways from the manufacture and distribution of physical goods (see, *e.g.*, Cass and Noam, 1989). The problems this has caused have not only been noted by economists such as Babe and Parker, who explore these problems at length here; it has caused problems for negotiators as the US is repeatedly stunned when, during international discussions, they are told, for example, that information flows have cultural and political value, or that other nations value "balance" as well as "freedom" of its information flows. While as Babe and Parker point out, it is in the political economy of the field that these analytical tools, with their attendant and well-developed methodological applications, fit into existing policy-making structures and processes, it is also increasingly acknowledged that the results of policy-making that derives from this perspective are not always survival-oriented. Environmental problems seem to be having the largest impact in this regard.

Rejection of Mainstream Economics

A second approach to problems faced when trying to treat information economically has been to argue that the emergence of these problems only illuminates long-standing contradictions within the neoclassical school. Differences here derive from base assumptions that differ in the conceptualization of the information economy. Those who use a definition based on the statistical proportion of information industries and flows to the economy, as do Babe and Parker, argue that the inherent contradictions in neoclassical economics are increasingly exacerbated because they are particularly provoked in dealing with information and its flows.

While Babe and Parker agree on their fundamental critique of neoclassical economics, and both work in the domain of theory and deductively, they point to alternative paths forward. Babe focuses on the possibility of an alternative exchange mechanism to drive the economy, such as gift-giving. I would be interested in knowing what Babe would think of either Antonelli's interdependencies comprised of information flows or the deviation-amplifying mutual causal processes and other generative mechanisms of second order cybernetics as described by Maruyama (1963), Jantsch (1989), and others as other alternative exchange mechanisms. It is the particular advantage of periods of turbulence that a number of different alternatives can be explored before settling on one around which to organize a new equilibrious state.

Parker emphasizes the communicative aspects of the market, leading him to semiotics. Parker is interested in semiotics as a way of discovering the actual impact of the existing economic system. In this his views share something with the work of certain business and economic historians, such as those in a recent (1991) book edited by Temin, who are looking at the construction of the economic information collection and flows (with which any theory must deal), their interactions with organizational form and motive direction, and their ultimate impact on economic competitiveness and related matters. Johnson (1991), for example, notes that the kinds of information collected internally about corporate activities significantly changed when ownership patterns changed, and that they did so at the loss of attention to the significant human values within organizations. Such an approach in a sense exemplifies Parker's call for a semiotics of the economy, and it could be interesting to see Parker's work engage with this stream of literature in the future.

Theoretical Adaptation from Within

A third approach by economists trying to deal with information creation, processing, flows, and use has been to work towards theoretical adaptation moving forward from existing commonly used terms. Antonelli (1992) provides a premier example of this in his development of network economics. Beck (1992) offers another effort of the scope of that of Antonelli with his concept of the "risk society," in which every exchange involves the distribution of risk as well as wealth. Because calculations of risk are today as important as those of wealth, the politics of information flows are critical and our understanding of social relations must come to incorporate class divisions based to a significant extent on risk, not wealth.

Some other efforts in this vein include attempts at reformulating measurement tools by beginning with reconceptualizing quantification methods (e.g., Berndt and Triplett, 1990; Hooper and Richardson, 1991). These quantification tools provide the basis for implementation of policy. One might also class efforts at restructuring the legal system to fit new economic realities—and opportunities (on the part of transnational lawmakers)—such as in the work of Huber (1987), Petersmann (1986, 1991) and Dezalay (1989, 1990), here.

There is a particular self-reflexivity in the literature about making law that deals with information and its flows, for those are exactly the constituent elements of any organizational form; thus communications policy-making is fundamentally decision-making about how to constitute ourselves as a society.

Policy-making Considerations

As one chooses which path among the multiple available to follow, it makes sense to keep in mind that a primary reason for developing an economics of information is to serve the policy-making process. That places certain demands upon the development of concepts that need ultimately become validly and feasibly operationalizable. (It is success in achieving at least methodological feasibility that underlies what is referred to in these chapters as the political economy of economics—the acceptance of certain economic theories and theorists by those in power.) Here, rhetorical, procedural, and strategic issues that arise out of the needs of policy-making will be discussed. Rhetorical and procedural decisions of course have strategic implications.

Rhetorical Issues

Rhetorically, there are two distinct problems. First, the structure of any argument must match the ongoing norms of specific decision-making arenas. Certainly any study of key arenas for communications policy must note not just the number at any given governmental level, but the diversity of decision-making cultures (contrast UNESCO, for example, with the GATT, or the Voice of America with the Office of Management and Budget). These cultures are distinguished by their operational definitions, mode of argument, and dominant value hierarchy. Decision-making regarding the Voice of America, for example, defines information as power, uses a monotonal free flow of information argument, and has national security as its guiding value. The Office of Management and Budget, on the other hand, casts its discussion about information collection, processing, flows, and use within a cost-benefit argument, defines information as a commodity, and—seemingly—has cost effectiveness and efficiency as its guiding values.[1] Thus development of any economic theory that seeks to influence policy-making processes must pay some attention to the ongoing discussion within specific policy-making arenas to ensure that concepts ultimately developed are operationalizable within their terms.

Further issues regarding the procedural aspects of this problem are discussed below, but at the arena level it must also be noted that there can be a problem with what, for lack of a better word, must be described as tone. At its most extreme—*not* represented here—accusations of evil intention on the part of representatives of one theoretical or methodological approach and a claiming of the moral high ground for one's own group just doesn't work. Even the most limited of economists is generally trying to do his or her best to solve a set of problems to the best of his or her understanding—what differs is in the definition of the problem, the length of time and depth within the social structure to which its impacts must be traced, approaches to problem-solving, and resources and "capacity" available. Polarization along allegedly moral lines prevents fruitful discussions across perspectives from emerging.

Procedural Issues

Assertions that certain phenomena or processes cannot be validly quantified, irrespective of economic efforts to do so, must face the challenge levied by current decision-making processes in their demand for certain types of information in specific formats in order to be usable. Those who argue that existing procedures are incapable of validly dealing with significant dimensions of social life, including processes within the economic system, or that those decision-making procedures are inherently biased at the value level, have the responsibility of coming up with alternative and feasible decision-making procedures. Without a means of concretely implementing an altered vision of the goals and means of policy-making, the genuine effectiveness of any critiques is vastly diminished.

There are three alternatives:

1. Development of ways of quantifying previously unquantified values for the purposes of insertion into existing decision-making procedures.
2. Adaptation of existing decision-making procedures to take into account the need to deal with values, processes, and externalities that may not be quantifiable.
3. Development of alternative types of decision-making procedures.

It is now arguably possible, with the use of vast computerized intelligences and the evolution of organizational forms made possible by the use of new information technologies, to explore each of these three alternatives as we attempt to ensure that all pertinent values are incorporated into information and economic policy-making processes. New theoretical developments, in particular in the areas of second order cybernetics, chaos theory, and organizational theory, should be drawn upon to enrich the range of concepts upon which economists can draw, and to include in the development of economic theory those concepts which map most accurately onto the significant features of today's environment. In one example, those working within the field of second order cybernetics have noted that we know far more about negative feedback mechanisms—as found underlying much economic theory—than we do about those that are mutually beneficial. In another, these recently-developed bodies of literature provide insights into periods of turbulence, an issue of concern in most social and economic analysis today. As we move from here to there, however, incremental steps may well be more effective than those that seek to wipe the slate clean.

While Babe's emancipatory vision is moving, it also seems to require a set of transformations unlikely at this point to occur—when cast in terms of a "gift" economy. Much of Babe's thrust, however, maps onto some of Antonelli's ideas. Coordination and cooperation can, after all, be understood as forms of gift-giving, or gift-giving as an example of a way of structuring coordination and cooperation. Thus Babe's ideas might well be developed in such a way that they usefully enrich the latter.

Parker strikes off in a different direction. His focus on the communicative aspects of market transactions leads him to suggest semiotics as an analytical approach to understanding the effects of the economic system. While this approach may be seen as even more adventuresome intellectually, it is actually less radical politically than the direction indicated by Babe because it does not immediately lead to policy prescriptions. But like the work of Babe, Parker's semiotic approach to the economy could well be developed in such a way that it enhances the operationalization of Antonelli's ideas about network economics.

Strategic Issues

Theoretical and conceptual development legitimately occur separate from the positioning of ideas in environments in which decisions are made on a short time scale that will have both short- and long-term impacts in multiple dimensions. The question of positioning, however, while always of political import, becomes extremely interesting during periods of such turbulence as we are experiencing today. As mentioned above, it is a characteristic of turbulent periods that a number of alternatives will arise. Ultimately, however—if there is to be successful transformation from chaos to order—one among those alternatives will be chosen as the new organizational approach, and resources thrown behind it.

In a turbulent period, therefore, to claim the central position has particular strategic value: to speak and act as if you are the mainstream will take you some distance towards assuming that position as a new order coalesces. To do so in a turbulent period is *not* to claim the identity of those who have previously held the position, but to claim a *new* identity for the holder of the position.

From this regard, Babe and Parker take a more conservative stance than does Antonelli. The ideas of each of the three are as radical and strike as deeply at the heart of economics as those of the others. Antonelli, however, presents himself as within the "mainstream," takes that position, while Babe and Parker explicitly place themselves on the margins. In doing so, of course, Babe and Parker participate in the reproduction of their own marginalization. As a result, the ideas of Antonelli are more likely to be taken up in the short-term by working policy-makers.

Babe and Parker do both make strong claims for the continued importance of the field of economics itself as a source of the types of theoretical, conceptual, and methodological developments that will be needed. Should they choose to take a more aggressive stance regarding the centrality of their own ideas to the field in this time of turbulence—and should they find ways of operationalizing their concepts for policy-making processes—they may go further in dragging the field in their own direction without in any way indicating even a shift in their own identities or in the nature of the tools they intend to use. While it is true that there may be significant ontological and deontological consequences of taking particular theoretical positions, it is not on those grounds that the arguments are fought.

Conclusions

In these two chapters, Babe and Parker do a persuasive and provocative job of unravelling a number of the problems economists face when trying to cope with information with neoclassical analytical tools. Babe's work, in particular, has over time built this case ever more strongly, and he has an appreciated skill for identifying useful concepts and approaches that litter the history of economic theory.

Both of these chapters, however, take us just up to the edge of a vision of where we should go next. As each of these economists, and others, step down the paths identified, they are encouraged to take into account theoretical developments in other fields, the pragmatic and interpersonal needs of decision-making processes, and empirical developments.

Some criticisms can be made. Both authors may want to find opportunities to unfold at more length extremely compressed arguments. Various among us may have more specific quibbles.

But it has been a number of years now during which folks have been complaining, in trying to understand the information society for prescriptive purposes, that the old categories don't work. Here Babe and Parker take adventuresome steps in the direction of identifying new categories for analysis. And while it is suggested that their largely theoretical and deductive work take into account the results of empirical research, both deductive and inductive, as well as policy-making needs, it is also strongly urged that those doing empirical research and formulating policy questions and procedures seriously incorporate the insights offered by Babe and Parker.

Finally, it is worth noting that Babe and Parker, along with Antonelli and, increasingly, business and economic historians, are all offering views—though widely disparate—of an economics that has become self-reflexive as a consequence of its efforts to deal with information. In this information economics shares with other approaches to understanding the information society, such as the various post-modernisms, a sense that there has been a tilt in the relationship between society and the material and symbolic worlds.

References

Antonelli, Cristiano. (1981). *Transborder Data Flows and International Business: A Pilot Study*. OECD Directorate for Science, Technology & Industry, DSTI/ICCP/81.16.

Antonelli, Cristiano. (1984). "Multinational firms, international trade and international telecommunications." *Information Economics and Policy* (1): 333–343.

Antonelli, Cristiano. (1992). "The economic theory of information networks." In Cristiano Antonelli (ed.), *The Economics of Information Networks*. Amsterdam: North-Holland, pp. 5–27.

Baudrillard, Jean. (1983). *Simulations*. New York: Semiotext(es).

Beck, Ulrich. (1992). *Risk Society: Towards a New Modernity*. London: Sage Publications.

Berndt, Ernst R., and Triplett, Jack E., eds. (1990). *Fifty Years of Economic Measurement: The Jubilee of the Conference on Research in Income and Wealth*. Chicago: University of Chicago Press.

Braman, Sandra. (1990a). "Trade and information policy." *Media, Culture and Society* (12):361–385.

Braman, Sandra. (1990b). "The CSCE and Information Policy for the New Europe." Presented to Second Conference, Europe Speaks to Europe, Moscow, USSR, December.

Braman, Sandra. (1991). "Contradictions in Brilliant Eyes." *Gazette* (47):177–194.

Cass, Ronald A., and Noam, Eli M. (1989). "Services Trade and Services Regulation in the United States." Presented at Symposium on Rules for Free International Trade in Services, Tel Aviv, Israel, March.

Chandler, Alfred D. Jr. (1977). *The Visible Hand: The Managerial Revolution in American Business*. Cambridge: Belknap Press.

Dezalay, Yves. (1989). "Putting Justice 'into Play' on the Global Market: Law, Lawyers, Accountants, and the Competition for Financial Services." *Tidskrift fur rattssociologi* 6(1–2):9–67.

Dezalay, Yves. (1990). "The BIG BANG and the Law: The Internationalization and Restructuration of the Legal Field." *Theory, Culture & Society* (7):279–293.

Hooper, Peter, and Richardson, J. David, eds. (1991). *International Economic Transactions: Issues in Measurement and Empirical Research*. Chicago: University of Chicago Press.

Huber, Peter. (1987). *The Geodesic Network: 1987 Report on Competition in the Telephone Industry*. Washington, D.C.: U.S. Department of Justice, Antitrust Division.

Ito, Youichi. (1991). "*Johoka* as a Driving Force of Social Change," *KEIO Communication Review* (12):33–58.

Jantsch, E. (1989). *The Self-Organizing Universe*. New York: Pergamon Press.

Johnson, H. Thomas. (1991). "Managing by Remote Control: Recent Management Accounting Practices in Historical Perspective." In Peter Temin (ed.), *Inside the Business Enterprise: Historical Perspectives on the Use of Information*. Chicago: University of Chicago Press.
Kroker, Arthur. (1984). *Technology and the Canadian Mind: Innis/McLuhan/Grant*. New York: St. Martin's Press.
Kroker, Arthur. (1992). *The Possessed Individual: Technology and the French Postmodern*. New York: St. Martin's Press.
Maruyama, Magoroh. (1963). "The Second Cybernetics: Deviation-Amplifying Mutual Causal Processes." *American Scientist* (51):164–179.
McLuhan, Marshall. (1964). *Understanding Media*. New York: McGraw-Hill.
McLuhan, Marshall, and Nevitt, Barrington. (1973). "The Argument: Causality in the Electric World." *Technology and Culture* 14(1):1–18.
McLuhan, Marshall, and Powers, Bruce. (1981). "Ma Bell Minus the Nantucket Gam: Or the Impact of High-Speed Data Transmission." *Journal of Communication* 31(3):191–199.
Petersmann, Ernst-Ulrich. (1986). "Trade Policy as a Constitutional Problem: On the 'Domestic Policy Functions' of International Trade Rules." In Heinz Hauser (ed.), *Protectionism and Structural Adjustment*. Grusch, Switzerland: Verlag Ruegger, pp. 243–277.
Petersmann, Ernst-Ulrich. (1991). *Constitutional Functions and Constitutional Problems of International Economic Law*. Fribourg, Switzerland: University Press.
Porat, Marc U. (1977). *The Information Economy: Definition and Measurement*. Washington, D.C.: Office of Telecommunications, U.S. Department of Commerce.
Temin, Peter, ed. (1991). *Inside the Business Enterprise: Historical Perspectives on The Use of Information*. Chicago: University of Chicago Press.
Woolf, Douglas. (1992). Personal communication of author.

Notes

1. The Clinton Administration is in the process of radically redirecting this information policy.

4 THE POLITICAL ECONOMY OF COMMUNICATION: LESSONS FROM THE FOUNDERS

Vincent Mosco

Introduction

When Harvard economist Jeffrey Sachs, a leading architect of economic reconstruction in the former Communist world, was asked about his work in the region, he began by calling it "the greatest moral challenge of our time" (Rusk, 1991, p. B8). When his colleague Benjamin Friedman wrote a book (1988) attacking the excesses of Reagonomics, he introduced each chapter with a Biblical citation. In their recent overview of the political economy of communication, Golding and Murdock (1991, pp. 18–19) maintain that what distinguishes critical political economy is that "perhaps most importantly of all, it goes beyond technical issues of efficiency to engage with basic moral questions of justice, equity and the public good." These are examples from across the spectrum of perspectives in economics and political economy that there is some unease with what has become the customary practice of separating science from morality. They inspire the effort in this chapter to expand our conception of the political

---

The author acknowledges the assistance of a grant from the Canadian Social Sciences and Humanities Research Council.

economy of communication by returning to the thinking of some of the discipline's founding figures.

In essence, this chapter argues that we have established Western traditions of social science, political science, and economics that need some major fixing if we are to understand the world better and to change it for the better. Among the many ways to go about doing this, this chapter resurrects some of the dinosaurs of political economy, itself a dinosaur discipline (or at least prehistoric to the disciplinary wars of modernity). Specifically, I am interested in how political economy might provide some insight into how social scientists address fundamental problems in communication and information. For this we need the dinosaurs because we are losing sight of one of the central purposes for the development of social science.

To understand this point, it is useful to return to the prehistory of social science, to the discipline of political economy as it was understood by Adam Smith, David Ricardo, Thomas Malthus, and Karl Marx, among others. Even a limited reading of their work conveys a sense that these founding figures posed questions and defined a terrain of analysis in far broader terms than we are willing to do today. Our disciplines have, for a variety of reasons, taken on a narrow, empiricist, or worse, positivist, vision. Simply put, according to this view reality is that which is objective, rational, and empirically testable. The view is deeply reluctant to raise questions about subjectivity and moral philosophy. Among the social sciences, current mainstream economics has proceeded furthest down the positivist road much to the dismay of economist Donald N. McLoskey who argues in *The Rhetoric of Economics* that "philosophers agree that strict logical positivism is dead. The length of time it has been dead raises the question whether economists are wise to carry on with their necrophilia" (McCloskey, 1985, p. 12).

To convey a sense of the gap between the prehistoric and the contemporary and what the former have to teach us, we need to consider three central dimensions of their intellectual project: a commitment to history, to the analysis of the social totality, and to moral philosophy.

History

In an article well ahead of its time, Baran and Sweezy (1965, p. 29) attacked neoclassical economists for giving up the classical economists' concern for history:

> If the neoclassical concern for reform has been jettisoned, how much more complete has been the abondonment of the older classical economists' passion

to discover in the present the shape of the future, and to single out for intensive analysis whatever forces seemed to hold promise of new and better times to come. Anti-historical to the core, present-day bourgeois economics scorns any effort to investigate the nature of the changes that are taking place or where they are leading. The great quest *Quo vadis?* which occupied not only Adam Smith and David Ricardo and John Stuart Mill but also in our time Joseph Schumpeter has simply disappeared from the agenda of bourgeois economics.

Much of our social science today considers the post-World War II period as the watershed of understanding. Having given birth to nuclear weaponry, the computer, and television, it is the defining historical moment. This has enabled some of the leading analysts in the field of communication and information to argue that there is no real history until the birth of the computer, television and the Information Society. Implicit in this view is the notion that our technologies of communication and information have almost literally dropped out of the sky, *Deus ex Machina*, just in time to solve the problems of the modern age (for example, Naisbitt, 1982).

For all of their differences, the dinosaurs of political economy would hardly tolerate such ahistorical thinking. Their work teaches us that there is more continuity to the development of social, cultural, and technological forms than contemporary futurists and utopians of the information age acknowledge. Specifically, they have shown how Western society has built its system of social relations around creating commodities for the marketplace, in a global process that turns use values into exchange values. Unfortunately, with all too few exceptions, contemporary students of information and its technologies lose sight of the market base and mainly see the technology—the bells, whistles and glitz—as unique and historically transformative. Yet, even as this utopian vision, what I have called the "push-button fantasies" of the information age, continue to receive popular attention, we are creating structures to subject communication to the same process of commodification that Adam Smith described in *The Wealth of Nations*. This is because information is encased in structures that are centuries old: the market, the production of commodities, exchange, pricing, and so on.

Social Totality

In addition to their concern for the historical, the founders of political economy determined that the discipline should be firmly rooted in an analysis of the wider social totality. This incorporates a recognition that analysis must address the constraints of social structure, the values of cultural life, and the agency of individuals and social groups aiming to make sense of social experience. Structures, like markets, cultural values, like the value of labour, and agency, the intervention of individuals and classes who make history, even as they recognize that it is done under conditions that are not of their own making, all of these comprise the bedrock of political economic analysis as it was traditionally understood (Murdock, 1989, pp. 436–440).

Today, much of our social science is based on disciplinary turf wars whose battlefield is comprised of problems, ideas, methods, and theories that academics define as unique to a particular discipline. Social class "belongs" to sociology; the government to political science; the market to economics. Though there is some serious research of an interdisciplinary nature, it is the exception to the rule of academic protectionism: stake out turf; protect it with language; preserve it with rules governing entry, proper conduct within a discipline and the extent of visiting rights on other turf. The dinosaurs of political economy were not bound by such restrictions and consequently did not back off from what today might be called an excessively ambitious effort to address the social totality (Jacoby, 1987). As one follower of the classical thinkers put it in 1923 (Ely, p. 4):

> As to the place of economics in the general system of the sciences, it holds that the study of wealth cannot be isolated, except temporarily and provisionally, from the other social phenomena; that it is essential to keep in view the connections and interactions of the several sides of human life. There is, in fact, properly speaking, but one great Science of Sociology, of which Economics forms a single chapter which must be kept in close relation to the others.

Those of us who examine the Information Age can incorporate this lesson by situating information and the technologies that are used to produce and distribute it within this wider social totality. One consequence of a narrow disciplinary focus is that those of us who examine the *social* dimension are restricted to one corner of a discipline—limited to examining social impacts. The study of the social totality leads us to recognize that information does not just affect social relations, it embodies them. In essence, technology is, a *congealed social relationship*. In the broader socio-cultural sense, technology only has meaningful existence as the embodiment of the social relations that enter its design, production, distribution, and use. The second lesson is that the social, cultural, political, and economic are one; when we examine information and technology, our study should be guided by a recognition of the unity of the social totality.

Moral Philosophy

The third lesson and perhaps the most controversial one that these founding figures have to teach us is their commitment to moral philosophy. Adam Smith, professor not of economics but of moral philosophy, offers a vision of how to advance the social good, not through self-interest, as he would later argue in *The Wealth of Nations*, but through systematic social benevolence:

> And hence it is that to feel much for others, and little for ourselves, that to restrain our selfish, and to indulge our benevolent affections, constitutes the perfection of human nature; and can alone produce among mankind that harmony of sentiments and passions in which constitutes their whole grace and propriety. (Smith, 1976 (1759), Pt. 1, Sec. 1, Chap. 5, p. 71)

Similarly, Thomas Malthus, son of a preacher, warns of the moral consequences of unchecked population and Karl Marx gives us the critique of political economy to create a society based on satisfying human needs rather than on class power.

However we respond to their specific visions and values, we cannot deny that visions and values were central to their analyses, that the moral sphere was integral to their work. It would be left for later analysts to take "this branch of ethics" and turn it into a discipline "that is striving to be a science" (Robinson, 1962).

There are two types of lessons to be learned here. First, the moral, cultural, or spiritual domain is itself the central subject of analysis. The Information Age is inflected with the moral dimension of our life. Adam Smith chose to write *The Theory of Moral Sentiments* before his analysis of the divison of labour in the marketplace because it was essential to understand the moral basis of a rising commercial society that was accelerating in Britain in the latter half of the eighteenth century. He felt that it was a better work than *The Wealth of Nations* and returned to it near the end of his life because, according to Lux (1990, p. 98), "there was a more serious problem with unmoderated commercial motives than he was aware of earlier." Similary, Marx, began with moral philosophical treatises that are too readily dismissed as the writings of the "young Marx," but which form the core of understanding the value of a growing industrial society.

These people were moral visionaries in another sense. They felt that an essential element of their responsibility as social philosophers was identifying visions of a morally appropriate way of living. For them, the moral vision became the very definition of reason. Our age has stripped away the moral component and has left us with rationality, logic, and positivism; the moral dimension is diminished or eliminated entirely from analysis. One is permitted to go only so far as Max Weber (1946) who felt that it was acceptable to be motivated by moral concerns, but that the canons of science left no room for them in one's analysis; the dinosaurs of political economy simply did not accept such divisions.

Today, it is fashionable to talk about the ways that communication and information technology will define the vision of future generations. Such thinking makes it essential to revisit the founding figures of political economy. For them, it was not technology that would shape the moral climate. Rather, it was moral individuals acting from a moral philosophical perspective who would determine the form of technology and its social uses.

The Political Economy of Communication

Taking into account the lessons from the founders of political economy, we take a closer look at how a political economist thinks about communication and information technology. Recognizing that this is a tall order for one chapter, we focus on key elements and general contours.

Economic Restructuring

Economic changes occurring in the media sector are a part of wider changes taking place across most major industry sectors. There has been a tendency to perceive these narrowly as simply the growth of market-based competition. However, as Anthony Smith (1989, p. 22) has noted, "Perhaps the language for describing the shift of doctrine has been badly chosen. We are not really dealing with an extension of competition or an intensification of accountability of enterprises through the market, so much as with a general reorganization of enterprises."

Globalization, the development of an electronic services marketplace, and new corporate structures and relationships are three dimensions of economic restructuring. *Globalization*, the process by which nationally and locally owned businesses are concentrated in international enterprises, has always played a role in the media business. As the former Associated Press head Kent Cooper reminded us in his 1942 *Barriers Down*, AP fought a tough battle to overcome the global cartel that Reuters, Havas, and Wolff engineered in the nineteenth century. Nevertheless, there is something new in the current pattern of globalization. In the past, though business might operate in international markets, a company's link to its national home was more than symbolic.

Today, globalization means the declining significance of the national base. Robert Reich (1991, p. 8) asks, "So who is 'us?'" Neither the profitability of a nation's corporations nor the successes of its investors necessarily improve the standard of living of most of the nation's citizens. They are becoming disconnected from their home nations." We are slow to accept this change. We would rather think that though they are multinationals, at least they are *our* multinationals. Hence, we worry about the consequences of having almost half the Hollywood majors under foreign control; we tend not to ask what makes the rest American. Or why the United States should continue a decades-old practice of permitting "our" Motion Picture Export Association to avoid anti-trust oversight when it operates in foreign markets. U.S. telecommunication policy makers worry about the loss of its manufacturing market share to Northern Telecom, a "Canadian" company headquartered in the United States with more of its work force in the United States than anywhere else. Americans rarely question the national identify of IBM, half of whose revenues are earned outside the United State, or what makes Ameritech, which, according to Judge Greene, has used its regional monopoly to buy half of New Zealand's telephone system and the German publisher of Yellow Pages, American. Who is us? The answer is less clear than ever.

Economic restructuring also means the decline of traditional industrial divisions. Our common language, statistical base, and forms of regulation are founded on divisions among print, broadcasting, telecommunications and information industry sectors. But these are eroding quickly and the loosening of regulations allows companies to move from one to another, strengthening cross-ownership concentration. But loosened regulation reflects more than just the clout of a few media powers or a change in government philosophy. It also acknowledges that a common digital language and technology makes it easier to move among these sectors and less likely that one can sustain the differences. Newspapers spawn on-line information services; cable companies create intercorporate data networks; telephone companies bring us a $1.2 billion "900" industry that supplies everything from recipes to baseball scores.

The old divisions are all the more difficult to sustain as traditional consumers of communication services, particularly large banks, insurance companies, retailers and others, come to recognize that—even if they don't agree with the head of Citibank who claims to be in the information business—information production, distribution and exchange is central to their primary business. Private data networks, in-house video services, and just-in-time inventory control systems are just a few of the rapidly growing business sectors that make major producers of these traditional consumers. In essence, traditional categories and the legal, regulatory, and policy apparatus that came with them are collapsing. What separates an American from a Japanese company; a telephone from a cable from a computer company; a producer from a consumer? All of these differences are tending to disappear as we move into a global *electronic services marketplace*. Much of the heat coming out of the battles among media firms results from an understandable tendency to cling to old categories as we puzzle over how to think about this new reality.

Many companies are carrying out economic restructuring by adopting *new organizational structures* that combine the power to command resources and the flexibility to respond to changing markets. According to the economic geographer David Harvey (1989, p. 147), this form of restructuring "rests on flexibility with respect to labour process, labour markets, products and patterns of consumption." It results in "entirely new sectors of production, new ways of providing financial services, new markets, and above all, greatly intensified rates of commercial, technological, and organizational innovation." Finally, it leads to what he calls a new round of "time-space compression"—the time horizons for decision-makers shrink while declining transport and communication costs make it possible to spread decisions over a wider and more diverse space.

One obvious consequence is the rise of what Anthony Smith (1991) calls the "behemoths": Time-Warner, Matsushita, Bertelsman, News Corp., Disney, and Sony. These firms integrate vertically by securing control over production, distribution and exhibition; horizontally across a range of media products, including hardware and software; and globally by taking advantage of an international division of labour that makes possible the flexible and cost-effective use of labour, capital, research and development.

These companies embody enormous concentrated economic power. Nevertheless, you don't need to be a Maxwell employee shorn of a pension, a creditor hoping for a few cents on the dollar, or a Time-Warner investor wondering if the company will ever get out from under its debt load, to recognize that the conglomerate form is not the only or even the most effective form of corporate response to global restructuring. The integrated conglomerate benefits from competition within as it flexes its market power without. But it does so at a price, measured in debt and in the difficulty of getting big beasts to respond to a changing environment.

Economic restructuring sometimes leads to the conglomerate but the key is to develop flexible structures that can take on new forms rapidly to meet changing demands. The communication industry offers numerous examples. It is not ironic that amidst all the war talk we see a growth in joint ventures: AT&T, US West, and TCI team up in pay-per-view. These extend across borders. NBC gets much of its foreign news from Reuters-owned Visnews. AT&T works with Japan's NEC to supply and market memory chips, with Dutch-onwed Philips to make and market telecommunication switching equipment, and with Japan's Mitsui on value-added networks. Similarly, IBM joins with Mitsubishi for value-added networks, with Toshiba on computers, with Siemens for disk drives, and with Italtel and Siemens for switching equipment.

A UN report (1990) identified the growth of international "vertical linkages" among industrial, media and advertising firms. The latter are small relative to their partners but act "as a catalyst that drives the growth of media firms."

Though Hollywood is arguably more conglomerate than ever, commentators have also noted the increasing reliance on independent producers. But as Aksoy and Robins (1991) have shown, Hollywood majors are stronger for having shorn off elements of the riskier side of the business because they retain control over financing and distribution. You don't have to *own* a supplier to control the relationship. Similarly, the TV networks cut back sharply on expensive foreign bureaus and now rely on independents like WTN and Visnews. In addition to externalizing risk, restructuring by streamlining enables companies to rely on a small collection of highly skilled workers and avoid the range of costs that come with a large group of unionized employees. Or in the words of the executive vice president of Fox News (Waite, 1992, p. F5), "it is phenomenally less expensive compared to doing it yourself."

Paralleling this form of labor restructuring is a changing relationship to consumers. Across the electronic services industry, firms are moving away from mass production for largely undifferentiated consumers and toward a deepening of the relationship to more valuable segments, even if that means cutting off some of the mass. This is perhaps most advanced in telecommunications where the demands of large users, backed by court-ordered restructuring, permitted greater attention to customizing services to business customers and an end to a traditional system that kept local rates low.

Similar tensions can be felt in television, where the drive to deliver pay-per services to higher-income customers has intensified, where cable companies seek relief from must-carry rules and make revenue-sharing deals with televised shopping channels, and where NBC, which *The New York Times* describes as "willing to forsake prime-time leadership in order to pursue greater profits," dropped two of its most popular shows because they tilted toward older viewers who, in the words of one commentator "are not avidly sought by most television advertisers" (Carter, 1992, p. D1). Economic restructuring means rethinking the balance between mass and skilled labor and between mass and targetted marketing.

In conclusion, global restructuring offers numerous opportunities to expand control from the conglomerate form to the range of flexible alternatives. The chief requirements: control central points in the production, distribution and exchange process (outright ownership is one among numerous alternatives) and remain flexible to respond to changing markets and technologies.

The Media Commodity

Economic restructuring brings out tensions that increase talk of media wars. So too does the expansion of the market with the growth of the primary media commodity. Business has deepened and extended two of the elements essential in creating a commodity: with the considerable help of new technologies, it has markedly improved the capacity to *measure* the product and to *monitor* its exchange.

Pay-per-view television, local measured telephone service, on-line information systems, people meters, and computers that count keystrokes are examples of how we are refining what has traditionally been a rather fuzzy commodity. Satellite dish and cable converter pirates are living evidence that there is considerable slippage in the commodifiction process, but one can hardly deny that we have moved very rapidly from over-the-air television to monthly cable bills that now include per-channel and per-view charges. Though there is always backsliding and detours occur (who predicted that videocassette rentals would constitute the first major example of pay-per-view TV?), the tendency is clear: it has become increasingly cost effective to market pay-per media and information products.

But this is only part of the picture. Information products and processes are indeed cybernetic. The very process of creating and exchanging information produces new products. According to the president of Olivetti Canada (DeSimone, 1992), this changes our conception of value:

> From the value that is *intrinsic* in the product to values associated with the knowledge of who needs it, who supplies it and what it does. You buy a magazine and pay for it with a credit card. A simple transaction? Hardly. The *information* about who you are and what magazines you prefer—recorded by a computer—is worth as much as the return on the sale of the magazine. The information can be variously packaged. It can be marketed to others. Moreover, all the internal processes are affected by your decision—from marketing to purchase to finance. Today, all organizations are in the information business.

Even after discounting for the hyperbole, we are left with a sense that it is more useful than ever to envision information as both a commodity and a form of control central to the creation of new commodities.

Restructuring Government

It is not uncommon for media warriors to decry government intervention even as they seek its protection from competitors, typically characterized as predatory, self-interested, creamskimming and/or profit-grabbing. The same sort of confusion that Anthony Smith noted about misuse of language in the communication business applies to the regulation of the business. Words like competition and market discipline are "badly chosen" because they miss economic restructuring; words like deregulation and procompetitive policies miss the restructuring of government.

There is remarkable agreement across political lines about the source of the change in government. On the left John Kenneth Galbraith (1992) calls it "the culture of contentment." For liberal Robert Reich (cited in Murray, 1991) it is the "secession of the successful." And conservative Charles Murray (1991), agreeing explicitly with Reich, sees the rise of "a conservative caste."

"Try to envision," says Murray, social policy adviser to President Reagan, "what happens when 10 or 20 percent of the population has enough income to bypass the social institutions it doesn't like in ways that only the top fraction of 1 percent used to be able to do." He adds that for this group the U.S. Postal Service is "all but irrelevant" to how they communicate, as are public schools to their thoughts on how to educate (Murray, 1991, pp. 17–18). In essence, governments in the eighties learned the lessons that many marketers have been quick to pick up: reorganize to support the niche market, whether you are marketing automobiles or government policies.

In the United States, United Kingdom, and elsewhere this meant policies that support a fraction of the population, numerous, wealthy, and powerful enough to strengthen government programs from which they benefit (farm income supports, bank bailouts, practically free use of the radio spectrum for commercial gain) and to erode and eliminate those that provide few benefits. The results are now coming in. The Congressional Budget Office reports that between 1977 and 1989 three-fourths of the increase in pretax income and 60 percent of the after-tax income went to the top one percent of the income ladder. The top 20 percent received almost all of the pretax gain and all but 6 percent after taxes. On the other hand, the poorest fifth of the population received a smaller share of the national income than at any time since the New Deal, the last major government restructuring (Nasar, 1992, p. 1).

The restructuring of government communication policy was driven in part by the increasing ability to make information and entertainment products marketable commodities. It was also an important instrument to advance the interests of Murray's new caste. The governments which had operated communication systems out of a public service mandate either privatized them or cut back funding to favor private competitors. In the United States, this meant the erosion of government funding for public broadcasting. More significantly, the U.S. government ended regulations on commercial limits, eliminated the fairness doctrine, loosened ownership concentration regulations, and even made it easier for local monopolies like telephone companies and cable franchises to charge whatever a nearly captive market would bear. Television is now a sea of commercial stations, home shopping channels, program-length "infomercials" and product tie-ins masquerading as children's programming.

In telephony this amounted to the redistribution of billions of dollars from local residential subscribers to large users, all in the name of cost-based pricing, a phrase that Anthony Oettinger, Chairman of Harvard's Program on Information Policy, refers to as a "fairy tale" that reflects the latest shift in power (1988). Additionally, the government shifted massive amounts of information, produced and processed from tax revenues, to the private sector for commercial use. Meanwhile, the American Library Association reports that the state of public libraries is worse than during the Great Depression (*The New York Times*, July 8, 1991, p. A8). And the public school system is in such a sad state that many schools are left to assemble their students before a television monitor to watch news and commercials in return for some badly needed equipment.

Moral Pressure Points: Information Poverty in a Surveillance Society

A few marginal voices in government publicly acknowledge the growth of information inequalities. According to a report (for which I served as a consultant and advisory board member) from the congressional Office of Technology Assessment (1990, p. 243):

> OTA found that changes in the U.S. communication infrastructure are likely to broaden the gap between those who can access communication services and use information strategically and those who cannot. Moreover, the people most likely to be adversely affected will be those for whom the new communication technologies are held out as a means to improve their circumstances—the poor, the educationally disadvantaged, the technologically isolated, and the struggling small business.

Government has limited or abandoned principles that get in the way of global restructuring and the electronic services market. It no longer tends to see information as a public good and a right of citizenship. Market power, not the need for political democracy, increasingly determines access to communication resources.

Local residential users have borne much of the burden for transforming the telecommunciations system to meet the needs of large users. In a December 1991 report, the Consumer Federation of America concluded that the monopoly Baby Bells have overcharged their customers by about $30 billion since the 1984 breakup of AT&T (Ramirez, 1991). According to FCC data about 17 percent of unemployed households and about the same percentage of black and hispanic homes do not have a telephone (U.S., F.C.C., 1991).

Deregulation of cable has, according to a *New York Times* correspondent, "driven many of its customers to outrage with price increases of between 50 and 60 percent in the past five years for service that has ranged from indifferent to exasperating" (Carter, 1992b, p. E2). What is crucial here is that since most people acquire their news from television and since broadcast television has shifted much of the news burden to cable, it is more vital than ever that people have access to cable. Yet, in part owing to substantial rate increases, cable systems, which are available to 90 percent of American homes, appear to have reached a subscriber plateau of 60 percent. This means that as networks like CNN and C-Span become the arena for a presidential campaign, large segments of the population cannot afford the price of admission. A recent report from the Office of Technology Assessment (U.S., Congress, O.T.A., 1991) sees particular cause for concern in rural areas where the telecommunications gap is a chasm.

Similar developments are taking place across the electronic services marketplace. In the name of "paperwork reduction" the federal government has cut back on data collection, privatized for commercial use data that was available free to the public that paid for its collection, and has shifted much of its information to on-line data banks accessible to those who can afford access to the technology. According to its biannual publication *Less Access to Less Information by and About the U.S. Government*, the American Library Assocation reports that "during the past nine years, this ongoing chronology has documented Administration efforts to restrict and privatize government information" (cited in Schiller, 1991, p. 45).

Meanwhile, back at the workplace, numerous studies point to the development of a massive service sector divided into two distinct tiers. Highly skilled people are trained to use information technologies that, in the words of Harvard Business School professor Shoshana Zuboff (1988), enrich or *informate* their work. But more people tend machines that simply automate their work.

The increased ability to measure and monitor information transactions and the growing market value of information acquired about consumers and workers in the course of doing business raise a second significant social problem: the threat to privacy. One company, Lotus Marketplace, using information aquired from a major credit bureau, has already proposed to market profiles on 80 million American households. Citicorp has announced plans to sell marketers access to its files on 22 million credit-card customers. By 1995, it expects to be gathering and selling data on 40 million households that will process information on 30 billion transactions a year at 14,000 nationwide retail outlets (Quint, 1991, p. 1).

Even as traditional a mass medium as the newspaper is learning about the value of selling customer data. According to the press observer Alex S. Jones (1991, p. 22), "Americans are only beginning to realize that when they call a newspaper's sports line to get a score or send for a free brochure about car maintenance, they are probably also entering a data bank as a prospect for advertising about golf clubs or tires." As a result, he concludes, "privacy looms as a potential land mine." For the vice president of advertising for the *Atlanta Journal and Constitution*, which has one of the most sophisticated of such systems, "It's part of the future of the newspaper business."

The same monitoring activity affects the workplace as companies use the telephones and computer terminals that people work with to measure worktime (calls taken per minute, keystrokes per hour, groceries scanned in a shift, and so on) and monitor performance (number and duration of break times). Again, the temptation is strong to measure and monitor whatever the technology makes feasible, marketable, and controllable. Though accounts on the subject often summon the spectre of Big Brother, in most cases there is no irrational drive to heavy-handed domination. In some respects, this is a new form of power, one that does not physically coerce but rather insinuates almost naturally what Michel Foucault (1982) has called the capillary system of the body politic. Monitoring is seen as an extension of normal business practices in a competitive environment. T.W.A. monitors its reservation agents and distributes weekly and monthly report cards on computer measured time spent on the phone and a supervisor's assessment of phone conversations. According to a company executive, "I don't think we're different from any other type of workplace. From he standpoint of productivity, we believe it's possible for all agents to maintain the bench marks. We want to make sure the customers, paying hard-earned dollars, are getting what they paid for" (Kilborn, 1990, p. 8).

Absent considerably more attention to these issues, we will see more of a familiar pattern. Where public opposition fails to develop, the tendencies to eliminate impediments to economic restructuring and the commodification of information will continue. We can expect deepening inequalities and the advance of sophisticated monitoring systems. When pressure mounts, as it has over rate increases in cable and telephone, Congress and the FCC step in and either get bogged down over what constitutes a monopoly (are three players a cartel or a contestible market?) or reinvent the wheel of failed welfare programs. At about the time that the United States reached a consensus that traditional welfare programs are not the best way to deliver services to the needy, the FCC and state regulators stepped in to start a national telephone welfare program. Packaged in euphemisms like Link-up and Lifeline, they amount to a national patchwork of state and federal programs that will subsidize a phone hookup and monthly bill provided you pass a means test that differs in every state. If you live in South Carolina you can only get Link-up, must be a recipient of one of four types of welfare assistance and pass an income test administered by the phone company. If you live in Oregon you can get both Link-up and Lifeline, but must receive Food Stamps and pass an income test administered by the state. Means tests, policing, bureaucracy, and underenrollment (by January 1991, 3 percent for Link-up and 32 percent for Lifeline), all in the name of deregulation. (U.S., F.C.C., 1991)

There is no doubt a need for strong government action. No one put it better than Adam Smith in his justification of government banking regulations:

> Such regulations may, no doubt be considered in some respect a violation of natural liberty. But these exertions of the natural liberty of a few individuals which might endanger the security of the whole society, are, and ought to be, restrained by the laws of all governments; of the most free, as well as the most despotical. The obligation of building... walls, in order to prevent the communication of fire, is a violation of natural liberty, exactly of the same kind with the regulation of the banking trade which are here proposed. (Cited in Lux, 1990, p. 104)

Had U.S. policymakers paid more attention to Adam Smith, the country may have been spared the half trillion dollar losses that were brought about by the Savings and Loan industry scandal. If we are interested in doing more than repeating old mistakes, however well meaning the effort or however well they quell the complaints, we need to build on the work of those whose thoughts run to more fundamental questions.

What are the communication and information needs of people who live and work in an electronic services society? We conduct needs assessments in housing, transportation and other essential areas—what about information needs? How do we deepen and extend the concept of the public interest which was once expanded from a transportation model into the broadcasting system? How do we extend it further to information systems? Similarly, universality once applied to the telephone system, where the U.S. made great progress but still lags behind several countries including Canada which has the largest land mass of any nation. How can we build networks and price services so that we guarantee to all an evolving package determined to be the minimum essential for a responsible democracy?

Challenges

This is an ambitious program for a renewed political economy of communication. Nevertheless, there are additional challenges that none of the founders of the field foresaw, but which provide important areas for future research.

The strength of political economy is bound up with understanding institutions and social groups; who owns and controls information. It situates power in large organizational forms. But there is still something missing here, a missing link suggested in the work of the French philosopher Michel Foucault (1982). Foucault suggested that power is not simply an institutional form embedded in the macro-structures of social life. For him, power is most interesting and effective when it enters the personal level of life, what he aptly called the capillaries of society, the small blood vessels of life's circulatory system. The political economist is effective in examining global systems of power, but needs to consider how these systems translate into the experiences of individuals. In essence, political economy would benefit from an encounter with the ethnography of power which uses anthropological methods to examine the interplay of structured power and human agency (Pendakur, 1993).

The need to step into the microstructures of power became all the more evident when reflecting on the issue of gender. As Jansen (1989) has pursuasively noted, gender has been a major blindspot, "a socially structured silence" in most studies of technology, including communication and information technology. Both prehistoric and contemporary political economists have tended to ignore the patriarchal nature of industrial society. In choosing to emphasize class and state power, political economists have contributed substantially to understanding the major forces at work in modern society. But in doing so, they have generally ignored the gendered nature of power. Political economy can learn a great deal from feminist analyses that have uncovered the skewed nature of so much of our analyses, whether they support or oppose dominant systems of power.

Conclusion

In sum, the political economy of communication needs to renew itself by revisiting the work of its founders who taught the value of history, the social whole, and moral philosophy. It needs to apply these lessons to understand the role of communication and its technology in modern society by examining global economic transformations, the growth of a controlling commodity, the rise of concentrated information power, and in the development of an integrated electronic services market. Additionally, it needs to consider the moral significance of growing information poverty amidst a vast expansion of information technology and the ability of this technology to undermine personal and social privacy. Finally, political economy needs to learn from the work of anthropologists who understand power in its cultural and interpersonal dimensions and from feminist research which has examined the gendered nature of power.

This admittedly substantial program would help us to move beyond the superficialities of the "information society" and beyond the overdisciplined nature of contemporary social science. The dinosaurs would be pleased.

References

Aksoy, Asu, and Robins, Kevin. (1991). "Hollywood for the 21st Century: Global Competition for Critical Mass in Image Markets." Newcastle upon Tyne, UK: Centre for Urban and Regional Development Studies, University of Newcastle.
Baran, Paul A., and Sweezy, Paul M. (1965). "Economics of Two Worlds." *On Political Economy and Econometrics*, Oxford: Pergamon, pp. 15–29.
Carter, Bill. (1992). "Broadcasters Take a Bite Out of Cable in the Ratings." *The New York Times*. March 9, D1.
Carter, Bill. (1992). "Now or in 1993, Cable TV Meets the Regulators." *The New York Times*. March 8, E2.
Cooper, Kent. (1942). *Barriers Down*. New York: Farrar.
DeSimore, Mark. (1992). "Information is Value." *The Globe and Mail*. March 3.
Ely, Richard. (1923). "Introduction." *A History of Political Economy*. London: A&C Black.
Foucault, Michel. (1982). *Power/Knowledge*. New York: Pantheon.
Friedman, Benjamin M. (1988). *Day of Reckoning: the Consequences of American Economic Policy under Reagan and After*. New York: Random House.
Galbraith, John Kenneth. (1992). *The Culture of Contentment*. Boston: Houghton Mifflin.
Golding, Peter, and Murdock, Graham. (1991). "Culture, Communication, and Political Economy." In James Curran, and Michael Gurevitch (eds.), *Mass Media and Society*. London: Edward Arnold, pp. 15–32.
Harvey, David. (1989). *The Condition of Postmodernity*. Oxford: Basil Blackwell.
Jacoby, Russell. (1987). *The Last Intellectuals*. New York: Basic Books.
Jansen, Sue Curry. (1989). "Gender and the Information Society: A Socially Structured Silence." *Journal of Communication* 39(3):196–215.
Jones, Alex S. (1991). "Newspapers Try, Carefully, to Investigate Subscribers." *The New York Times*. May 27, 22.
Kilborn, Peter T. (1990). "Workers Using Computers Find a Supervisor Inside." *The New York Times*. December 23, 1, 8.
Lux, Kenneth. (1990). *Adam Smith's Mistake*. Boston: Shambhala.
McCloskey, Donald N. (1985). *The Rhetoric of Economics*. Madison: University of Wisconsin Press.
Mosco, Vincent. (1989). *The Pay-per Society: Computers and Communication in the Information Age*. Toronto: Garamond.
Murdock, Graham. (1989). "Cultural Studies: Missing Links." *Critical Studies in Mass Communication* (December):436–440.

Murray, Charles. (1991). *Harper's Magazine*. October, 17–18.
Naisbitt, John. (1982). *Megatrends*. New York: Warner.
Nasar, Sylvia. (1992). "Even Among the Well-Off, the Richest Get Richer." *The New York Times*. March 5, 1.
Oettinger, Anthony G. (1988). *The Formula Is Everything: Costing and Pricing in the Telecommunications Industry*. Cambridge, MA: Harvard University Program on Information Resources Policy.
Pendakur, Manjunath. (1993). "Political Economy and Ethnography: Transformations in an Indian Village." In Janet Wasko, Vincent Mosco, and Manjunath Pendakur, *Illuminating the Blindspots: Essays in Honour of Dallas Smythe*. Norwood, N.J.: Ablex.
Pool, Ithiel de Sola. (1983). *Technologies of Freedom*. Cambridge, MA: Harvard University Press.
Quint, Michael. (1991). "Banks Looking More Closely at their Credit Card Holders." *The New York Times*, May 27, 1.
Ramirez, Anthony. (1991). "Phone Customers Overpay, Consumer Group Contends." *The New York Times*. December 18.
Reich, Robert. (1991). *The Work of Nations*. New York: Knopf.
Robinson, Joan. (1962). *Economic Philosophy*, Chicago: Aldine.
Rusk, James. (1991). "The Greatest Moral Challenge of Our Time." *The Globe and Mail*, February 19.
Schiller, Herbert I. (1989). *Culture, Inc.* New York: Oxford.
Schiller, Herbert I. (1991). "Public Information Goes Corporate." *Library Journal*. October 1, 42–45.
Smith, Adam. (1976). *The Theory of Moral Sentiments*. Indianapolis: Liberty Classics.
Smith, Anthony. (1991). *The Age of Behemoths*. New York: Priority Press.
Smith, Anthony. (1989). "The Public Interest." *Intermedia* 17(2):10–24.
United Nations, International Labour Office. (1990). *The Emergence of Global Multi-media Conglomerates*. Geneva: ILO.
U.S. Congress, Office of Technology Assessment. (1990). *Critical Connections: Communications for the Future*. OTA-CIT-407. Washington, D.C.: U.S. Government Printing Office, January.
U.S. Congress. (1991). *Rural America at the Crossroads: Networking for the Future*. OTA-TCT-471. Washington, D.C.: U.S. Government Printing Office, April.
U.S., F.C.C. (1991). *Monitoring Report*. CC Docket No. 87-339, Prepared by the Staff of the Federal-State Joint Board in CC Docket No. 80-286, Washington, D.C.: Government Printing Office, January.
Waite, Teresa L. (1992). "As Networks Stay Home, Two Agencies Roam the World." *The New York Times*. Sunday, March 8, F5.
Weber, Max. (1946). "Science as a Vocation." In *From Max Weber: Essays in Sociology*, ed. Hans Gerth, and C. Wright Mills. New York: Oxford.
Zuboff, Shoshana. (1988). *In the Age of the Smart Machine*. New York: Basic Books.

5 ECONOMIC THEORY: RHETORIC, REALITY, RATIONALIZATION

Walter Adams and James W. Brock

"C'est regrettable," the French economist Sismondi wrote in 1827, "that we see political economy in England every day adopting a more sententious language, enveloped in calculations increasingly difficult to follow, losing itself in abstractions and becoming, in every way, an occult science, above all in an epoch when the sufferings of humanity demand that this science should talk a popular language, that it should accord to the needs of all, that it should come nearer to the common understanding and that it should apply itself to realities." In this predicament, he warned, "humanity should be on guard against all generalization of ideas that causes us to lose sight of the facts.... There is perhaps no manner of reasoning that exposes itself to more errors than that which consists of constructing a hypothetical world entirely different from the real world, for the purpose of applying one's calculations" (1827, pp. 3–4).

The Rhetoric of the "New Economic Science"

Alas, the sententiousness of economics has not abated since Sismondi's day. Draping themselves in the mantle of "science," brash devotees of the "new economics" have fearlessly engaged in ever more grandiose theorizing about every conceivable aspect of human—and lately, of nonhuman—affairs. They have constructed a pristine, simplistic world uncomplicated by human failures, faults, and imperfections. Reflexively applying their cant and incantations, and blithely redefining terms and concepts as best befits their purposes, they believe themselves to have found the keys to the secrets of the animate universe.

They redefine economics as "the science of rational choice" (Posner, 1986, p. 3). They do "not draw conceptual distinctions between major and minor decisions, such as those involving life and death in contrast to the choice of a brand of coffee; or between decisions said to involve strong emotions and those with little emotional involvement, such as in choosing a mate or the number of children in contrast to buying paint..." (Becker, 1976, pp. 7–8). Nor is the reach of their new science limited to economic affairs alone; its high priests claim it "may well be on its way to providing a unified framework for all behavior involving scarce resources, nonmarket as well as market, nonmonetary as well as monetary, small group as well as competitive" (Ibid., p. 205).

They redefine "rationality" as comprising behavior consistent with their theoretical deductions. In their Alice in Wonderland world, human consciousness is irrelevant: "Rational maximization should not be confused with conscious calculation. Economics is not a theory about consciousness. Behavior is rational when it conforms to the model of rational choice, whatever the state of mind of the chooser" (Posner, 1986, pp. 3–4). Realism, too, is *declassé*: "abstraction—reductionism, if you like—is of the essence of scientific inquiry.... [L]ack of realism, far from invalidating the theory, is the essential precondition of theory" (Ibid., p. 16). Circular reasoning is a strength, not a weakness: "Microeconomic theory rests upon a few empirical premises... Once a few such basic premises are accepted, the rest follows like a proof in geometry. The system is entirely circular, which is its strength because circular logic is not rebuttable" (Bork, 1984, p. 16). Even the irrational is grist for their theoretical mill.[1]

Thus, in the argot of the new economic science "a person decides to marry when the utility expected from marriage exceeds that expected from remaining single or from additional search for a more suitable mate. Similarly, a married person terminates his (or her) marriage when the utility anticipated from becoming single or marrying someone else exceeds the loss in utility from separation, including losses due to physical separation from one's children, division of joint assets, legal fees, and so forth." In sexual matters, "[e]conomic analysis, with its useful concepts of substitution and complementarity, search costs and signaling, inferior goods and externalities, and much else besides [can explain] much of the variation in, and many of the puzzles and peculiarities of, human sexual behavior and customs, ancient and modern, Western and non-Western..." (Posner, 1992, p. 434). And death is synonymous with suicide, because all deaths "could have been postponed if more resources had been invested in prolonging life" (Becker, 1976, p. 10).

Of late, the exponents of the new economic science consider all species—not merely humankind—to fall within the explanatory power of their science of rational choice: Cast in their phraseology, "all species must 'decide' whether to mate in monogamous or polygamous systems, whether to produce many offspring and devote little care to each one or produce few and devote more care to each, whether to have a sharp division of labor by sex and in other ways, and whether to behave selfishly or altruistically toward offspring and others..." (Becker, 1991, p. 307). Indeed, they suspect that "the economic approach may well be *more* powerful in understanding the long-run behavior of other species even though it was developed for human behavior"[2] (Ibid., p. 322; emphasis in original).

The Problem of Economic Power

In all their prestidigitations, however, the apostles of the new economic science may have committed the Sismondian sin of evading fundamental economic problems, and drawing erroneous or irrelevant conclusions about hypothetically constructed worlds far removed from reality. They may have engaged in what Kenneth Boulding characterizes as fashioning the celestial mechanics for a nonexistent universe (1966, pp. 1–13).

Perhaps nowhere is this more evident than in the failure of the new economists to confront the problem of economic power and its consequences. As Kurt Rothschild puts it, "If we look at the main run of economic theory... we find that it is characterized by a strange lack of power considerations. More or less homogeneous units—firms and households—move in more or less given technological and market conditions and try to improve their economic lot within the constraints of these conditions." This model has been explored in great detail, and has yielded important insights into the working of the market mechanism. But, Rothschild points out, "that people use power to alter the mechanism itself; that uneven power may greatly influence the outcome of market operations; that people may strive for economic power as much as for economic wealth; these facts have been largely neglected" (1971, p. 7).

Absent such considerations, the new economics is in danger of becoming a pseudo-scientific rationalization for the status quo—the rhetoric for an apologetics that ignores contemporary economic problems, that misdiagnoses or trivializes them, and that provides public policy prescriptions congenitally incapable of resolving them. The spread of the new economic science to the field of industrial organization provides a graphic case in point, particularly with regard to its twin touchstones of Pareto optimality and economic Darwinism.

Pareto Optimality and the Power Problem

Superficially, the concept of Pareto optimality seems unobjectionable: It describes a state of affairs in an economic system such that no individual's welfare can be enhanced without, at the same time, reducing the welfare of at least one other person. In the new economic science lexicon, however, Pareto optimality is a rosetta stone for draining economic terminology of its everyday meaning, for redefining it in obscure ways, and for redeploying it as a primary weapon in a campaign for radical laissez-faire.

Robert Bork, a leading advocate of the new economic science, redefines "competition" itself as Pareto optimality: Competition, he claims, "may be read as a shorthand expression, a term of art, designating any state of affairs in which consumer welfare cannot be increased by moving to an alternative state of affairs through judicial decree." Bork contends that this definition of competition "is consistent with everyday speech" (1978, pp. 6, 61). He recasts the meaning of "efficiency," too, in terms of consumer welfare. "Efficiency," Bork says, "is a normative concept and is defined and measured in terms of consumer welfare. Since a free market system assumes that consumers define their own welfare, it follows that economic efficiency consists in offering anything, whether products or services, that consumers are willing to pay for . . ." (Ibid.).

The result is not merely obfuscation. It is to root the meaning of consumer "welfare" and "efficiency" in the concept of Pareto optimality and, in turn, to interchangeably assert each as the sole goal of public policy. According to William Baxter, another exponent of the new economic science and the first antitrust chief during the Reagan Administration, "the antitrust laws are a 'consumer welfare prescription'—that is, they are intended to promote economic efficiency, broadly defined." Mr. Baxter insists that the "sole goal of antitrust is economic efficiency" and, further, that this redefinition of "efficiency" provides "the only workable standard from which to derive operational [antitrust] rules and by which the effectiveness of such rules can be judged" (1992, p. 22, and 1983, pp. 619, 621).

This, of course, is sheer tautology: From the assumption that consumers make choices in attempting to maximize their individual wellbeing, apostles of the new economic "science" leap to the doctrinaire conclusion that the existing pattern of consumer choices must represent the highest possible attainable level of consumer welfare. What is chosen maximizes consumer welfare. How do we know? Because it is welfare maximizing to choose it!

More significantly, they ignore the capacity of those wielding market power to artificially restrict the range of options from which consumers are permitted to choose. For example, confronted by a monopolist selling only vanilla ice cream, the fact that consumers purchase vanilla would be interpreted by the new economic scientists as "proof" that vanilla maximizes consumer welfare—even though consumers might have chosen chocolate or strawberry if these flavors had been provided, and even though consumer welfare would have been greater as a result of this expanded menu of choice.

Likewise, the mere fact that firms' offerings are purchased is, according to the new economic scientists, "proof" of efficient resource allocation—again, regardless of how narrow the actual range of products made available to choose from, regardless of the terms exacted for them, regardless of whether consumers would have bought other products if they had been made available, and regardless of whether the latter outcome would have resulted in a better, more efficient and entirely different allocation of society's resources. In other words, if an ice cream monopolist produces only vanilla, then according to the new economic science, this represents the most "efficient" use of society's resources. What is produced is efficient. How do we know? Because it is efficient to produce it!

Buttressed by the Pareto optimality criterion, then, the new economic "science" is not only tautological, it also begs the core questions of political economy: What consumer choices would have been made if the opportunity set from which they chose had been more expansive and more diverse? Would not a different array of options lead to a different pattern of consumer choices and greater consumer welfare? Would it not result in a different, more efficient allocation of society's resources? More fundamentally, new economic scientists' use of Pareto optimality, and their allied distortion of language and terms, evades the central questions of the political economy of power: Who determines the options from which consumers are permitted to choose? Who thus governs the allocation of society's resources? According to what criteria? With what consequences? For whom? And with what assurance that the outcomes will be in society's best interests?

"Pareto optimality," "consumer welfare," and "efficiency" are the shibboleths with which the new economic science removes economic power from the picture—where economic power includes the capacity to manipulate the options from which the public is permitted to choose, to dictate the cost of those options, and thus to govern the allocation of society's resources. It fails to recognize that concentrations of economic power will yield patterns of consumption choices different from those that would be produced under competitive conditions. It fails to recognize that a different power structure will produce a different array of consumer options, with different consumer choices, and a different allocation of resources. Above all, it fails to recognize that "voluntary" choice within the confines of restricted range of alternatives maximizes neither consumer welfare nor efficiency in any meaningful sense.

In sum, the fatal flaw of the new economic science and its Holy Grail of Pareto optimality is that it is blind to the problems of economic power. It sanctifies the status quo and the existing power distribution. It is compatible with the most egregious inequities. It legitimizes coercion, so long as such force is exerted by private power concentrates. It is tantamount to defining 'consumer welfare" and "efficiency' as equivalent to whatever outcomes private power commands. It is neither a valuefree prescription for promoting economic efficiency, nor a scientific policy for maximizing consumer welfare.[3]

Economic Darwinism and the Power Problem

Economic Darwinism is the second touchstone of the new economic science. According to Robert Bork, there is a close analogy between a free market system and the Darwinian theory of natural selection: "The environment to which the business firm must adapt is defined, ultimately, by social wants and the social costs of meeting them. The firm that adapts to the environment better than its rivals tends to expand. The less successful firm tends to contract—perhaps, eventually, to become extinct." Nor should society be concerned by corporate consolidation and trends toward corporate giantism and industrial concentration. When they occur, Bork contends, such trends are "prima facie evidence that greater concentration is socially desirable. The trend indicates that there are emerging efficiencies or economies of scale . . . which make larger size more efficient. This increased efficiency is valuable to the society at large, for it means that fewer of our available resources are being used to accomplish the same amount of production and distribution" (1978, pp. 205–206). How do we know? Because if consolidation and corporate bigness were not efficient—if they were not in society's best interest—market forces would punish them with losses and, in the extreme, would inflict economic death (Ibid., pp. 118–119). Hence, public policy should not be concerned or interfere with mergers and private concentrations of economic power. Laissez-faire will produce optimum results (1979, p. 86).

This argument suffers from at least two fatal flaws:

1. The Post Hoc Ergo Propter Hoc Fallacy

Neo-Darwinists assume that corporate giants attain, and maintain, powerful positions *solely* by virtue of their superior economic performance. They thus conveniently ignore the fact that, in reality, corporate bigness and market dominance can be achieved in ways unrelated to superior performance in the market—most notably, by mergers and consolidation. They also ignore the fact that once attained, such dominance can be sustained by virtue of the market control thereby amassed, as opposed to superior economic performance conventionally understood.

In the American cable television industry, for example, a massive merger movement during the 1980s has concentrated horizontal and vertical control in the hands of a few giant firms which, in turn, have exercised their market power to throttle and contain potential competitors in the field (Adams and Brock, 1989, pp. 79–91). In 1986 alone, the number of cable system mergers had a combined value of $8.6 billion—an amount greater than the combined sum spent on all cable mergers over the preceding decade. By 1988, horizontal cable consolidations reached an even higher level of $12.2 billion. Tele-Communications Inc. (TCI), America's largest cable firm, spent nearly $3 billion acquiring more than 150 local cable operations between 1984 and 1987; the Time-Warner consolidation of 1989 combined together the nation's second and fifth largest operators of local cable systems. At the same time, this handful of cable giants has also been vertically integrating into the control of programming by acquiring substantial ownership stakes in most of the country's largest program producers and distributors. Observing that "a few large vertically integrated firms control large segments of the domestic cable market," the House Committee on Energy and Commerce reports that access to cable programming by potential cable competitors (such as direct satellite broadcasters) "has been limited and, in some cases, denied completely"; that fledgling new rivals attempting to compete are burdened by the cable giants with "severely discriminatory terms and conditions," including program access prices in some cases as much as 460 percent higher than those charged the giants' affiliates; and that competition in the industry "has been impeded, in part, by the unreasonable refusal of some [of the largest] video program vendors to deal with" smaller potential competitors—evidence scarcely indicative of superior performance rewarded by an autonomous marketplace (U.S. Congress, 1990, pp. 36, 40, 42, 44).

In airlines, an eruption of anticompetitive mergers during the 1980s— e.g., Northwest/Republic, Texas Air/Continental/Eastern/People Express, Delta/Western, TWA/Ozark, American/Air Cal, USAir/Piedmont —notoriously concentrated control of the American industry in the hands of a few giants, produced fortress hub monopolies at major cities across the country, and inflicted flight frequency cutbacks, service deteriorations and fare hikes on the flying public (Adams and Brock, 1989, pp. 99–106).

Meatpacking is another American industry that has succumbed to a furious consolidation frenzy during the merger-mania of the 1980s. ConAgra, for example, has become the nation's second largest beef-packer by acquiring Armour, Northern States Beef, Monfort, E. A. Milller, and Swift meatpackers; it also employed corporate acquisitions to become the nation's second largest pork producer, second largest poultry processor, largest lamb producer, and largest seafood processor (Western Organization of Resource Councils Factsheet, 1989, and Weiner, 1990). As one result, concentration in the field has skyrocketed, with the combined market share of the four largest packers leaping from 28 percent in 1975 to more than 70 percent by 1988. As another consequence, giant packers are coming to exert increasing influence over cattle and meatpacking markets (U.S. General Accounting Office, 1990 and 1991; U.S. Congress, 1991; Kilman, 1992, p. B3).

Obviously, mergers like these—and the number of examples can be multiplied[4]—produce size, dominance and power, but without meeting the market test of success achieved by internal growth and "efficiency" in pleasing consumers. As such, the reality of anticompetitive mergers and acquisitions refutes deductions by the economic Darwinists that size and market power are primarily the result of superior economic performance, that they automatically promote economic welfare, and that public policy should never disturb them.

2. The Political Ramifications of Private Economic Power

The new economic Darwinism also conveniently ignores the broader political ramifications of private economic power—most notably, the capacity of corporate giants to capture government, to manipulate the state to preserve their positions, and to thereby escape market sanctions for deficient economic performance. It assumes that extreme laissez-faire will perform perfectly so long as government refrains from intervening in the private marketplace. What the apostles of the new economic science fail to recognize is that by permitting concentrations of private economic power to form, they thereby unleash powerful vested interests able to capture government and to pervert it in order to subvert the very marketplace they profess to cherish.

In the hypothetical world of the economic Darwinists, such power is nonexistent: Corporate giants abstain from influencing government to obtain private privilege and succor. They dutifully obey neatly drawn boundaries between "economics" and "politics." They do not retain high-powered lobbyists, nor do they exert undue financial pressure on the state. In this mythical world, corporate giants silently suffer the market's penalties for poor performance; seeking neither protection nor preferment, they sacrifice themselves on the altar of laissez-faire free enterprise.

Of course, this fantasy bears no resemblance to the real world. In reality, politics and economic concentration are not hermetically isolated spheres. In reality, corporate bigness complexes do not meekly submit to market-inflicted punishments when confronted with the consequences of their delinquent economic performance. Instead, they mobilize the vast political resources at their command—funds, employees, executives, labor unions, contractors, subcontractors, suppliers, elected representatives—to manipulate the state and to evade or to re-write the rules of the free market game.[5]

For example, corporate bigness complexes can lobby the state to immunize them from foreign competition, to subvert the market, and to protect them from the self-inflicted consequences of their own deficient economic performance, but at exorbitant cost to the public (as the American steel giants have successfully done for more than 20 years, at an annual cost of billions of dollars in artificially high steel prices inflicted on the American economy, and a concomitant loss of tens of thousands of jobs imposed on steel-using U.S. firms, whose competitiveness has been eroded by steel prices 20–40 percent above world levels).

They can capture the regulatory power of the state, pervert it into an instrument of cartelization and monopolization, and luxuriate in a cozy cost-plus environment (as the U.S. trucking industry did for decades, with an annual burden of billions of dollars imposed on the public in artifically inflated transportation prices as a result of imbecilic route restrictions, government-sanctioned cartel rates, anticompetitive mergers, and upwards of one-half of all American trucks travelling empty due to backhaul restrictions).

Overriding the market, corporate giants can successfully lobby the state for financial sustenance (as the nuclear electric power industry has done for decades in obtaining government subsidies for research and production, while producing astronomical cost overruns, billions of dollars of hopelessly uneconomic and abandoned power plants, multi-million dollar rate hikes, deception of the public concerning health and safety threats, and a lethal, steadily mounting bounty of radioactive wastes for which no safe method of disposal has yet been devised.)

They can extract tax favors, tax privileges, and tax loopholes worth hundreds of millions of dollars (as United Airlines and Northwest Airlines recently proved in whipsawing communities against each other in locating their aircraft maintenance facilities).

Once they attain mastadonic size, private economic power blocs acquire a potent sabotage power—the capacity to threaten to shut down operations, and inflict economic catastrophe on society—if their demands aren't met (as defense weapons giants have repeatedly demonstrated in forcing government to pay huge cost overruns on under-performance weapons systems).

And if they are big enough and incompetent enough, corporate giants can enjoy the ultimate perversion of free enterprise—government bailouts—because they are perceived to be too big to be allowed to fail. They then confront a free society with a Hobson's choice between the principles of private enterprise and the principles of representative democracy: allow giant firms to collapse, while ignoring the economic harm to the citizenry, or avert economic disaster through bailouts, but destroy the economic discipline of the market. As the Chrysler, Lockheed, and Continental Illinois debacles demonstrate, the political economy of bigness and concentration of economic power give rise to reverse Darwinism: Corporate giants survive, not because they are better, but because they are bigger—not because they are fitter, but because they are fatter!

In their hatred of government, the apostles of the new economic Darwinism thus fail to recognize the critical distinction between government intervention that makes the competitive market work by decentralizing and dispersing economic power (e.g., antitrust policy), and government intervention that subverts the market as a result of disproportionate political pressure exerted on the state by private economic power blocs (e.g., restraints on foreign competition). They thus fail to recognize that the extremist laissez-faire policies they advocate contain the seeds for the destruction of the private enterprise system they proclaim to protect, and beget the counterproductive kinds of government policies they so vehemently deplore. As a result, they are like Henry David Thoreau's neighbors who, he observed, "invite the devil in at every angle and then prate about the garden of Eden and the fall of man."

Conclusion

Rationalism, it has been observed, renounces life in order to preserve truth. The same might be said about the exponents of the new economic science: They imbue their rhetoric with the sententious language of Pareto optimality, "efficiency," "welfare," and "survival of the fittest." They proclaim themselves to be the *nouvelle vague* of value-free, modern scientific positivism. They construct brilliantly intricate edifices of internally consistent premises, deductions, theorems, and mathematical proofs. But in evading the reality of economic power, and by redefining terms and concepts to systematically exclude power from their glass bead games, these new economic "scientists" preserve their truths by sacrificing their relevance. The outcome is the kind of rationalizations, anesthetic platitudes, and politically animated nostrums that Sismondi warned against long ago.

Notes

1. "[P]erhaps the main conclusion of this study is that economic theory is much more compatible with irrational behavior than had been previously suspected" (Becker, 1976, p. 154).

2. Sane economists reject this simplistic extremism masquerading as "science." In his 1991 Ely Lecture to the American Economic Association, for example, economist George Akerlof (1991, pp. 1–19) questioned the validity of this new economic approach, on the basis of findings by cognitive psychologists that individuals choose actions without fully comprehending how their actions will affect them in the future; that human beings possess cognitive structures of which they are unaware; that there are many important instances of such behavioral pathologies; that in these cases the principle of revealed preference cannot validly be cited to assert that the options chosen are superior to those not chosen; and that a "more modern view of behavior, based on twentieth-century anthropology, psychology, and sociology is that individuals have utilities that do change and, in addition, they fail fully to foresee those changes or even recognize that they have occurred."

Similarly, Herbert A. Simon (1991, p. 29), Nobel laureate in economics and founding father of artificial intelligence, warns that "any model of human behavior that focuses on decision making gives us an overrational ideal of humans." He points out: "It is one thing to decide to climb a mountain. It is quite another to be on top of it."

Frank Knight (1956, pp. 121–122) long ago warned economists against attempting to ape the natural sciences. He pointed out that "the fundamental revolution and outlook which represents the real beginning of modern natural science was the discovery that the inert objects of nature are not like men, that is, subject to persuasion, exhortation, coercion, deception, . . ." He admonished economists to combat the erroneous inference "that since natural objects are not like men, men must be like natural objects."

3. The disturbing implications of examining the Pareto optimality criterion in juxtaposition with some of Pareto's other theories are analyzed in Walter Adams, James W. Brock, and Norman P. Obst. (1991, pp. 11–13).

4. For one recent survey, see Business Week (1991, pp. 86–94).

5. For further elaboration of these points, and for more detailed examinations and documentation of the examples that follow, see Walter Adams and James W. Brock (1986 and 1991).

References

Ackerlof, George A. (1991). "Procrastination and Obedience." *American Economic Review Proceedings* 81 (May):1–19.

Adams, Walter, and James W. Brock. (1991). *Antitrust Economics on Trial: A Dialogue on the New Laissez-Faire*. Princeton, N.J.: Princeton University Press.

Adams, Walter, and James W. Brock. (1986). *The Bigness Complex*. New York: Pantheon Books.

Adams, Walter, and James W. Brock. (1989). *Dangerous Pursuits: Mergers and Acquisitions in the Age of Wall Street*. New York: Pantheon Books.

Adams, Walter, James W. Brock, and Norman P. Obst. (1991). "Pareto Optimality and Antitrust Policy: The Old Chicago and the New Learning." *Southern Economic Journal* 58 (July):1–14.

Adams, Walter, and James W. Brock. (1989). "Vertical Integration, Monopoly Power, and Antitrust Policy: A Case Study of Video Entertainment." *Wayne Law Review* 52:79–91.

Baxter, William F. (1992). "Interview." *Wall Street Journal*, March 4.

Baxter, William F. (1983). "Responding to the Reaction: The Draftsman's View." *California Law Review*, 71 (March):618–631.

Becker, Gary S. (1976). *The Economic Approach to Human Behavior*. Chicago: University of Chicago Press.

Becker, Gary S. (1991). *A Treatise on the Family*. Cambridge, Mass.: Harvard University Press.

Bork, Robert, H. (1978). *The Antitrust Paradox*. New York: Basic Books.

Bork, Robert H. (1979). "Antitrust and the Theory of Concentrated Markets." In Eleanor M. Fox, and James T. Halverson (eds.), *Industrial Concentration and*

the Market System. Chicago: American Bar Association.
Bork, Robert H. (1984). "Judicial Precedent and the New Economics." In Eleanor M. Fox, and James T. Halverson (eds.) *Antitrust Policy in Transition: The Convergence of Law and Economics.* Chicago: American Bar Association.
Boulding, Kenneth. (1966). "The Economics of Knowledge and the Knowledge of Economics." *American Economic Review Proceedings* 56 (May):1–13.
Business Week. (1991). "The Age of Consolidation." October 14.
Kilman, Scott. (1992). "IBP Gobbles Up Weak Rivals in Meatpacking Industry." *Wall Street Journal*, August 31.
Knight, Frank H. (1956). *On the History and Method of Economics.* Chicago: University of Chicago Press.
Posner, Richard A. (1986). *Economic Analysis of Law*, 3rd edn. Boston: Little, Brown.
Posner, Richard A. (1992). *Sex and Reason.* Cambridge, Mass.: Harvard University Press.
Rothschild, Kurt. (1971). *Power in Economics.* London: Penguin Books.
Simon, Herbert A. (1991). "Interview." *New York Times Book Reivew*, March 17.
Sismondi, Jean Charles Leonard. (1827). "Nouveaux Principes d'Economie Politique." In Guy Routh (1975). *The Origin of Economic Ideas.* London: Macmillan Press Ltd.
U.S. Congress, House. (1990). H. Rep. 682, Cable Television Consumer Protection and Competition Act of 1989, 101st Cong., 2d sess.
U.S. Congress. (1991). House, Subcommittee on Government Information, Justice, and Agriculture, Hearing, Integration of the Meatpacking Industry: Its Effect on the Farmer and Consumer, 101st Cong., 2d sess.
U.S. General Accounting Office. (1990). "Beef Industry: Packer Market Concentration and Cattle Prices." Rep. No. RCED-91-28, Dec.
U.S. General Accounting Office. (1991). "Packers and Stockyards Administration: Oversight of Livestock Market Competitiveness Needs to be Enhanced." Rep. No. RCED 92-36, Oct.
Weiner, Steve. (1990). "How Josie's Chili Won the Day." *Forbes*, February 5.
Western Organization of Resource Councils Factsheet. (1989). "Monopoly Power in the Beef Industry." October.

Commentary by Herbert I. Schiller

For at least the last twenty years, American capitalism has been on a rampage, knocking down and trampling people's social defenses that had been built up by bitter historical struggles for improved living standards since the early days of industrialism.

Laissez faire economic doctrine—let capital do whatever it wants—cast into disrepute by the Great Depression of the 1930s, in the post-World War II era, and especially in the twelve Reagan-Bush years, once again became revered principle.

Following the upsurge of American global power after 1945, corporate business, grown fat on war orders, government contracts and foreign aid markets, regained and surpassed its prewar strength. With the reemergence of German and Japanese competition in the 1970s, American Big Business's response was to demand (and achieve) the dismantling of as many as possible of the checks that were originally imposed to forestall another crisis as well as to protect the working population against the effects of unrestrained market forces.

But that was yesterday. Today a new political atmosphere may be emerging, softening the tone of what up to recently was an uncritical adulation of so-called market forces, an out-of-hand rejection of the idea that government can fulfill a social role and a sweeping disrespect of any kind of planning of the overall economy. Even the likes of John Maynard Keynes—the acknowledged theoretical exponent of a managed capitalist economy—may begin to receive an occasional approving nod.

Walter Adams' and James W. Brock's essay "Economic Theory: Rhetoric, Reality, Rationalization" was written before the 1992 elections swept the Reagan-Bush Administration out of office. It remains helpful all the same in understanding where the attention of a good number of the country's social scientists and intellectuals has been focused, at least up to the day after the elections. It is also a valuable reminder of the service that theory often provides to power.

Adams and Brock lay bare the premises of doctrines that have underpinned dominant economic thinking in recent years. They find, as have others examining similar phenomena in earlier years, that dominant economic thought is, for the most part, a massive escape from reality. It generally is more concerned with justifying the status quo than it is with explaining the mechanics of power and social control.

In fact the authors demonstrate that "the problem of economic power and its consequences," invariably, is absent in the studies of dominant school economics. The currently prevailing doctrine-rational choice-has its own specificities but it bears a close ressemblance to earlier theories in its disregard for the underpinnings of the economic order. How structure affects the allocation of resources and the distribution of income and power are not the concern of rational choice theory. Adams and Brock emphasize the current doctrine's unwillingness to confront". . . the capacity of corporate giants to capture government, to manipulate the state to serve their positions, and to thereby escape market sanctions for deficient economic performance . . ." (p. 133).

The everyday record of economic and governmental affairs confirms this charge. This provokes an interesting question. How do ideas and theories that are so patently wrong-headed and incapable of genuine explanatory power, that are contrary to the experiences of most people, take root and flourish?

Perhaps the simplest explanation for this phenomenon is implicit in Adam's and Brock's observation that the corporate giants "have the capacity to capture government and manipulate the State" to their own ends. If this is the case, and the evidence that supports this conclusion is overwhelming, it is hardly a demanding task for the same resource-rich companies to capture economists, to say nothing of political scientists, jurists and whichever other professional cadres are useful in providing legitimation and material protection. Economics is especially susceptible to this fate because, with the exception of engineering, no other profession has such organic ties to business.

No crude corporate stimulus-response relationship need be invoked. The process by which this occurs extends from the primary school through the university, from the selection of a profession to the assumption of a job in the field. Taking years to be fully effective, once it is, a respectful attention to the propertied perspective will be its mark of success. Conversely, a demonstrated lack of respect for property is sure to be regarded as a failure of the socialization process and can be expected to affect adversely a poorly socialized individual's advancement in no uncertain measure. Where, in fact, if not in government and the corporate sector, are the jobs that professionals trained in the social sciences seek?

This being so, prevailing economic doctrine, however lacking in realism and social applicability, as long as it is compatible with, or better still, an endorsement of the established corporate order, can rely on its widespread dissemination. But beyond this elementary conditioning mechanism, deeply embedded in the general practices of the institutional system, there are still other, powerful instruments encouraging people to think positively, that is, non-disturbingly about economic relationships. [Harvard University's Department of Government, for example, offers a hard-to-match illustration. In a recent [late 1992] educational advertisement there is this listing: "Postdoctoral Fellowships in Positive Political Economy in 1993–1994." Did Adam Smith, Thomas Malthus, David Ricardo and John Stuart Mill realize they were writing "positive" political economy?]

Today, one of the most compelling components of power, hardly less influential than industrial strength itself, is the media/informational/cultural sphere. How control is exercised here is of no little consequence to popular thinking and the level and quality of national consciousness. What has been happening in this sphere, at an astonishing pace, is the extension of the developments at work in meatpacking, cable television and the airlines industries that Adams and Brock detail in their chapter. Mergers, consolidations and giantism now also describe the cultural industries.

Massive corporate conglomerates of cultural production, based in a few metropolitan centers, produce and sell the bulk of the world's entertainment, news and pop culture. Time-Warner, Disney, Murdock's News Corporation, Bertelsman, Sony, Matsushita, El Globo, Hachette and a number of similar combines, largely but not entirely resident in North America, Western Europe and Japan, preside over what the global audience sees, hears and reads.

These combines have been the main beneficiaries of an explosion of new information technologies—television, satellite communications, cable TV, computerization, fibre optics—which provide instantaneous worldwide transmission and reception of messages and images, with economies of scale that reduce costs and allow the media products of these corporate giants to overwhelm local inputs.

At the same time, corporations engaged in producing, collecting, organizing and disseminating information have emerged, or grown larger if they already existed, alongside the pop culture combines. These include financial and business service companies and electronic data base producers who assemble vast stockpiles of information which can be accessed electronically, at a price, wherever terminals exist. Accordingly, the Dow-Jones Company, McGraw Hill, Knight Ridder, Mead Data and a handful of similar firms, have become the producers and custodians of a good part of the world's information, and to a certain extent, the global memory. They also use their already considerable economic weight to accelerate the process by which information is transformed into a saleable good, available only to those who can afford to pay for it.

What do these developments have to do with what Adams and Brock are discussing, that is, the irrelevance of much of current economic theory? The connection is hardly mysterious.

If it is true, as Adams and Brock insist, that corporate industrial giants can "capture government" and "manipulate the state" to serve their interests, how much more may this be the case when these same forces have at their disposal an imposing instrumentation to influence, if not shape, popular consciousness? This is not only a matter of directing a flow of messages and images with the corporate perspective to the national public. This, without exception, is the daily fare of the vast unseen audience. But beyond this preemption of informational/cultural space for the corporate point of view, there is another less visible impact. It is the marginalization, sometimes elimination, of weaker and alternative voices and outlooks.

The big communication/media combines are inextricably part of the industrial order's general framework. They follow the basic institutional practices insofar as they employ wage labor, invest capital in their business and rely on the financial support of the main goods and services producers. It follows that the objectives and interests of corporate industry are shared by the media/cultural industries, and these latter provide their viewers, listeners and readers with a daily dosage of messages and images, however abundant, that are generally unquestioning and supportive of the established order.

In this not entirely but still largely controlled cultural arena, all sorts of views, as long as they are not seen as system-threatening, are given an airing. Indeed, the more bizarre and/or outrageous, frequently, the greater the opportunity for exposure that is offered by the cultural guardians. There is, consequently, a continuous succession of fads and fashions, in ideas and in cultural matters no less than in clothes and personal adornment. Madonna's antics and rational choice theory are both at offer in the cultural-intellectual supermarket. Sales are stimulated at the same time as the perception is strengthened that a wide range of thought and creativity exists.

This satisfies, in turn, the ideological need to demonstrate the openness and freedom of a social system that is actually pretty tightly sealed when it feels it has to be e.g., the clampdown on criticism during the Persian Gulf War (Mowlana, Gerbner and Schiller, 1992). Economic theory, as could be expected, invariably reflects the general social condition. Its assumptions and distortions are no less, and possibly more egregious, than those that may be found in most other fields of social knowledge. The most casual literature search in almost any social sphere will turn up startling evidence of an ideological imprint.

In some disciplines, the actual origins of the field record direct systemic demand and specific purpose. Anthropology, for example, can be considered an offspring of European colonialism, however distant the field may be today from its initial motivations. Communication, a relatively recent sphere of academic inquiry, includes scholars still alive, who were engaged in the original marketing, psychological warfare and economic developmental studies that comprise a good part of the theoretical foundations of communication theory.

Throughout Asia, Africa, and Latin America, there are countless individuals who studied at U.S. universities and took home with them the theoretical perspectives that derived from American corporate global interests in the post-World War II years. The field of development communication offers a striking example of theory elaborated to serve the interests of expanding American communication and media industries, as well as the systemic aims of a world market order—under American direction at the time (Rogers, 1978, and Simpson, 1992).

In the case of development communication theory, the theorists' prescriptions were especially capable of adoption and application. To this day, most of the new nations that emerged from the old colonial empires, are still laboring under development programs whose parentage, in significant part, was U.S. communication and development theory.

The installation of advanced telecommunications systems throughout the less industrialized regions, bear witness not only to the strength of communication "theory," but, more to the point, its service to the transnational corporate system whose members are the main users and beneficiaries of highly developed communication instrumentation. This technology has facilitated the massive movement of capital to locales where wages are low, governments are compliant and markets are open to exploitation. The electronic informational networks that have been installed around the world allow the transnational corporations to administer a global structure of production, promotion and distribution.

A hard-to-miss feature of this pattern of "development," is the shocking differential at most of these global sites between the availability and range of information services to the corporate sector alongside the glaring absence of these services to the population-at-large. One study which examined these arrangements in several less industrialized countries—the Philippines, Mexico, Malaysia, Brazil, India, Singapore and so on, carried the dedication: "For the humble folk not invited to the 'communication revolution'" (Sussman and Lent, 1991).

Communication departments in American universities are often remodeled journalism or speech departments. In many of these departments (schools), advertising and marketing constitute an important part of the curriculum. This makes sense, of a sort, since U.S. television, radio and cable, to say nothing of the press and publishing, are heavily, sometimes totally, dependent on advertising. Imagine, in such an academic setting a young nontenured, faculty member examining critically the structure of American communications! It does happen but the weight of the corporate sponsor is never too distant from the classroom, or, more indirectly but no less threateningly, the Dean's office.

Those who scoff at the possibility of ideological influence of the corporate system on academic life and theory-making in particular, rely on the incontestable fact that monolithic dominance doesn't exist and that, to the contrary, there are examples enough that demonstrate a wide range of unhampered intellectual and theoretical academic activity.

The response to this is that ideological influence does not require total domination. A hegemonic condition is sufficient. Hegemonic control represents something less than absolute cultural dictation. It is all the more effective for its lack of being all-encompassing.

What the concentration of industrial production, financial resources and media/cultural outputs have in common, is the coexistence in each of these spheres of a number of small to medium-size businesses. The essential shared feature of these "competitors" is that they are incapable of seriously challenging the big, concentrated companies. They exist, in fact, at the suffrance of the dominant power wielders, though there can be occasions when one or another marginal unit can take advantage of some extraordinary condition and become a major stakeholder. This in no way disturbs the general terrain of concentrated power alongside marginalized cohorts.

In the communication sector the same situation prevails. There are the dominant voices, transmitted and amplified by the media networks. There are also a fair number of weaker voices that circulate through thin and restricted circuits. *The Nation*, for example, after 130 years of continuous publication of critical commentary, reaches 100,000, or less subscribers. *Time, Newsweek*, and the like, have weekly sales in the millions.

So too with theory! Here the circuits are relatively narrow and the audiences far smaller. But the factors that determine how wide the theory gets disseminated, and how much attention it will receive, are the same that govern the supply of popular culture and the daily news flow. Sometimes there is a unique additional feature, at least in the academic arena. For example, in touting a special brand of economic theory, the awarding of a Nobel prize can be a valuable promotional asset. Offered by a Swedish Bank, the prize confers international status on the recipient and his (never her) thinking. In accordance with the growth of conservative views in recent years, the Nobel committee has chosen for the award, four years running, an economist from the University of Chicago—an acknowledged center of conservative thought. In 1992, the prize went to Gary Becker, whose writings on rational choice theory are scrutinized by Adams and Brock.

Much like the journalism and publishing fields, that revel in bestowing awards on themselves for outstanding achievement, economics legitimates and extols those who find that all is well with the resource allocative process—despite a mountain of contrary evidence.

Given the breadth of the resources and ideological capability arrayed against it, how does thinking that is contrary and oppositional, escape total marginality in the contemporary corporate system? Here, only the briefest and most general explanation can be offered.

The reality, which rational choice, and many other schools of economists, prefer to ignore, does in fact exist. This reality does not accommodate itself to constructed models that disregard its fundamental dynamic. It follows that there have been, there is now, and there will continue to be, economic crises in a market economy. These crises, whatever their specific character and origins, are experienced by millions of people—some directly, many indirectly. Questions are asked, answers are sought, especially if a crisis is prolonged and the human costs are extended. At such times, the hollowness of dominant economic thinking is illuminated. In November 1992, "supply side" economics, though it was not specifically on the ballot, all the same, received a resounding rejection by an economically illiterate but materially hard-pressed electorate.

Professors Adams and Brock can be reassured. Economic theory which satisfies corporate power, may circulate in schools, journals, the media and political speeches but it has a dated shelf life. Invariably, it loses its lustre when cyclical reality intrudes. So too, the mind management machine, extraordinary as it has become, cannot conjure away unmet mass medical needs, unemployment and homelessness. Whose rational choice accounts for these conditions?

References

Hamid Mowlana, George Gerbner, and Herbert I. Schiller, ed. (1992). "Triumph of the Image: The Media's War In The Persian Gulf, An International Perspective." Boulder, CO: Westview.

Everett Rogers. (1978). "The Rise and Fall of the Dominant Paradigm." *Journal of Communication* 28(1):64–69.

Christopher Simpson. (in press). "Mass Communication and Counter-Insurgency After 1945: An Investigation of the Construction of 'Scientific Reality.'"

Gerald Sussman, and John A. Lent, ed. (1991). "Transnational Communications: Wiring the Third World." Newbury Park, California: Sage.

6 THE POLITICAL ECONOMY OF COMMUNICATIONS RESEARCH

William J. Buxton

Communications Research and its History

As Paul Lazarsfeld recounted the early history of mass communications research:

> I remember one day, a friend of mine, in 1937 or so, introduced me to a group of colleagues and said, "this is a European colleague who is an utmost authority on communication research," and he saw that no-one was especially impressed, so he wanted to press the point and said "as a matter of fact, he is the only one who works in this field."[1]

A dozen years later, a jest of this kind would have been impossible to make. By 1949, under the leadership of Lazarsfeld, the Bureau of Applied Social Research at Columbia University, extending the earlier initiatives of the Princeton Research Project, had produced a considerable of body of work on mass communications.[2] As Lazarsfeld and his co-editor Frank Stanton noted in the introduction to the last of their three volumes summarizing research that had taken place under the auspices of the Bureau over intermittent periods, "It is no longer necessary today either to justify communications research as a special discipline or to outline its general scope. Because the field has developed so rapidly and because its pioneers have been a rather closely knit group, it has been taught in a surprisingly similar way at many universities."[3] The "closely knit group" in question had been quite active in publishing the results of their studies as the decade drew to a close. In addition to the final volume edited by Lazarsfeld and Stanton, numerous works sharing the same general perspective made their appearance.[4]

The studies undertaken by the Bureau investigators and other early communications researchers, while generally accepting the framework of commercial broadcasting as a given, dealt with a broad range of issues. As such, they were largely discrete and unconnected studies responding to a variety of problems in understanding the media. Beginning in the 1950s, however, this body of work began to be defined much differently. As communications began to consolidate as a field, an effort was made to establish its credentials by defining the foundations upon which it was built. Accordingly, particular aspects of the Bureau's work were singled out for emphasis. Lazarsfeld himself was a key participant in the process. In conjunction with Elihu Katz, he established the "two-step" flow of communication as the leitmotif defining much of the communications research in the previous fifteen years.[5] In recognition of his contributions to the field of communications Lazarsfeld was hailed as a founding figure[6] whose early work in communications had attained "milestone" status.[7]

This version of the history of communications research had gained virtually unchallenged ascendancy by the 1970s. It viewed the body of work produced by Lazarsfeld and his collaborators as one of a series of foundational works in communications studies. Such a depiction of the field's lineages may have helped to define the field in relation to other more developed disciplines. But it resulted in little more than a cursory history of the body of work produced during the early Lazarsfeld epoch. Rather, particular aspects of the research programme—such as the effects of media and the two-step flow of communication—were appropriated from their original contexts and incorporated into whatever analytical framework the commentator in question had constructed. This approach to the history of communications research shares many features with what George Stocking, commenting on trends in the historiography of the social sciences, termed "presentism" or "the Whig version of history."[8] This involves viewing past thought as a repository of ideas that can be selectively drawn upon for solving current analytical problems. Given the assumption that each generation of social scientific practitioners builds upon the work of its predecessors—as it were, "standing on the shoulders of giants,"—it was concluded that current fields of social-scientific knowledge had evolved in a progressive manner from earlier initiatives. In this sense, they were viewed as a culmination of a program of research that had emerged out of the critical breakthroughs achieved in an initial set of studies. A variation of presentism was behind a number of the historical accounts of communications research that took their lead from Katz and Lazarsfeld's initial assessment of the trajectory of communications research. In true Whiggish fashion, history was written backwards. The research agenda of the "limited effects model" subscribed to by the authors implicitly gave meaning and direction to the narrative they provided of progressive developments in the "two-step flow of communication." In effect, the behavioral approach to communications research which they supported was vindicated because it culminated the efforts of a group of researchers who progressively built upon the early work of Lazarsfeld and his collaborators.

This widespread tendency to treat the legacy of the Lazarsfeld approach in an uncritical fashion received a severe challenge by Todd Gitlin in 1978.[9] Relying upon the then fashionable work of Thomas Kuhn, Gitlin argued that the approach to the study of mass communications, as consolidated in *Personal Influence*, constituted a particular paradigm, possessing a distinct method and a shared conception of what constituted valid research problems. In describing the Lazarsfeld approach in this manner, Gitlin did not differ radically from the school's proponents. However, Gitlin parted company with them by making the claim that the "paradigm" was rooted in a particular social order. He argued, moreover, that the research was designed to aid and abet corporate and governmental decision-makers. He sharply criticized Lazarsfeld's administrative approach as predicated upon "the search for specific, measurable, short-term, attitudinal, and behavioral 'effects' of media content."[10] This form of research had previously been labelled "abstract empiricism" by C. Wright Mills.[11] However, as Gitlin claims, the empiricism of mass communications research was not at all abstract; it was firmly rooted in "a concrete social order" and "a concrete system of power." As such, it served to deflect public attention from the domination and power of the media, as aligned with the state and powerful interests.

In effect, Gitlin's move corresponded to some extent to what elsewhere has been called the historicist or contextualist approach.[12] However, unlike contextualists who argue that particular schools of thought can only be understood in relation to a broader system of ideas, Gitlin suggests that communications research had practical implications for the order in question. While generally suggestive, Gitlin largely fails to explore what either the "concrete social order" or the "concrete system of power" were which underpinned administrative research. To be sure, he does offer an account of the origins of the Lazarsfeld approach during its formative period in the 1930s and calls attention to the Rockefeller Foundation's support of early studies of radio. But he fails to explore in detail how the designs of Rockefeller philanthropy affected the origins of mass communications research.

A similar failure to follow through on the practical implications of Lazarsfeld's early work can be detected in the work of Morrison and Delia.[13] After tracing the interplay between mass communications research, the Rockefeller Foundation (RF) and the needs of commercial broadcasters, Morrison rather surprisingly concludes that "in understanding the genesis of mass communication research it ought to be underscored that it was not influenced, or stimulated, as an academic field, by the industry's commercial research, it developed along an independent path guided by intellectual and social considerations.[14] Along similar lines, Delia makes the claim that "more so than any other individual or group, Lazarsfeld cemented the emerging bridge between academic and commercial interests in communication research and established the theoretical relevance of communication research based on applied problems.[15] This statement, however, largely goes unexplored. Instead, Delia is at pains to qualify the view that "Lazarsfeld's research practices ... were shaped by the interests of administrative and marketing research." He calls for a "more complex understanding," which emphasizes how the "theoretical significance" of Lazarsfeld's approach can explain its success within the sociology of communication.[16]

While the accounts of Gitlin, Morrison, and Delia all allude to the practical implications of the early radio research, they all fail to follow through on these claims. Arguably, this failure is rooted in their implicit presentism, and their concern to demonstrate the relevance of the early radio research to the field of communications. The texts examined are treated in a reified fashion, only in so far as they relate to subsequent developments in the discipline. Little attention is given to the way in which the texts were the sediment of socially rooted ideas and precepts. Moreover, no consideration is given to how the production and circulation of texts had particular social consequences. Given these oversights, a full exploration of how the early research was practically linked to its context cannot be made. While their work is quite suggestive, these critical historians of communications research are prisoners of a historiography whose ultimate frame of reference is the current field of communications.

These deficiencies suggest the need for a historiography which is more closely attuned to the practical interplay between communications research and its context. To some extent it builds upon some of Gitlin's insights into the strategic basis of "administrative research." It also heeds the suggestion of Delia that the history of communications research should pay closer attention to the institutional context in which it arose.[17] But it would differ from these accounts in a fundamental respect. Rather than simply deriving the context from a certain reading of communications research, as does Gitlin, or treating the context as a simple backdrop, as does Delia, it tries to show the way in which the communications research was intended to change that context itself. This corresponds to what I have elsewhere termed an "activist" approach.[18] With this emphasis upon how research is implicated in the construction of reality, it is closer to the approach used by Rowland, who emphasizes how communications research developed as part of a "shared ritual" of the "four tribes" (politicians, broadcast industry executives, reformers, and academic researchers):

> As they dance around the fire of contemporary tensions and uncertainties, as they marvel at the powers and dangers of modern communication technology, and as they invoke the deity of science in an effort to allay those fears and technology, [they] create a certain definition of reality and in the process reveal much about the structure of their society and its political, economic, and cultural values.[19]

Rowland uses this "dramatic reconstruction" form of analysis to shed some insights into the significance of the early radio research. But like Gitlin, he relies far too heavily on secondary sources, which means that he tends to "read in" imputed linkages to external forces and interests rather than examining in more concrete detail how communications research was socially implicated. Rowland's work illustrates the danger of simply deducing from the published material on the early Princeton radio research project what the political economical context *must have been*. To do so is to impose one's own view of the context rather than seeking to understand what context was relevant to those involved and how it affected their course of action.

The Princeton Radio Research Project and its Context

In order to understand what context was meaningful to those involved in radio research and how it set the terms for their activities, one must go beyond the usual published accounts by exploring more thoroughly unpublished sources. Fortunately, there is an abundance of material relevant to the origins of The Princeton Radio Research Project at the Rockefeller Archive Center in Pocantico Hills, New York. This collection reveals that the Radio project, of which Lazarsfeld eventually became the driving force, originated in a set of institutions and practices that were beginning to congeal in the mid 1930s, under the guidance of the Rockefeller Foundation. On the basis of a particular approach to how problems facing the broadcasting system could be solved, Rockefeller philanthropy embarked on its program of support for initiatives in communications.

Accordingly, if we are to understand the "concrete social order" in which the Princeton radio project was grounded—setting the stage for the series of studies conducted under Lazarsfeld's leadership—we must give particular attention to the system of broadcasting that had taken shape in the United States by the late 1930s,—what some commentators refer to as "Radio's Golden Age."[20] The term is usually applied metaphorically, referring to the number of households with radio sets, the size and attentiveness of the audience, and the extent to which radio personalities had captured the popular imagination.[21]

Even if one does not accept the notion that this set of features constitutes a golden age, one must concede that the commercial networks had come to dominate radio broadcasting. Correspondingly, small and independent broadcasters, serving local audiences with educational and informational programming had been all but obliterated.[22] Accepting that the decline of educational radio was necessary and inevitable, the early proponents of radio research chose to assume the framework of commercial radio as a given. Their studies, moreover, with their emphasis upon media effects, defined the boundaries for subsequent discussion of communications.[23]

Yet less than a decade earlier, the theory and practice of radio broadcasting was very much contested terrain. In response to the growing commercialization of radio mirrored by the sharp decline in educational broadcasting, a broadly based oppositional movement began to take form. It not only raised fundamental issues about the growing ascendancy of commercial radio, but elicited a vigorous public debate about the nature and purpose of broadcasting.[24] This opposition to commercial broadcasting lasted until the passage of the Communications Act of 1934, which marked both a victory for commercial radio, and the beginning of a sharp decline in public controversy about the direction of radio broadcasting.[25]

In explaining the triumph of commercial radio mirrored by the demise of the educational radio movement, one must assign central importance to the regulatory process in the United States. The trajectory of radio broadcasting in the United States can only be understood if one pays close attention to the major regulatory milestone (the Communications Act of 1934) and the political process that it engendered. While the Act set the framework for the incorporation of educational interests into the commercial broadcasting system, it did not provide the resources, programs, and expertise through which this reconciliation between educators and broadcasters could take place. As I will argue, the role of charting the path of cooperation between educational and broadcasting interests fell to the Humanities Program of the Rockefeller Foundation. Specifically, the Princeton radio research project, in conjunction with a number of other initiatives, was intended to provide the basis for the incorporation of educational and cultural concerns into commercial radio broadcasting. In effect, the Rockefeller Foundation assumed a task that neither broadcasters, educators, nor state officials were willing or able to undertake. In more concrete terms, this involved the integration of educational broadcasting into the programming of commercial networks, the commercialization of certain educational broadcasters, the improvement of relations between broadcasters and educators, and the shift of public discourse and understanding about issues related to radio. However, before examining the activities of the Rockefeller Foundation, I will trace the development of radio broadcasting that set the stage for its intervention into this arena.

Early Development of Radio

On November 2, 1920, station KDKA broadcast the results of the presidential election to what could only have been a handful of listeners. This event, generally recognized as the first broadcast by a radio station in the United States, ushered in a communications boom in the United States, unrivalled until the appearance of television a quarter of a century later.[26] By 1922, nearly 600 stations were in operation. Mirroring this dizzying expansion of broadcasters, the demand for radio receivers increased exponentially.[27] In effect, broadcasting had begun as a free-for-all. Regulation was minimal, as the only statute covering communications policy (that of 1912) was intended to regulate telegraphy. Little control was exercised over the granting of broadcasting licenses, with the result that the airwaves were overloaded with broadcast signals, making reception extremely difficult. Despite the chaos and confusion, a wide variety of groups and organizations had the opportunity to produce and broadcast programs. Many of these small broadcasters were educational or public service organizations, working on limited budgets with volunteer help and small transmitters. Overall, between 1921 and 1926, 158 broadcast licenses were issued to educational institutions.[28]

The Federal Radio Commission (FRC) was established in 1927 with the intent of bringing order to the airwaves. It did so by setting stringent standards for equipment and the quality of transmission, which resulted in the elimination of numerous small stations. Particularly hard hit were educational broadcasters, many of whom lacked the financial resources to meet the broadcasting standards set by the FRC. At the same time that the educational stations were closing down their operations, commercial broadcasting was thriving, as evidenced by the rapid expansion of the NBC and CBS chains in the late 1920s. Realizing that educational broadcasting was in jeopardy, its supporters began to organize themselves into action groups. However, from the very outset, the ranks of educational broadcasters were divided into two opposing factions. One group, the National Advisory Council on Radio in Education (NACRE) came into existence on July 1, 1930. Its director was Dr. Levering Tyson, of the American Association for Adult Education. Funded by the Carnegie Corporation of New York and John Rockefeller Jr., it advocated co-operation between educators and broadcasters. The other group, The National Committee on Education by Radio (NCER) took a less conciliatory stance in relation to commercial broadcasting. Organized by William J. Cooper (U.S. Commissioner of Education) with a small grant from the Payne Foundation, it met for the first time on December 30, 1930.

In keeping with their much different perspectives, the groups pursued divergent courses of action. In the early 1930s, NACRE put its efforts into developing high quality educational programs, in the hope that commercial broadcasters would be persuaded to make use of them. It also held annual meetings from 1931 through 1935. Their purpose was to provide a forum for discussion of central issues in education by radio, based on presentations by authorities in the field.

NCER, in contrast, directed it efforts into lobbying Congress and building public support for the preservation of educational radio.[29] In particular, it supported a bill of Ohio Senator Simeon D. Fess which called for the reservation of a minimum of fifteen percent of all radio broadcasting channels for educational institutions. The bill, however, was never reported out of committee. Along similar lines, NCER sought support for the amendment to the Communications Act proposed by

Senator Robert F. Wagner of New York and Senator Henry D. Hatfield of West Virginia. It called for a full twenty-five percent of channels to be distributed to non-commercial organizations. While the Wagner-Hatfield amendment did gain a good measure of support in Congress, it was defeated on the floor, paving the way for the passage of the Communications Act of 1934.[30]

To a large extent, the act built upon the earlier act of 1927, favoring the interests of commercial interests. It also specified that the new Federal Communications Commission (FCC) should "study new uses for radio, provide for experimental uses of frequencies, and generally encourage the larger and more effective use of radio in the public interest."[31] More specifically, this lead to the calling of a meeting to reconcile differences between commercial and educational radio.

The 1934 Act represented a severe setback for those who believed that educational broadcasting was incompatible with commercial broadcasting. The failure of NCER to convince Congress of its position increased its alienation from NACRE and from the newly created Federal Communications Commission. On the other hand, NACRE's position was not only vindicated; its advocacy of cooperation between educators and broadcasters became FCC policy.

It was in the bitter aftermath of the passage of the Communications Act of 1934 that the Rockefeller Foundation became involved in the radio-broadcasting controversy. Given the earlier funding ties to NACRE, it was consistent that the Foundation now broaden and deepen its support for cooperation between educators and broadcasters. But this increasing commitment to intervene in the aftermath of the "radio war" cannot be understood simply as an extension of the earlier pattern of support. The growing involvement in issues pertaining to radio reflected, in turn, a fundamental reorientation in the Rockefeller Foundation Humanities Division. As part of a thoroughgoing review a "committee of three" on "appraisal and plan" was struck to examine the purpose and future direction of the various Rockefeller boards. In its section on the Humanities Division, the committee implicitly criticized the "cloistered kind of research" that the Humanities Division had previously supported. This shift of emphasis "toward greater effect on contemporary society," meant a fundamental reorientation for the Humanities Program. Rather than focusing on "a few highly trained scholars as interpreters of the past," officers were to now take into account "those men and methods able to influence contemporary taste in large masses of population." Given that drama, film, radio and popular print—"the obvious sources of influence on public taste of today—are mediums of slight interest to scholars," the officers were to be "released from relations with much of the scholarly world... Their new contacts were to be with men outside universities and colleges." By virtue of this shift towards the new communication media the Humanities Program would help to find better means for reaching minds effectively.[32]

The formal task of changing the direction of the Humanities Program fell to its director, David H. Stephens. However, the actual implementation of the changes were to be carried out by the newly appointed assistant director, John Marshall. Indeed, evidence suggests that Marshall, as the official with the day-to-day responsibility for monitoring, assessing, and implementing Humanities program policy, almost single-handedly gave coherence and direction to the assorted Rockefeller projects related to the relatively new media of mass communication. Accordingly, Marshall's encounters, perceptions, and actions will figure prominently in my analysis.[33]

The Rockefeller Foundation and the Development of Radio

The new direction in the Humanities Programme began to take shape in 1935. Taking his mandate from the new Foundation guidelines, Marshall sought to explore "the possibilities of radio as a means of bringing humanistic values to application in present-day life."[34] To this end, he arranged interviews with those who were closely involved with the ongoing controversy about the relationship between educational and commercial broadcasting. It is instructive to examine in some detail Marshall's diary entries in this period, as his interviews with broadcasters and educators provide the basis for the subsequent course of action taken by the Humanities Program.

Marshall quickly discovered not only that the broadcasters and the educators had diametrically opposed views on the place of educational programming in broadcasting, but that the educators themselves were seriously divided on the question. Marshall initially relied heavily on the views and advice of Levering Tyson, Director of NACRE.[35] Tyson's position was that "little if anything can be accomplished through men within the industry. The educational directors of the two large broadcasting circuits seem to... have no conception of the educational possibilities of the radio." Accordingly, Tyson was of the view that any initiative must come from outside the industry, preferably from the government.[36] The government itself could not be relied upon, as the

FCC was "still dominated by surviving members of the old Radio Commission." This meant that the "majority of the present Commission are refusing to accept recommendations which the radio division is pressing. The recent report submitted by the division with regard to giving access to the air to non-profit seeking groups was regarded as quite unacceptable in its original form."[37]

Marshall also arranged interviews with those who had been pushing for a fixed amount of programming to be allocated for educational purposes. Armstrong Perry, council for NCER, recognized that a fixed portion of radio facilities for educational uses had provoked a good deal of opposition. He was nonetheless convinced that "educational activities will be severely hampered so long as broadcasting remains a commercial enterprise which draws its major support from advertising." This meant in turn that "educational programs . . . cannot succeed till they are assured of being granted the same radio time over a period sufficiently long to build up a listening audience." Perry argued further that because of the censorship practised by broadcasters, the freedom of speech for educators was extremely difficult to realize.[38] While Marshall was sympathetic to the National Committee's point of view, he ultimately sided with the position held by Tyson and NACRE. According to Tyson, a fixed allocation of facilities for educational broadcasting was unwise for two reasons. Not only could it potentially lead to the political control of broadcasting, but it was doubtful whether there was sufficient educational programming available to be utilized for educational purposes. Tyson was of the view that an ambitious program of educational broadcasting could only be attempted when the personnel had been sufficiently developed.[39]

Marshall not only solicited the views of educators; he also sampled the standpoint of the broadcasters. Among those with whom he met was Frederic A. Willis, assistant to the president of CBS, who described how his employer had "borne the brunt of the educators' attack on the broadcasting companies." Willis was completely dismissive about the efforts of educators to provide programming. In his view, they were totally unwilling to recognize the degree to which their talks failed to arouse interest among listeners. He emphasized, moreover, that "attempts to assist educational speakers to put their materials in a form adapted for broadcasting purposes have seldom been successful." Labelling the Committee on Education by Radio as "irreconcilable," he feared that they would now seek to accomplish their purposes by lobbying in Congress.[40] Other persons whom Marshall interviewed offered him insight into what kind of action might be taken. Bethuel Webster (former member and special counsel for the Federal Radio Commission) felt that discussions between broadcasters and educators could only advance if a "middle group", capable of adapting broadcasting techniques to educational interests, were to emerge. He suggested the need for an agency to select "competent representatives of the various interests involved who are qualified by temperament to profit from experience in broadcasting procedures."

Based on his experience with the Radio Commission and the newly formed Communications Commission, he doubted whether a government agency was capable of carrying out the kind of impartial study that was necessary. Such a study could be best carried out "by qualified experts working under the direction of a small commission composed of carefully selected engineers, lawyers, publicists, and educators."[41]

Marshall also gained insight on broadcasting through his interviewees' speculations on the outcome of the upcoming Conference on Radio, in which the issues dividing the two camps would be aired. Cline M. Koon (radio specialist, United States Office of Education) doubted whether anything would result from the conference.[42] According to Koon, cooperation between broadcasters and educators could only be worked out through "some smaller group, carefully selected with a view to the individual competence of its members."[43] Both Koon and Bethuel Webster noted that there were serious divisions among the educators themselves. In particular, NACRE was viewed as "a tool of the broadcasting industry." Hence it was "by no means certain that the cooperation of all concerned could be counted on if the conferences were organized by the Council."[44]

Much of what Marshall had learned about the broadcasting controversy was corroborated by the discussions at the joint session of the National Advisory Council for Radio in Education and the Ohio Institute for Education by Radio, held in Columbus from May 6 to May 8, 1935. For the most part, educators and broadcasters were able to find little common ground. Marshall, nevertheless, noted some encouraging developments. Chairman Anning S. Prall of the FCC, after "pointing out the deficiencies in the present practice of both educators and broadcasters ... affirmed once again the Commission's determination to find some practical means of making cooperation between the two groups effective."[45]

While Marshall's diaries are written in a detached and factual manner, one can nonetheless detect an emergent interpretive standpoint which gradually came to provide the basis for the Humanities policy on broadcasting. His overall view of the broadcasting dispute was heavily influenced by NACRE's position (as articulated by Levering Tyson) that commercial and educational interests were ultimately reconcilable.[46]

Consistent with Foundation practices in relation to perceived social problems, Marshall then proceeded to "diagnose" the basis for the divided interests within broadcasting. Finally, he sought to understand how a reconciliation through new institutions, initiatives, and funding could be brought about. As we will now examine, an obvious vehicle for these actions materialized at a meeting between educators and broadcasters held in Washington on May 15 and 16, 1935.

The meeting had been called by the FCC to develop increased cooperation between educators and broadcasters. Aware that the failure of the Fess bill and the Wagner-Hatfield amendments had exacerbated the already strained relations between educators and broadcasters, FCC officials expressed their hope that the meeting would begin a process of reconciliation between the two groups. However, given that the legislative initiatives over the previous eight years had served to consolidate the supremacy of commercial broadcasting, their real task was to find ways of incorporating educational programming into the corporate broadcasting framework.

Not surprisingly, the discussions at the conference did little to increase cooperation between the two sides. However, one important development did occur. The FCC announced its intention to appoint a committee to "formulate plans for furthering cooperation between broadcasters and the various non-profit groups." Known as the Federal Radio Education Committee (FREC), it was to be composed of representatives from both broadcasters and educators. Its chair was Commissioner of Education John W. Studebaker, who urged the need for "a thoroughgoing study of how educational broadcasting is to be financed, or more particularly how the expence involved is to be shared by the broadcasters, educational agencies, the foundations, and possibly the government."[47] As I will now examine, Marshall took a close interest in FREC and its initiatives, as it represented the best institutional basis through which cooperation between broadcasters and educators could be realized.

From the Federal Radio Education Committee to the Princeton Radio Research Project

In April of 1935, The Rockefeller Trustees gave their approval for "limited support to cooperative efforts of the radio industry and noncommercial agencies that are directed towards the greater cultural effectiveness of sustaining programs and towards a broader range of public service." Their interest in helping to reconcile the differences between broadcasters and educators through conferences and the anticipated activities of FREC, was just one aspect of a broader program. The overall goal of increased cooperation was also to be realized "through aiding regional centers, especially where strong cultural forces and local radio stations develop friendly relations and . . . through training personnel qualified to plan and produce radio programs of educational and cultural value."[48] Along these lines, the Humanities Program supported the "World Wide Broadcasting Foundation (WWBF) operating through short-wave station W1XAL at Boston." The WWBF was considered to be a worthy exemplar for educational broadcasting because it did not compete with the radio industry, supplementing "what is offered commercially by providing programs of a more serious nature for those who wish to hear them."[49] Similarly, the Foundation sought ways to provide further training for broadcasting personnel, so they might "compare favorably in technical finish with commercial broadcasting." This was considered "essential to any effective exploration of the possibilities of radio for educational and cultural purposes." To this end, the Foundation, largely through the General Education Board, funded fellowship appointments at NBC and CBS.[50]

The "natural and desirable" corollary of these two initiatives (support of local broadcasting, and training of qualified personnel), was "a limited program of research" on how commercial broadcasting could be more educationally and culturally oriented. It was for this reason that the Foundation took such a great interest in the proposed activities of FREC. With its emphasis upon research, it seemed to parallel Foundation concerns, albeit in a manner that seemed "less practical and more ambitious." Nevertheless, this convergence suggested that the Foundation was indeed "providing a firm basis for such cooperation as the Studebaker Committee aims at."[51]

But it had already become abundantly evident that the Studebaker Committee was having difficult achieving its stated goals. H. B. McCarty of the Wisconsin State Broadcasting Station reported that a meeting of the subcommittee on conflicts of FREC "was of little use, being largely given over to general and somewhat aimless discussion. The one specific case of conflict between educators and commercial broadcasters was not taken up." McCarty concluded that the meeting had been called only to demonstrate that the committee was still functioning.[52] Moreover, as Levering Tyson reported, the work of FREC was held up for lack of funds. He had even urged foundations interested in radio (including the Rockefeller Foundation) not to undertake any large projects on radio until the various subcommittees of FREC submitted their proposals for consideration. Tyson expected few results from the activities of the subcommittees, except for the technical subcommittee under the direction of Hadley Cantril which "may be able to arrange for research of general significance."[53]

Three days later, Marshall interviewed Cantril, who was highly critical of FREC, and "inclined to question the value of most of the projects planned... on the grounds that they are artificially limited by the conception of what constitutes educational activity by radio." Cantril believed that much more could be gained by sampling "general listener interests and wants... invoking the procedures of various current polls of public opinion and of marketing research." Obviously quite impressed by Cantril's ideas, Marshall suggested to him that if he "wished to formulate his interests in a definite project, [he] JM would be glad to look into what might be done to finance the work involved."[54]

Cantril responded to Marshall's suggestion by submitting a request for an annual grant of $25,000, extending over two years. This was to support a study of "what listeners find of interest in radio programs and... why these interests exist." He hoped to enlist the services of Frank Stanton, the assistant director of the research department at CBS to help him.[55] As part of his project, Cantril wished to undertake a thorough analysis of techniques with their later applications to broader population groups. He believed that this would be "of incalculable value to the educational and commercial broadcasters, and the general welfare of radio in this country."

In his view, neither educator nor commercial broadcaster was in a position to undertake research of this kind.

> The educator is not equipped, either financially or technically, to carry out such a program of research; the broadcaster is interested in more immediate problems and is not likely to see certain psychological factors underlying the interests of listeners. Furthermore, the commercial broadcaster has worked for so long within a definite framework that research conducted on a commercial basis is apt to be biased at the beginning by certain conscious or unconscious presuppositions.

What he proposed was a "highly centralized" research project "conducted by technically trained individuals aware of the problems at hand and not bound by any rigid commercial or educational sponsorship." Cantril maintained that "an objective, coordinated program of research" of this kind would be able to produce "a closely knit, well integrated body of data."

As a member of the technical subcommittee of FREC, Cantril had submitted a similar proposal for consideration. However, because of the "apparent lethargy of the Office of Education" he believed "that the investigations my committee submitted will probably never be carried out."[56] Because he was anxious to get started on his project, he had decided to seek foundation support instead.[57]

Marshall's reply on January 9, 1937, did not address the substance or direction of Cantril's research project *per se*. Rather he wished to inform Cantril of his (Cantril's) "appointment to a small committee to consider further the 16 projects set up by the Federal Radio Education Committee as preliminary studies that must be undertaken before the Committee can take up or suggest steps looking toward better cooperation between educators and broadcasters." In effect, as a member of this committee, Cantril would be in the position of evaluating the merits of his own proposal! Moreover, the same proposal had been submitted to the Rockefeller Foundation for its support. This set of circumstances undoubtedly led Marshall to encourage Cantril to state that he had submitted a project to the Foundation for financing, should Cantril agree to join the committee. As Marshall explained his suggestion to Cantril,

> The need for doing so will doubtless be evident as the committee's discussions progress. For it was more or less agreed at a conference in Washington yesterday that some of the outcomes aimed at in the FREC's list of projects might well result from studies undertaken outside the committee.[58]

Marshall was referring to a "Conference on January 8, 1937, regarding the Future of the Federal Radio Education Committee." Judge E.O. Sykes, chairman of the broadcasting division of the FCC and Studebaker had "called together representatives of the three broadcasting chains, the National Association of Broadcasters, and several educators including representatives of educational foundations, for the specific purpose of exploring the possible sources of funds with which to finance the work of the committee." In order to reduce the projected costs of its studies, those present at the meeting proposed the formation of a committee of six (three broadcasters and three educators), who would be charged with the responsibility of combining some of the studies in order to reduce its costs.[59] The three broadcasters chosen were Frederic Willis, Assistant to the President, Columbia Broadcasting System, James Baldwin, Executive Director of the National Association of Broadcasters and John Royal, Vice-President in charge of operations, National Broadcasting System;

the three educators were W. W. Charters of Ohio State University, Tyson, and Cantril.[60]

Marshall was undoubtedly pleased at the composition of the "informal committee." The three educators represented were firmly in the Rockefeller camp, and the industry spokesmen had views congenial with the thinking in the Humanities program radio project. Not only would this review committee provide direction to the proposed projects, but it could serve as a mediating body between the Rockefeller Foundation, and FREC—the larger body of representatives from industry and education whose mandate from the FCC was to develop better cooperation between the two interests.

Cantril accepted the offer to join the reconstituted executive committee, and began to take part in deliberations about how the projects could be streamlined. Succumbing to the conflict of interest that his simultaneous status of both assessor and assessee entailed, Cantril used the review process as an opportunity to gain further support for his own research proposal. His general comment on a report summarizing the studies proposed by the various FREC subcommittees was that those concerned with the drafting of the report "had no consistent ideas in mind." As he observed, "the studies do not seem to hang together and accomplish any single purpose. Many of them presuppose information and knowledge that does not already exist; others seem isolated in their specificity and of no practical or theoretical value." In Cantril's view, the proposed studies had largely failed to overcome the biases of the broadcasting and educational interests, respectively. He maintained that "if the various committees involved in these deliberations are to achieve any results of lasting value, broadcasters and educators must meet on a cooperative, not an antagonistic basis." Accordingly, he suggested that the various proposals ought to be reorganized as "a well coordinated research project, conducted by trained investigators to study *the essential value of radio to all types of listeners.*" In effect, Cantril suggested that his own research was to serve as the organizing framework for all of the studies under consideration. As he described the proposed reorganization,

> This general research project would include, then, all of the research now included in the Committee's 16 projects. As conceived here it would be directed from a central bureau so that there would be no duplication of effort and so each project would have maximum significance for both the educator and the broadcaster.

Cantril also proposed that a committee composed of experts from broadcasting and education be appointed to "arrange for some first-class educational programs to be put on as net-work features at good hours."[61]

At the same time that the review committee of FREC was deliberating on the research proposals submitted by its various subcommittees, Cantril's own proposal was under review by the Trustees of the Rockefeller Foundation. Indeed, it had been placed on the "hotlist," presumably reserved for projects of particular merit. However, it wasn't the substance of the proposal itself which accounted for the Trustees' interest. Rather, what made the proposal attractive was its connection to the activities of FREC, whose membership included "representatives of most of the more important non-profit agencies concerned with broadcasting and of the more important commercial broadcasting organizations." Moreover, "present indications are that the FREC will come to be recognized as a national council on educational broadcasting comparable in importance to the ACLS, the SSRC, the NBC, and the ACE." The informal committee had formulated a total of nine study projects, four of which were to be financed by the broadcasting industry over a two-year period, at a cost of not less than $83,000. In addition, the industry had agreed to pay for an executive secretary to coordinate the various studies. This meant that the other five studies, including that proposed by Cantril, would hopefully be funded by foundations and other sources.[62] By virtue of the formation of the "informal committee" which in turn was to become an executive committee, the FREC, in the eyes of the Rockefeller officials, had become transformed from an ineffectual body to one which could serve as a useful conduit for the exercise of influence.

Cantril's revised proposal (Project I), submitted in May, 1937, outlined a study of "the value of radio to all types of listeners." It argued that "if radio in the United States is to serve the best interests of the people, it is essential that an objective analysis be made of what these interests are and how the unique psychological and social characteristics of radio may be devoted to them." In addition to generating data along these lines, a major aim of the study was to develop methodological techniques appropriate to the issues in question. This would involve consultation with "consumer survey organizations such as Dr. George Gallup's 'American Institute of Public Opinion.'"[63]

In a letter to Marshall of May 11, 1937, Cantril sought to clarify "the exact ways in which Project I will supplement and go beyond the research now being carried out by the radio industry." This letter had been prompted by a telephone conversation of the previous day in which Cantril had sought to respond to Marshall's questions about the relationship between Cantril's project and the work that had previously been carried out by commercial radio researchers. Cantril emphasized that

"Project I will build on the techniques now known as the result of both commercial and non-commercial research, and will, at the same time, go far beyond any program of investigation that the industry itself is likely to undertake in the next several years." Cantril then proceeded to elaborate in some detail how his project would both build on the foundations of earlier research and would move into areas that the radio-industry researchers would be incapable of exploring.

First, Cantril addressed the issue of "what data are available regarding the tastes, habits, and attitudes of the radio audience" as well as "what techniques have already been established to study the value of radio to listeners of various types." He noted that a certain amount of data was available on the habits of the listening audience. What was lacking, however, was knowledge on "the listening habits of various age, vocational, and educational groups," as well as the more fundamental questions of "*why* people listen, and what effect their listening has on their attitudes, conduct, and information." Cantril claimed that his project would not only "fill in the existing gaps," but "do almost pioneer work in discovering and using techniques to understand the complex problem of why people of various types do listen."

Second, Cantril emphasized that the Project I would "utilize the available information regarding research techniques." He was at pains to stress that much of the research in the field of radio had been carried out by market researchers who had kept both their findings and their techniques confidential. However, in his capacity as associate editor of *The Public Opinion Quarterly*, responsible for research activities, Cantril claimed that he had been in "close contact with such workers as Crossley, Gallup, Link, and Starch." Not only was he familiar with the methods used and the research problems that had been faced, but Cantril was confident that these experts would provide him "advice and aid." All the same, as he noted, "the practical and immediate interests of these workers makes it impossible for them to indulge in what seems to be more basic investigation, concerned with problems other than who listens to what."

Third, Cantril stressed that the techniques developed in Project I, would "differ from the research already accomplished by the industry." In particular, private interests dictated the frame of reference used by commercial researchers. This led them to concentrate on estimating "the size and distribution of the listening audience at various times of the day, and to various programs." Findings of this kind were of little interest to the educator or the social scientist, who was concerned not with the lowest common denominator for the mass audience, but wished to know how "a specific educational program should be designed for a selected minority of the population," and "the role which radio plays in the lives of citizens whose education, age, vocation, or financial status places them in a separate category from the majority of their fellow citizens."

Finally, Cantril provided several reasons why the radio industry would neither develop technique further nor promote the further gathering of data. He noted that the broadcaster was primarily interested in the listener only as a purchaser. He pointed out that it was against the interests of the researchers to explore difference in the tastes of the audience. They were unable to examine how tastes of the audience differed from one another, for to do so would then reduce the scope of the broadcaster's audience, meaning that the rates would be reduced as well. Moreover, program preferences could not be examined, because such information would reflect unfavorably on sponsors and programs, thereby discouraging advertisers. Along the same lines, the industry did not wish to examine what the members of the audience were doing while listening, because this would might reflect badly on programmers. Overall, commercial interests were reluctant to undertake more than rudimentary research, because, as Cantril suggested,

> business is so "good" in broadcasting that the industry is not inclined to spend money for research until they are forced to do so, not only because of the embarrassment such data might cause, but because business does not demand it. Ultimately the industry will have to go deeper, in a research sense, in order to maintain its position. This will be in the distant future, perhaps. In the meantime, we might obtain data to guide the educator and direct the appeal of broadcasts.

Cantril concluded his remarks by explaining that he had examined these problems at such length, largely to account for the fact that the industry had chosen not to provide any support for Project I.[64]

That Marshall found Cantril's arguments convincing is indicated in a memorandum he wrote making a case for his proposed research project. He noted at the outset that "it has to be taken for granted that virtually all of the industry's activities are governed by commercial considerations."[65] At the same time, however, he emphasized that broadcasting should be based on service to the public. After reiterating the points raised by Cantril about how the project would do what commercial research was incapable of doing, he stressed the fact that the project was part of a broader program of research within FREC, which had been supported by the radio industry. Not only had the industry's representatives supported the Committee of Six as a coordinating agency, but had agreed to underwrite some of the projects "at an expense of not less than

$80,000 during the next two years," as well as to cover "the salary and office expenses of the executive secretary to the extent of $15,000 annually during that two-year period." Marshall concluded that

> the purpose of the present proposal is to set a new style in radio research.... the broadcasters do not at present feel that they can afford to initiate research of this kind for themselves. If the present project succeeds, as I expect it will in demonstrating the feasibility and significance of studying the actual and potential public service of radio to its total audience it will set a style which the broadcasters cannot afford to disregard.... Support of this project seems to me a strategic move for the Foundation to make at this time.[66]

As the trustees evaluating Cantril's proposal attested, work of this kind was "fundamental for the success of the co-operative efforts of the radio industry and non-commercial agencies that are directed towards broadening radio's range of public service." The three representatives of industry on the committee that reviewed the proposal (from NBC, CBS, and National Association of Broadcasters), agreed that the proposed study was important "for the development of radio's public service." Industry, however, was not able to undertake research of this kind, largely because of pressures from advertisers. Though it was "willing to have such research undertaken by outside agencies," industry was not prepared "to run the risk of taking the initiative." Finally, the trustees found the prospects for influence within the industry very much to their liking.

> The informal committee of six ... will shortly become the Committee's Executive Committee. As findings are to be released only through this Executive Committee, they will automatically carry the approval of three representatives of the industry whose authority cannot be questioned. At the same time, the presence on the Executive of three prominent educators assures due protection for educational and cultural interests.

Apparently persuaded that the linkage of Cantril's study to FREC would ensure that its activities would be closely monitored and its findings influential, the Rockefeller trustees approved a grant of $67,000 over two years to be administered by the School of Public and International Affairs at Princeton University.[67]

Conclusion

This analysis raises numerous issues about how one can best understand the relationship between Rockefeller philanthropy, early communications research, and the nexus formed by political economy and the American state in the 1930s. In particular, it serves to highlight how the trajectories of private philanthropy, communications research, and communications policy were mutually implicated. And it points to the degree to which a wealthy and powerful private philanthropy can shape, influence—and possibly even determine—the policy-formation process. To be sure, the Rockefeller Foundation did not establish broadcasting policy in the United States. The formal guidelines, as set out in the Communications Act of 1934, were to be implemented by the Federal Communications Commission. This agency, with its powers consolidating several former jurisdictions into a single office, gave it the appearance of authority and control. Yet the newly formed Commission was given neither the resources nor the powers to deal with the problems of regulation. The mandate of the Commission, "to act in the public interest" approximated what some have called a "holy-grail" goal; what constituted the public interest, was largely left undefined.

However vaguely the public interest may have been defined, there was an immediate issue of social harmony that demanded action, namely, the chronic hostility between commercial and educational broadcasters. Recognizing that the Communication Commission's proposed "solution" to the crisis—the FREC—was both unwieldy and unworkable, the Humanities Division of the Rockefeller Foundation took decisive action to achieve reconciliation between educators and broadcasters. Quite remarkably, this line of policy was largely pursued *within* the institutional framework put in place by the Communications Act of 1934. In effect, The Rockefeller Foundation, for a time, operated as a *de facto* arm of the American state.

The Foundation's strategy of reconciliation was a complex one, operating on several fronts involving a range of institutional actors. Its overall goal was to find a place for educational programming within the primarily commercial framework that had been consolidated under the 1934 Communications Act. Rejecting the NCER's aims of developing a vigorous and autonomous network of educational broadcasters, it sought instead to transform *particular* educational broadcasters by drawing on the resources of their commercial counterparts. This involved the provision of training grants at commercial broadcasters for promising persons within the educational sector, and the support of particular educational broadcasters who had demonstrated that their programming had audience appeal.

Most of the RF's efforts and resources, however, were directed towards the private broadcasting sector. Above all, it sought to find ways of convincing private broadcasters that educational programming could have an appeal to their audiences. If this were to be achieved, it was necessary to have a better understanding of the tastes and interests of the listening audience itself. Because of their concern to convince advertisers that the programs they sponsored were attracting large audiences, the commercial broadcasters relied on rating surveys that would deliver data which only addressed audience size. In effect, their vested interest in maintaining good relations with advertisers prevented them from gaining a more precise understanding of the make-up and tastes of their audience. It was assumed that once the private broadcasters had a clearer sense of what their audience wanted (assumed to be a greater diversity of noncommercial fare), then they would begin to offer more educational, artistic, and public interest programming. Given that the commercial broadcasters were unwilling to provide the resources for sophisticated surveys and analyses of the tastes of the listening audience, The RF took it upon itself to build up the foundations for studies of this kind. It was assumed that such a program of research would lead to an increase in educational programming in commercial broadcasting. This would mean, in turn, that the tastes and standards of the listening audience would be elevated. While such a goal might now seem quite naive and unrealistic, it was fully consistent with the Humanities Division's notion that radio could be used as a vehicle for enhancing the cultural levels of the mass public.

In order to put this research programme in place—under the auspices of the Princeton Radio Research Project—the RF worked through a public agency, in the form of the FREC established by the Federal Communications Commission. Seemingly through informal persuasion, it saw to it that the diffuse authority of FREC gave way to a smaller steering committee whose members were all in the RF camp. Through the support of this committee, the RF was able to generate funding from a variety of sources for a focused set of research initiatives. After having established the credibility of this committee in this manner, John Marshall was then able to make a compelling case to the RF trustees that any funding that was allocated would be subject to review by a group who had "the public interest" of radio broadcasting in mind. In effect, it was only after having, for all intents and purposes, taken over the workings of a state agency, that the RF was prepared to acknowledge that the institution in question was adequately serving the public interest.

This study suggests the need for a historiography capable of shedding light on the intertwined interests of philanthropy, social science, and political economy. Most analyses, as a matter of course, have dealt with these realms in a compartmentalized manner, with little attention given to how institutional interests are realized through collective action. However, if one uses the contested terrain of knowledge and power as a point of departure, then it becomes possible to bring these three areas into simultaneous focus. In the case of "the radio war" between educators and broadcasters, a resolution of the dispute was contingent upon a redefinition of their relationship. This, in turn, could only be accomplished through more precise knowledge about matters such as the nature of the listening audience and the production of educational programming. Given that each of the two sides in the conflict pursued its ends in a headstrong manner, the prospects for reconciliation were not favourable. Recognizing the intractability of the conflict, the state sought to intervene. Yet it lacked both the will and the means to resolve the differences. It was at this point that the role of social scientists and philanthropists became crucial. Certain social scientists came to the conclusion that research into communications could contribute to the reconciliation between educators and broadcasters. However, they lacked either the resources or the institutional leverage to undertake the studies that they envisioned. Rockefeller officials, recognizing the potential of communications research for helping to mediate the conflict, were prepared to provide the resources and direction to get studies of this kind underway. In effect, Rockefeller philanthropy was able to deploy social-scientific knowledge to redefine the public policy framework, thereby pursuing their private interests more effectively. While these interests were couched in terms of public service, it was assumed that the public could best be served by a capitalist system of ownership and control. The Rockefeller Foundation officials saw themselves as mediating between commercial and educational interests, with a view towards helping develop a system of broadcasting that would better serve the general public. It was recognized that capitalists, because of their narrowly defined self-interest, were unable to deal effectively with either tensions in the relation of production (radio broadcasting) or in the sphere of circulation (consumption of radio broadcasting). Accordingly, Rockefeller philanthropy intervened on several fronts, thereby approximating (to borrow a phrase from German political economy) the "ideal collective capitalist"[68] of the commercial broadcasting system in the United States.

Notes

Quoted material has been published with the permission of the Rockefeller Archive Center. This chapter has been researched and written with the support of a research grant from the Social Sciences and Humanities Research Council of Canada.

1. David Morrison, "The Beginning of Modern Mass Communication Research," *Archives of European Sociology*, XIX, (1978):347.
2. This work included Paul F. Lazarsfeld, *Radio and the Printed Page* (New York: Duell, Sloan, and Pearce, 1940); Paul F. Lazarsfeld, Bernard Berelson, and Helen Gaudet, *The People's Choice* (New York: Duell, Sloan, and Pierce, 1944); Paul F. Lazarsfeld, and Frank Stanton (eds.), *Radio Research, 1941* (New York: Duell, Sloan, and Pearce, 1941); *Radio Research, 1942-43* (New York: Duell, Sloan, and Pierce, 1944); *Communications Research, 1948-49*, (New York: Harper and Brothers, 1949); Paul F. Lazarsfeld and Harry Field, *The People Look at Radio* (Chapel Hill: University of North Carolina, 1949); Paul F. Lazarsfeld, and Patricia Kendall, *Radio Listening in America: The People Look at Radio—Again* (Englewood Cliffs, N.J.: Prentice-Hall, 1948).
3. Lazarsfeld and Stanton, *Communications Research, 1948-49*: xiv, quoted in Willard D. Rowland, *The Politics of TV Violence* (Newbury Park, CA: Sage):70.
4. Lazarsfeld and Kendall, *Radio Listening in America*; Lymon Bryson (ed.), *The Communication of Ideas* (New York: Institute for Religious and Social Studies, 1948); Wilbur Schramm (ed.), *Communications in Modern Society* (Urbana, University of Illinois Press, 1949); *Mass Communications* (Urbana: University of Illinois Press); Joseph Klapper, *The Effects of Mass Media* (New York: Bureau of Applied Social Research, Columbia University, 1950). In the introduction to the influential anthology that he edited in 1949, Wilbur Schramm dedicated the volume "to Paul Lazarsfeld who has done perhaps more than any other man toward bringing the social sciences to bear on the problems of communications", quoted in Emile McAnany, "Wilbur Schramm, 1907-1987: Roots of the Past, Seeds of the Present, *Journal of Communications*, 38, 4, 1988:113.
5. Elihu Katz, "Communication Research and the Image of Society: Convergence of Two Traditions." *American Journal of Sociology* 65, 8, (1960):435-440; Elihu Katz and Paul F. Lazarsfeld, *Personal Influence* (New York: Free Press, 1955).
6. Bernard Berelson, "The State of Communication Research," *Public Opinion Quarterly*, 23, (1959):1-6.
7. Shearon Lowery and Melvin L. DeFleur, *Milestones in Mass Communication Research: Media Effects*, 2nd edn (New York: Longman, 1983): chs. 4 and 7.
8. George Stocking, "On the Limits of 'Presentism' and 'Historicism' in the Historiography of the Behavioral Sciences," *Journal of the History of the Behavioral Sciences*, 1, 1965:211-17.
9. Todd Gitlin, "Media Sociology: The Dominant Paradigm," *Theory and Society*, 6, 1976:205-253.
10. Ibid., 207.
11. C. Wright Mills, *The Sociological Imagination* (New York: Oxford University Press, 1959).
12. Robert Alun Jones, "New History of Sociology," in Ralph H. Turner (ed.), *Annual Review of Sociology*, v.9 (Palo Alto: Annual Reviews Inc., 1983); Charles Camic, "The Utilitarians Revisited," *American Journal of Sociology* 85, (1979):516-50.
13. Morrison, "Beginnings of Modern Mass Communications Research," Jesse Delia, "Communication Research: A History." in Charles R. Berger and Steven H. Chaffee (eds.), *Handbook of Communication Science* (Sage: Beverly Hills, 1987).
14. Morrison, "Beginnings of Mass Communications Research,": 354.
15. Delia, "Communication Research,": 51.
16. Ibid., 52-53.
17. Delia, "Communication Research."
18. William J. Buxton, *Talcott Parsons and the Capitalist Nation-State: Political Sociology as a Strategic Vocation* (Toronto: University of Toronto Press, 1985); William J. and

David Rehorick, "The Sociology of Knowledge: Toward Redemption of a Failed Promise." *International Journal of Politics, Culture, and Society* 2(1), Fall, 1988:66–80; William J. Buxton, "The Marshall Lectures and Social-Scientific Practice. *Sociological Inquiry*, February, 1991.
   19. Rowland, *Politics of TV Violence*: 16.
   20. Christopher H. Sterling and John M. Kittross, *Stay Tuned: A Concise History of American Broadcasting* (Belmont, CA: Wadsworth, 1978): ch. 5.
   21. A better case could be made to consider the golden age of radio in more literal terms, as the profitability and power of radio industry was creating at around the same time as the Princeton Radio Research project had its modest beginnings. The May, 1938 edition of *Fortune* provides a vivid account of how lucrative the business community had found the radio industry. The issue featured no less than four major articles on radio; three of which were given titles capturing the monetary value of the subject in question: "a $140,000,000 art," "a $45,000,000 talent bill; "a $537,000,000 set business." As the editors of *Fortune* glowingly described it, "Radio is a hot subject for more than the simple reason that it is big business. It is a very special kind of big business, combining art, show business, and science—and exists on the sufferance of a government bureau" (*Fortune*, May, 1938).
   22. Carroll Atkinson, *Broadcasting to the Classroom by Universities and Colleges* (Boston: Meador, 1942); S. E. Frost, *Education's Own Stations* (New York: Arno Press and the New York Times [1937] 1971, originally published by the University of Chicago Press).
   23. This was reflected in Bruce Lannes Smith, Harold D. Lasswell, and Ralph D. Casey. *Propaganda, Communication, and Public Opinion: A Comprehensive Reference Guide* (Princeton: Princeton University Press, 1946). One searches in vain for any reference to ownership or control of the media. However, there is plenty of discussion of media effects, media content, and propaganda.
   24. Tracy F. Tyler, (ed.), *Radio as A Cultural Agency: Proceedings of National Conference on The Use of Radio as a Cultural Agency in a Democracy* (Washington: The National Committee on Education by Radio, 1934), James Rorty, *Order in the Air!* (New York: John Day, 1934).
   25. Eric Barnouw, *The Golden Web: A History of Broadcasting in the United States. Volume II- 1933 to 1953* (New York: Oxford University Press): 26–27.
   26. Charles Siepmann, *Radio, Television, and Society* (New York: Oxford, 1950):4–5; Eric Barnouw, *A Tower in Babel: A History of Broadcasting in the United States. Volume I- to 1933* (New York: Oxford University Press: 68–72).
   27. This demand was largely filled by a conglomerate of General Electric (GE), Radio Corporation of America (RCA), American Telephone and Telegraph (AT&T), and Westinghouse. Formed within 8 months of the first broadcast at KDKA, these allied companies had joined forces to control the anticipated broadcasting boom. As Barnouw describes the GE-RCA-AT&T-Westinghouse agreements,

> The making of receivers and parts would be done by GE and Westinghouse; the marketing of these receivers and parts would be done through RCA under RCA trademarks. RCA would assign 60 percent of all manufacturing to GE, 40 percent to Westinghouse. The sale of transmitters would be mainly an AT&T concern (Barnouw, *Tower of Babel*: 81).

   28. Frost, *Education's Own Stations*: 4.
   29. Tyler, *Radio as a Cultural Agency*.
   30. Robert J. Blakely, *To Serve the Public Interest: Educational Broadcasting in the United States* (Syracuse: Syracuse University Press, 1979:57–59); Barnouw, *Golden Web*: 23–27).

31. Quoted in Rowland, *Politics of TV Violence*: 54.

32. "The Humanities Program of the Rockefeller Foundation: A Review of the Period 1934 to 1939." Rockefeller Foundation archives. RG 3. Series 911. Box 2. Folder 11:15. Rockefeller Archive Center, Pocantico Hills, New York (hereafter RAC).

33. For a more detailed account of Marshall and the Humanities Division, see William J. Buxton and Charles R. Acland, "Reaching Men's Minds," (manuscript in progress).

34. John Marshall officer's diary, January 23, 1935 entry. Rockefeller Foundation Archives. 905 MAR. RAC.

35. Founded in 1930, the Council took a moderate position in relation to the dispute about Broadcasting. It had received its funding support from both the Carnegie Corporation and the Rockefeller Foundation, which could explain why Marshall relied on Tyson's judgment.

36. Marshall diary, January 23, 1935.

37. Ibid.

38. John Marshall, officer's diary, February 7, 1935 entry. Rockefeller Foundation archives. 905 MAR. RAC.

39. John Marshall, officer's diary, January 31, 1935 entry. Rockefeller Foundation archives. RAC.

40. John Marshall, officer's diary, February 8, 1935 entry. Rockefeller Foundation archives. 905 MAR. RAC.

41. John Marshall, officer's diary, February 2, 1935 entry. Rockefeller Foundation archives. 905 MAR. RAC.

42. John Marshall, officer's diary, March 19, 1935 entry. Rockefeller Foundation archives. 905 MAR. RAC.

43. Ibid.

44. John Marshall, officer's diary, March 7, 1935 entry. Rockefeller Foundation archives. 905 MAR. RAC.

45. John Marshall, officer's diary, May 6-8, 1935 entry. Rockefeller Foundation archives. 905 MAR. RAC.

46. NACRE, however, was becoming less sanguine about the prospects of commercial and educational radio reconciling their interests. This was evident in a study it released in 1937 in which it "denounced cooperation between educators and commercial broadcasters as unworkable and failed." Robert McChesney, "The Payne Fund and Radio Broadcasting, 1928-1935," (chapter submitted to proposed book on the Payne Fund, Garth Jowett et al. eds.): 34.

47. Marshall diary, May 15-16, 1935.

48. John Marshall, Statement on Radio. June, 1936. Rockefeller Foundation archives. RG 3.1. Series 911. Box 5. Folder 51:1. RAC.

49. Ibid.

50. Ibid., 4. Among those for whom the Foundation provided a training fellowship at NBC was Allen Miller, of the University Broadcasting Commission [UBC] in Chicago. Judith Waller of NBC noted that "Miller and UBC would profit substantially from Miller's having a chance to gain a direct acquaintance with commercial methods." Moreover, "she ... would definitely prefer M[iller]'s studying commercial methods in this country ... he could in this way consolidate his relations with the chains to which he must look for outlets for his programs." John Marshall, officer's diary, December 8, 1936 entry. Rockefeller Foundation archives. 905 MAR. RAC.

51. John Marshall, "Statement on Radio,": 9-10. The First National Conference on Educational Broadcasting, (organized by FREC) held in Washington from December 10-12, 1936, gave Marshall further reason to believe that circumstances were propitious for

a research project on broadcasting. The conference discussions were particularly successful because representatives from the industry were present in unprecedented numbers. Marshall concluded from the conference that only through some kind of collaboration between industry and education in the study of common problems could greater cooperation be realized. In particular, "collaboration in studies of the actual effects of present broadcasting and its opportunities to extend its public service, thus seem to promise a knowledge of present conditions which forecasts better understanding of the real issues on both sides." (John Marshall, officer's diary, December 10–12, 1936, 905 MAR RAC.)

52. John Marshall, officer's diary, October 9, 1936. Rockefeller Foundation archives. 905 MAR. RAC.

53. John Marshall, officer's diary, October 16, 1936 entry. Rockefeller Foundation archives. 905 MAR. RAC. Tyson's views echoed those of Edward R. Murrow, director of talks at CBS, who had met with Marshall on August 11, 1936. As Marshall noted in his diary,

M[urrow] is also much interested in the critical appraisal of the effects of educational broadcasting. In a recent conference with Studebaker he stressed the urgency of work of this kind, as contrasted with other sponsored by the Studebaker Committee of the FCC, and is recommending to CBS that it cooperate in financing only this phase of the Committee's plans... Murrow feels that the Technical Subcommittee under Cantril's chairmanship can be looked to for significant research. (John Marshall, officer's diary, August 11, 1936 entry. Rockefeller Foundation archives, 905 MAR. RAC.)

54. John Marshall, officer's diary, October 19, 1936 entry. Rockefeller Foundation archives. 905 MAR. RAC.

55. John Marshall, officer's diary, December 21, 1936 entry. Rockefeller Foundation archives. 905 MAR. RAC.

56. This was to be a study of the effect of radio-listening upon children, modelled on a similar study of movies and children supported by the Payne Fund.

57. Hadley Cantril to John Marshall, 31 December, 1936. Rockefeller Foundation archives. RG 1.1. Series 200. Box 271. Folder 3233:4–5. RAC.

58. John Marshall to Hadley Cantril, 9 January, 1937. Rockefeller Foundation archives. RG 1.1. Series 200. Box 271. Folder 3234. RAC.

59. J. W. Studebaker, "Report of Progress of Federal Radio Education Committee." Address delivered at Second National Conference on Educational Broadcasting, Chicago. November 30, 1937. General Education Board. GEB Advisory Committee. Series 1, Subseries 2. Box 359. Folder 3706:2. RAC.

60. Rockefeller Foundation Program in Broadcasting, 1937. Rockefeller Foundation archives. RG. 1-1. Series 200. Box 271. Folder 3234:1–2. RAC.

61. Hadley Cantril to John Marshall, 2 February, 1937. Rockefeller Foundation archives. RG 1-1. Series 200. Box 271. Folder 3234. RAC.

62. Rockefeller Foundation, "Hotlist", April 28, 1937. Rockefeller Foundation archives. RG 1-1. Series 200. Box 271. Folder 3234. RAC.

63. Hadley Cantril, "Project I". May, 1937. Rockefeller Foundation archives. RG 1-1. Series 200. Box 271. Folder 3234. RAC.

64. Hadley Cantril, Letter to John Marshall, 11 May, 1937. Rockefeller Foundation archives, RG 1-1. Series 200. Box 271. Folder 3233.

65. John Marshall, "Memorandum on Cantril's Proposal," May, 1937:8–9. Rockefeller Foundation Archives. RG 1-1. Series 200. Box 271. Folder 3234:1. RAC.

66. Ibid., 8–9.

67. Memorandum of May 21, 1937 approving grant to School of Public and International Affairs, Princeton University. Rockefeller Foundation archives. RG 1.1. Series 200. Box 271. Folder 3233. RAC.

68. For a discussion of this concept in relation to discussions of the capitalist state, see Bob Jessop, *The Capitalist State: Marxist Theories and Methods* (Oxford: Martin Robertson, 1982).

7 ALL THE EDITORIALS FIT TO PRINT: THE POLITICS OF "NEWSWORTHINESS"

Edward S. Herman

In his article "Are U.S. Journalists Dangerously Liberal?" Herbert J. Gans claims that mass media news choices rest on a foundation of "professional values" and rules of news judgment that "call for ignoring story implications." Thus, while extremists of the right and left may complain about news bias against themselves, this is largely sour grapes (Gans, 1985).[1] Insofar as there is bias in news selection, Gans contends that this is mainly because of the nature of sourcing and related efficiency considerations (Gans, 1979),[2] with a resultant tendency to exclude nonstandard and dissident suppliers. His policy recommendations are thus oriented mainly to strengthening these suppliers and encouraging media receptivity to their messages (Gans, 1979, pp. 313ff, 328ff.)

An alternative view of news choices was given in Warren Breed's article "Social Control in the Newsroom: A Functional Analysis," where it was contended that newspapers generally have a "policy" on a number of strategic issues, which reporters must learn and apply in order to prosper and even survive in their jobs. This policy is determined, in Breed's view, by the proprietors (Breed, 1955, p. 326), and reflects their values and weighting of factors that affect the newspaper's success. The implication is that the news is skewed by a combination of economic factors and political judgments imposed from above, which override professional values.

In the tradition of the Breed approach, Noam Chomsky and I have put forward a "propaganda model" (Herman and Chomsky, 1988), which spells out a number of market and structural factors that, in our view, powerfully shape the U.S. mass media's treatment of news and opinion. Proprietary interests are among those that define the framework within which journalists operate. But we also include the role of advertisers, sourcing, flak, and anticommunist ideology as constraining forces. These may operate in part by influencing proprietary choices, in part through their effects on the overall intellectual and news environment within which journalists operate.

In this paper, I will argue and present empirical data in support of the view that there is a dominant policy and/or ideological basis for decisions on newsworthiness in a number of areas of news-making in the U.S. mass media, which often overwhelm professional values. In the next section, I will discuss briefly "professional values," "policy," and "ideology," and then describe and illustrate the ways in which policy and ideological bias manifest themselves and can provide the materials for testing. In the subsequent section I will compare and analyse the *New York Times*'s coverage of Cuba and El Salvador for a six week period in early 1990, using several criteria of objectivity, professionalism and the influence of policy and ideology. This is clearly a small sample and will not in itself sustain major generalizations. Nevertheless, this material is suggestive, and takes on more meaning in conjunction with other analyses of the media's treatment of a variety of issues, which I will cite and discuss.

Manifestations of Policy Bias

I interpret "professional values" to encompass two things: First, it implies "objectivity" in the sense of presenting a variety of sides to a story, searching out facts without political constraint, and presenting these fairly and impartially. It is, of course, important to distinguish between *nominal* and *substantive* objectivity. The latter refers to the attempt to meet the objectivity standard in substance, not just form. Nominal objectivity refers to the use of the forms of objectivity alone, sometimes as a cover for de facto bias, as in citing two sides of a story, but giving a preferred side prominence and space for a full argument, allowing the other side only a feeble and empty riposte.[3] Another important mode of nominal objectivity is quoting officials on a point, but failing to provide historical or other context that would allow a reader/listener/watcher to understand the purpose and evaluate the truthfulness of the statement. Adherence to nominal objectivity facilitates news management by the government and other powerful sources. This may be understood and approved by the cooperating journalists and media officials as they work with government officials toward a common end (see the material that follows, especially under "5. The 'Gullibility Quotient'").

A second element of professional values is determining what is newsworthy on the basis of consistently applied news values and not in pursuit of an identifiable policy agenda, biased by ideological premises, or compromised by strategic or profitability considerations. "Policy" means that a line or news gathering procedure is imposed by proprietors and editors that pre-determine news choices, emphases, framing, tone, and investigative zeal in accord with a political agenda or in response to the influences of power or profit. This would include allowing oneself to be used by a source to get over its line, as well as fixing a policy position from within. Policy may extend to few or many topics, leaving professional values intact in the residual areas. It may be tightly or loosely enforced and it can change over time.

Ideological assumptions are implicit value judgments, or premises about fact that are debatable and rest on value judgments. The assumptions that national leaders have benevolent intentions and speak the truth, whereas those of hostile states have ill- or self-serving motives and are not truthful, are ideological. The assumptions that free enterprise and free trade are good and government enterprise and regulation, and constraints on free trade, are bad, are ideological. Herbert Gans lists a number of assumptions, such as "ethnocentrism," "altruistic democracy," and "responsible capitalism," which he also calls "enduring values," that are taken for granted by U.S. journalists (Gans, 1979, pp. 42–55). He gives them the term "paraideology," but he contends that their presence as an underpinning of newswork does not constitute a violation of objectivity. Because they are already built into news judgments "they do not conflict with objectivity—in fact, they make it possible. Being part of news judgment, the enduring values are those of journalism rather than of journalists; consequently, journalists can feel detached and need not bring in their personal values" (Gans, 1979, pp. 196–197). But if premises that reflect the dominant ideology are already incorporated into news judgments, objectivity is compromised in advance and Gans' journalists don't have to introduce "personal values" because this is already done for them. He salvages journalistic objectivity by the semantic shift of the ideological bias and nonobjectivity to "journalism" and away from journalists.[4] But the penetration of ideology, including "paraideology," into the newsmaking process at any stage is incompatible with meaningful conceptions of objectivity and professional values.

It is well established that important media proprietors have had definite, strong political views which they imposed on their media outlets,[5] and there is episodic evidence that a great many less strongly ideological proprietors have had a distinct and well understood ongoing influence on media policy choices.[6] Close connections and reciprocal service between media top owners and executives, on the one hand, and U.S. presidents and State Department, CIA and Pentagon officials, on the other hand, are also easily documented.[7] For some reason these cases, though numerous and applicable to many important media institutions, are given little weight and are rarely mentioned in discussions of the sources and direction of media bias.[8]

Although there is extensive evidence of proprietary influence, it is often difficult to prove on an ongoing basis. Policy is likely to be transmitted to the lower echelons in subtle ways, including the hiring of top level editors known to fit the owner's "general outlook" and sensitive to proprietary demands; politically based reporter selection, promotion and encouraged exit;[9] and editorial judgments on story selection, emphases and tone that instruct underlings on what is expected of them.[10]

Equally important, it is difficult to distinguish between proprietor-editor policy and mere profit-seeking. It should be recognized, however, that a decision to focus strictly on profitability, which calls for sticking closely to establishment sources and avoid disturbing advertisers and other powerful constituencies, is a major and conservative "policy" decision in its own right. We may distinguish between an explicit and intended policy line, and a policy by default, where a proprietor trying to maximize profits follows the line dictated by dominant sources, which will be cheap ("efficient") and will not offend the powerful. Those who fit the latter category, unwilling to absorb the costs necessary to provide more accurate and balanced news, have a policy by default that conflicts with "professional values."

Dominant ideologies tend to reflect the interests of the powerful. Thus, policies imposed by proprietors often incorporate such ideologies as suitable premises and frames of reference. Reporters who treat these uncritically are hired and rewarded; those that do not are either not hired, adapt, or fall by the wayside.

Whatever the evidence of "smoking guns" showing high level intervention, and despite the problem of separating out intended policy bias from mere profitmaking, it is still possible to test the relative strength of policy and ideology, on the one hand, and professional values, on the other, by examining their effects on news outputs. Whether the bias is planned or derivative, and based on too ready dependence on official sources and uncritical acceptance of ideological assumptions, there are limits to such bias if professional values are operative.

Let me enumerate and illustrate briefly a number of ways in which policy and ideological bias may be manifested and where the limited role of professional values is correspondingly displayed.

1. Differential Tone and Language

It is elemental that professional values will not permit a dichotomous use of language, in which "snarl" words are regularly applied to disfavored people, groups, and countries, whereas "purr" or neutral language is applied to those looked upon with favor. For example, when the United States was withdrawing from UNESCO in 1983–1984, editorial opinion in the U.S. mass media was uniformly hostile to UNESCO and its head Amadou M'Bow. This was reflected in a spectacular dichotomization of language, with M'Bow "autocratic," "ripping off" the Third World, "wily," "evasive"; UNESCO "wasteful," "totally deformed," "scandalous," "abominably managed," "corrupt," etc. On the other hand, the U.S. officials engineering the withdrawal and their allies were treated with wholly neutral language, and the United States was portrayed as a benevolent parent "goaded beyond endurance."[11]

In another enlightening case, when the Soviet Union shot down Korean airliner KAL 007 in 1983, the U.S. media used freely words like "atrocity," "deliberate," "wanton," "barbarian," "criminal," and "murder," whereas when the Israelis shot down a Libyan civilian airliner with 110 civilian casualties in 1973, the dominant phrase was "tragic error," and the word "criminal" was used only in citations from the Arab press (Herman, 1986, p. 192). That "policy" underlay this word usage was suggested explicitly in a *New York Times* editorial of March 1, 1973, discussing the tragic error: "No useful purpose is served by an acrimonious debate over the assignment of blame for the downing of a Libyan airliner in the Sinai peninsula last week." That is, the "useful purpose" of news was acknowledged to influence the paper's coverage; it was not "ignoring story implications" (Gans).

2. Double Standard in Intensity of Coverage

Just as the *New York Times* found it not "useful" to focus heavily on the Israeli shootdown, so by contrast it cooperated enthusiastically with the

Reagan administration in giving intensive coverage to the Soviet downing of KAL 007; the ratio of column inch space in the two cases was 5.7/1 (Herman, 1986, p. 189). This was a politically congenial story, and while newsworthy by standard rules, the frenetic play it eventually received had little or nothing to do with efficiency or professional news values.

The same point may be made for innumerable other cases of dichotomization between what this writer refers to as "worthy" and "unworthy" victims, the division based on political preference and serviceability in politically motivated propaganda campaigns. For example, of 22 cases in which human rights victims were given intensive coverage in the *New York Times* between 1976 and 1981, 21 involved victims in the Soviet sphere of influence; only one was a victim of a western state (Herman, 1982, p. 197).[12] As there was a plentiful supply of human rights abuses in the West during this period,[13] this selectivity was clearly a product of ideological preference and policy, not the application of professional news values.

3. Double Standard in the Application of Relevant Principles

An even more dramatic illustration of the application of a double standard was afforded by the media's coverage of elections in El Salvador, Guatemala, and Nicaragua in 1984, where the media used a varying set of criteria of evaluation in elections held in the same year, in accordance with a political agenda. The U.S. government sponsored or supported elections in the first two countries in order to help legitimize their governments (Herman and Brodhead, 1984). It opposed the 1984 election in Nicaragua, because the government there was not to its liking and it was busily engaged in trying to remove it. The U.S. government and its official observers did not call attention to the fact that in El Salvador and Guatemala the press had been attacked and journalists murdered,[14] that the left was off the ballot, and that state terror had created a climate of fear—they focused on long lines of voters, turnout, the personalities of candidates, army support of the election, and guerrilla threats. In the case of Nicaragua, however, the U.S. official position was that Nicaraguan government constraints on the newspaper *La Prensa*, the refusal of Arturo Cruz to run, which allegedly caused the "main opposition" to be off the ballot, and Sandinista control of the army, made the Nicaraguan election a farce (Herman and Chomsky, 1988, chap. 3).

U.S. mass media coverage followed this government agenda in detail, focusing heavily on *La Prensa*'s difficulties in Nicaragua, but wholly ignoring the condition of the press in El Salvador and Guatemala, attending closely to Arturo Cruz as the "main opposition" in Nicaragua, but barely mentioning and not considering relevant the exclusion of the left in El Salvador and Guatemala, and finding the murderous armies of El Salvador and Guatemala to be "protecting" the election, the Sandinista army a threat to election integrity. The conclusion of the U.S. media, paralleling their government's official position, was that El Salvador and Guatemala had elected governments, whereas Nicaragua's government had put on a charade.

Qualified independent observers at the Nicaraguan election found it a valid election, and those who had witnessed both the Salvadoran and Nicaraguan elections found the latter superior.[15] It may be argued that this result merely shows the extent to which the media depend on the government for framing and sourcing; but where the mass media allow the government frame to be reversed in elections held in the same year, the media has failed to meet elemental standard of neutrality and intellectual integrity. Many of the independent observers who gave an alternative view were highly credible. The failure to tap them was incompatible with professional values.[16] Media policy was adjusted to government policy in a remarkable, even Orwellian, display of doublethinking bias.

4. Double Standard: Politically Biased Selection of Facts

Selectivity based on framing merges indistinguishably into that based on prior belief and simple fit to policy. For example, once the U.S. news establishment had adopted the idea that the Bulgarians and KGB were behind the shooting of the Pope in May 1981, events and facts that would cast doubts on this idea were often found unnewsworthy.[17] The evidence for a tie-in of the shooting to Bulgaria and the KGB was based entirely on the confessions of the Turkish rightist, Mehmet Ali Agca, made in an Italian prison many months after his incarceration. He confessed after lengthy interviews with members of the Italian secret service agency SISMI and the Investigating Magistrate, Ilario Martella.

There were numerous reports in the Italian press in 1982–1984 that Agca had been coerced, threatened, and bribed to implicate the Eastern Bloc. None of these reports made it into the *New York Times* or network TV. The Italian Parliamentary Report on the extreme rightwing P-2 conspiracy, issued in July 1984, was also never even mentioned in these same news outlets, although the report described the penetration of this conspiracy into the secret service agency SISMI and the judiciary. In July 1985, a court in Milan found that high officials of SISMI had been guilty of forgery and other crimes, including a coverup of the people responsible for the Bologna terrorist bombing. Michael Ledeen, a U.S. rightist who served as a regular commentator on the Bulgarian Connection in the U.S. press and on the McNeil Lehrer News Hour was mentioned in this report as affiliated with SISMI. This important story was given very muted coverage in the *New York Times* and was rarely mentioned elsewhere in the U.S. mainstream media. Ledeen's role was entirely ignored.

The mainstream press, liking and having accepted the Bulgarian-KGB connection as true, and certain members having contributed substantially to the origination of the plot,[18] simply ignored evidence that the Agca confession was contaminated. Claims and reports of bribery and pressure on Agca would suggest this. So would evidence indicating that the Italian secret services and judiciary were corrupt, forged documents, and protected rightwing terrorists. The papers were full of tiny details on the Investigating Magistrate's visits to sites where Agca claimed to have visited Bulgarians and they assiduously searched out the opinion of notables like Zbigniew Brzezinski and Italian prosecutors on whether the Bulgarians and Soviets would do this sort of thing (Herman and Brodhead, 1986, pp. 174–181), but documents and opinions pointing to possible coaching and manipulation of Agca in prison were ignored.

5. The "Gullibility Quotient" and the Transmission of Lies

A closely related test of policy and ideology versus professional values may be termed the "gullibility quotient." The hypothesis is that where official handouts or media-generated themes like the Bulgarian Connection are congenial to ideological biases and media policy, the media news managers will often be extremely gullible, and will accept dubious stories without feeling any obligation to verify them. Professional values, if operative, would call for caution and insistence on evidence. The mass media's handling of the 1981 shooting of the Pope falls into this high gullibility quotient class. In the case of the Libyan "hit squad" allegedly sent to the United States to kill President Reagan in 1981, the U.S. mainstream press jumped on this bandwagon with enthusiasm, despite the convenience of the claim to ongoing government strategies, its implausibility, and the absence of evidence (Perdue, 1989, pp. 50–57). The alleged shipment of MIG airplanes to the Nicaraguan government in early November 1984, an Office of Public Diplomacy strategem designed to push the Nicaraguan election out of the headlines, was taken at face value (Herman and Chomsky, 1988, pp. 137–139).

Another important illustration is the U.S. mass media's receptivity to the official claim that in client states, where the government is killing large numbers of civilians, the killing is being done by extremists of the right and left who the moderates in the government are allegedly unable to control. This view of the Argentine military regime's holocaust of 1976–1983 was faithfully transmitted to readers of the *New York Times* by its reporter, Juan deOnis: "The military junta headed by Lieutenant General Jorge Raphael Videla, Commander in Chief of the army, has been unable to control the rightwing extremists, who are clearly linked to the military and police" (De Onis, 1976).

The official view of El Salvador in the 1980s was that the moderate government was having difficulty containing the extremists. John Bushnell of the State Department told congress in 1980 that "there is some misperception by those that follow the press that the government is itself repressive in El Salvador" when in fact the violence is "from the extreme right and extreme left" and "the smallest part" of the killings come from the army and security forces" (Bonner, 1984, p. 172). On September 27, 1981, Alan Riding wrote in the *New York Times* that "under the Carter administration, United States officials said security forces were responsible for 90 percent of the atrocities," not "uncontrollable rightwing bands" (Riding, 1981). Nevertheless, despite this isolated admission, widely confirmed by independent sources, *Times* editorials and virtually all of its news articles from 1980 to the present have maintained the distinction between the government, on the one hand, and the people on the extreme right and left who kill. In 1987, e.g., *Times* reporter Lindsey Gruson wrote that "Today, death squads of the right and left no longer terrorize the population into submission and silence" (Gruson, 1987). In 1990, the paper still has the president of El Salvador "bravely" pressing criminal charges against the killers of the six Jesuits. "By so doing, he defied the zealots in his own rightist camp" ("Light in El Salvador," 1990). The alternative and extremely plausible frame, that Cristiani or any other leader would have to engage in at least a *nominal* effort to investigate charges against the army, when not doing so would seriously jeopardize the flow of U.S. funds, is not suggested by the *Times*. When it was finally disclosed that Cristiani had personally approved army surveillance of the Jesuit victims three days before their murder, the *Times* gave this very muted coverage. It treated in very low key, also, the evidence that the investigation and case were falling apart. In other words, there was still a moderate in command, deserving support as he fought extremists of the right and left.

When the priest Jerzy Popieluszko was murdered by the Polish police in 1984, the *Times* never suggested that this was a killing by police extremists whom the government must bring to justice—this was the Polish *government* in action. The consistent distancing of agents of the government who murder from the government itself in Argentina, Guatemala, and El Salvador is an expression of ideology and policy that flies in the face of professional values.

6. Lack of Investigatory Zeal

Professional values would call for a determined search for confirmation or disproof where propaganda agencies make convenient but implausible claims. The failure to ask questions and seek evidence is the corollary of a high gullibility quotient. This failure is applicable to all the cases mentioned earlier. For example, in the instance of the disclosure that the administration had lied in the case of KAL 007 when claiming that the Soviets knew they were shooting down a civilian plane, the *Times* acknowledged editorially that it had been taken in ("The Lie That Wasn't Shot Down," editorial, Jan. 18, 1988), but the editorial neglected pointing out the paper's own failure to question and investigate from the beginning. Furthermore, the information that contradicted the lie was provided by Congressman Lee Hamilton using Freedom of Information Act procedures available to the *Times* and other mass media organizations, but unused by them.

7. Unwillingness to Correct Error

Another possible check on the force of policy/ideology versus professional values is the willingness of the media to correct error. In principle, if a paper or broadcast station transmits a lie, it should be anxious to clear the matter up and straighten out the record. The cost of admitting gullibility should be more or less offset by a desire to get back at the victimizer. True integrity would demand featuring the correction at least as prominently as the original lie, and explaining who was responsible for the deception.

On the other hand, if the errors reflect a politically based gullibility and bias, the points scored against enemies (the Soviet Union and Libya), and the protection afforded allies (pre-1983 Argentina, El Salvador), are desirable and correcting error would cancel out some or all of the benefits of policy. While professional values would call for assiduity in correction, ideological and policy bias would militate against it.

The U.S. mass media almost never give corrections equal prominence with original fabrications, and often don't admit error at all.[19] When the *New York Times* did admit it had transmitted a lie claiming Soviet knowledge of the fact that KAL 007 was a civilian plane, the editors blamed it on the government, and gave the news correction only back page treatment ("Reagan Said to Ignore Data on Downing of Jet," 1988). The *Times* has never acknowledged error in reference to the Libyan hit squad story of 1981. Although the hit squad never surfaced, the mainstream U.S. press simply dropped the story. It was revealed in the British *New Statesman* of August 16, 1985 that the source for the claim of a hit squad (about which the president of the United States had said "we have the evidence and [Qadaffi] knows it"), was Manucher Ghorbanifar, an individual linked to Israeli intelligence, whose hit squad list was of a Lebanese group strongly hostile to Qadaffi (Campbell and Forbes, 1985).

In the case of the U.S. withdrawal from UNESCO in the years 1983–1984, and up to the present, the *New York Times* has repeatedly asserted that "UNESCO" favored a New World Information and Communication Order that would license journalists and allow governments to control the media (Preston et al, 1989, pp. 246–247, 267–273). UNESCO officials kept writing to the *Times* (and other papers as well), pointing out that UNESCO had never even voted on, let alone passed proposals approving, the licensing of journalists or a NWICO; that UNESCO officials had varying opinions on the subject; and that it was entirely improper to say that "UNESCO" favored these things. In one reply to such a UNESCO complaint, the Foreign Editor of the *Times* acknowledged that this mode of expression was not "fully fair," but the *Times* did not publish the letter and, most important, continued to make the same error in 1989 and 1990 (Preston et al, 1989, pp. 273–277; on the 1989–1990 continuation, Herman, June 1990, pp. 17–18). This reflected a clear *Times* policy of hostility to UNESCO that led to manifestations of bias at many levels.

A Comparison of the New York Times Coverage of Cuba and El Salvador in Early 1990

I turn now to an examination of recent *New York Times* coverage of Cuba and El Salvador as a case study and test of the explanatory value of professional values versus policy and ideology. The government position as regards the two countries in early 1990 was clear. Cuba was viewed as an enemy state and was subject to an official boycott, regular disparagement, and other manifestations of hostility. The Salvadoran government was a U.S. ally and was given military and economic aid and diplomatic support. The U.S. government had maintained a multi-year campaign to get Cuba condemned in the United Nations for human rights abuses, whereas it consistently sought to downplay and excuse those of its Salvadoran client.

The editorial position of the *New York Times* was close to that of the government, although it occasionally took the government to task for tactical mistakes. Hostility to the Castro regime has been unremitting and intense: Castro is a "tropical dictator-for-life," a "crabbed caudillo," heading a country "rooted in stagnation," loaded with political prisoners, an "armed camp, despite the security from attack promised by Washington in 1962" ("Thirty Years of Fidel Castro," 1989).[20] El Salvador, despite the many regrettable killings by the extreme left and right, is always headed by well-meaning moderates trying to control the extremists; these moderates need support and nudges. There is always "light," "surprises," "brave stands," and "brave experiments" under way.[21] Unlike the moderates in power—the "weak centrist government . . . beset by implacable extremes" in 1980 (ed., April 28, 1980), Duarte, and Cristiani—the rebels are Marxists-Leninists, i.e., very bad people who cannot be allowed to take power.

From the standpoint of a propaganda model or one that stresses the importance of policy, the government's position and *Times* editorial stance would be expected to yield news and comment consistently hostile to Cuba and supportive of the Salvadoran government. This should be reflected in all the forms of bias and dichotomization discussed in the previous section. The dominance of professional values would, of course, preclude such a result.

The expected dichotomization by the U.S. mass media had been displayed in dramatic fashion in 1986, when the prison memoirs of Armando Valladares were published, unleashing a torrent of press coverage, reviews, editorials, and interviews, all flattering to Valladares, uncritical of him and his work, and extremely hostile to Cuba. Among the phrases employed were "bestial prisons," "unhuman torture," "institutionalized torture," "the hell that was the Cuba [Valladares] lived in" (*New York Times*), "tyrant" and "dictatorial goon" (Castro), etc. (phrases cited in Chomsky, 1989, p. 138). At virtually the same time as the Valladares claims were making their mark in 1986, members of the Salvadoran human rights commission, including the late Herbert Anaya, were imprisoned and tortured in El Salvador. While in prison, Anaya and his associates compiled a 160-page report based on the testimony of 430 tortured political prisoners. This document, along with a videotape of prisoner testimony, was smuggled out of the Salvadoran prison at the height of the furor over Valladares and the Cuban prison system, and was offered to the U.S. media. The material was of no interest, however, and was comprehensively ignored (Chomsky, 1989, p. 138).

There is other evidence that a pattern of policy-based tone and selectivity characterized coverage of Cuba and El Salvador in earlier years (Platt, 1987; Herman and Chomsky, 1988, chaps. 2–3). I want to focus now, however, on a sample of all *Times* news articles and opinion pieces on Cuba and El Salvador in the six week period from March 1 through April 15, 1990. The period chosen was selected arbitrarily—the most recent six weeks at the time the research was undertaken. I will examine this material for comparative tone and language, intensity of coverage, and selectivity.

Tone and language

During the period March 1–April 15, 1990, the *New York Times* had 27 news articles, one Op Ed column, two book reviews and one editorial on Cuba. In the same period it had eight news articles, one Op Ed column and one editorial on El Salvador. The tone of many of the items on Cuba was negative, resulting in part from the choice of topics (discussed below under Selectivity), but also from the use of invidious words in headings and text. The difference in treatment of Cuba and El Salvador was so marked that a comparison of the use of invidious language in the titles of articles alone will suffice to demonstrate the point. In the ten items on El Salvador no invidious word appears in any title, and the editorial invokes the warming language "Light in El Salvador" (April 10, 1990).

In the 31 entries under Cuba, by contrast, a substantial number included gratuitously slanted language observable in their headings (emphases below are added):

"Havana Journal: When Castro Talks, the Generation Gap *Yawns*," (Howard French, April 13, 4A)

"Castro *Unbending* on Cuba's Future," (French, April 5, 5A)

"Is Castro Planning *Another Mock Trial*?," (Herberto Padilla and Belkis Cuza Male, Op. Ed., March 27, A27)

"Castro *Piqued*, Says Quayle is 'a Dandy'," (Reuters, March 24, A14)

"*Setback* for the Cubans Benefits the Dominicans," (Special to NYT, March 19, D11)

"Soviet Press *Snaps Back* at Castro, Painting an *Outdated Police State*" (Bill Keller, March 8, A1)

"Rights Panel *Scolds* Cuba, Not China" (Paul Lewis, March 7, A3)

"A Writer in Castro's *Stifling* Shadow" (Herbert Mitgang, March 3, A14)

As El Salvador certainly presented at least as many opportunities for critical reporting and strong language in 1990 as Cuba, it would be hard to explain the differential word use in terms other than policy and ideological bias.

Intensity of Coverage

The coverage of Cuba was intense for the six weeks under review, with better than an article every other day. It was sufficient, I believe, to create an atmosphere of excitement and expectation and—given its hostile and negative content—to provide support for the more aggressive strategies against Cuba underway in Washington. Several weeks earlier, the *Times* had run a front page article by David Pitt, "Dreaming of an End of Castro, Cubans in Miami Are Abuzz" (Feb. 20), based on no specific news event, but reflecting and contributing to atmospherics. Developments in Eastern Europe, Nicaragua, and the Soviet Union had left Cuba more isolated, and the U.S. administration was escalating its propaganda and policy actions against Cuba, including the commencement of operations of TV Marti. Four of the 27 news articles and the single *Times* editorial on Cuba in this period related to the TV Marti controversy. Many of the others, like the February 20 piece, were pegged solely to the environment of administration and media hostility to Cuba, and served to reinforce negative public attitudes toward a target of state policy, thereby giving the state greater freedom of action. This news performance was a function of policy and ideology, not professional news values.

The point is reinforced by the contrast with the relatively slight coverage of El Salvador. Many potentially newsworthy events took place in El Salvador in March and April, but most of them—like the human rights document leaked from the Salvadoran prison in 1986—were about matters the U.S. administration did not want publicized. It *had* wanted a stepped-up focus on El Salvador at the time of the elections of 1982, 1984, and 1989, in order to legitimate the ruling power. Subsequently, with government murders and other ongoing abuses tending to delegitimize, the administration wanted the media to avert their eyes from El Salvador.

The *New York Times* followed the state agenda closely in both the election periods and the interludes.[22] As one illustration of the paper's earlier drastic underreporting in relation to abuse levels, for the first six months of 1988, the El Rescate Human Rights Department Chronology of Events in El Salvador[23] listed 1,679 violations of human rights, including 256 murders and disappearances [El Rescate, 1988]. During that period the *Times* had a grand total of eight articles on abuses in El Salvador, of which six were about "rebel" violence (Herman, 1989, pp. 24–26).

In the period March 1 through April 15, 1990, the *New York Times* did not run a single article on the course of the Jesuit murder inquiry or on any other murder, disappearance, or investigation or trial for human rights violations and crimes. The El Rescate Chronology gives the names of victims of fresh political murders and disappearances on 13 separate days during this time, and the Jesuits' murder case was in the news in El Salvador on at least eight different days. The wire services also carried a steady stream of reports on human rights violations and trials. These were simply ignored by the *Times*.

Selectivity

In covering Cuba in our six week period of review, the *Times* did not find a single topic that put Cuba in a good light. Several were neutral, but most referred to accusations of abuses and difficulties encountered by Cuba's leaders. Both Reuters and Interpress carried a report in early April that on March 30 Cuba had begun receiving hundreds of Soviet children suffering effects of the Chernobyl disaster for specialized treatment in Cuban hospitals. This was not newsworthy for the *Times*, in contrast with the report that a foreign maker of expensive cigars had stopped buying Cuban tobacco (the subject of articles on March 16 and 19). An A.P. report of March 27, "Cuban Tobacco Chief Challenges Cigar Company to Taste Test," was not newsworthy, nor were a number of other A.P. reports which allowed Cuban officials to get over a point or had connotations incompatible with U.S. and *Times* policy. Among these were:

> George Gedda, "Cuban Leader Confident, Despite Setbacks, U.S. Hostility," April 4, 1990.

Virginia Byrne, "Suspect in Social-Club Arson Was an Army Deserter From Cuba," March 27, 1990.

Robert Weller, "U.S. Supplies to Angolan Rebels Stepped Up," March 25, 1990.[24]

Catherine Wilsin, "Six Florida Stations Pick Up Castro Speech," March 25, 1990.

Ruth Sinai, "Angolan President Wants Cease-Fire, Talks With Rebels," March 20, 1990.

George Gedda, "Castro Still Has Strong Following But Questions Linger," March 17, 1990.

George Gedda, "Diplomat Debunks Notion That Cuba Will Fall," March 1, 1990.

Even in areas where the *Times* did report news on Cuba, politicized selectivity is apparent. Brazil's main news magazine *Veja* reported that Fidel Castro "won the title of the international star" at the inauguration of Brazilian president Fernando Collor de Mello; he was interviewed by the major Brazilian media and was guest of honor of the governor of Sao Paulo on a visit following the ceremonies. The U.S. journal *Cuban Update* reports that "everywhere he went he was mobbed by the press. Besides holding press conferences with hundreds of journalists, he was interviewed on four national television stations by Brazil's best known journalists." He also met with every major Latin political leader. *Cuban Update* also reports on Castro's message, which urged Latin unity and integration as the only means of escaping U.S. control and recolonization ("President Castro in Brazil," 1990, p. 12.)

None of the three *Times* news reports on Castro's visit give any sense of the excitement and welcome he received and the extent of his interaction with political leaders and media, nor did they present or discuss his ideas. The only one of the three articles with any vitality characteristically featured a story that put Castro in a bad light, namely, Brazil's insisting on the return of arms and personnel sent from Cuba as security insurance (James Brooke, "Brazil Returns 10 Tons of Arms Sent by Cuba for Castro's Security," March 8, p. 8).

The *Times* ran a front page article on Soviet press attacks on Cuba (March 8), but Soviet statements and actions in support of Cuba were not newsworthy. For example, in a press conference in Washington on April 6, Soviet Foreign Minister Eduard Shevardnadze spoke warmly of Cuba, saying that "I do not perceive any problems that may cause concern, as I know the situation in this country is normal, stable, they have their own plans, they have their own view of the world, and we wish them well. We wish them success in the realization of those plans" (Fed. Inf. Systems Corp., 1990). A Cuban-Soviet trade accord worth $14.7 billion for 1990, representing an 8.7 percent increase over 1989, which was reported by Reuters on April 17, never made it into the *Times*. As regards the new TV Marti, a stream of foreign denunciations of this U.S. enterprise as illegal and provocative, offered by Interpress Service in early April, from Mexico, Ecuador, by the Rio Group of eight Latin American countries, and by the U.N. International Telecommunications Union, were ignored by the *Times*.

The *Times* news coverage of El Salvador in the period March 1–April 15 included five articles on the proposed negotiations between the FMLN and Cristiani government (including Bush administration reactions to them), one article on the proposed amnesty for the military, and two articles on rebel threats to renew the fighting. As noted, there was a large universe of facts about ongoing state terror in El Salvador which the *Times* simply ignored. In addition to the murders and disappearances, there were numerous seizures of civilians, ransacking and looting of offices of unions and human rights organizations,[25] and trials of army and civil defense forces for murder, all unnewsworthy. A West German church delegation press conference denouncing state terror in El Salvador, a petition signed by 263 members of the Italian Parliament calling for an end to aid to that country, and two separate U.S. congressional press statements calling for an end to military aid were unreported in this period. The congressional statements were both available in A.P. wire dispatches on March 22 and 23. A.P. also had reports by Carl Hartman, "Court is Asked to Curb U.S. Trade With Labor Rights Violators" (March 29) and Douglas Mine, "Rights Group: Violations at Worst Levels Since Early 1980s" (March 23), focusing on human rights abuses in El Salvador, and unnewsworthy.

On April 4, 1990, charges against Jorge Alberto Miranda in El Salvador for allegedly killing human rights activist Herbert Anaya were dropped. On the following day the Salvadoran human rights commission, of which Anaya had been head, called for an investigation into who the actual killers were. The *Times*'s failure to report this incident is enlightening. When Miranda, a student, confessed to doing the killing on behalf of the FMLN in January 1988, after a long and illegal stint with the Treasury Police, the *Times* took this seriously and gave it substantial coverage— more attention, in fact, than all the state killings in the first half of 1988. As I have shown elsewhere, this was a case of what appeared to be knowing gullibility (Herman, 1989, pp. 65–69), closely geared to the

Times (and U.S. administration) policy of focusing on alleged rebel violence and playing down state terror. When Miranda was released briefly in February 1988, he quickly recanted and stated that he had confessed under torture.[26] The *Times* reported this in very muted fashion (in a six paragraph A.P. dispatch, "A Salvadoran Recants Confession in Slaying," 1988), without any reflection on its own gullibility. Shortly thereafter, Miranda was arrested again and has been in prison ever since. The rearrest and then the court decision that his trial was "full of errors" and that his confession "could have been coerced" were never mentioned in the *Times*.

Although the *Times* prime focus in its news columns of March 1 through April 15 was on the new negotiating efforts and plans, its selectivity in this area is also revealing. For example, on April 1, Salvadoran Archbishop Arturo Rivera Damas called on the *government* to make a serious move in the negotiations process.[27] Bishop Rosa Chavez asserted in a statement reported on Salvadoran TV that conditions in the country were still not such as to permit the rebels to participate in political life. These statements were unreported in the *Times*. The FMLN, in a new analysis and proposal in early March, asserted that one of the crucial problems in El Salvador was that the army controlled the country. President Alfredo Cristiani replied on Salvadoran TV that this was not so, but in discussing the Jesuits murder case, he explained on TV (and to the *Washington Post*) that he felt "frustrated" by the fact that the leader of the group who killed the Jesuits, Colonel Benavides was living in a luxury apartment and visiting the armed forces beach resort, and "probably" would not be prosecuted, "but the armed forces have their rules." Cristiani also got himself embroiled in controversy by a public statement that the death squads were a response to rebel and left violence. He was assailed in El Salvador for an implicit defense of the death squads. None of this found its way into the newspaper of record.

Conclusions

Back in 1920, in a famous analysis of the *New York Times* coverage of the Russian Revolution, Walter Lippmann and Charles Merz concluded that the paper's editorial policy "profoundly and crassly influenced their news columns (Lippmann and Merz, 1920, p. 42). Despite the greater polish developed over the intervening 70 years, as in 1920 policy and ideology still inject observably profound bias into the news coverage and commentary on important topics like El Salvador and Cuba. In language and tone, intensity of coverage, and the pattern of selectivity on newsworthiness, a political agenda clearly overwhelms professional values. Moreover, that the paper continues to reiterate the view which it has applied to each successive leader of El Salvador in the 1980s—that he is a moderate, and that the primary violence of El Salvador is attributable, not to the leadership and government but to a separate category of extremists of the right and left—shows that "policy" is based on a patriotic lie of Orwellian dimensions.

Notes

1. "The beliefs that make it into the news are *professional* values that are intrinsic to national journalism and that journalists learn on the job. . . . People with a strong interest in ideological matters have often been dissatisfied with the news media, but their dissatisfaction is also the product of certain rules of news judgment. . . . The rules of news judgment call for ignoring story implications [except for libel and national security matters]." Gans, 1985, pp. 32–33.

2. This point is developed in his book *Deciding What's News*, New York: Vintage Books, 1979, where he says that "The considerations [of journalists in choosing among sources] are interrelated because they have one overriding aim: efficiency." p. 128. See also pp. 281–2. In this complex and detailed work, Gans also brings in other factors, including the *power* of dominant sources, but the main thrust of his argument is the dominance of the efficiency factor.

3. This distinction is implicit in Gaye Tuchman's discussion of the rules of objectivity [Tuchman, 1972, pp. 660–79], which stresses that while the media's rules of objectivity could provide the basis for a serious approximation to true objectivity, their primary role is ritualistic and formal, to protect the media from complaints of unfairness and libel suits.

4. Gans also contends that paraideology is less biasing than other ideologies: "in the final analysis it encourages them [reporters] to be somewhat more open-minded than would an integrated ideology." [Gans, 1979, pp. 277–78]. This claim is unconvincing. A journalist who doesn't even recognize his bias is hardly likely to be more objective than one who does. The former need not make any concessions for balance as the truth is entirely clear.

5. Famous cases are those of Henry Luce and his *Time-Life-Fortune* empire, the Hearst press, Colonel Robert McCormick and the *Chicago Tribune*, the Wallace family's *Reader's Digest*, William Knowland's *Oakland Tribune*, Rupert Murdoch's papers, the Moon-sponsored *Washington Times*, Walter Annenberg's *Philadelphia Inquirer*, and the Copley papers. There are many others.

6. Turner Catledge, the top *New York Times* editor for 17 years, noted that the paper's chief owner, Arthur Hays Sulzberger, was in the habit of "making his likes and dislikes known," and that "he sought executives who shared his general outlook, and he tried, by word and deed, to set a tone for the paper." Catledge, 1971, p. 189. It is clear that during the later era, when A. M. Rosenthal was Managing Editor of the *Times* and imposed a distinct structure of policies on the paper, that this was in accord with the political preferences of the publisher Arthur Ochs Sulzberger. See Hess, 1985, p. 125; also, Goulden, 1988. Similar conclusions can be drawn from histories of the *Washington Post*, CBS, and the *Los*

Angeles Times. For the *Post*, see Deborah Davis, 1984 and Halberstam, 1981. On CBS, see Halberstam and Paper, 1987. On the Los Angeles Times, see Halberstam.

7. David Sarnoff, head of RCA and NBC, received the title of Brigadier General during World War II for his armed services propaganda effort. In the late 1940s he chaired an organization called the "Armed Forces Communication Association, where he pressed numerous Cold War propaganda themes. See *Broadcasting*, 1950 [1], p. 21 and *Broadcasting*, 1950 [2], p. 21. On the extensive connections of Paley and CBS to the government and CIA, see Paper, 1987, pp. 303–4; Schorr, 1978, pp. 204, 275ff. The revolving door between top level government and media officials has been extremely active. James Hagerty went from President Eisenhower's press secretary to chief of ABC News. David Gergen went from Reagan's White House media staff to a high editorial position at *U.S. News and World Report*. Edward W. Barrett resigned as Under Secretary of State for Public Affairs to work for NBC. Before he went to State he was editorial director of *Newsweek*. See Adams, *New York Times*, 1952. On the *Washington Post* official links to government and CIA, see Davis, 1984.

8. In the numerous neo-conservative tracts on media bias, I believe this point is never brought up and evaluated. In other instances, cases of strenuous proprietor intervention are dismissed as reflecting a distant past, before the rise of professional management, etc. Many great media firms, however, are still owner controlled, and in the instance of the Murdoch empire, e.g., the intrusion of the proprietor's political views into the newsmaking process is as blatant as in the classic Luce, Hearst and Wallace cases (see Kiernan, 1986, pp. 198–322). One reason for citations to the past is that it is often only for the past that compelling documentation is accessible. Furthermore, professional management and a more rigorous profit orientation may bring its own form of policy biases that conflict with professional values (see the text).

9. According to Deborah Davis, at Ben Bradlee's interview for a top job at the *Washington Post*, Katherine Graham asked him how he planned to cover the Vietnam war, which she consistently supported. "Bradlee said he didn't know, but that he'd hire no 'son-of-a-bitch' reporter who was not a patriot." Davis, 1984, p. 302.

10. See Breed, 1955; Soloski, 1989, pp. 207–28.

11. This dichotomization of language is laid out in Tables 5 and 6, in Preston *et al.*, 1989, pp. 248–50.

12. "Intensive coverage" is defined there as a case where an individual received attention six or more times in the news columns in any consecutive 30-day period, as recorded in the *New York Times Index*.

13. In its Annual Report for 1975–76, Amnesty International noted that "more than 80 percent" of the urgent appeals involving torture were coming out of Latin America [p. 84].

14. Thirty or more journalists were murdered in El Salvador between 1979 and 1986 by official and affiliated paramilitary forces, 48 were killed in Guatemala between 1978 and 1982, and none were known to have been killed in Nicaragua between July 1979 and 1986. See Committee to Protect Journalists, 1986.

15. See Herman and Chomsky, 1988, for a summary of the findings of the Latin American Studies Association and Irish government teams, contrasted with the treatment by the U.S. mass media.

16. Stephen Kinzer of the *New York Times* did cite a report of the International Human Rights Law Group on the 1984 Guatemalan election, but only to the effect that the election was "procedurally fair." The main finding of the group, that there was an intense climate of fear in Guatemala during the election, Kinzer did not see fit to mention. See Kinzer, 1985, p. 4.

17. This statement and the account that follows are based on Herman and Chomsky, 1988, pp. 154–167; Herman and Brodhead, 1986, chap. 7.

18. This propaganda campaign was to a considerable extent media rather than government sponsored, with the *Reader's Digest*, NBC-TV, and the *New York Times* playing especially important roles. See further, Herman and Brodhead, 1986, pp. 174–181 and ff.

19. An article by Edwin Diamond, A. Biddle Duke and Isabelle Anacker [Diamond et al., 1987], stressing the unwillingness of TV networks to correct errors, notes that newspapers have developed standard practices for doing this through correction boxes, letters to the editor, etc. The authors cite a Gannett Center research report that on average, large newspapers publish "a correction every other day." The authors, however, never discuss the meaning of "error," make no attempt to assess the relationship of number of corrections to the number of actual errors, and fail to note the possibility that the large papers correct a few trivial errors but fail to correct more subtle and important ones. Their undoubtedly just criticism of TV's correction failures is thus juxtaposed with a highly credulous apologetic for the large print media.

20. The amazing final statement of the editorial just quoted illustrates well the built-in "gullibility quotient": if Washington "promised" something, then it must be true. After 1962 there were numerous U.S.-sponsored assassination attempts on Castro and periodic acts of terrorism carried out against Cuba by U.S.-sponsored forces, all documented but ignored by the *Times* editorialists. See especially, Hinckle and Turner, 1981.

21. "Two brave experiments are under way in El Salvador,..." "High Noon in El Salvador," ed., Nov. 25, 1987; "Surprise in El Salvador," ed., March 6, 1989; "Brave Stand for Justice in El Salvador," ed., Jan. 9, 1990; "Light in El Salvador," ed., April 10, 1990.

22. That this was the state agenda, and was followed by the mass media, is the theme of Massing, 1983, pp. 42–49. For a description of the mass media's intense coverage of the 1982 election, see Herman and Brodhead, 1984, pp. 126–152.

23. This church-based group, located in Los Angeles but with representatives in El Salvador, puts out a chronology of events on a monthly basis, as well as individual reports on specialized subjects such as the murder of the six Jesuits, peace negotiations, and Salvadoran economic conditions.

24. Cuban troops were attacked by Savimbi's forces during the period under review, causing Cuba to threaten to halt its withdrawal and to retaliate. The *Times* did not report on these events.

25. The El Rescate Human Rights Department Chronology gives a number of cases in this time frame, and I rely on it for otherwise unidentified statements below. A number of these cases also appeared on the wire services as well.

26. This duplicated a 1983 episode of imprisonment, torture, TV and press-oriented confession, then release and recantation. Although this previous case was well-known, it was never mentioned in the *Times* series on the Miranda case. See Herman, 1989.

27. The facts in this paragraph are taken from the El Rescate Chronology.

References

Adams, V. (1952). "NBC's Secret Project." *New York Times*. Aug. 3.
Bonner, R. (1984). *Weakness and Deceit*. New York: Times Books.
Breed. W. (1955). *Social Forces*. 326–35.

Brooke, J. (1990). "Brazil Returns 10 Tons of Arms Sent by Cuba for Castro's Security," *New York Times*. March 8.
Campbell, D., and Forbes, P. (1985), "Tales of Anti-Reagan Hit Squad Was 'Fraud'." *New Statesman*, Aug. 16.
Catledge, T. (1971). *My Life and The Times*. New York: Harper and Row.
Chomsky, N. (1989). *Necessary Illusions*. Boston: South End Press.
Committee to Protect Journalists. (1986). *Journalists Killed or Disappeared Since 1976*. Dec.
Associated Press. (1990). "Cuban Tobacco Chief Challenges Cigar Company to Taste Test." A.P. report. March 27.
Davis, D. (1987). *Katherine the Great*. Bethesda, Md.: National Press.
deOnis, J. (1976). "Rightist Terror Stirs Argentina." *New York Times*, Aug. 29.
Diamond, E., A. Duke, and I. Anacker. (1987). "Can We Expect TV News to Correct Its Mistakes?" *TV Guide*, Dec. 5.
El Rescate. (1988). "Chronology of Human Rights Violations in El Salvador, for Jan. 1-June 30, 1988." Los Angeles: El Rescate.
Fed. Inf. System Corp. (1990). *New Report from Cuba*. April 6.
Gans, H. (1979). *Deciding What's News*. New York: Vintage.
Gans, H. (1985). "Are U.S. Journalists Dangerously Liberal?" *Columbia Journalism Review*, Nov.–Dec.
Goulden, J. (1988). *Fit to Print: A. M. Rosenthal and His Times*. Secaucus, N.J.: Lyle Stuart.
Gruson, L. (1987). "Peace Is Still a Long Shot in El Salvador." *New York Times*. Sept. 27.
Halberstam, D. (1981). *The Powers That Be*. New York: Alfred Knopf.
Herman, E. (1982). *The Real Terror Network*. Boston: South End Press.
Herman, E. (1986). "Gatekeeper and Propaganda Models." In P. Golding, G. Murdoch, and P. Schlesinger. *Communicating Politics*. Leicester: Leicester University Press.
Herman, E. (1989). "Disinformation as News Fit to Print: Lemoyne and the Times on the Murder of Herbert Anaya." *Covert Action Information Bulletin*. (Winter):65–69.
Herman, E. (1989). "Labor Abuses in El Salvador and Nicaragua: A Study of New York Times Coverage." *EXTRA!*. (Summer):24–26.
Herman, E. (1990). "How Paul Lewis Covers UNESCO." *Lies of Our Times*. (June):17–18.
Herman, E., and N. Chomsky. (1988). *Manufacturing Consent: The Political Economy of the Mass Media*. New York: Pantheon.
Herman, E., and F. Brodhead. (1986). *The Rise and Fall of the Bulgarian Connection*. New York: Sheridan Square Publication.
Herman, E., and F. Brodhead. (1984). *Demonstration Elections*. Boston: South End Press.
Hess, J. (1985). "The Culture Gulch of the Times." *Grand Street* (Winter).
Hinckle, W., and W. Turner. (1981). *The Fish Is Red: The Story of The Secret War Aginst Castro*. New York: Harper & Row.

Kiernan, T. (1986). *Citizen Murdoch*. New York: Dodd, Mead.
Kinzer, S. (1985). "Christian Democrat Takes Big Lead in Guatemala." *New York Times*, Nov. 5.
"Light in El Salvador." (1990). *New York Times* (editorial). April 10.
Lippmann, W., and C. Merz. (1920). "Test of the News." *New Republic*, Supp., Aug. 4.
Massing, M. (1983). "About-face on El Salvador." *Columbia Journalism Review*, Nov.–Dec., 42–49.
Paper, L. (1987). *Empire: William S. Paley and the Making of CBS*. New York: St. Martin's Press.
Perdue, W. (1989). *Terrorism and the State*. New York: Praeger.
Pitt, D. (1990). "Dreaming of an End of Castro, Cubans in Miami Are Abuzz." *New York Times*. Feb. 20.
Platt, T., ed. (1987). *Tropical Gulag*. San Francisco, CA: Global Options.
"President Castro in Brazil." (1990). *Cuban Update*. Summer.
Preston, W., E. Herman, and H. Schiller. (1989). *Hope and Folly: The United States and UNESCO 1945–1985*. Minneapolis: University of Minnesota Press.
"Reagan Said to Ignore Data on Downing of Jet." (1988). *New York Times*. Jan. 13.
Riding, A. (1981). "Duarte's Strategy May Work Better in U.S. Than in El Salvador." *New York Times*. Sept. 27.
"Sarnoff Plan." (1950). *Broadcasting*. July 17.
Schorr, D. (1978). *Clearing the Air*. New York: Berkeley Medallion Books.
Soloski, J. (1989). "News Reporting and Professionalism: Some Constraints on the reporting of News." *Media Culture & Society*, April, 207–228.
"Thirty Years of Fidel Castro." (1989). *New York Times* (editorial). Jan. 2.
Tuchman, G. (1972). "Objectivity as Strategic Ritual." *American Journal of Sociology* (77)4.

Commentary by Gertrude J. Robinson

Notes on the Political Economy of News Production and Communication Research

Ideological Criticism and its Assumptions

William J. Buxton's "Rockefeller Philanthropy, Commercial Broadcasting and the Princeton Radio Research Project" as well as Edward S. Herman's "All the Editorials Fit to Print: The Politics of Newsworthiness" both belong to the genre of communication analysis which has been called "ideological criticism." Ideological criticism is preoccupied with power relations in the economic, political and symbolic spheres. Such criticism had its origin in Marxist theories of culture and is concerned with the ways in which cultural artifacts produce and reproduce particular types of knowledges and interpretive positions for reader/viewers. These knowledges and positions link the audience member with program content and make possible the reception of class based values and outlooks. It is argued that since cultural artifacts, be they news reports or media research, are produced in a particular historic context by and for specific social groups, these groups' interpretive positions change with time and so do the values and views which are embedded in media content.

Over the past thirty years various versions of Marxist theory have been developed. Classical Marxism construes society in terms of a base/superstructure model in which the crucial organizing factor is the economic base, or what is called the "mode of production." As a consequence, the cultural artifacts produced within a given mode of production reflect the values and interests of the dominant class in society. Classical Marxist cultural theory has been most eloquently espoused by the Frankfurt school (Horkheimer and Adorno, 1940s/1971) who introduced the notion of "cultural industries" and began to demonstrate their effects on radio programming. In particular, they were interested in analyzing how culture as a form of expression makes class-based values and beliefs publicly available and how the public receives and interprets these artifacts.

Subsequent elaborations of the concept of ideology can be ranged on a theoretical continuum from the classical position, to those espoused by Antonio Gramsci (1971) who substituted the concept of "hegemony" to explain ideological practices, to that of Louis Althusser who revised the simple base/superstructure model itself. He argued that ideology is not constituted by one, but by three types of social practices: the economic, the political and the ideological (Althusser, 1971). Ideological practices, for Althusser refer to systems of representation (images, myths, ideas) in which individuals experience their relationship to the material world. He argues that because each of the three spheres may operate quite independently from the others, it is impossible for systems of representation to function as *direct expressions* of the class interests manifested by economic practices. Instead, systems of representation found in newspapers for instance, constitute a battleground for competing and contradictory interpretations, which may speak to different aspects of the reader's identity, including class, professional formation, age, gender and race.

Even the elaborated Althusserian conception of society and ideology is however not without problems and limitations and has itself been criticized since the seventies (Clarke et al, 1980). In spite of this the Althusserian reinterpretation provided a foundation for the elaboration of yet another Marxian cultural theory. This more "open" and "complex" theory was propounded by communication theorists in Birmingham England. In it, Stuart Hall and his colleagues rejected the simple notion of ideological determinism to explore the polysemic nature of texts and the active participation of reader/viewers in meaning creation. The "cultural studies" school shifted the theory of ideology further from the conventional model of political economy, and drew on concepts from earlier political theorists, linguistics and literary theory (Hall, 1977). In the process it developed a new understanding of the social determinacy of texts and media contents. Hall points out that because individuals make meaning actively in particular times and places, there is no such thing as being "outside" of one's culture's ideology. Ideology, instead, presents itself as the "natural" way of looking at and understanding the world and thus serves to naturalize a particular set of beliefs and ways of representation. In Hall's words "when we contrast ideology to experience or illusion to authentic truth, we are failing to recognize that there is no way of experiencing the "real relations" of a particular society outside of its cultural and ideological categories (Hall, 1979, p. 105). Consequently, the point of ideological criticism is not to find unadulterated truth or unbridled manipulation "beneath" or "behind" a given text or system of representation, but to understand *how* a particular system of representation offers us a way of knowing or experiencing the world (White, 1987, p. 141).

For people living in the North American privately owned media context, the ways of knowing and experiencing the world are primarily those of a potential consumer, one who will presumably purchase some of the promoted products. To address audience members as consumers means an overemphasis on entertaining rather than fact based program content, as well as the sale of audience "segments" as commodities to relevant sponsors. In the process, it is argued the political knowledge base which guarantees the democratic functioning of the state can become seriously eroded (Garnham, 1982). The 1992 U.S. presidential election campaign, where voters turned to talk show hosts for information on Bush and Clinton, rather than to media journalists, is a graphic instance of public disgust with a messenger industry which itself has become corrupted.

The Herman Study: An Example of the Classical Approach

Edward S. Herman's study of American news values as represented by the *New York Times* coverage of various South American political issues, belongs to the "classical" school of Marxist analysis which assumes a direct and determinate relationship between the elite production base and the expressive values found in textual reports. Herman's argument is straight forward. He argues "there is a dominant policy basis for decisions of newsworthiness in a number of areas of newsmaking in the U.S. mass media, which often overwhelms professional values" (Herman, 1993). The professional values which are being overwhelmed are of two kinds. The first is "objectivity" defined as "presenting a variety of sides to a story, searching out facts without political constraint and presenting these fairly and impartially." The second concerns the application of news values without pursuing an identifiable policy agenda, where "policy" is defined as "a line or news gathering procedure imposed by proprietors." Substantial amounts of evidence of owner likes and dislikes, selective coverage, incomplete evidence, excluded information, etc. are presented in the article to prove that "bias" exists in US reporting procedures and in the descriptions of events. Herman summarizes seven kinds of policy bias discovered by Noam Chomsky and himself (Herman/Chomsky, 1988). Among them are: differential tone and language; double standards in intensity of coverage and in the application of relevant principles; politically based selection of facts; the transmission of lies; a lack of investigatory zeal and the unwillingness of *Times* editors to correct error. The classical theory of materialism which is implied in "bias" studies, makes two types of assumptions which are difficult to embrace for contemporary communication scholars. Philosophically it requires one to affirm that there is a reality "out there" which is directly apprehensible by the observer. In addition it assumes that there is a one-to-one type of correspondence between facts/events and their descriptions (Robinson, 1984). About fifty years ago, Walter Lippmann (1922) and others noted that it is virtually impossible to come up with "unvarnished" or "pristine" facts against which "objectivity" can be established, as a portrait photo establishes the identity of the passport bearer. Classical materialism is additionally criticized on theoretical grounds. Here the major concerns are an overly forceful economic determinism in which culture and politics are reduced to reflections of economic interests, values and power. Such a reductionism is unable analytically or historically to account for the infinite variety of human social organization associated with capitalist or with socialist countries.

A related criticism notes that classical political economy "functionalizes" culture in the service of ideological production (Knight, 1982). The assumption that culture is ideology and thus primarily concerned with system reproduction, leaves no room for contradiction, opposition, resistance and human agency, all of which are evident in communicational behaviour. The privilege of dominance, contemporary scholarship shows, does not lie in the subordinate groups' unquestioned acceptance of ideological dictates, but in the dominant descriptions' ability to pay less attention to alternative meanings (Bourdieu, 1990). Hegemony is an "expansive" rather than a "restrictive" confrontational process which functions through the *incorporation* rather than the exclusion of alternative and oppositional meanings which have been stripped of their original context.

The Buxton Study: An Example of the "Cultural Studies" Approach

William J. Buxton's insightful analysis of the political economy of early radio research, which establishes how the Princeton radio project received its 1937 mandate, does not suffer from the same kinds of methodological criticisms levelled against classical Marxist cultural theory. The reasons are that Buxton implicity subscribes to the more "open" version of Marxism in which both the notions of power and ideology have been reconceptualized along Gramcian and Althusserian lines. Though he describes himself as an "activist" reconstructor of the Rockefeller radio story, his approach is close to that of the British "cultural studies" group (Buxton, 1993, p. 9). He, like they, works from the inside out and uses situational, qualitative and contemporary evidence interlacing individual agency with institutional settings and goals. In the process he is able to illuminate the strategic basis of what C. Wright Mills (1959) calls "administrative research" and the institutional context in which it arose. Instead of "reading in" interpretations of the 1930s from the 1990s perspective, Buxton relies on contemporary evidence and demonstrates the double hermeneutic involved in communicational activities, the ways in which research *itself* is implicated in the construction and reconstruction of the social activity of radio research (Giddens, 1983).

Buxton's reconstruction of the intellectual and institutional origins of the Rockefeller sponsored Princeton radio study adds to the growing amount of scholarship which is refocusing on Lazarsfeld's contributions to media research (Sills, 1987; Morrison, 1988; Robinson, 1990) independently from his opinion and methodological innovations. In the recent past his contributions to survey research have received much more sustained attention than his communications work (Converse, 1987; Hyman, 1991), possibly because it spanned only ten years of his extensive career. All of these studies heed my 1988 call for careful "historiographical" work in our field (Robinson, 1988). Proper historiographies, as Jones (1983) notes are designed to systematically trace the intellectual, institutional, socio-political and media interconnections which have set the research agendas for North American communication research since the turn of the century. One of the important early scholars and definers of this field was doubtlessly Lazarsfeld who gained entry into the US academy through the Rockefeller project.

Yet, the conceptualization of this project and how it fit in with government regulatory issues and how the triumph of the commercial over the educational potentials of radio were achieved, has up to now remained unrecorded. Buxton's great contribution is to provide this missing link and to demonstrate that "the Rockefeller Foundation assumed a task that neither broadcasters, educators, nor state officials were willing or able to undertake.... This involved the integration of educational broadcasting into the programming of commercial networks, the commercialization of certain educational broadcasters ... and the shift of public discourse and understanding about issues related to radio" (Buxton, 1993) where a fierce power battle had previously raged. Buxton elucidates that the Foundation's three tiered strategy for reconciliation began in 1935 and subsequently took shape through the participation of key Rockefeller advisors in various government and broadcast committees. The first initiative consisted in providing research grants to particular educational broadcasters, like Boston's "World Wide Broadcasting Foundation" (WWBF) to improve the "appeal" of their programs. A second step was to convince private broadcasters through Frank Stanton's budding Research Department at CBS that educational programming could have audience appeal. This was to be documented by sponsored research into audience likes and dislikes, headed by social psychologist Hadley Cantril at Princeton. John Marshall's third initiative grew out of his conviction that a better understanding of audience interests would ultimately lead to increased educational programming in commercial stations, an idea with which the FCC was in agreement.

Buxton's reconstruction provides an answer to the question why the Princeton Radio Project initially received such a vague mandate. The December 1936 request by Cantril for an annual grant of $25,000 extending over two years, for support of a study of "what listeners find of interest in radio programs and . . . why these interests exist," incorporated the Foundations three conciliatory goals. It also noted that Cantril "hoped to enlist the services of Frank Stanton to help him with the research" (Buxton, 1993). In an August 1937 letter, wooing Lazarsfeld for the directorship of the project, Cantril described its purpose "to determine the role of radio in the lives of different types of listeners, the value of radio to people psychologically and the various reasons why people like it" (Stanton file, Columbia University Archive, box 26, file 10, p. 1).

Buxton's holistic research based on contemporary documents demonstrates that a "cultural studies" approach which uses "the contested terrain of knowledge and power as a point of departure "offers an efficacious strategy for reconstructing the past. It provides a means for identifying the relevant institutional actors, tracing their strategic moves to achieve varied institutional goals. It also permits one to understand why and how a particular research objective is constructed and how it becomes studied. In the process Buxton finds that the contesting institutions, the governmental regulatory environment and the research goals of the Rockefeller sponsored team are mutually adjusted, rather than fixed, linear and pre-determined as classical Marxist theory would predict. My own research shows that this adjustment of goals is achieved through John Marshall's pressure on Lazarsfeld to publish a coherent set of results for the Princeton project before a second Rockefeller grant will be entertained. This is accomplished through the publication of *Radio and the Printed Page* (1940) (Robinson, 1993 forthcoming).

Communicationally, Buxton demonstrates that ideas and interpretations matter and that individual agents like Lazarsfeld, Stanton and Cantril in the process of their collaborative work, transformed the original purposes of the Princeton project. Preexisting research concerns and personal circumstances are involved in such transformations. Allan Janik and Stephen Toulmin (1972, p. 27) note how important preexisting intellectual sedimentations (Problemstellung) are to the ways in which intellectuals approach new research projects. Though they were all trained in social psychology, Hadley Cantril, Frank Stanton and Paul Lazarsfeld brought very different background knowledges to the Princeton project, which also precluded their developing a common theoretical outlook. Between 1937 and 1940 they published independently. Personal circumstances also undermined a possible collaboration. Cantril objected to Lazarsfeld's administrative style and non-experimental approach, whereas Stanton was drawn into Lazarsfeld's orbit and began talks about what became the Stanton/Lazarsfeld program analyzer (Converse, 1987, pp. 150–151). In 1940 Cantril dropped out of the project and set up his own Princeton based public opinion research organization, and Lazarsfeld received a visiting appointment at Columbia. As a consequence, a common perspective for radio and ultimately communications research was delayed until Lazarsfeld encountered Robert K. Merton in 1941, when both were hired into Columbia's sociology department. Their close intellectual bond and the department's supply of graduate students laid the foundation for the emergence of an influential new "school" of media research in the Columbia Bureau of Social Research (Robinson, 1990, pp. 96–98).

References

Althusser, Louis. (1971). "Ideology and Ideological State Apparatuses." In *Lenin and Philosophy*. trans. Ben Brewster. New York: Monthly Review Press, pp. 127–186.

Bourdieu, Paul. (1990). *In Other Words*. Cambridge: Polity Press.

Buxton, William. (1993). "Political Economy of Communications Research: Rockefeller Philanthropy, Commercial Broadcasting and the Princeton Radio Research Project." In *Information and Communication in Economics*. Robert Babe (ed.), Boston: Kluwer.

Clarke, Simon et al (1980). *One Dimensional Marxism*. London: Allison & Busby.

Converse, Jean. (1987). *Survey Research in the United States: Roots and Emergence 1890 to 1960*. Berkeley: University of California Press.

Garnham, Nicholas. (1982). "Film and Media Studies: Reconstructing the subject." *Film Reader* (5): pp. 177–183.

Giddens, Anthony. (1983). *Central Problem in Social Research*. Berkeley: University of California Press.

Gramsci, Antonio. (1971). *Selections from the Prison Notebooks*. Ed. & trans. by

Quentin Hoare & Geoffrey Newell-Smith. New York: International Publishers.
Hall, Stuart. (1977). "Culture, the Media and the Ideological Effect." In J. Curran, M. Gurevitch, and J. Wollacott (eds.), *Mass Communication and Society*. Beverly Hills: Sage, pp. 315–348.
Hall, Stuart. (1979). "Signification, Representation Ideology: Althusser and the Post-structuralist Debates." *Critical Studies in Mass Communications*. (2):2.
Herman, Edward S. and Noam Chomsky. (1988). *Manufacturing Consent: The Political Economy of Mass Media*. New York: Pantheon Press.
Horkheimer, Max, and Theodor Adorno. (1972). "The Cultural Industry: Enlightenment or Mass Deception." In *Dialectic of Enlightenment*. trans. John Cumming. New York: Seabury.
Hyman, Herbert H. (1991). *Taking Society's Measure: A Personal History of Survey Research*. New York: Russell Sage Foundation.
Janik, Allan, and Stephen Toulmin. (1973). *Wittgenstein's Vienna*. New York: Simon and Schuster.
Jones, Robert A. (1983). "The New History of Sociology." *Annual Review of Sociology*, no. 9, pp. 447–469.
Knight, Graham. (1982). "Property, Stratification and the Wage-reform." *Canadian Journal of Sociology* (7): pp. 221–231.
Lippmann, Walter. (1922). *Public Opinion*. New York: Harcourt Brace.
Mills, C. Wright. (1959). *The Sociological Imagination*. New York: Oxford University Press.
Morrison, David E. (1988). "The Transference of Experience and the Impact of Ideas: Paul F. Lazarsfeld and Mass Communication Research." *Communication* (10): pp. 185–209.
Robinson, Gertrude J. (1984). "Television News, The Quebec Referendum and the Claim to Facticity." *Interpreting Television: Current Research Perspectives*. Bruce Watkins & W. Rowland (eds.). Sage Annual Reviews of Communication Research. Beverly Hills: Sage, pp. 199–222.
Robinson, Gertrude J. (1988). "Here Be Dragons: Problems in Charting the U.S. History of Communication Studies." *Communication* (10): pp. 97–119.
Robinson, Gertrude J. (1990). "Paul F. Lazarsfeld's Contribution to the Development of US Communication Studies." In *Paul F. Lazarsfeld: Die Wiener Tradition der empirischen Sozial und Kommunikationsforschung.*, Wolfgang Langenbucher (ed.). Munich: Olschlager Verlag, pp. 89–112.
Robinson, Gertrude J. (1993). "The Paul R. Lazarsfeld & Robert K. Merton Collaboration at Columbia: Master Surveyor meets Master Codifier." *Freedom Forum Media Studies Center*. New York: Columbia.
Sills, David L. (1987). "Paul F. Lazarsfeld 1901–1976." *Biographical Memoirs*, vol. 56.
White, Mimi. (1987). "Ideological Analysis of Television." In Robert C. Allen (ed.) *Channels of Discourse: Television and Contemporary Criticism*. Durham: University of North Carolina Press, pp. 134–171.

Reply by Edward S. Herman
"Reburial" of Ideology

Gertrude Robinson does not really comment on my paper at all. She evades this task by resorting to what we may call the "taxonomic placement putdown ploy." That is, she locates the paper in a taxonomic class, and then enumerates the alleged deficiencies of that category, quite independently of the content of the paper. This saves her the labor of examining the paper itself. The paper is placed in the "classical Marxist" category, which is the reductionist pit of the Marxist genre, "preoccupied with power relations," assuming a "direct and determinate relationship" between base and superstructure, and therefore "implying" other intolerable assumptions: "That there is a reality 'out there' that is directly apprehensible" and 'a one-to-one' relationship "between facts/events and their description." There is more on functionalism, reductionism and the inability of the alleged methodology "to account for the infinite variety" of human experience.

Robinson doesn't relate any of these horrors to the modest aims and analyses of the paper, which examines the concepts of objectivity and professionalism, and criticizes the claims of the media and some of their liberal critics that the rules of objectivity and professional values control media news performance and are not overpowered by media proprietors' profit/policy agendas and ideology. The paper shows how media performance is in fact subject to a systematic bias in language, framing and other qualities, that seems to be explicable in terms of preconceived policy and ideology. The methodology is simple: exploring a straightforward hypothesis of bias, with extensive empirical testing that shows radically dichotomous treatment of similar matters that have different policy/ ideological power relationships. It is true that the hypotheses are built on power relationships, but neither they nor the testing methods have anything to do with—or are legitimately criticized by reference to— "classical" or any other kind of Marxism. The test of the hypotheses in the paper is their ability to explain and give insight into some small part of reality. Robinson does not subject them to this test. Dismissing them because their alleged taxonomic class cannot explain the "infinite variety" of reality is an irrelevant copout.

Robinson's mode of criticism is also illegitimate in denying (and misunderstanding) my individuality and integrity as a scholar. I am trying to understand and explain media reality and have been seeking hypotheses and constructing models without any prior commitment to classical or any other Marxism. My methodology is rooted in my own structural analyses of the corporate system (e.g., a critical but non-Marxist book, *Corporate Control, Corporate Power*, Cambridge University Press, 1981), experience in observing and continuously reflecting on how the media work, and the successful use of the dichotomous methodology employed in the present paper for many important news episodes. I have long been perfectly well aware of media complexity, the "partial autonomy" of the media, and interactive processes, along with the fact that my own analyses and methods do not explain everything. Thus a criticism indicating that "classical Marxism" does not take these matters into account and cannot explain everything is singularly unhelpful.

In a way, Robinson's criticism fits and extends Stuart Hall's well-known analysis in his essay "The 'Rediscovery' of Ideology" (in Michael Gurevitch et al, *Culture, Society and the Media*, Methuen, 1982). Hall describes the pre-"rediscovery" school as one of pluralist/denial-of-ideology scholars who arose in the post World War II era of U.S. triumphalism and hegemony. They decried the Frankfort school theorists and other analysts of domination and hegemonic power and control as unscientific and ideological. But they themselves were unconsciously highly ideological, not all that scientific, and well integrated to the demands of western power centers. As Hall describes it, the emergence of critical studies (the "rediscovery of ideology") put "power" to the fore once again, with a consequent great release of creative energies in the media field. Gertrude Robinson's comment, openly critical of studies of an "ideological" bent that are "preoccupied" with power and domination, making assumptions "difficult to embrace for contemporary communications scholars," seems like a throwback to the earlier era. As we are in a new age of Western triumphalism and growing importance of the market, could her comment be a harbinger of a rerun of the earlier phase of media end-of-ideology adaption and "*reburial*" of ideology?

8 THE INFORMATION ECONOMY IN A SPATIAL CONTEXT: CITY-STATES IN A GLOBAL VILLAGE

Mark Hepworth

Introduction

As a field of study, the geography of the information economy is concerned with the distribution of jobs, investment and services between cities, regions and countries. For example, at a global scale, it may consider the international allocation of high technology production, with a key policy focus on the relative competitiveness of Europe, Japan, or the United States (the central issue for the European Commission's 1994–1998 framework program on telematics research and development). At a national scale, attention may focus on regional uneven development in the information economy, perhaps with reference to the spatial impacts of computer networking in multilocational firms. In seeking to address these types of distributional issues, economic geographers are simply moving with the times, shifting their traditional concerns with uneven spatial development into the so-called "information age" (Hepworth, 1989).

This paper discusses a key structural characteristic of the information economy—its geography of metropolitan dominance. It looks at two basic aspects of urban development in the information economy. The first relates to the intensifying competition between cities for new jobs and new investment—one that is fuelled by geopolitical upheavals across the world and by a deepening world recession. The construction of "electronic highways" are drawing cities closer together—but, with this newly created proximity—the technical platform of the global village—cities see threats and opportunities from a variety of different standpoints. For example, the competitiveness of British cities as manufacturing locations may be eroded as Eastern European cities open their doors to foreign direct investment—a teleport for a future high tech Budapest or a 30-channel, ATT international exchange linking Kiev directly to U.S. business centres (rather than via Moscow)? Similarly, whilst British cities continue to woo Japanese electronics industries through expensive marketing strategies, these investment flows are being short-circuited by intervening opportunities closer to Tokyo: the powerful regional platform for electronics production being built around low-cost metropolises in the Far East and China (Henderson, 1989).

The second aspect of the information city I wish to highlight is the impact on urban form and functioning of technological and organisational change. This area is littered with futuristic scenarios of cities disappearing under the influence of telematics, with vast swathes of the workforce migrating to the countryside as inhabitants of electronic cottages. During the 1980s, these scenarios were contradicted by an apparent strengthening of the world's big cities—London, New York, Tokyo and others—as the massive income-generating power of the financial revolution pushed back the limits to urban growth or the locational costs of urban centrality. But now in the recessionary, early 1990s, and with telematics innovation being more geared to cost-cutting than income-generation as a way of increasing productivity, there are signs that the new technologies could change the face of the city. These new tendencies in the information city and what they broadly signify are discussed with particular reference to London.

Global Competition Between Cities

The political economy of international competitiveness is mostly discussed in terms of nation states and increasingly the regional blocs now taking shape in the Americas, Europe, and Japan-Asia. Below this level, there is another struggle for global economic competitiveness, one fueled by the erosion of national frontiers within these blocs—a contest of economic strength between cities. Thus, while the stated ambition of the British national government is to be at the center of Europe, the aim of British city governments is to be at the center of the European space economy—what is now dubbed the "Euromegalopolis." This split-level geopolitics of the information economy is evident in all regions of the world.

A Place in the Euromegalopolis

The real importance of the 1992 Olympics to Barcelona was that it put the Catalonian capital firmly on the world map—the momentary centre of a global village created by satellite television. In effect, Barcelona laid a powerful claim to world city status, having long been overshadowed by Madrid; at the same time, backed by European Community funding and publicity, the city pressed home its case for being seen as a dominant economic and cultural centre of the Mediterranean region within the new post-1992 Europe. The extravagant fireworks display at the end of the Games did seem to have its desired effect of intimidating the opposition in the rest of Europe. For example, the London Evening Standard was moved to write off Manchester's chances of hosting the 2000 Olympics on the grounds that the northern English city could not possibly muster the logistical and economic muscle to match (and surpass) Barcelona's performance as a world-class metropolitan center.

Within the European Community, economic competion between cities is taking place along a broad front, with information created by academic research and the media playing an important role in pushing the claims of rival centres. This is most clearly illustrated by the war of words between Frankfurt and London in their bids to capture the future European Central Bank, a competition which Manchester has now withdrawn from due to its belief that Britain's humiliating exit from the European Exchange Rate Mechanism has ruined its prospects for success.

The struggle between British cities and their continental rivals is driven by the perceived need to develop within the so-called "Euromegalopolis," a vast heartland of economic activity formed by transnational integration between Europe's most powerful metropolitan regions. This is a new geographical entity in name only, but it is one which conveys a powerful imagery of a centralized Europe in the making, with its own system of urban winners and losers. The French national planning agency, DATAR, has drawn up a map of the Euromegalopolis (see Figure 1) which I have seen reported in the English press. Even if its cartographical representation is vulnerable to national bias, the concept of Euromegalopolis neatly captures the essence of what concerns and motivates city governments right across the Community: the need to compete for a central place in the future European space economy.

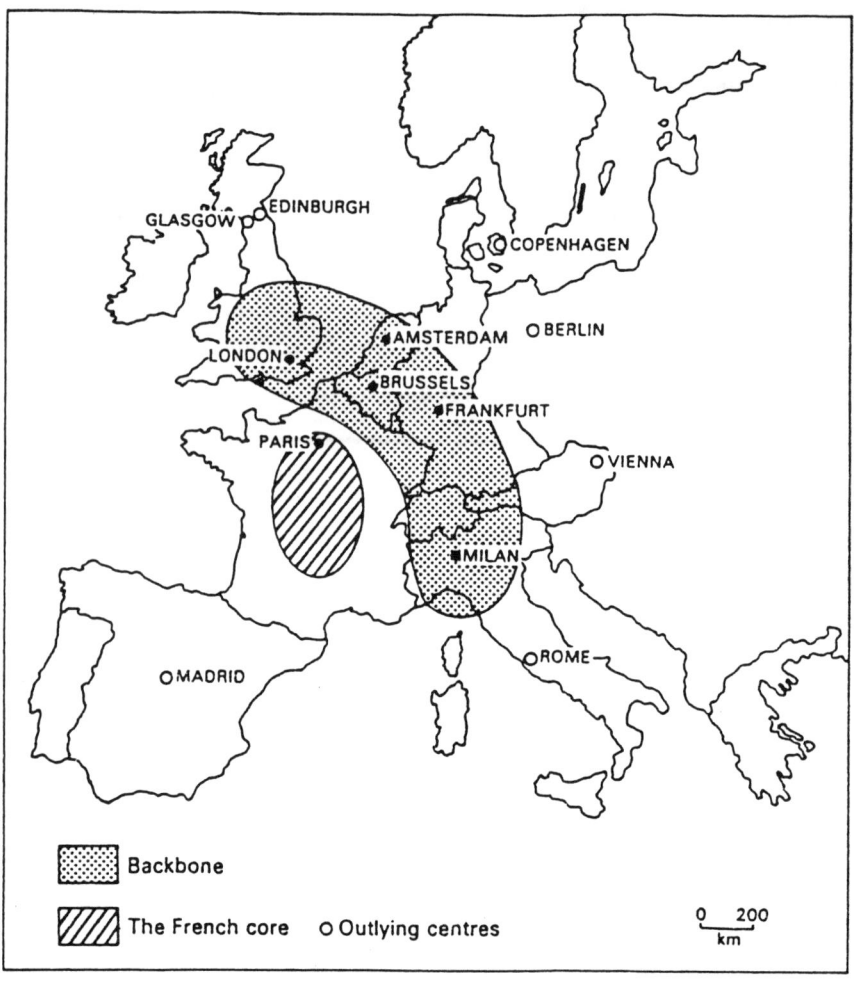

The drive to become an integral part of Euromegalopolis has led to British city governments taking a greater interest in the role of telecommunications in local economic development (Graham and Dominy, 1992). From being mainly a regional interest shared by northern English cities and Scottish cities, where the pressures of economic renewal and geographical peripherality are strongest, there is now a universal interest in the competitive advantages which telecommunications is believed to offer local economies—the result of the recession's devastating impacts on southern England and Greater London (London Research Centre, 1992). This interest has been translated into urban-regional telecommunications initiatives of different shapes and sizes: teleports for Glasgow and Edinburgh, a simple metropolitan area network for community development and small firms in Manchester (the "Manchester Host") and so on.

Importantly, the drive to differentiate one information city from the next—the basis for achieving a competitive advantage—depends ultimately upon funding. Since British local authorities have been stripped of economic development powers by the Conservative government, the process of urban innovation is now based on private-public sector partnerships secured and orchestrated by central government, and to a lesser extent the European Commission in Brussels. The real winners in this new political economy of urban generation are the information brokers who offer gateways to fund-holding private and public decision-makers—the big management consultancies, commercial developers, urban planning specialists, and so on. In this context, the wider social and economic potential of telecommunications is paid lip-service, with the main thrust of urban innovation being channelled into the closed world of site-by-site property development—a wonderland of high technology theme parks prefaced by adjectives such as *smart*, *intelligent*, *science*, and so on.

The key issue, though, is whether packaging urban sites and whole cities in the this way really produces the desired results. That is, will marketing Manchester as the information city or Glasgow as the communicating city, for example, lead to firms relocating to these places or to mobile investment from the rest of the world settling there? I doubt it! Research on firms in the U.K. shows that accessibility to good old-fashioned road transport is by far the dominant factor in influencing corporate location decisions—the electronic highways of the infermation economy trail in last on the list of locational factors (Diamond and Spence, 1989). Another example of the seemingly limited value of high tech labelling relates to the massive run-down Park Royal industrial area in west London. Without any labels to boost its image, and without dressing up the area's offer to prospective inward investors (the public-private sector partnership has no money to spend), Park Royal is soon to become home to AT&T's entire European network operations.

Beyond the Euromegalopolis

What will matter more to the future competitiveness of British cities—and their rivals in the rest of western Europe—is not what AT&T is doing inside the Euromegalopolis but what it is doing outside it. The American telecommunications giant has set up direct communications links between U.S. business centres and Moscow, Yerevan, and St. Petersburg—it has also started up a joint venture to supply communications equipment with a St. Petersburg company, Dalnyaya Svyaz. Reflecting the Ukraine's new autonomy, AT&T's telephone links between Kiev and American cities do not go via Moscow; but, perhaps ironically, Moscow's international traffic is being channelled through British Telecom's switching exchanges in London.

Eastern Europe has indeed become a vast field of new electronic highways construction, which is underwritten by international funds for technology transfer and economic cooperstion—for example, the World Bank's aid funds, the European Commission's PHARE programme and the complicated voucher systems for investment-trade credit run by the United States, the United Kingdom, and other capitalist countries. Under a cooperation protocol, a German consortium made up of Bundespost Telecom, ATN-Bosch-Telekom and Deutsche Aerospace are involved in project "Romantis," the construction of a three-satellite system for carrying telephone, data and television traffic in the state of Kazakhstan. AT&T has already signed an agreement to supply Kazakhstan with one million lines of digital switching over the next ten years, also involving the creation of an inter-city business communication network linking into Alma Ata, the state capital. There are plans, led by the Japanese giant KDD, to construct a transcontinental fibre link between Copenhagen and Tokyo via Moscow, in order to meet the expected growth in demand for telecommunications between Asia-Pacific countries and the former states of the Soviet Union. In Poland, a consortium composed of British Telecom, Fintelcom, and Swedish Telecom will be providing a mobile phone service, starting in Warsaw and then extending to other major cities. Cable and Wireless, U.S. regional Bell companies, France Telecom, and others are positioning themselves in readiness for the privatisation of Hungary's telephone system (where U.S. West aleady has a joint venture in cellular phones with Hungary Telecom)—fittingly, the advisers to the Hungarian Government on telephone privatisation are Rothschild, one of the City of London's premier merchant banks.

The wiring of Eastern Europe in this way, of course, opens up new telecommunications markets for American, Japanese, and European carriers, together with the entire "filiere" of information technology goods and service industries that have developed in capitalist economies over the last few decades. Importantly, the cities which will develop on these electronic highways—including the global private networks of multinational corporations now setting up production all over the CIS—are likely to emerge as rival industrial locations and trading centres to Euromegalopolis soon into the next millenium. Rather like Third World industrialisation, there will be an initial emphasis on serving the local market—for example, Pepsi's new bottling plant, McDonald's burger restaurants, and Tampon's base in Kiev are positioned to exploit a 300 million consumer monopoly—and the establishment of off-shore export production platforms—for example, both Ford and Fiat have announced joint ventures to set up car assembly lines. In the years ahead, western European and North American cities will face economic competition from Eastern European cities which are still shrouded in political uncertainty.

Whilst the competitive threat of Eastern Europe will evolve over the next decades, cities in North America and western Europe have already experienced the impacts of global competition from East Asia and the Pacific Rim countries. This threat has widened from textiles, squash rackets, shoes, and the like to high technology. As Jefferey Henderson's (1989) excellent analysis of the new international division of labour in semiconductor production shows, Japanese and American multinationals have built a regional production hierarchy covering South Korea, Taiwan, Hong Kong, Malaysia, the Phillipines, Singapore, Thailand, and Indonesia. In search of even cheaper export platforms and new product markets, Motorola is building a $300 million semiconductor plant in China, where Peking has been promoting investment in high-technology industries; NEC of Japan, BTM of Belgium, and Philips (the Dutch consumer electronics group) have all recently set up joint ventures in China.

The shift in Japan's strategic orientation in favour of Asia is commented upon by the president of Mitsubishi Electric Corporation, Moriya Shiki as follows: "Friction between Japan and the United States is not likely to disappear any more than friction between Japan and Europe. What is important for Japan is to attach greater importance to Asia" (Keidanren Review, April 1992, p. 8). In fact, Mitsubishisi, like other Japanese multinationals, manages and coordinates its operations on a global scale, using the company's private international computer network called MIND. From its headquarters in Tokyo, MIND connects into central London—to support videoconferencing with top management in the newly established European Coordination Centre—and into its regional production centres in Singapore (the so-called intelligent island) and Hong Kong. In June 1992, Mitsubishi opened an elevator factory (it has 50 percent of Japan's elevator market) in Bangkok, after collaborating with Thailand's telephony company to upgrade the local communications infrastructure—including the construction of a MIND-Thai Regional Communications Centre to support the network operations of other companies.

Against this background, British cities are still looking to Japan for inward investment in high technology sectors. The realities are that the "goalposts have shifted" as Japan channels more and more of its new investment into countries nearer to home. Even in Silicon Valley, the "cradle of high technology industrialization," there is a rising tide of bankruptcies and unemployment. The Valley has lost 30,000 jobs since 1984, and venture capital investment has fallen by 25 percent to a total of $750 million (1991). The same story of decline is evident in Britain's silicon corridor (the westward motorway stretch between London and Bristol), silicon fen (around Cambridge), and silicon glen (Scotland). Not only is information technology production not generating jobs—IBM and British Telecom have just cut 100,000 jobs between them—but the jobs that are being created are staying in Asia. They are going to Bangkok and Manilla, not Sheffield or Manchester.

A further threat to the blissful future which cities imagine leading inside Euromegalopolis comes from the newly emerging electronic colonies of the Third World. In this case, it is not manufacturing but the back office sector of the urban economy which is vulnerable to competition from cities on the other side of the world. As Robert Reich (1992) observes, "The foot soldiers of the information economy are the hordes of data processors stationed in back offices at computer terminals linked to worldwide information banks." Increasingly, these routine information-processing services—accounting for about one-third of the information workforce in big cities like London and Toronto (Hepworth, 1989)—are being shipped "over the wire" to offshore platforms in the Caribbean, the Phillipines, and Singapore. Thus, next to the tourist beaches, we find teleports operating or being built in Jamaica, Barbados, St. Lucia, and the Dominican Republic. According to one report, from beginning as an information age slave economy, the Caribbean information processing industry has recently seen "a definite shift to the higher value-added type of processing activities" (*Financial Times*, 9 April, p. 3). Again, we find AT&T heavily involved in these distant but fully-connected outposts of the global information economy; similarly, whilst Cable and Wireless builds up China's intercity electronic highways and modernises Moscow's industrial communications networks, it can also be observed up-grading several national telecommunications systems in the Caribbean islands.

For British cities, press reports on the development of these sunny electronic colonies—where wages for information workers are only a small fraction of those paid in world city labor markets—must surely give cause for concern. London's back-offices have been and still are a key target for northern cities in the U.K.—the same is true of New York and Paris and their respective fields of office migration. But today, with the recession laying waste to the capital's white-collar jobs, London can not afford to be complacent about the possibility of a back-office exodus. The rise of the Caribbean information services industry cannot be dismissed that easily, particularly when it is set alongside the migration of information goods production to other exotic places in the East.

Inside the Information City

The creation of a global village in which cities struggle for economic supremacy is one side of the urban impacts of the information technology revolution. The other side, given more emphasis by geographers and planners, relates to the impact of telematics or computer network technologies on urban form and functioning. What will cities look like in the twenty-first century? Will cities resist the space-and-time adjusting power of telematics or will their spatial monopoly of the information economy decline steadily in the years ahead?

In Search of New Engines of Growth

Through the 1980s, the world's great metropolitan cities—London, New York, Tokyo, and other international business centres—underwent explosive growth generated by the revolution (dubbed "big bangs") in capital markets. In terms of its direct impacts on cities, therefore, we saw the power of information technology operating through major restructuring in the financial sector: the use of global computer networks for product innovation—the creation of new financial instruments—and for process innovation—new methods of transacting business. The income-generating capacity of this paper revolution outweighed the rising costs of urban centrality—escalating commercial rents and wages, inflated house prices, congested public services, and so on—such that the limits to urban growth were increasingly pushed back.

The 1990s has, of course, seen this financial "engine of growth" crash with devastating consequences for not just property developers and financial industries, but also for workers and house-owners who depend upon the services-based economy of metropolitan cities. In the U.K. case, London has gone from boom to bust within a space of five years, and the recession has hit the capital harder than anywhere else in the country. About 20 percent of central London's office space is empty and 12 percent of the capital's workforce is unemployed—half of London's inner-city boroughs have unemployment rates of 20 percent or more. Unlike the early 1980s, this recession is devastating London's white-collar information labor force and, for many observers, it is thought to mark the widening of deindustrialisation from manufacturing to the service sector.

In a recent article (Hepworth, 1992), I have argued that cities like London will need to find new engines of growth based on marriages between telematics and sectors other than financial services, as a basis for economic renewal and future growth. At the same time, these marriages need to be consistent with structural trends in the information technology sector itself, characterised by market shifts toward the growth areas of systems integration in computer networks, high value added services and new types of applications. Reflecting these trends, John Diebold highlights the future potential of applications such as intelligent road systems, environmental monitoring, and health care. Indeed, whilst cities like London are unlikely to develop as production centres for information technology goods, they may successfully develop as knowledge-based centres of innovation and creativity in the evolving high value added, growth markets of information technology services.

Thus, my own bias in finding new marriage partners for telematics is towards sectors such as transport, health, education, environment, recreation, and other types of services which are still predominantly supplied as public goods by local and central governments. Transport, for example, is crying out for renewal and innovation in all metropolitan cities, where traffic congestion wreaks havoc with an economy increasingly running on just-in-time principles, with an environment polluted by the toxic vehicle emissions, and where the safety of children and old people is under daily threat. In the book *Wheels and Wires*, which I co-authored with Ken Ducatel of Manchester University, it was argued that European cities could benefit from investments in advanced transport telematics—passenger information systems, electronic road pricing, urban freight logistics, and so on—as part of a general program of modernization in urban infrastructure. At the same time, this investment could create major platforms for economic growth based on a host of marriages between the most powerful sectors of the modern economy—transport, including vehicles manufacturing ("wheels") and telecommunications, including computer systems ("wires") (Hepworth and Ducatel, 1992).

The transport telematics market in the European Community alone is reckoned to be worth 100 billion ECUs (European Currency Units), and similar figures have been attached to the future markets for environmental and health telematics. It is these new markets which offer the best hope for cities looking for economic growth in the information age, rather than the manufacture of high tech memory chips, personal computers and other standard bits and pieces which can now be produced and assembled by cheap, low-skilled labor. These new markets will, however, be open to global economic competition between cities and the real winners will be the metropolitan centres who not only introduce the new products and services as part of strategies to upgrade urban infrastructure, but also who create the new products and services for themselves and for export to the rest of the world.

Clearly, the new marriages I favor can only succeed if they are integrated within a wider framework of new public investment in the infrastructure of cities—and in the transport networks which link together cities within countries and across national boundaries. In Europe, the creation of transEuropean networks which include transport, energy, and telecommunications is being given high priority by the European Commission, and the Commission's DRIVE research and development program on transport telematics is matched by large infrastructure projects in the United States and Japan. Within this context, infrastructure projects are squarely organized around national and international city systems, the main concentrations of traffic and the highways which interconnect their economies.

The dual objectives of building high-technology transport infrastructure—a convergence of physical and information highways—are to create new global markets for the telematics industries and transport industries whilst generating wider social and economic benefits, including improvements to the environment and to public safety and more efficient transport networks for other sectors. As such, the creation of this information age infrastructure tends to cut across different and perhaps competing policy domains. For example, within the European Commission, transport telematics is the responsibility of Directorate General XIII, the division charged with promoting information industries and building electronic highways, whereas the responsibility for the physical highways actually lies with the transport policy Directorate (DG VII). Indeed, this untoward and anachronistic division of responsibility (exacerbated by territorial jealousies within the Commission) is a general barrier to telematics innovation in the public services, including at the policy level of city governments. As a result, the new marriages I have highlighted as being important to the future of cities are emerging slowly and without being integrated into wider strategies for overhauling the urban infrastructure which, at least in London's case, is more or less the same as the urban streets used by Victorian firms and residents during the last century.

In Japan, where national systems of advanced information cities are being constructed as platforms for global economic competition, public investments in transport telematics are integrated into both long-term industrial and urban strategies. There is a clear recognition that the information economy moves on "wheels" and "wires": most information comes embodied in physical goods and in the brains of commuters who travel to offices concentrated in the central city. Given this physical dimension of the information economy, the competitiveness of cities will depend upon the quality of their transport infrastructure, a simple but fundamental point which is overlooked in much of the telecommunications-centered literature on the highways of the twenty-first century, the wired city, and their expected impacts on urban economic and social life.

In advocating new engines of urban growth that link telematics with social overhead capital I am banking on a return to Keynesian economic policy, a U-turn from the free market ideology of Thatcherism and Reaganism which has led to a serious deterioration in pubilc infrastructure over the past two decades. Without major programmes of public capital investment the new marriages I favor will not materialize and cities are unlikely to reach the twenty-first century as dynamic economies and better places to live.

The Shrinking Information-Based Organisation

Geographers and planners have been impressed by the fact that cities have not dissolved in the spaceless-timeless world that telematics was expected to create. In this resistance to the all-consuming power of telematics, they point to an urban paradox—the geographer's equivalent to what western economists call the productivity paradox: why have massive investments in information technology not generated higher rates of productivity and economic growth as they were expected to do? In commenting on the economist's paradox, Paul David (1990) wisely observes that—like all revolutions—the impacts of the information technology revolution will come about in the long-term, owing to the gradual evolutionary nature of institutional change in capitalist societies. As economic institutions, firms are subject to the inertia of past investments in organization:

The information structures of firms (i.e., the type of data they collect and generate, the way they distribute and process it for interpretation) may be seen as the direct counterparts of the physical layouts and material flow patterns of production and transportation systems. In one sense they are, for they constitute a form of sunk costs, and the variable cost of utilising such a structure does not rise significantly as they age. Unlike those conventional structures and equipment stocks, however, information structures per se do not automatically undergo significant physical depreciation. Although they may become economically obsolete and be scrapped on that account, the mere passage of time to create occasions to radically redesign a firm's information structures and operating modes. Consequently there is likely to be a strong inertial component in the evolution of information-intensive production organisations.

Changes in the information structures of firms are at the heart of industrial reorganization throughout the economy, including the development of new information-intensive methods of manufacturing and distribution—factories of the future (Drucker, 1990), flexible specialization between networks of firms (Piore and Sabel, 1984), and the advanced logistics of just-in-time distribution (Hepworth and Ducatel, 1992). Geographical research suggests that information-intensive production has a variable spatial logic, but one that generally underlines the metropolitan bias of change in an increasingly globalised information economy:

- The greater use of specialist information services (R&D, production engineering, marketing, etc.) and highly-skilled labour in information-intensive production favours metropolitan regions.
- The transaction cost-minimising behaviour of firms organised around flexible specialisation and just-in-time production favours metropolitan regions.
- Metropolitan economies are increasingly locked into a new international division of labour being established by multinational corporations, whose "global reach" has been strengthened by transborder data flows over computer networks.
- The creation of supply chains based on electronic logistics favours "entrepot" cities as international trade-distribution centres, with this aspect of metropolitan dominance extending to cities with major airports for business travel and the shipment of high value-added/low weight products.

While cities appear to be favored by information-intensive production—within the context of global inter-urban competition—they are threatened by parallel technological and organisational changes which strike at the core of the metropolitan economy: information-based office activities. For over a century, and particularly after the decentralization of manufacturing industry, the metropolitan economy has been dependent upon the growth of office-based, information services. And historically, this growth of the metropolitan information economy has been concentrated in the great private and public bureaucracies, the command and control hierarchies of big firms and big governments. This is reflected in the city's built environment and mass transit systems, the tall or sprawling office blocks which are home to armies of white-collar commuters. There are now signs that these bureaucracies—the cornerstones of the twentieth century metropolitan economy—are starting to crack up in the face of organisational and technological innovation.

The intellectual and ideological attack on bureaucracies has come from two directions. First, within the private sector, the business schools are spearheading a "managerial revolution" based on new models of corporate organisation which involve streamlining, downsizing, and de-layering as the route to improved competitiveness, quality, and lower overhead costs. Second, within the public sector, these prescriptions for organizational change have converged with a wider politically motivated set of institutional reforms, which are intended to reduce the state's role as a direct provider of information services and public services generally in favour of the private sector. Thus, whereas the 1980s saw productivity rising due to income-generation, this decade's productivity growth will be fuelled by a mangerial revolution aimed at creating lean and mean organizations: the coming of the cost-cutter's knife.

For the metropolitan city, the coming of what Peter Drucker (1989) calls the information-based organisation has wide-ranging implications. My current research in the London Borough of Croydon, the sixth-largest office center in the U.K. confirms that corporate managers in all sectors are implementing the radical innovations prescribed by the managerial revolution. The general thrust of this organisational restructuring is towards reducing the costs of creating information for decision-making, with computer network technology playing a central role. In all sectors, shrinking the organization has involved reducing the number of management layers between the boardroom and employees closest to customer or supplier—the ideal number appears to be 3–4 management layers, with bounded rationality limiting the manager's spproximate scope of command to 20-person teams. Thus, I interviewed an insurance company which had shifted from a 12-layer to a 4-layer information structure of management—over 200 middle and junior managers lost their jobs as a result.

There are numerous aspects to downsizing as a general way of transforming the firm's information structure. Insurance companies are cutting out middlemen (brokers) by selling directly to customers over the telephone, with local area computer networks backing up the transaction; telebanking is being driven by the bank's efforts to cut back-office costs; noncore informational functions are being contracted out to specialist firms (e.g., credit checking and information technology services); electronic data interchange is creating direct links between manufacturers and retail/wholesale distibutors, so reducing the office labor time spent on paper-pushing (order-entry, invoicing, etc.); branch office networks are being scaled down, with routine information-processing services being concentrated into high tech data factories; and, full-time, permanent information workers are being replaced by part-time, short-term contract information workers (e.g., seasonal data-entry clerks, word-processing temps, interim managers, and telemarketing staff working twilight shifts between 6:30 P.M. and 9:00 P.M. to catch potential customers at home).

My interviews with Croydon employers have revealed all of these types of changes in the information structures of firms. There are also important spatial dimensions to corporate strategies aimed at cutting information costs. Relocating back office activity to cheaper urban locations is fairly common—for example, a credit information firm sends its data entry work to the Phillipines and India; an insurance company has concentrated all of its back office, support services in the low-cost northern towns of Oldham and Halifax. This predictable flow of back office information services to cheap-labor locations is widespread, but other intervening opportunites are being taken up by employers which short-circuit or run counter to long-distance spatial decentralisation. Several Croydon employers are using teleworking to decentralize routine information-processing work to local residential areas. More broadly, the recession has made London and South-East England more competitive as a mass information-processing location, as office rents and wages have fallen dramatically over the last few years. At the same time, the new technology has down-scaled the total labor and space requirements of back office work, creating options for firms to centralize routine information-processing functions at existing sites, whether these are located in half-used central London buildings or at branch/divisional offices in the capital's extensive outer-metropolitan hinterland.

The Croydon research suggests that changes in information structures at the level of the firm will have profound impacts on urban form and functioning. In general, the shrinking information-based organization needs less space and less people to generate more turnover and more profit. The physical manifestation of this shrinkage is that Croydon's office buildings are either empty or part-empty, and the new high tech office buildings are compact low-rise structures rather than capacious high-rise or lengthy structures. What is going to happen to all of this office space which dominates Croydon's town center? The same question applicable to the whole of London. In part, it is being demolished (both old and new buildings) or being rendered uninhabitable (to avoid business property taxes), or even being converted into residential dwellings.

But, the depressing reality is that vast and growing stocks of buildings and land—what Porat (1977) calls information capital—are going to waste and falling into dereliction. In this, I see obvious parallels with the physical havoc caused by deindustrialisation in manufacturing—wastelands of empty factory buildings and run-down infrastructure that developers and urban regeneration programs have failed to revive to any real extent. Looking into the future and assuming that present trends continue, I believe that downsizing in the information economy will produce the same results in the twenty-first century city.

The Lean-and-Mean City: Some Concluding Remarks

Just as the leanness and meanness of the information city threatens to wreck the urban physical environment, it poses an ugly threat to many people living and working in the metropolis. Before downsizing became part of business orthodoxy, occupational trends pointed to the development of a dual labor market, since job growth during the 1970s and 1980s was confined to relatively well-paid information occupations and poorly-paid lower-order service occupations (Hepworth, 1989). Both of these growth components have been extinguished by what is dubbed a white-collar recession. With downsizing cutting into information occupations, consumer services have been hit by a consequent fall in purchasing power. The engines of job-generation which carried cities through the 1970s and 1980s have ceased to function, and double-digit structural employment threatens to become a key feature of the 1990s. Metropolitan cities also have been hit hardest by this collapse, since their occupational structures have developed on the basis of highly polarized growth in information services and lower-order consumer services.

This recession has indeed hit white-collar workers, a full range of information occupations previously thought to be recession-proof, but it has also decimated blue-collar and service jobs in factories, warehouses, mines, shops, hospitals, and seemingly everywhere else. In the European

Community, there are now 20 million people out of work and the unemployed total is expected to climb higher as strong economies like Germany and the Benelux countries slide now into recession. In addition to carrying forward deeply-entrenched racial and gender inequalities into the twenty-first century, competition in the future labor market threatens to revolve around so called ageism. At one end of the spectrum, unemployment rates amongst young people (up to 25 years of age) are far greater that for the rest of the workforce—over 25 percent in Greater London; at the other end, the average age for what is euphemistically called early retirement has come down to 55, leaving 25 percent of the population with only their pensions to subsist on—ironically, just as life expectancy in industrialized countries has risen to beyond 70 years of age. My research in Croydon shows a new preference for recruiting amongst the so called Third Age population (Handy, 1989), employers calling back their retired staff on a contract basis rather than finding new trainees through local school and college recruitment drives. Employers justify this age discrimination on the grounds that young people are badly educated and have poor interpersonal communication skills, at a time when firms are developing more sensitive, customer-centered approaches to market competition. So, what are young people good for?

Against this gloomy background, the information city is developing without safety nets for a growing underclass of poor, homeless people cut off from decent health care, public transport, and other basic human services. In the U.K., at least, town halls are no longer battlegrounds for grassroots politics but function as information shops created by the Tory government's "citizen's charters," paper-scrolls which set out the rights of local public service consumers. Since public services have been cut back, local people are becoming information-rich and materially poorer—the window-shoppers of the information city. Basically, the cost-cutter's knife is laying waste to what remains of the Welfare State, and subjecting basic human services to the vagaries of the market which has left more and more people homeless, cut off from hospital care and abandoned by the educational system. According to national governments, there is no money to tackle these mounting social problems. The public sector borrowing requirement is already too mountainous and out of control, they say, and rebuilding the Welfare-Keynesian State is politically unrealistic in a world of tax-phobic citizens and inflation-phobic monetarist authorities.

The urban crisis is a political minefield that governments are reluctant to enter. In this context, global economic competition between cities has turned into a struggle for survival—a war for jobs, investment, and services fought below the level of nation states.

References

David, P. (1990). "The Dynamo and the Computer: A Historical Perspective on the Modern Productivity Paradox." *Papers and Proceedings of the American Economic Association*, 80(2):355–361.

Diamond, D., and Spence, N. (1989). *Infrastructure Costs and British Industry*. London: Department of Trade and Industry, HMSO.

Drucker, P. (1990). "The Emerging Theory of Manufacturing." *Harvard Business Review* (May–June):94–102.

Drucker, P. (1989). *The New Realities*. New York: Harper and Row.

Graham, S., and Dominy, G. (1991). "Planning for the Information City: The U.K. Case." *Progress in Planning* (33):169–248.

Handy, C. (1989). *The Age of Unreason*. London: Arrow Books.

Henderson, J. (1989). *The Globalisation of High Technology Production*. London: Routledge.

Hepworth, M. (1993). "Croydon: The European Communications City." London: Borough of Croydon Publication.

Hepworth, M. (1992). "Telecommunications and the Future of London." *Policy Studies* 13(2):31–45.

Hepworth, M. (1989). *Geography of the Information Economy*. London: Belhaven Press.

Hepworth, M., and Ducatel, K. (1992). *Transport in the Information Age*. London: Belhaven Press.

London Research Centre. (1992). *Telecommunications in London: The Role of Local Authorities*. London: LRC publications.

Piore, M., and Sabel, C. (1984). *The Second Industrial Divide*. New York: Basic Books.

Reich, R. (1992). *The Work of Nations*. New York: Simon and Schuster.

Commentary by Nicholas Garnham

It is well known that in Marxist political economy the basic structural contradiction is the antagonistic relationship between capital and labour. Many of the social problems created by the capitalist mode of production stem from the tendency within such a mode of production to treat human labour as a commodity like any other and thus create a system of commodity fetishism which makes human beings work for it rather than it working for human beings.

One form the antagonistic relation between capital and labor takes is their differential potential for spatial mobility. Capital having no necessary permanent physical embodiment can flow relatively freely through global time and space. The human laborer on the other hand is inevitably spatially and temporally rooted. The school of economic geography within which Hepworth works focuses on this problem and on the processes of uneven development that result.

In recent years economic geographers have in particular been concerned with the impact on the spatial organization of production in general and on the future of cities in particular of developments in information technology and global communication networks. A central thesis of the post-industrial, information society thesis was that cities were the product of a historical period in which economic activity was dominated by large-scale manufacturing production and the costs of transport meant that huge competitive advantages stemmed from exploiting the economies of propinquity. According to the post-industrialists the shift to a service based economy allied to the development and convergence of electronic information manipulation, storage and communication would lead to the inexorable decline of cities as the efficient economic scale of organisations declined and as work could come to workers rather than vice-versa. This development was seen as socially benign. Urban centers were endowed with the negative images of "dark satanic mills," congestion, dirt, and crime rather than with their classic positive image as the very fount of civilized living. The positive image of the new built environment was that of suburbia on the U.S. model and Alvin Toffler's "electronic cottage" calm, peaceable, environmentally friendly, inhabited by autonomous professional workers, active in their communities, and linked by electronic rather than physical highways.

Hepworth valuably undercuts this misleading new age nostalgia. He is concerned with two questions in relation to the global development of the information economy. First the question of the continuing survival of metropolitan urban centers and second the impact of the information and communication technology revolution on urban form itself. In answering those questions he presents a black picture with which it is hard in general to disagree.

He argues that the first phase of the information revolution, particularly the growth of the financial services sector and of information based office work, far from destroying metropolitan urban centers reinforced their advantages. However these sectors now experience the same impacts of global competition previously experienced by traditional manufacturing and the continuing health of metropolitan centers is now threatened by the crash of the world's financial service sector and a resulting intense global competition between them to locate jobs and investment. In this process established centers in Western Europe and North America are vulnerable to competition from Eastern European and Asian urban centers. This trend is further accelerated by the ability to use communication networks to send routine information work offshore to low wage Third World locations. At the same time his research shows that those economic activities typically located in urban centers are now being down sized and that all urban centers are now suffering from the de-industrialization of information work. This is creating a massive devaluation of information capital in the shape both of the existing urban built environment geared to servicing the office economy and of the skilled, urban based, information work force.

Hepworth argues that the only possible response to this crisis is a major policy shift. He advocates a combination of public sector led Keynesian investment in urban infrastructures and services ranging from public transport to health, education and cultural services which recognises that the information economy continues to run on "wheels" as well as "wires" and that the economic advantage of the metropolitan urban center lies in the flexibility and variety of its human capital. Linked to this investment strategy he sees a linkage of telematics to the service sector, in for example urban transport and health care, as the locus of the new engine of economic growth that such urban centers need. It is here that I part company with his argument. First given the generally intense global competitive environment within which his cities are, he argues, operating it is hard to see where the policy change he advocates is likely to come from. How will any such urban center be strong enough, on its own, to sustain the deficit financing that such a strategy would require on a declining tax base. This reveals the essential weakness of an urban centered analysis abstracted from the national and international political economy within which such centers are located. Such an analysis still has too much of the nostalgia for the city state, as opposed to the nation state with its metropolitan center or centers, which this tradition of urban geography inherits, and which has been revived by the post-modern fashion for localism, and too easily assumes that the days of the nation state are numbered in the face of globalisation and that industrial districts are the new flexibly specialized answer to the problems of economic development in these new times. Secondly supposing the new technologies and associated expertise he advocates, for instance in transport telematic systems, were to be developed, why should they remain located in the center which originated them? Will they not also be subject to the same processes of global competition and mobility that Hepworth analyses as undermining both the economic health and physical structure of our contemporary metropolitan centers?

9 THE EMERGING MASS MEDIA ENVIRONMENT

Barry R. Litman and Scott Sochay

I. Globalization

Trends

The late 1980s saw the beginnings of two important trends in the communications industry. The first was a series of mergers in which four of the seven major Hollywood studios combined with other corporate conglomerates. The second is a continuing trend toward deregulation in the international entertainment industry that helped the first trend emerge.

In 1989, Sony purchased Columbia Entertainment, and Time, Inc., and Warner Communications merged. In 1990, Pathé Communications acquired MGM/UA and Matsushita bought MCA. The strategic momentum behind these mergers is the concept of globalization.[1]

Globalization can best be understood as a two-pronged approach focusing on the changing global media market. First, the growth of foreign markets (especially in Europe) and the rapid development of new electronic technologies have greatly increased demand and the revenue streams for entertainment programming. Second, to fill this increased demand, there is a growing perception in the communications industry that to survive in the marketplace, it is essential to become a global media colossus.

This perception is fueled by the economics of the motion picture entertainment industry which is characterized by high fixed costs and high risks. An entertainment company needs the financing and marketing clout to produce enough software to give itself more opportunities to bring home a hit. By merging or consolidating, an entertainment company can not only spread its risk, but through vertical integration can back up its product with distribution and sales outlets as well. When a consumer electronics firm such as Sony or Matsushita acquires a portion of the entertainment industry, in effect, it merges the hardware and software markets (*The Economist*, March 11, 1989, p. 65).

Mergers

A look at the four recent mergers demonstrates this strategy. Sony's strategy was to complement its strength in hardware (electronics) with a software (programming) library. Columbia's library of 23,000 television episodes and 2,700 films, along with its Loews circuit of theaters, and its previous acquisition of CBS Records, allows Sony to produce software to play on its electronic components such as its 8 mm format videocassette and DAT audiocassette players. It may also help Sony become a leader in the developing market for HDTV, global satellite networks and other future technologies (*Time*, October 9, 1989, p. 70; *Institutional Investor*, January, 1990, p. 139).

Time Inc.'s merger with Warner Communications came about partly because of its need to become more competitive in the international market and partly because it feared that it might be relegated to second class status in the emerging global lineup. Time-Warner saw its merger as an opportunity to have a stronger impact on film and television programming in the European market (*Advertising Age*, March 20, 1989, p. 16).

Pathé Communications' acquisition of MGM/UA was part of an overall strategy to create a wide ranging international conglomerate. MGM/UA gave Pathé network television and syndication capabilities as well as a 1,200 title film library to mesh with its 1,000-theater network in Europe (*Broadcasting*, March 12, 1990, p. 31).

The last mega-merger saw Matsushita (the world's largest consumer electronics firm) acquire MCA. With growth in the electronics market slowing, Matsushita pictured Sony's move into the entertainment industry as a competitive challenge. Sony's acquisition of Columbia had given it an edge in software which, in turn, could direct the consumer electronics market to purchase Sony products. Acquiring MCA gave Matsushita equivalent access to music through MCA Records, films through Universal Pictures and film distribution through Cineplex Odeon theaters. Matsushita now had software of its own to complement its electronic hardware. It also wanted to position itself to be a leading marketer of HDTV and enhance its international image (*Time*, October 8, 1990, p. 63; December 10, 1990, p. 68; *Wall Street Journal*, September 26, 1990, p. A6).

Issues

The MCA deal has heightened American awareness of the Japanese economic presence in the United States and has raised fears of foreign control over American culture. The Japanese invested $12 billion in American entertainment companies between 1988 and 1990 and project this industry to be the fastest growing global industry in the next decade (*Fortune*, December 31, 1990, p. 50).

Worldwide, when people want to experience pop culture they are turning increasingly to exports from the United States. American software, movies, music, television programming and home video are at the top of the American export list, outranked only by the aerospace industry. In the past five years, the overseas revenues of Hollywood studios doubled, and in a few years should surpass domestic revenues (*Fortune*, December 31, 1990, p. 50).

The common consensus is that American movies are the only ones that are truly international; and nobody knows how to make commercial motion pictures better than the Hollywood studios. Simply put, Hollywood has developed product that the Japanese and Europeans can't improve on. As a result, both have bought large portions of the United States entertainment industry and seem positioned to acquire more. Strategically and economically, it makes more sense for these foreign firms to acquire a Hollywood studio that gives them a preexisting library of programming to plug into the growing international market than to build their own studios from scratch.

This chapter will build on the globalization context discussed above and analyze the emerging mass media environment of the 1990s. It will focus on three main areas: conglomeration, cross-media ownership and synergy. The analysis begins with a closer look at globalization; the driving force behind much of the increasing conglomeration in the mass media.

II. Conglomerate Mergers: Theory

Overview

The communications industry is in the midst of a corporate revolution that has been dubbed "globalization." At the heart of this process is the idea that for a corporation to stay competitive in the changing international communications industry it must continue to expand in global dimensions. This picture is complicated by the fact that not only are communications companies expanding through mergers and joint ventures, noncommunications firms are diversifying into the communications field by acquiring existing media firms.

Table 9–1 provides a brief profile on some of the major players in media globalization. Two extremes in diversification are evident. In some instances, large conglomerates are diversifying into the communications industry, yet are only involved in one segment of the industry. General Electric illustrates this type of diversification. Communications revenues account for only five and one half percent of total corporate revenues and these revenues are concentrated within one segment; broadcasting. On the other end of the spectrum, Time-Warner derives one hundred percent of corporate revenues from the communications industry yet, is extremely diversified within segments of the industry; deriving roughly one quarter of its revenues from each of the four communications segments it is involved in; cable television, filmed entertainment, recorded music, and consumer and business magazines. In between lie various combinations of conglomerates with differential amounts of diversification into and within the communications industry. Such size and diversification greatly complicates the analysis of market structure, conduct and performance.

This section will attempt to explore the recent trends in conglomerateness within the context of the dynamics of the current communications markets. Such an analysis is no easy task and must be preliminary in its conclusions since the current dynamics are still in the beginning stages of transforming the communications industry as we know it.

The difficulty of the task is well expressed by Mueller (1990) when he says:

> The power that conglomerates have within a particular industry depends on their market position, not just in that one industry but in all their other lines of

THE EMERGING MASS MEDIA ENVIRONMENT

Table 9–1. Diversification of Selected Media Conglomerates ($ figures in millions)

Company	1990 Total Corporate Revenue	1990 Total Communications Revenue	Total Com. Revenue as % of total Corporate	TV & Radio B-casting 1990	%	Cable TV 1990	%	Filmed Entertainment 1990	%	Recorded Music 1990	%	Newspaper Publishing 1990	%	Book Publishing 1990	%	Consumer & Business Magazines 1990	%
Bertelsmann A.G.	2,659.5	2,616.2	98.4							1,804.0	69.0			812.2	31.0		
Capital Cities/ABC	5,385.6	5,385.6	100.0	4,283.6	79.5											1,102.0	20.5
CBS	3,261.2	3,261.2	100.0	3,261.2	100.0												
Walt Disney Co.	5,843.7	2,250.3	38.5					2,250.3	100.0								
Gannett	3,443.3	3,443.3	100.0	396.7	11.5							2,775.2	80.6				
General Electric (NBC)	58,414.0	3,236.0	5.5	3,236.0	100.0												
News Corp.	6,719.7	3,040.0	45.2	850.0	28.0			990.0	32.6			250.0	8.2			950.0	31.3
Paramount	3,869.0	3,869.0	100.0					2,446.7	63.2					1,422.3	36.8		
Polygram N.V.	3,108.0	3,108.0	100.0							3,108.0	100.0						
Sony	25,649.1	5,188.1	20.2					1,826.5	35.2	3,361.6	64.8						
Telecommunications Inc. (TCI)	3,625.0	2,942.0	81.2			2,942.0	100.0										
Time-Warner	11,778.0	11,778.0	100.0			3,017.0	25.6	2,904.0	24.3	2,931.0	24.9					2,926.0	24.8

Source for all tables: The Veronis, Suhler & Associates Communications Industry Report, 1986–1991 Annual Editions. Limitations for this table and all tables following: Data only includes publicly held companies and private companies that report publicly. Further, some conglomerates do not break out financial information for its communications subsidiaries and are therefore not included in the data.

business, at home and abroad. When the same huge firms are among the leading producers in separate industries, the industry lines themselves may become blurred. This does not mean that traditional industrial organization theory and research are meaningless, but rather, that conglomeration should be considered an additional structural variable when explaining behavior in many contemporary industries.[2]

This blurring of industry lines not only makes it more difficult to separate the effects of conglomerateness on the structure of a large firm from the structure of any individual market, but globalization also makes it difficult to separate these trends from more traditional concentration and cross-ownership activities.

The current worldwide demand for communications software (i.e., programming) has served to make previously infeasible markets ripe for development. To this end, prior constraints on economic growth in new markets no longer hold. This has fueled the pressure to expand and acquire production, distribution and exhibition bases in these new markets. However, for firms currently outside of established markets, capturing demand in these markets is more difficult. The existing barriers to entry may inhibit the development of new competitors. As a result, *it becomes easier to seek to acquire or merge with firms that are already established.* These realities also fuel the growth of worldwide conglomerate corporations. Firms wanting to be key players in the emerging global communications market realize that they need to have a base in Asia, Europe, and North America.

Globalization is fueled by more than the desire to be a corporate giant. Other factors such as the exponential growth of new technologies and the trend in the international deregulation of mass communication industries have become major forces in the changing face of the communications landscape. Each of these factors also has multiple consequences.

Technology

Irwin (1984) argues that the characteristics of technology impact the entry process into the telecommunications field. Technology has several important properties. It is diverse and spans a multitude of disciplines. Technologies also interact, couple and combine in new ways. They foster productivity—multiplying the features and functions of hardware and software (Irwin, 1984, pp. 45–46). As a result of these characteristics, product options expand (more and new substitutes), costs decline, prospects for profits increase, and capital investment as an economic barrier diminishes.

THE EMERGING MASS MEDIA ENVIRONMENT 239

Technology also erodes boundary lines. Not only can it alter the structural lines within an industry, it can also erode lines along geographic, spatial, sectoral and global dimensions. As a result, boundary lines are no longer static or isolated and every market enters into a dynamic flux in which the competitors of today and the competitors of tomorrow are not easily discerned.

Irwin (1984) characterizes this process by noting that the entry process facilitated by new technology tends to destabilize the familiar relationships and traditional lines of demarcation between buyers, sellers, customers, and suppliers. Such an environment can be depicted as shown in Figure 1.

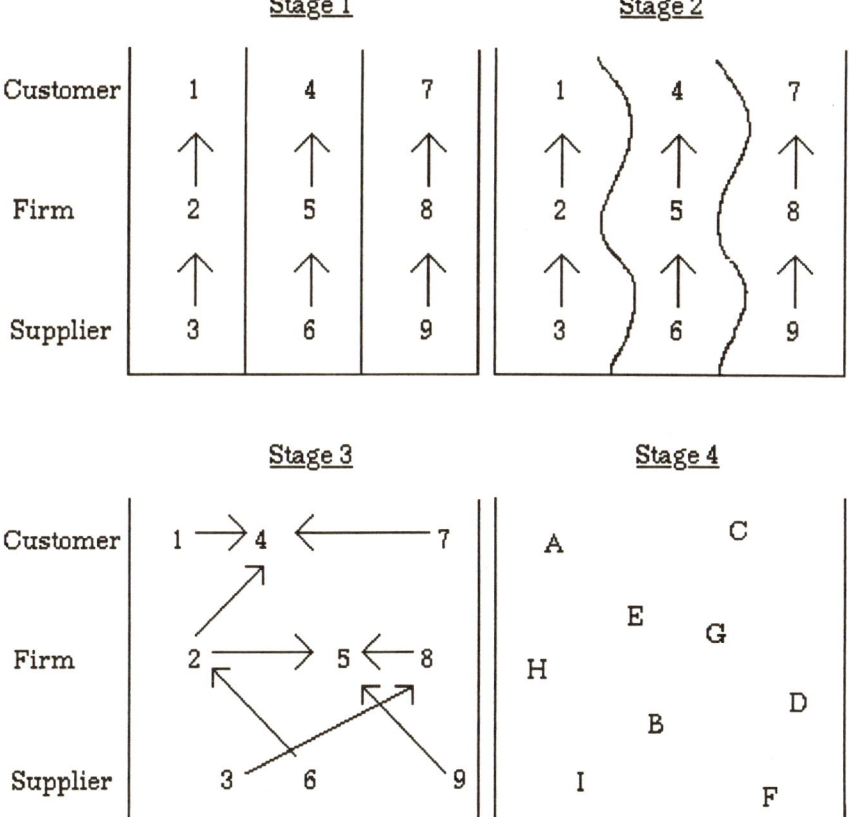

Figure 1.   Irwin's Model of the Erosion of Market Relationships
Source: Adapted from Irwin, Manley Rutherford (1984). *Telecommunications America: Markets Without Boundaries*, Quorom Books, Westport, CT, p. 68.

In stage 1, the environment for any given firm is relatively stable. Rivals and suppliers are known and boundary lines are fixed. As a result, market conditions are relatively peaceful. In stage 2, new technology is introduced. Boundary lines begin to blur as technology introduces new products and features. Still, relationships between firms are relatively stable. In stage 3, suppliers may become rivals, and rivals suppliers. Firms cross industry lines as technology fosters substitutes that blur the distinctions between two adjacent industries. In stage 4, everything is in a state of flux; industry lines have dissolved, and the relationships between rivals, suppliers and new entrants is difficult to ascertain from day to day. In fact, new entities emerge that defy the traditional categories of classification (represented by the alphabetical rather than numerical designations). This new environment contains combinations of media that haven't been seen before (Irwin, 1984, pp. 67–68).

As Irwin (1984) sums up this new environment:

> Technology and market entry impart a profound effect on the environment of the firm. Relationships uncouple not only within a single industry but also among adjacent and even remote industries. The erosion process produces an environment of intensified, even frantic competition. That new competition marks the essence of an emerging environment (pp. 71–72).

Current Technological Environment

The emerging media environment is typified by the recent negotiations between IBM and Time-Warner to seek ways to combine IBM's data transmission technology with Time-Warner's programming and cable television systems. This proposed joint venture would use IBM technology to store video images in compressed form and then deliver programming directly into viewers' homes. Digital technology will also allow the system to develop interactive television—along the lines of services currently offered by Prodigy or Compuserve, using the television set at home, in addition to video on demand. This venture merges computers, communications, mass media and home electronics technology into one package (*Wall Street Journal*, April 30, p. B1).

In addition, the telephone companies aren't standing idle as transmission technologies merge with the mass media. For example, Pacific Telesis Group's Pacific Bell is developing a transmission system that will allow movie studios to send films directly to theaters through fiber optic telephone lines. Sony Pictures is involved in the testing and development of this system (*Wall Street Journal*, April 30, 1992, p. B1).

From the above illustrations it can be seen that the interaction between technology and conditions of entry creates a new dynamic of intensified competition and an increased flow of new products. These factors fuel each other and intensify the process creating an ever accelerating spiral of new competition and barrier disintegration. This is the final stage in a process analogous to what Schumpeter called the "gale of creative destruction" and which has permeated the entire fabric of the communications industry.

In addition to technology, deregulation has similarly affected the structure of the communications industry. Deregulation serves as an instrument that tends to blur industry lines. As countries have moved to privatize their media structures, the relationships between public and private sectors, customers, firms and suppliers blurs. New entrants into previously state monopolized industries create new competition and new forms of relationships between competitors. Broadcasting is a good example of this trend toward deregulation. In some respects, broadcasting has benefited as national systems have been privatized. On the other hand, deregulation has also opened the door for rival delivery systems to compete for access and revenues.

III. Conglomerate Mergers: Research

Motives

These convergent forces raise questions relevant to the issue of conglomeration. Why do firms diversify, and what do they expect as a result of acquiring a firm in another industry?

A number of motives for conglomerate mergers can be posited. The most frequent justification cited is synergism. This concept can be expressed in the notion that the sum is greater than the parts, that is, the combination of two firms will produce efficiencies at a level greater than either firm alone could. One primary efficiency that is enhanced is economies of scale—the belief that management expertise can carry over to the acquired firm and improve its performance. Another belief is that debt capacity can be increased. A final justification springs out of the previous discussion; firms (especially those in established industries) must diversify and expand in order to survive.[3]

If these motivations are representative of the real reasons conglomerate mergers occur, then they should manifest themselves in improved corporate performance. Several studies exploring the performance of conglomerate mergers shed light on this question.

Research

Hogarty (1970) analyzed the past fifty years of research concerning the profitability of mergers and found that the consensus was that these mergers have "a neutral or negative impact on profitability." (Hogarty, 1970, p. 389). Mueller (1977), analyzed similar data and found that in general, conglomerate mergers did not improve profitability or stock values. In addition, he raised the question of whether the motivations for these mergers was really related to the increase of stockholder wealth (Mueller, 1977, p. 339).

Ravenscraft and Scherer (1987) analyzed the mergers of the 1960s and 1970s by looking at the premerger and postmerger performances of over 600 acquisitions. They found that typically, profitability and market share for the acquired company declined. This result was amplified when considering only pure conglomerate mergers (Ravenscraft and Scherer, 1987).

The most current analysis of conglomerate mergers was conducted by Lee and Cooperman (1989). They proposed other motivations for conglomerate mergers under the heading of agency theory. This theory suggests that "a separation of ownership from control permits managers to pursue personal goals including increased compensation by means of size maximization, ego satisfaction, and reduced unemployment risk" (Lee and Cooperman, 1989). If the traditional motivations held, then on average, conglomerate firms should out-perform nonconglomerate firms. If not, agency theories cannot be ruled out as prime motivations for conglomerate mergers. Their analysis showed that conglomerates exhibited some synergies in depreciation, interest expense, and administrative and marketing costs. They did not demonstrate efficiencies in production, nor did they perform better in terms of returns. A secondary analysis resulted in an interesting finding related to the degree of diversification, i.e., the number of industries in which the firm operates. They found that the more concentrated conglomerates, operating in three industries, demonstrated superior performance and that performance deteriorated as more industries were added (Lee and Cooperman, 1989, p. 51). This suggests that there may be a maximum number of industries that a conglomerate can efficiently be involved in.

In light of the majority of this evidence Mueller (1990) concludes:

> There is now overwhelming research evidence that considerations other than efficiency motivate most large conglomerate mergers. But a question still remains: Even though large conglomerate mergers generally do not promote efficiency, are there reasons for placing restraints on mergers? One reason for

concern with conglomerate mergers is that they result in greater overall concentration of economic power, with a concomitant increase in corporate political power (p. 325).

Effects

In addition to Mueller's concern, economists generally agree that there are three potentially harmful effects associated with conglomerate mergers; cross-subsidization, reciprocity, and competitive forbearance. It can be noted that these practices are not limited to conglomerates, vertically integrated firms may also engage in these practices.[4]

If a conglomerate generates excess profits in one market it has the ability to shift profits to other markets and cross-subsidize other operations. The impact of this practice may be to lessen competition through the ability of the conglomerate to engage in predatory pricing and have "deeper pockets" with which to survive a lengthy price war.

Further, a conglomerate can also engage in reciprocal selling. Its large purchasing presence in several fields can serve as leverage to induce suppliers to buy from the conglomerate. Such a situation short circuits the normal buying process in a market and may harm the ability of smaller firms to generate sales and thus compete on a level playing field.

Finally, conglomerates may come to realize that they have common interdependencies with other conglomerates in several markets. This may in turn foster a spirit of cooperation across industries as they forbear competition in one market to avoid competition in another. Such an arrangement serves to lessen the amount of competition that would occur in an otherwise free marketplace.

How real are the effects of these potential practices? Measuring their impact is not a simple matter. Cross-subsidization information is generally proprietary and not available for analysis. Reciprocity is hard to ascertain without access to the bidding processes. Mutual interdependence and competitive forbearance inferences tend to be anecdotal in nature.

There has been one study that has attempted to get at the heart of these issues. Under these conglomerate practices, economists generally agree that small firms will find it difficult to survive and grow. Gort and Swanson (1983) tested this assumption by hypothesizing that if conglomerate mergers and subsequent practices affect the ability of small firms to compete then small firms should exhibit lower growth rates relative to conglomerates in the postmerger period, and the number of small firms in a market should decrease as well. They studied the 50 largest conglomerate mergers between 1947 and 1977 and found that there was no support for the assumptions that large firms would exhibit better growth rates or reduce the number of small firms in a market (Gort and Swanson, 1983). Such a result calls into question the real impacts of conglomerate mergers.

Given the above discussion, how have firms in the communications industry reacted to the new forces and trends shaping the markets of the future? Smith points out corporations are coming to realize that control over information and software is critical to long term survival (Smith, 1991). Not only is it cheaper to acquire control over programming, it also minimizes risk. No matter what new delivery systems emerge due to technological innovation, programming will be needed to fill the new capacity. A company with control over programming (and its distribution rights) is somewhat insulated from the new competitive pressures and faces less risk. However, firms also find it advantageous to be involved in delivery systems in order to insure access for its programming when the new delivery system is launched.

To better understand the dynamics of the changing communications industry, one must look at recent structural changes. It is to this type of empirical analysis that we now turn our attention.

IV. Structure And Trends in the Communications Industry

Measures

If it is difficult to assess the impact of conglomerate mergers it is equally as difficult to specify measures of conglomerateness. Litman (1991) highlights this when he says:

> There are several techniques for assessing absolute firm size and conglomerateness. The simplest is to seek some sort of ranking such as the Fortune 500 or 1000 and identify those firms whose corporate parents occupy such positions. Alternatively, one can calculate the sales or assets of the firm in the product line under investigation and compare them to those of the parent corporation.... There are no standard rules of thumb for assessing the degree of conglomerateness or absolute size differentials. One can only look for wide variations between firms in an industry as possible explanations for unconventional or unusual market behavior (pp. 25–26).

In addition to the measures Litman proposes, Dimmick and Wallschaeger (1986) have proposed a measure of diversification from the resource dependence perspective. This measure indexes the proportion of pretax profits contributed by each division within a diversified firm and indicates a firm's survival potential in a changing environment (Dimmick and Wallschlaeger, 1986, pp. 3–5).

The following analysis will incorporate some of the measures noted above as well as other measures developed from the data set.[5] No single measure tells the complete story of the conglomerateness of the communications industry; rather, each measure reveals a different facet of the phenomenon.

1. Fortune 500 Rankings

The first measure of the structural changes in the communications industry is indicated by the Fortune 500 rankings of the 100 largest diversified services companies in the United States. In 1986, eight communications firms made the list and two were in the top ten. By 1991, twelve communications firms were listed and four were in the top ten. It is illustrative to note that in 1986, CBS was ranked in the top ten (8th), and American Broadcasting was ranked seventeenth. In 1991, CBS was still the highest ranked broadcasting concern but its ranking had fallen to thirty-first. Turner Broadcasting was the only other broadcasting firm to make the listing, coming in at number seventy-three. While it is not reasonable to draw conclusions from such gross measures, they do provide a backdrop for the data that follows. These figures would seem to indicate that relative to other industries, the communications industry has undergone considerable corporate growth over the past five years. It would also seem to indicate that broadcasting firms have not been blessed by this growth trend. It remains to be seen how much of the growth in the communications industry can be attributed to conglomerate mergers.

2. Market Power

The next two measures can be considered rough measures of market power.[6] The first of these measures is the distribution of communication company size as a function of revenue. If the number of large firms is growing at a significantly greater rate than the number of small firms it would indicate that conglomerate merger activity is present in the communications industry. Table 9–2 shows exactly that trend. The number of companies with revenues of one billion dollars or more has doubled in the last five years. This is four times the growth rate of the next fastest growing segment. Further, the two smallest firm categories are down 24 and 32 percent respectively; the only two categories to show declines over the last six years. Given stability in the number of firms, the redistribution of size favoring very large firms suggests the simultaneous occurrence of mergers and new entry.

Similarly, using another data series extending back to 1981, within the communications industry universe the overall number of firms with one billion dollars or more in assets has increased from two in 1981 to thirty-nine in 1990. Within these industries it can be seen that significant market power is potentially possible in television/radio broadcasting (from 1 to 7 firms), cable systems (from 1 to 10 firms), and filmed entertainment (from 1 to 9 firms). While some of this growth can be attributed to internal expansion, the majority of firms have attained this size through acquisition. Taken together, these two measures show an increase in conglomerate size both in the communications industry as a whole and within important segments, thus enhancing the potential to wield market power.

3. Cross-Ownership

Another approach is to examine two measures of cross-ownership of communication firms. The more diversified firms are within the industry, the more opportunities there are for reciprocity and mutual forbearance. One measure looks at the number of segments in the communications industry that companies participate in. Table 9–3 shows that overall, diversification within the industry has been relatively stable. The number of companies operating in two segments of the industry is up slightly but this is appears to be at the expense of the number of companies that are in three segments.

The next measure tries to get behind this aggregate data to see what is actually happening in each segment of the communications industry. Table 9–4 shows that some segments (newspapers, film, books and magazines) are becoming more diversified, while other segments (TV/Radio, cable) are either stable or less diversified.[7] Such trends may reflect the relative attractiveness of each industry. For broadcasting, this would suggest an unfavorable competitive position vis-a-vis newspapers, film, and books and magazines. In combination, the print segments demonstrate relatively more diversification than the broadcast and programming segments.[8] Correspondingly, while the film, and print industries (books and magazines) are becoming more diversified, the number of companies

Table 9-2. Distribution of Company Size as a Function of Revenue (B = Billion, M = million)

Company Size	1990		1989		1988		1987		1986		1985	
	# of Cos.	%	# of Cos.	%	# of Cos.	%	# of Cos.	%	# of Cos.	%	# of Cos.	%
$1 B+	40	14.6	34	12.7	28	10.2	26	9.8	20	7.5	20	7.2
$500M–$1B	22	8.0	22	8.2	19	6.9	19	7.2	23	8.6	18	6.4
$100M–$500M	69	25.2	67	25.0	68	24.7	61	23.0	57	21.3	66	23.7
$50M–$100M	39	14.2	32	11.9	27	9.8	33	12.5	29	10.9	31	11.1
$10M–50M	52	19.0	56	20.9	64	23.3	61	23.0	68	25.5	68	24.4
$1M–$10M	52	19.0	57	21.3	69	25.1	65	24.5	70	26.2	76	27.2
Total	274	100	268	100	275	100	265	100	267	100	279	100

Table 9–3. Number of Segments of the Communication Industry that Companies Participate in

Category	1990		1989		1988		1987		1986	
	# of cos.	share	# of cos.	share	# of cos.	share	# of cos.	share	# of cos.	share
1 Segment	223	81.4	217	81.0	229	83.3	217	81.9	219	82.0
2 Segments	39	14.2	38	14.2	30	10.9	30	11.3	29	10.9
3 Segments	5	1.8	5	1.8	9	3.3	10	3.8	12	4.5
4 Segments	7	2.6	7	2.6	7	2.5	8	3.0	6	2.2
5 Segments	0	0.0	1	0.4	0	0.0	0	0.0	1	0.4
Total	274	100	268	100	275	100	265	100	267	100

THE EMERGING MASS MEDIA ENVIRONMENT

Table 9–4. Distribution of Single Segment Companies by Segment

Segment	1990 A	1990 B	1990 C	1989 A	1989 B	1989 C	1988 A	1988 B	1988 C	1987 A	1987 B	1987 C	1986 A	1986 B	1986 C
TV/Radio	35	64	55	37	67	55	38	67	57	36	67	54	35	66	53
Cable	34	44	77	35	46	76	38	50	76	33	45	73	36	53	68
Film	28	38	74	36	48	75	43	53	81	40	50	80	38	49	78
Music	3	6	50	3	6	50	2	4	50	3	6	50	2	5	40
NP's	11	38	29	12	39	31	9	36	25	11	37	30	11	34	32
Books	13	25	52	13	25	52	12	20	60	15	24	63	18	28	64
Mags.	10	24	42	10	24	42	15	28	54	12	29	41	14	29	48
Bus. Info	44	52	85	28	35	80	23	28	82	24	31	77	24	31	77
Ad Age.	9	9	100	11	11	100	10	11	91	9	9	100	9	10	90
Misc.	36	44	82	32	40	80	39	47	83	34	41	83	30	39	77
Total	223	344	65	217	341	63	229	344	67	217	339	64	217	344	63

A = number of companies with no other communications business
B = total number of companies in segment
C = single segment company share of market

with no other communications business besides film or print, respectively, has dropped in the same period. Since the single segment firms tend to be the smaller firms, this runs counter to the findings of Gort and Swanson and suggests that increasing conglomeration in the film and print industries may be having an adverse effect on competition within these industries.

4. Conglomerateness

The final measures are more direct measures of conglomerateness. If the proportion of companies in which noncommunication interests are primary is increasing, and/or communication related revenue as a proportion of total corporate revenue is declining, we can surmise that the level of conglomeration within the communications industry is increasing.

The first of the conglomerate measures looks at the relationship between the number of companies that have communications or noncommunications as their primary line of business. The percentage of companies in which communication is the primary or only business has decreased at a slow rate (from 86.9% of the communications industry in 1986 to 82.1% in 1990). Reversing this finding, the percentage of communications companies in which noncommunications interests are primary is increasing, but again only at a very slow rate (from 13.1% in 1986 to 17.9% in 1990).

The next two measures explore this finding in greater detail. These measures look at the proportion of total revenues companies derive from communication segments. If the proportion of corporate revenues attributable of communications interests is declining, this is an indication that conglomerateness and presumably conglomerate power in the marketplace is increasing.

Table 9–5 shows the results of the first of these measures in comparing the contribution of communication revenues to the corporate revenues of the industry as a whole. The data show a marked decrease in the proportion of communications revenue as a proportion of total corporate revenue. Before commenting on the implications of this finding, it would be best to incorporate the results of the next measure which looks at similar data for the top ten percent of the firms in terms of revenues in the communications industry. If this data show similar patterns, conclusions drawn about the impacts of conglomeration are heightened in significance since intuitively larger conglomerates would have more opportunities to engage in anti-competitive practices.

Table 9-5. Percentage of Communication/Non-Communication Revenues for Communication Industry ($ mil.)

Year	# of Cos.	Total Revenues	Com. Revenues	% Com/Total
1990	274	388,403.3	141,733.7	36.5
1989	268	324,565.8	122,400.8	37.7
1988	275	185,504.9	98,111.7	52.9
1987	265	171,895.3	88,751.7	51.6
1986	267	156,265.5	77,103.0	49.3

This second measure indeed shows a similar pattern. The proportion of communications revenues as a function of total corporate revenues has decreased dramatically since 1989. Further, the gap in these proportions has increased at a faster rate for the top 10% of the firms than for the communications industry as a whole. Hence, the largest corporations are driving the trend.

Taken together, these last two measures indicate a significant movement towards conglomeration that was masked by the initial measurement in this section. It now remains to compare the results of the data analysis with the theories of conglomerate impact outlined in section one. It will be instructive however, to explore two other areas related to conglomerateness; cross-ownership and synergy, before coming to any conclusions.

V. Cross-Ownership

Preliminary Considerations

Even with trends toward conglomeration and the globalization philosophy, the ability to acquire and merge with communications industry firms is not absolute. In many countries, these industries are nationalized; hence, private acquisitions of the media aren't possible. However, as privatization of the media moves outward from Europe to Eastern Europe and beyond, new opportunities open for media conglomerates to expand. New technologies and new delivery systems also provide opportunities to expand global communications networks.

Several forces keep global media giants from getting bigger. The first is non-regulatory—the finite capital available in financial markets that fuel the acquisitions process. The second is regulatory. In the United States, this involves both anti-trust and FCC cross-ownership rules. It is to FCC policy that we now turn in order to analyze trends in the FCC's philosophy of media ownership.

FCC Regulations

Beginning in the late 1930s, the FCC began to promulgate rules that affected broadcast ownership. Beginning with AM radio and later expanding to FM, television, newspapers and cable, regulations were put forth that restricted ownership both within and across media and markets. These regulations had a dual purpose; they were designed to maximize competition and to promote diversity in the number of voices on the airwaves. Consistent with the public interest philosophy of broadcast regulation, cross-ownership rules were designed to promote "the widest possible dissemination of information from diverse and antagonistic sources essential to the welfare of the public" (McGregor, 1988).

As early as 1944, the FCC looked into prohibitions against ownership of a newspaper and a broadcast station in the same market. The FCC was concerned that such a combination could lead to a monopoly on information in a given community. In 1975, the FCC prohibited the ownership of either AM, FM, or television stations by daily newspapers in the same market. Although some existing combinations were grandfathered, many were ordered to divest. To date, despite the trend toward deregulation, no serious movements have been made to change these ownership restrictions (Second Report and Order, 1975; Zuckman et al., pp. 403–404).

In 1984, the FCC revised its thirty year old "7-7-7 rule," which limited the number of stations broadcasters could own. The new rule allowed for a single broadcaster to own up to 12 TV, AM and FM stations (up to 14-14-14 if at least two of each type of station was minority-controlled) with certain restrictions. One key restriction limited a broadcaster's potential audience to twenty-five percent of the nation's households. The FCC also retained the duopoly rule which prohibited ownership of more than one AM, FM or TV station in a single market.

The revision of these ownership regulations was prompted by the substantial increase in the number of "nonbroadcasting" media sources such as cable TV, multi-point distribution services (MDS), satellite master antenna television (SMATV), and VCRs. These developments negated the initial rationale concerning the diversity of voices in the marketplace. With the expansion of media voices, concerns over potential ownership concentration of the traditional broadcast media lessened.

Following these revisions, did ownership concentration increase? Howard (1989), in a study of group and cross-media ownership of television stations found that between 1982 and 1989, ownership patterns showed a substantial numerical increase in the number of group owned stations. Of more importance is the answer to the question of how many ownership groups actually expanded beyond the former 7-7-7 limitations. By 1989, five groups had reached the new limit of twelve stations, and twenty-four other groups held between eight and eleven licenses. Of these, only three groups were approaching the twenty-five percent limitation of potential households (Howard, 1989). Thus, it appears that the increase in the number of stations any one group could own did not provoke a massive rush to acquire stations up to the new limit. However, it does seem to imply that there were at least a few players who would willingly go beyond the new limits if given the opportunity.

Changes in FCC Regulation

The 1990s have seen momentum grow for a further relaxation of ownership restrictions. As before, the further emergence and viability of alternate delivery systems and the lessened importance of public policy toward guaranteeing diversity played a part in the move to allow greater ownership in broadcast stations. Two new factors have also contributed to the current situation. First, a reversal of the maximizing of competition argument. Previously, ownership was restricted so that new delivery systems and new technologies would have a chance to survive and eventually compete with broadcasting. Now, these new systems such as cable and VCRs were doing so well that the future viability of broadcasting itself is being threatened. Market power is now seen as residing in the newcomers, and some sort of deregulation of broadcasting is needed to allow broadcasting to remain competitive.

Second, in line with the trend toward globalization, new arguments arose that argue that cross-ownership and vertical integration, once viewed as a danger to competition, are in actuality the key to the new global communications industry. As a result, the United States, it is argued, needs to drop "outmoded" restrictions so that the "new way of thinking," i.e., more mergers along the lines of Time-Warner, could continue to take place (*Broadcasting*, April 23, 1990, p. 59).

1. Radio

Since 1990, the FCC has begun to review ownership rules for radio, television, cable/telephone and cable/networks. Revisions in the radio ownership rules were the first to be proposed. While the final form of the new regulations has yet to be decided, the initial proposal permitted ownership of up to sixty radio stations (30 AM & 30 FM) and up to six in a single market. In one sweep these new regulations not only more than doubled the permissible number of radio stations that could be owned they also did away with the duopoly rule. Ownership would now be permitted of up to three to six stations in a single market depending upon the size of the market. Further, there would be caps placed on the size of the potential audience share that any one ownership group could control in a single market (*Broadcasting*, March 16, 1992, pp. 4, 11).

Will these changes result in a new wave of mergers? When the change was made to allow up to 12 AM and 12 FM stations the same fears were present. Under this cap, the minimum number of owners if each owned the maximum of stations, was 415, yet there are still thousands of different owners of radio stations. Under the new limits, the theoretical minimum is 166 broadcasters (*Broadcasting*, March 23, 1992, pp. 5–6). While it is certain that if these new rules are upheld there will be a new buying spree, yet, attributing new acquisition activity to globalization would be premature. At this point in time there is a glut of stations on the market waiting for buyers. Many of these stations will be acquired not to set up global networks but simply to fill gaps in the coverage of regional networks. Others will be acquired because of deeply discounted prices that will attract speculators. In terms of globalization, the intriguing developments are in the potential of raising the ownership caps for television.

2. Television

Following on the heels of the radio ownership changes came proposed changes for television ownership. Proposals are generally in the range of raising the ownership cap to between twenty and twenty-four stations and increasing the potential national audience share to thirty-five percent. Other proposals would permit UHF-VHF cross-ownership in a single market and eliminate bans on radio-TV cross-ownership in the same market (*Broadcasting*, March 23, 1992, p. 44; April 20, 1992, p. 10; April 27, 1992, pp. 4, 15).

No matter what form the new proposal eventually takes, the outcome is all but certain—an increase in the number of television stations that a group may own. The results from the Howard study would suggest that there are media groups that would seek to acquire stations up to the new limit. The potential to set up a fifth network also looms as a possibility if a group can acquire a full complement of stations in strategic markets.[9] The increased programming power from a larger broadcast group may also attract attention from media conglomerates. Those conglomerates involved in video production may see synergies in owning a broadcast group; guaranteeing a venue for programming product.

3. Cable

Finally, regulations concerning cross-ownership in cable are coming under increased scrutiny. Ownership regulations that restrict telephone company (telco) entry into cable television are destined to change in the near future (*Broadcasting*, April 20, 1992, p. 27). What form the new regulations will take is impossible to predict but the changes will further blur the lines between broadcasting, common carriers, computers, and information services. Changes in the ownership regulations will allow new giant conglomerates into the media field such as the regional Bell operating companies (RBOCs), who are already actively engaged in cable and other delivery systems overseas.

Similarly, the FCC is also revising its network-cable cross-ownership rules. It is becoming increasingly clear that cable doesn't need to be protected from broadcasting. What isn't so clear is if local broadcasters need protection from potential network moves into cable. Lobbying groups from the Network Affiliated Station Alliance (NASA) to the networks themselves to related industry groups such as the National Cable Television Association (NCTA) and the Motion Picture Association of America (MPAA) have developed competing proposals of what new cable-network cross-ownership rules should look like (*Broadcasting*, March 30, 1992, pp. 39–40). Recently, the FCC issued regulations allowing the three major networks to buy cable systems that serve no more than ten percent of cable homes nationwide and up to fifty percent of cable homes in a local market. Restrictions barring networks from owning a broadcast station and a cable system in the same market were upheld. This effectively bars network ownership of cable in systems in key cities such as New York, Los Angeles and Chicago. The FCC plans to review this regulations in three years to see if further deregulation is needed (*Broadcasting*, June 22, 1992, p. 19).

Taken as a whole, these changes in cross-ownership across media will contribute to the further blurring of the lines between the various communications industries. Limited research findings suggest that globalization will have at least a small impact in the emerging American media structure. We now turn toward the second area related to conglomerateness; synergy, and explore its impact on the emerging media environment.

VI. Synergy

Evidence for and Against

Synergy is often cited as one of the major reasons behind the recent wave of communication industry conglomerate mergers. The question can justly be raised, what evidence is there these that talked about synergies do indeed exist?

There are examples of synergies taking place before the most recent wave of merger activities. Warner Bros took comic book characters such as Batman and Wonder Woman from its DC Comics division and turned them into feature films, TV series and paperback books. Paramount turned the Star Trek television series into a successful feature film and book franchise. And Fox turned the "Alien Nation" feature film into a Fox television series (*Newsweek*, June 26, 1989, p. 54). This evidence points out that at least some of the global media conglomerates of today were able to develop synergies in their premerger form but further expansion did not multiply these opportunities.

Recently, Sony Pictures Entertainment (SPE) and Time-Warner completed multimedia deals with several entertainment superstars that have been touted as proof of the new synergism. SPE signed Michael Jackson to make and produce records, appear in videos, star in video games and CD-ROM interactive projects, and act in movies. A year after this deal was signed, only the record and video projects had become a reality; and neither had lived up to expectations. "Dangerous" became the fastest selling album worldwide, but failed to claim that distinction in the all-important U.S. market. Videos for the album were shot by the same director slated to direct Jackson in upcoming movies and subsequently shown in the Loews theater chain. However, other development projects have languished (*Variety*, February 10, 1992, pp. 1, 102).

Time-Warner has signed Madonna to a multimedia deal that includes film and TV projects in addition to recording albums. Estimated to be worth up to twenty-five million dollars, Time-Warner forged ahead with the agreement despite the failure of a less ambitious deal Madonna previously had with Columbia, and which Columbia opted not to renew after it failed to produce as expected. On the other hand, in what appears to be the most successful synergistic arrangement to date, Time-Warner has benefited from a cross-media deal with Quincy Jones, which has led to successful film, television, video, print, and music projects (*Variety*, February 10, 1992, pp. 1, 102).

Other evidence points out that synergy may not be as extensive as it is touted to be. Time-Warner points to its cross-media endeavors with its *Sports Illustrated* Swimsuit franchise that has been spun off into video (both for programming on HBO and video rental and sell-through) by HBO Video (*Variety*, February 10, 1992, pp. 1, 102). However, this synergy was in place before the Time-Warner merger, hence, it cannot be claimed as a successful synergy as a result of the merger. Other Time-Warner arrangements support this lack of additional synergies. Time Inc. has publicized its ability to develop cross-media advertising synergies. For example its recent thirty-five million dollar contract with Chrysler and its eighty million dollar arrangement with GM featured Time-Warner's ability to structure an ad campaign across its various magazine imprints. Time-Warner has cited the fact that each deal offered the potential of using Lorimar Television for video production, Warner Bros. for music, and Six Flags as venue for showing cars. It should be noted that in neither of these deals were these potential synergies used. Again, the structure of these contracts is no different from what Time Inc. was capable of doing before the Time-Warner merger (*Mediaweek*, April 15, 1991, pp. 18, 22–23).

In another example of the lack of Time-Warner synergies, Little, Brown, a subsidiary of Time-Warner, recently purchased book rights to a new PBS series on the West to be produced by Ken Burns. Although the oversized book would seem to lend itself to Time-Warner's Book-of-the-Month Club, Time Life Video, and Time-Warner's CD-ROM division, Time-Warner New Media, the division responsible for CD-ROM, didn't even know about the acquisition and the book club and direct mail divisions will have to bid separately for the ancillary rights. As one publishing CEO put it, "I've yet to see a single example of synergy starting out of a book division" (*Variety*, June 1, 1992, pp. 1, 84).

Investors have questioned the importance of synergy as a motivation for the merger as well. They have cited concerns ranging from marketing and distribution capacities to the fact that Warner Bros. studios and music have yet to see any real synergies. Further, some argue, to make the merger work, "massive alliances with partners in Europe and Asia" would still be needed to create synergies overseas (*Business Week*, July 22, 1991, pp. 70–74).

News Corp., as mentioned above, has demonstrated that it is capable of creating synergies, but has often refused to do so. Twentieth Century Fox produces shows for the Fox network, but charges the network market prices. It's even more competitive for Sky Cable which actually has to engage in competitive bidding to acquire Fox programming. In addition, Fox produces some of the Big Three networks top shows such as *LA Law* which it doesn't even make available to the Fox network. Another piece of evidence against synergy is that the Fox network isn't automatically assured of favorable coverage in the News Corp. owned *TV Guide* (*The Economist*, August 18, 1990, pp. 61–63).

The emergence of Bertelsmann as potentially the next big acquisition conglomerate on the scene demonstrates that large media conglomerates still cite synergy as a motivation for acquisitions even if past evidence counterargues the point. In 1986, Bertelsmann bought RCA Records and Doubleday Inc. After transition difficulties, both have finally started to show profits. Neither however, had demonstrated the ability to create cross-media megahits. RCA hasn't had a major album since 1987s *Dirty Dancing* soundtrack, and at one point in the fall of 1990, it didn't have a single album in Billboard's Top 50 (*Business Week*, November 12, 1990, pp. 72, 74–75). Doubleday suffered from an inflated book list and posted large losses in both 1988 and 1989. Doubleday regained a profitable status only by paring down and cutting back, not by exploiting synergies. Still, the lure of Hollywood as a source of programming for Bertelsmann's German television interests (RTL Plus and Premiere), and a cash war chest marked for expansion may bring Bertelsmann back into the synergy mindset (*The Economist*, November 16, 1991, p. 90).

Bertelsmann has decided in some cases not to take advantage even of the synergies it currently has. Despite owning printing plants worldwide and owning the Literary Guild book club, Bertelsmann continues to print books at competitors' plants and sells books through Time-Warner's Book-of-the-Month Club (*Newsweek*, June 26, 1989, p. 54).

The News Corp. and Bertelsmann examples demonstrate that even if potential synergies exist, if it is more cost effective and profitable to outsource products/services, then in-house synergies don't always make sense and shouldn't be attempted (*Newsweek*, June 26, 1989, p. 54). Is this viewpoint realistic? Is there evidence of when synergies may or may not be effective from a business efficiency standpoint?

Research Findings

Research by Clarke and Brennan (1990) state that as multinational enterprises diversify they tend to create strategic business units (SBU's) to manage each product/service area (e.g., a film division, a music division, a television division etc., each separately managed). Such an organizational structure has led to firms taking a portfolio approach to managing resources. The problem as they see it is that shared resources form the heart of synergistic relationships, yet SBUs fundamentally tend to drive out synergies by duplicating resources instead of sharing them with other SBUs. They propose that synergy can be better measured and managed in terms of Product Market, Resource, Customer, and Technology portfolios. Such an approach allows synergies to be viewed simultaneously across SBUs, rather than having SBUs compete separately. This approach can also help conglomerates analyze potential acquisitions by anchoring moves around identified synergies in products, resources, customers and technologies (Clark & Brennan, 1990).

In addition, Crompton (1990) notes that in industries such as telecommunications, businesses have found that interrelationships (analogous to Clarke & Brennan's shared resources) are so great that synergies are lost under a decentralized structure (analogous to Clarke & Brennan's SBUs). He further notes that firms that are facing global competition and those built around a single core business have led a trend away from decentralized operations (Crompton, 1990).

Both of these lines of research directly apply to the communications industry. The "globalization" phenomenon illustrates the concept of media firms in a single core business facing the pressure to diversify in the face of global competition. However, communications firms have been attempting to create synergies by decentralizing operations and creating new SBUs. Clarke and Brennan state this is precisely the wrong approach to take to develop synergies. Further, the trend toward joint ventures and small investment stakes in small and start-up companies further decentralizes business decisions and makes it more difficult to efficiently share resources. This research suggests then, that for the media conglomerates such as Time-Warner, SPE, News Corp., and Bertelsmann, the current line of acquisitions will not create the synergies they all proclaim are the driving forces and benefits behind diversification activities. This is the difference between "credible" and "incredible" diversification motives—the mythology and the reality.

VII. Implications of Conglomerateness

Review

The previous sections have focused on conglomerateness and two related areas, cross-ownership and synergy, in the communications industry. Various theories have been outlined that hypothesize a diversity of potential impacts from these trends. On the positive side, the gale of creative destruction evident in the increasing growth of new technologies has been posited to lower barriers to entry and enhance the role of competition in and across markets. On the negative side, the trend toward conglomerateness evident in the process of globalization suggests a lessening of competition due to the increasing market power of large firms in several of the communication markets. This potential is especially evident in the print and filmed entertainment markets which are not as susceptible to changes in technology as are some of the other communications markets. The data bear out this implication by showing that the number of single segment firms within these industries has decreased at the same time as diversification has increased.

The implications for broadcasting are almost the converse. Broadcasting has been hard hit by advances in technology that have fostered new programming delivery services. As a result, broadcasting faces the "gale of creative destruction" head-on. The implications of this are twofold. First, a shrinking market with existing firms becoming larger in absolute size (see table 9–2) foreshadows corporate giants slugging it out over a smaller and smaller revenue pie. And second, in order to survive broadcasting conglomerates will need to acquire firms in other industries and/or themselves develop and gain a foothold in new delivery systems.

Given the lack of availability of data concerning the practices of cross-subsidization, reciprocity, and mutual forbearance in the communications industry it is impossible at this stage to say which of these centripetal and centrifugal forces is stronger. It seems intuitive that in the early stages of globalization, change is occurring so rapidly, and the markets are is such a state of flux, that it is not feasible for conglomerates to solidify their positions to the extent necessary to successfully engage in anti-competitive practices. As markets mature, however, corporate giants will find themselves in positions of market power on a global scale heretofore unknown in the communications industry. Under these conditions, concerns over anti-competitive practices seem realistic. Irwin posits an ever increasing rate of technological change. It remains to be seen if the pace of technological development can move fast enough to prevent markets from solidifying. If such is the case, fears of conglomerate market power may be overstated.

The motives for conglomeration suggest that although synergies are most often cited as reasons for mergers, the postmerger performances of conglomerates suggests otherwise. Additional anecdotal evidence backs up the contention that mergers are motivated by reasons other than efficiencies. In theory, some of the new media corporate giants (i.e., Time-Warner, News Corp. etc.) have the ability to develop a creative work, put it into production across various media, and distribute it to a multitude of ancillary markets. The advantages of such flexibility are obvious in that the complexities of scheduling releases in multiple windows and negotiating distribution arrangements would all be handled in house between the appropriate divisions. The previous section demonstrated that these synergies aren't as real as they are proclaimed to be. Note a statement typical of these large media firms, in which the president of Bertelsmann Inc. (involved to some extent in music, publishing, video, television and radio) claimed "that cooperation among his half-dozen companies is unusual" (Smith, p. 26).

Foreign Investment Impacts

There has been little study done to analyze the potential effects of conglomeration on an international scale. All of the studies cited previously have looked at performance almost exclusively in the American market. One recent study by Ozanich and Wirth (1992) examined recent trends in foreign investment in mass media companies and how this will affect globalization in the future. They analyzed foreign investment by U.S. firms and by non-U.S. firms investing in U.S. media.

Ozanich and Wirth identified three components that spur foreign investment in media companies. They looked at the acquisition of foreign companies for investment or strategic purposes, investment in new technologies or in emerging markets (typically joint ventures and minority equity stakes), and the use of foreign capital markets for fundraising.

Their study found that investment in mass media companies in foreign countries will be limited by regulatory and economic constraints. Overall, the opening of markets through deregulation and trade agreements is considered crucial to increased investment but will be restricted by: the high debt loads of media conglomerates (and the subsequent lack of access to capital markets), the lack of well developed consumer markets for new technologies and new media products, and the uncertainty of changing (or emerging) technical standards that make investment in new technologies a risky proposition. Given these limiting factors, Ozanich and Wirth conclude that future investments in foreign media companies will likely focus on joint ventures, strategic partnering, licensing agreements and minority equity stakes (Ozanich and Worth, 1992).

The pattern Ozanich and Wirth suggest for future investment in foreign media companies is illustrated by Time Warner's ventures in European media. Time Warner's strategy is to invest in small media companies (especially cable systems) that they believe have strong growth potential. This low capital low risk strategy helps Time-Warner avoid some of the legal restrictions European countries place on foreign ownership of media companies (*Variety*, March 16, 1992, pp. 1, 80–81).

The potential benefits of efficiencies in such areas as marketing, management and promotion are counterbalanced by the need to develop communication strategies tailored to each national culture. It remains to be seen if the implementation of a unified marketing campaign worldwide can be successful. As a result, it is difficult to posit advantages for international conglomerate mergers beyond agency theories or strategies motivated by survival considerations.

The Film Industry

As the introductory remarks highlighted, one of the key industries in which globalization and conglomeration will play a significant role is the film industry. The changing communications market is beginning to emphasize control over information and programming as the key to economic success. In practical terms this has meant a growing interest in the acquisition of Hollywood studios. The "majors" are expert in the worldwide distribution of feature films and dominate virtually every market they compete in. Given all this, it is no wonder that in the last six years, Twentieth Century Fox, Columbia, MGM/UA and MCA/Universal have been the objects of conglomerate mergers. As a result, entering the U.S. film market is no longer easy.[10]

If it is true that the film industry is considered both the key to future economic success in the communications industry, and that it also may have a propensity for anti-competitive practices, a deeper look at some of the current corporate trends may be helpful to discern the future direction of the communications industry as a whole. Several questions come to the fore. How have the majors performed in the post merger period? And, what can be expected of new entry? If the majors have performed better in the postmerger period than in the premerger period and the number of firms in the film industry is expected to decrease, the potential for conglomerate power to alter competition is enhanced.

To answer the first question, one can look at the profits of Columbia (Sony), MCA/Universal (Matsushita), and Time-Warner and compare pre- and postmerger performance. In all three cases, these conglomerates have yet to realize any of the synergies that were predicted to yield high profits. Both Sony and Matsushita have cited their film divisions as the major reasons for declining corporate profits (*Variety*, September 9, 1991, pp. 105, 109; September 16, 1991, pp. 41, 50; November 25, 1991, p. 57). And, Time-Warner continues to report losses and its interest payments on the debt incurred in the merger continues to put a drain on profits (*Variety*, September 23, 1991, pp. 93-94; October 28, 1991, p. 66).[11] Although far from a complete analysis, even these preliminary findings indicate that these conglomerates are still far from being in a position that would enable them to alter the current level of competitiveness in the film industry.

Exploration of the question of entry into the film industry yields some interesting results. Many of the majors are struggling to raise the financing necessary to produce feature films. The standard method for raising capital has been for the majors to engage in joint ventures. But investors have grown wary of Hollywood accounting practices which often put returns to investors at the back of the revenue line. As a result, Time-Warner reached a merger agreement with Toshiba and C. Itoh of Japan to sell each firm a 6.25% equity stake for a combined one billion dollars. This arrangement not only gives Time-Warner access to Japanese markets, it also gives it capital to both reduce debt and fund future media projects (*Variety*, November 4, 1991, p. 78).

Other corporations that want to gain a foothold in Hollywood are choosing a different route. Realistically foreclosed from direct acquisition of a major studio, a very recent trend toward building a Hollywood studio from scratch has emerged. Four large media conglomerates, Fujisankei, Canal Plus, Polygram, and Penta Entertainment have announced plans to make major investments into film production and distribution (*Variety*, October 21, 1991, pp. 1, 93). This represents a significant trend away from a philosophy of joint ventures and toward a more competitive marketplace.

Even within the majors there are signs of increased competition.

Disney is in the process of setting up its own overseas distribution network instead of relying upon Warner Brothers (*Variety*, September 30, 1991, pp. 1, 90). Such a move can only increase competition in overseas film distribution markets.

VIII. Conclusion

The answers to the questions raised above seems to be that conglomerates have not performed better financially in the postmerger period and, that the number of firms in the film industry is beginning to increase, not decrease. Both of these answers point toward a somewhat more competitive marketplace, and not yet one in which conglomerates can effectively lessen competition.

It would seem then, that if current trends in the film industry, which is better insulated from the effects of technology on barriers to entry than program delivery industries such as television and cable, are showing some signs of increased competition then it bodes well for the communication industry as a whole in terms of the effects of conglomeration. At this stage in the developing global structure in communications, it appears that competition may be enhanced—at least in the short run. However, concerns about the effects of conglomerate power in the long run cannot be easily dismissed.

The analysis above has also demonstrated that the blurring of industry lines will continue, possibly at a slower pace as Ozanich and Wirth imply. Although to date, examples of synergy are hard to find, future consolidation efforts by the media conglomerates may bring synergies to the forefront. However, as research indicates, "creative" products may not be easily adaptable to a portfolio approach.

Finally, the key role of regulation, privatization and the availability of capital in worldwide financial markets will greatly impact the rate of globalization in the future. As new technologies develop, the need for increased capital investment and healthy consumer markets will partially dictate the rate of technological implementation.

This chapter has taken a preliminary look at what the future holds for the structure of the communications industry. As we head towards the twenty-first century, this analysis shows that new combinations of technology and business structures in conjunction with the movement toward globalization will radically alter the communications landscape, and the once clear lines that separated communication mediums from each other will continue to blur.

Notes

1. See "The Entertainment Industry," *The Economist*, December 23, 1989, for general background on globalization and the film industry.
2. Quoted in Adams, Walter (ed.) (1990). *The Structure of American Industry, 8th ed.*, New York: Macmillian Pub. Co., p. 318.
3. For a detailed discussion of diversification in a mature industry, see Dimmick, John & Wallschlaeger, Mikel (1986), "Measuring Corporate Diversification: A Case Study of New Media Ventures by Television Network Parent Companies," *Journal of Broadcasting and Electronic Media*, 30, (Winter), pp 1–14.
4. The following discussion is drawn largely from Mueller, "Conglomerates: A Nonindustry, pp. 328–337 and Adams, Walter, & Brock, James W. (1986). *The Bigness Complex*, New York: Pantheon Books, pp. 185–191.
5. All data following with the exception of Fortune 500 information comes from the 1986–1991 annual editions of *The Veronis, Suhler & Associates Communications Industry Report*.
6. The following measures are all derived from Veronis & Suhler data. It can be noted here that most of the measures cover a five-year period. While it would be ideal to analyze a longer period of data, such was not available for the present analysis.
7. If anything, the data tend to underestimate diversification. For example, No attempt is made to separate cable, television, and film programming from within the film segment.
8. This would support Dimmick and Wallschlaeger's hypotheses concerning the level of diversification and the maturation of the particular industry. Their study focused on broadcast television networks, but it could easily be argued that the print industries also represent a mature market.
9. See Thomas, Laurie & Litman, Barry R. "Fox Broadcasting Company, Why Now? An Economic Study of the Rise of the Fourth Broadcast Network," *Journal of Broadcasting and Electronic Media*, Vol. 35, No. 2, Spring 1991, pp. 139–157.
10. No "major" is currently considered to be "in play" with the possible exception of MGM after current litigation involving ownership is settled.
11. The situation is complicated by several factors. Among them is the fact that Hollywood is in the midst of a financial slump which is putting a squeeze on profits, and, that Matsushita does not breakout financial data for MCA separate from corporate financial data. Further, the short amount of time since these mergers took place may not be long enough to factor out acquisition and transition costs that also affect profitability:

References

"II: A year of politic plans and pratfall." (1990). *Institutional Investor*. (January): 139.
Adams, Walter, and James W. Brock. (1986). *The Bigness Complex*. New York: Pantheon Books.
Adams, Walter, ed. (1990). *The Structure of American Industry, 8th ed*. New York: Macmillian.
Alexander, Garth. (1991) "Japan Jury Still Out on Sony's Showbiz Career." *Variety* September 9, pp. 105, 109.

Alexander, Garth. (1991). "Wiser and Choosier Dealing with Hollywood." *Variety* September 16, pp. 41, 50.
"America's Hottest Export: Pop Culture." (1990). *Fortune*, December 31, p. 50.
"Bertelsmann: When Being a Giant Isn't Enough." (1990). *Business Week* November 12, pp. 72, 74, 75.
Clarke, Christopher J., Kieron Brennan. (1990). "Building Synergy in the Diversified Business," *Long Range Planning* (April):9–16.
"Coming to America: The Sequal." (1991). *The Economist* November 16, p. 90.
"Commission May Capsize Its Ownership Limit." (1992). *Broadcasting* March 23, pp. 5, 6.
Crompton, Ron. (1990). "Brief Case: The Return of Synergy," *Long Range Planning* (October): 122–124.
"Cross-Media Megadeals Stoke the Synergists." (1992). *Variety* February 10, pp. 1, 102.
Dimmick, John, and Mikel Wallschlaeger. (1986). "Measuring Corporate Diversification: A Case Study of New Media Ventures by Television Network Parent Companies." *Journal of Broadcasting and Electronic Media 30* (Winter): 1–14.
"The Entertainment Industry." (1989). *The Economist* December 23, pp. 3–18.
"FCC Eyes Relaxing Television Rules." (1992). *Broadcasting*, March 23, p. 44.
Fleming, Charles, and Richard Natale. (1991). "Hollywood Seeks Visa for Foreign Exchange." *Variety* September 30, pp. 1, 90.
"From Walkman to Showman." (1989). *Time*, October 9, p. 70.
"Going Ape for Entertainment." (1990). *Time*, October 8, p. 63.
Gort, Michael, and Eric V. Swanson. (1983). "Conglomerate Size and Competition Between Large and Small Firms." *The Antitrust Bulletin* (summer): 337–348.
Groves, Don. (1992). "Time Warner forages in Euro media field." *Variety* March 16, pp. 1, 80–81.
"Here Come the Global Moguls." (1991). October 21, pp. 1, 93.
Hogarty, Thomas F. (1970). "Profits from Mergers: The Evidence of 50 Years." *St. Johns Law Review*, (special edition) 44 (Spring): 389.
Howard, Herbert H. (1989). "Group and Cross-Media Ownership of TV Stations: A 1989 Update." *Journalism Quarterly* (Winter): 785–792.
"IBM, Time Warner Discuss a Technology and Media Mix." (1992). *Wall Street Journal*, April 30, p. B1.
Irwin, Manley Rutherford. (1984). *Telecommunications America: Markets Without Boundaries*. Westport, CT: Quorum Books.
"Is FCC Rule 'Half a Loaf?" (1992). *Broadcasting*, June 22, p. 19.
Lee, Wilson B., and Elizabeth, S. Cooperman. (1989). "Conglomerates in the 1980s: A Performance Appraisal." *Financial Management* (Spring): 45–54.
"Let Us Entertain You." (1990). *Time*, December 10, pp. 68.
Litman, Barry R. (1991). "The Industrial Organization Model." *Economics of the Mass Media* (in preparation), Erlbaum publishers.
"Make Synergy Work." (1991). *MEDIAWEEK*, April 15, pp. 18, 22–23.
"Matsushita Net Drops in First Half." (1991). *Variety*, November 25, p. 57.

Max, Daniel. (1992). "Time Warner's 'West' flunks synergy test," *Variety* June 1, pp. 1, 84.
"MCA's Allure to Matsushita Lifts Stakes in Japanese Firms' Entertainment Aims." (1990). *Wall Street Journal*, September 26, p. A6.
McGregor, Michael. (1988). "Cable/Newspaper Cross-Ownership: Pre-empting Local Regulatory Options." *Communications and the Law* October pp. 19–27.
"Meet the New Media Monsters." (1989). *The Economist*, March 11, p. 65.
"Metzenbaum Says Diversity Will Protect Consumers," (1990). *Broadcasting*, April 23, p. 59.
Mueller, Dennis C. (1977). "The Effects of Conglomerate Mergers: A Survey of the Empirical Evidence." *Journal of Banking and Finance 1*: 339.
Mueller, Willard F. (1990). "Conglomerates: A Nonindustry." In Walter Adams (ed.), *The Structure of American Industry, 8th ed*. New York: Macmillan pp. 318–348.
"Murdoch's Kingdom: The Morning After." (1990). *The Economist*, August 18, pp. 61–63.
"The Myth of Global Synergy." (1989). *Newsweek*, June 26, p. 54.
Noglows, Paul. (1991). "Time Warner Finally Seals Japanese Deal." *Variety* November 4, p. 78.
Noglows, Paul. (1991). "Wartime at Time Warner?" *Variety* September 23, pp. 93–94.
Ozanich, Gary W., and Michael O. Wirth. (1992). "Trends in Globalization: Direct Foreign Investments in Media Companies 1985–1991." Presented to the Management and Sales Division of the 37th Annual Convention of the Broadcasting Education Assocation, April 12.
"Pathe' Buying MGM-UA for $1.2 billion." (1990). *Broadcasting*, March 12, p. 31.
"Radio's Magic Numbers: 30–30." (1992). *Broadcasting*, March 16, pp. 4, 11.
Ravenscraft, David J., and F. M. Scherer. (1987). *Mergers, Sell-Offs, & Economic Efficiency*. Washington D.C.: Brookings Institution.
Second Report and Order, 50 F.C.C. 2d 1046 (1975).
"Sikes Ready to Move on TV Ownership." (1992). "*Broadcasting*, April 20, p. 10.
Smith, Anthony. (1991). *The Age of Behemoths: The Globalization of Mass Media Firms*. New York: Priority Press Publications.
"Sony Sales up, Profits down." (1991). *Variety November 25,* p. 57.
"Squaring Off over Cable Crossownership." (1991). *Broadcasting* March 30, pp. 39–40.
"Telco Entry May Lead to Cable Bill Veto." (1992). *Broadcasting* April 20, pp. 27.
Thomas, Laurie, and Litman, Barry R. (1991). "Fox Broadcasting Company, Why Now? An Economic Study of the Rise of the Fourth Broadcast Network." *Journal of Broadcasting and Electronic Media*, 35(2):139–157.
"Time Warner: As debt Worries Mount, So Do Doubts About Steve Ross's Strategy." (1991). *Business Week* July 22, pp. 70–74.

"TV Dereg." (1992). *Broadcasting* April 27, pp. 4, 15.
"TW Clips Losses." (1991). *Variety* October 28, p. 66.
The Veronis, Suhler & Associates Communications Industry Report, annual editions 1986–1991.
"What's Motivating Mega-media." (1989). *Advertising Age* March 20, p. 16.
Zuckman, Harvey L., et al. *Mass Communication Law*, 3rd ed. St. Paul, MN: West Publishing.

Commentary by Gilles Paquet

The limits of scale and scope

These two papers examine the information economy in its spatial and industrial contexts. Hepworth's paper emphasizes the spatial aspects with an emphasis on the European experience and the Litman/Sochay paper builds its case mainly on the experience in the mass media sector in North America. Yet, even though cities are not the only component in space, and mass entertainment is only one sector of the information economy, both papers aim at generating propositions that transcend these segments, and argue that these components are important enough for their experience to be examplary.

The next few pages underline briefly some of the key ideas presented in those papers, and then present a few modest general propositions that would appear to emerge from these quite different papers.

Some Central Ideas in Telegraphic Style

While these papers are quite different in tone, style, and methodology, they are trying to grapple with the same general set issues: what is the likely outcome of the combined impact of the centrifugal and centripetal forces unleashed by the information economy on the concentration of power in industry and on the spatial concentration of economic activity?

In the Spatial Context

Mark Hepworth's work on the geography of the information economy examines the nature of metropolitan dominance and the impact of the technology and organization features of the information economy on urban form and functioning. This work focuses on two separate processes in the information economy: the intercity competition and the new intracity engines of economic growth.

At the intercity level, the central force is the erosion of the national frontiers and the emergence of competitive advantages built on informational resources. The myth of an Euromegalopolis at the core of Europe and the possibility that it might be capable of imposing its hegemony have been mesmerizing. This outcome now appears somewhat problematic: the construction of public and private electronic highways would appear to hold in store some advantages sufficient to compensate for the locational advantages of being within the core European space.

At the intracity level, the new engines of economic growth would appear to be the "mariages" between telematics and sectors other than financial services. These require massive new public investments in the infrastructure of cities. In this context, the weakening of the local government structure in the United Kingdom is bound to be a major impediment to U.K. competitiveness. Moreover, the shrinking information-based organization and the tendency to disperse its activities toward cheap-labor locations have already had some deleterious effects on the large cities within the core European space.

As a result of this dual set of forces, the metropolitan cities have been hit hard. Unemployment has grown exponentially, and residents of those informationally-rich metropolitan areas have often become materially poorer. On the other hand, peripheral cities that might benefit from such circumstances would appear to be ill-organized to position themselves strategically mainly because of the limitations and constraints imposed by nation-states on local governments.

In the Mass Media Environment

In the same way that national frontiers have been eroded, the boundary lines between products and industries have also become fuzzy. This is no where more apparent than in the telecommunications and mass media fields. Conglomerates covering a large number of segments of the industry and massive cross-ownership arrangements have become the rule.

Litman and Sochay describe carefully the extensive merger activities in the mass media sector and the blurring of boundaries that has ensued. Very much like in the case of the spatial context, centripetal and centrifugal forces are at work. What transpires from the Litman/Sochay survey is that the conglomerativeness factor has yielded little synergy effect, and that in the film industry (which is a significant segment of the industry), the number of firms is increasing, not decreasing.

As a result, there is some sense that nominal competition is increasing despite the efforts invested by conglomerates to tame it. However, the authors caution the readers that this may be only an observation pertaining to short-run effects. In the longer haul, technological change and consolidation efforts by the media conglomerates may foster the emergence of really effective synergies and the coalescence of global business structures capable of limiting competition much more effectively.

Three Modest General Propositions

The authors of these chapters are quite careful to avoid putting forward anything that might look like a modest general proposition. This is reasonable academic restraint in areas where little is known with great certainty. Yet some propositions would appear to flow naturally from their work. Our purpose in teasing them out of their arguments is not to burden the authors even obliquely with the responsibility for propositions they chose not to put forward, but to illustrate the extent to which the papers have heuristic power. The authors may have chosen not to be adventuresome, but this is not in the job description of a commentator or of an active reader.

The following propositions are not necessarily going to be borne out by future research, but since they are latent in the work of Hepworth and Litman/Sochay, they deserve at least some airing.

Limits to Scale and Scope

Both papers are making much of the fact that after some original hopes that economies of scale and scope might sweep existing structures in space and industry, and lead to megalopolises and conglomerates that would generate immense synergies and external economies, the experience of the last few years would not appear to bear this out. Indeed, both spatially and organizationally, there would appear to be a countermovement of some magnitude that one might called *a dispersive revolution*. This is well-documented in the literature on private (Stalk and Hout, 1990; Peters, 1992) and public management (Osborne/Gaebler, 1992; Rivlin, 1992).

Both papers illustrate very well those limits to scale and scope, and tend to suggest that despite the fact that the information economy literature has celebrated much these information economies, this may have been done to excess over the last decades.

Information May be Embezzled

A second general point toward which both authors would appear to converge is that synergies are omnipresent in the information economy and that proximity (in space or organization) may help to tap the surplus thereby generated. Moreover the authors hint at the fact that large organizations (be they megalopolises or conglomerates) have acquired in the process of growing a requisite dose of economic power that may lead them to hijack this surplus. Neither paper dares to enter the uncomfortable world of power analysis, and both take some consolation in the fact that countervailing peripheral powers capable of preventing information from being totally embezzled would appear to be emerging both in the urban and in the industrial landscapes. However, the authors are no Dr. Pangloss, and they alert the readers to the possibilities that large inter-territorial units may indeed use such power either to hijack the surplus or even to prevent the emergence of the best of all possible organizational worlds (Bartlett, 1989).

Both papers are in that sense perceptive when it comes to the possibility of markets being ineffective, but very cautious in allowing this line of reasoning to run its course. Consequently, there is little in the way of policy advice for action in the event that such an eventuality materializes.

The Virtual Corporation/Urban Unit

The authors are led to speculate on the nature of the spatial and organizational forms likely to prevail in the future, but they do not appear willing to be very bold. The information economy has obviously made location, technology and organization forms somewhat footloose (Paquet, 1989). This is bringing about the age of the "virtual product": produced instantaneously and customized in response to consumer demand, and commanding therefore the requisite adjustments in the locational, technological and organizational features of the sort of companies ("virtual corporations") and the emergence of new kinds of networks or compacts or strategic alliances (Davidow/Malone 1992).

High-quality multimedia communication and agile manufacturing demand subsidiarity in business and government, but the sort of decentralization that favours peripheral units and small and medium-sized enterprises may not entail a decentralization of power. What is likely to evolve is a federated network of project-based flexible units adapted to all the challenges of new circumstances, but quarterbacked by a very powerful organizing force within those transnational networks. The possibility that the regulation and governance of the world economy might be organized by those efficient and powerful deterritorialized compacts is not negligible.

* * *

Those are only some of the modest general propositions one may derive tentatively from the work currently done on the spatial and organizational contexts of economic activity in the information economy. Both the Hepworth and the Litman/Sochay papers have broadly sketched the background for developing these sort of propositions. Indeed, one may expect the readers to emerge from reading these pieces with a temptation to put forward some such propositions of their own. This is a testimony to the heuristic power of these papers that they naturally trigger such reactions. Those temptations should not be resisted.

References

Bartlett, R. (1989). *Economics and Power*. Cambridge: Cambridge University Press.
Davidow, W. H. and M. S. Malone (1992). *The Virtual Corporation*. New York: Harper Business.
Osborne, D., and T. Gaebler (1992). *Reinventing Government*, Reading. Mass.: Addison-Wesley.
Paquet, G. (1989). "Vers une nouvelle dynamique de la localisation des entreprises." In *Les conditions du développement technologique de l'entreprise en région*. Québec: Conseil de la science et de la technologie du Québec.
Peters, T. (1992). *Liberation Management*. New York: Knopf.
A. M. Rivlin. (1992). *Reviving the American Dream*. Washington, D.C.: The Brookings Institution.
Stalk, G., and T. M. Hout (1990). *Competing Against Time*. New York: The Free Press.

Commentary by Nicholas Garnham

A central issue for the political economy of communications has always been the relationship between the economic dynamics of the communication industries under conditions of market capitalism on the one hand and the provision of informational diversity that theories of the centrality of free expression for democracy require on the other. One school of thought has argued that privately owned and unregulated commercial media are the essential condition for freedom of expression, because only such a system avoids the dangers of State control of information—a view enshrined in the Ist Amendment to the US constitution. The opposing school argues, to the contrary, that the economics of the communications industry, in particular their reliance on technologies of reproduction that produce large and increasing returns to economies of scale, tend inexorably to produce concentration of ownership and a reduction of diversity that represent a threat to freedom of expression that only State intervention can effectively challenge. One school sees the State censor as the enemy of democracy, the other the media baron.

This debate has produced over the years a large number of studies which attempt to demonstrate whether or not there is growing concentration of ownership and whether, if there is, it does or does not lead to a reduction in informational diversity. In particular two differing threats to informational diversity have been identified. On the one hand there is concentration within a media sector which places control over newspapers or TV channels in fewer hands. On the other there is conglomerate diversification which, while it may not increase concentration of ownership within a media sector, presents the potential threat of placing decisions over information flows in the hands of those who would use them to pursue their wider economic and political interests—for instance in support of the capitalist system in general or particular probusiness economic policies in particular—or more specifically by, for instance, oil companies using media ownership to down play environmental or energy policy concerns.

This debate and its accompanying research has largely to date been national in focus. It was assumed that the market and regulatory environment being addressed was national in scope. In recent years however the focus has shifted to the global level. It is now claimed by many analysts that there is an accelerating tendency for the capitalist economy to globalize—that is to say increasingly goods and services are produced for and sold into global rather than national markets by firms which are transnational in character and within a financial environment characterised by rapid global capital flows with a global capital market. These trends it is argued are leading to a restructuring of production and distribution, to a new international division of labour and, in particular, to the undermining of the power of the nation state to determine policy in favor, depending on the school of thought, either of transnational corporations or of regional trading blocks or of uncontrolled and uncontrollable global market forces. Within the field of media it is now argued that these trends are increasingly affecting the production, distribution and consumption of media goods, services and related electronic hardware such that the world's media will soon be controlled by less than ten highly integrated global media/electronic conglomerates using communication networks controlled by perhaps three or four major telecommunications giants. In a market which has traditionally been highly regulated at the national level with the aim of protecting information diversity and national control over information production and distribution—for instance by restricting ownership of national media to national citizens—these trends raise the question of whether and if so in what form these new market powers can be regulated in the public interest.

Litman and Sochay's paper addresses this important debate. In doing so it itself exhibits the tension between the national and the global which is central to the debate, because it looks at the global exclusively from a US perspective using US market data and largely concerning itself with the impact of globalization on the US media environment.

What then is their argument and how well does it stand up? In my view it is riven with contradictions and reaches an unjustified conclusion. The paper concludes with the statement that their "analysis shows that new combinations of technology and business structure in conjunction with the movement towards globalization will radically alter the communications landscape and the once clear lines that separated communication mediums from each other will continue to blur," when in fact they have done no such thing as I will attempt to demonstrate. In particular the argument exaggerates the role of technology and the novelty of the processes which they observe.

First they argue, based upon Manley Irwin, that there is a trend towards globalisation which is primarily driven by an endogenous process of technological development that, by reducing entry costs and blurring sectoral boundaries, is leading to a Schumpeterian wave of creative destruction on a world scale. They argue that these technological developments have caused increased demand pull from the creation of new distribution channels, especially in Europe, and increased competition for these new markets the response to which has been the attempt to create corporations with global reach and cross sectoral span.

First no evidence is in fact presented that the costs of entry have lowered and it seems an unlikely proposition, especially in this context, since one of the primary arguments for the creation of the global mega corporation is precisely the need to access the ever larger capital sums required to stay in the game. Crucially however it is capital required for software production and marketing rather than for investment in technological distribution systems that has always been and remains crucial. Certainly it would be hard to argue that the costs of entry to the cable market were lower than those to terrestrial over-air broadcasting. Moreover the authors go on to argue that one of the major barriers to globalisation is shortage of capital.

As to the blurring of industry boundaries, this is a view that is fashionable under the name of convergence and has been much touted by the Harvard Program on Information Resources and its Information Industry Mapping project. But what is the reality? At one level such blurring is nothing new. It just depends how you look at the industry as a whole. The paper makes the mistake of defining industry divisions in terms of film and broadcasting for instance rather than looking at it from the point of view of an audio-visual entertainment production and distribution split. From this later point of view the Hollywood Majors have, since they came to terms with television, always seen the various technologies of distribution as alternative delivery mechanisms for the same product. Thus there has been no new blurring in production and concentrated control has been enhanced rather than undermined by technological developments which have expanded market demand while at the same time increasing the production industry's bargaining power. On the other hand the structure of distribution has been determined more by regulation than by technology, a factor which is surprisingly neglected in this paper. Thus the film/television distinction in the US, and the market structure that results, was largely created by regulatory distinctions not technological differences. The restructuring now going on thus takes very different forms in the US and in Europe with their different regulatory regimes in ways that cannot be explained in terms of technologically determined boundary blurring.

At the same time if one looks at a global corporation like News

International its expansion has been largely fuelled by profits from its stake in that most traditional of media industries the UK tabloid newspaper. Its only significant stake in "new media" is its stake in direct satellite broadcasting in the UK, an enterprise which was itself the result of a withdrawal from a satellite based transnational strategy in Europe and a refocussing on the UK national market. Here it is in competition with established broadcasters and its market share remains marginal. Its entry into the US audio-visual market was through buying Fox, a long established Hollywood major, largely for its film library, and through entry into the saturated market for conventional, over-air network broadcasting. This is a portfolio investment strategy with which technological development, in spite of the corporate PR hype which surrounds it, has very little to do. Indeed the author's themselves rightly critique the whole notion of cross sectoral synergy upon which the economic rationale for much cross media conglomeration is supposedly based.

I would also want to challenge the demand pull argument. We need to distinguish here between the demand, especially for films, popular TV series and sporting events, from channel controllers on the one hand and audience demand on the other. Because of an expansion of new electronic delivery media, and attempts by new market entrants to use those new channels, audio-visual entertainment product with proven audience pulling power has been at a premium. This has undoubtedly temporarily improved the bargaining power of the major producers of that product and thus their revenue streams. This has strengthened the market position of the corporations, the Hollywood majors, who control this market and has resulted in both the attraction of those corporations to predators, especially the Japanese hardware companies, and some new entrants. The expansion of their market may make it possible for one or two more major players to survive. But this is likely to be a temporary phenomenon simply because it is not reflected by expanding audience demand. On the contrary one of the trends driving globalization has been rising production costs against a background of static or declining consumer demand. While the balance between US and overseas revenues of the US audio-visual industry has shifted in favour of overseas revenues, overall revenue levels have remained stagnant. Overseas revenues were required to make up for static or declining real US revenues and rising costs. Declining trends in advertising and the impact of the current global recession on consumer media expenditure are likely to exacerbate this demand failure. Thus it is a demand squeeze that explains globalization trends not expanding demand pull.

The argument presented by Litman and Sochay is full of fascinating and pertinent data concerning the current state of the US media market. But it contains three major contradictions which should fruitfully generate further debate.

First it argues on the one hand that there are clear signs of increased concentration and conglomerate diversification, while on the other hand arguing that research shows that conglomeration is in general economically irrational—in the sense that such conglomerates are less profitable after merger than their component parts were premerger. This is now a well attested finding in the economic literature. In particular it mounts a wide ranging critique of the synergy thesis that corporations at least claim to be one of the key reasons for global conglomeration. Again this is now widely supported in the literature. The question which then presents itself, given the supposed profit driven economic rationality of the capitalist market, is what drives this irrational behavior. Is it power hunger and if so how long can such a power hunger be sustained in the face of market pressures? Is it driven by the needs of finance capital and if so for how long can those needs over ride the dynamics of the sector itself? Both these responses raise the question of whether current moves towards global conglomeration are or are not cyclical and whether therefore we do not need to worry over much because we will shortly witness a wave of demergers and a retreat back to national or at least regional bases. Certainly these questions raise question marks for me over whether there is likely to be the radical restructuring of the communication landscape the authors claim.

Second it argues on the one hand, based on Manley Irwin's work, that there are strong technologically driven trends to globalisation, but on the other, based on the research of Ozanich and Wirth, that there are severe economic and regulatory constraints to globalisation; the high debt loads of media conglomerates and thus shortage of capital, lack of well developed consumer markets for new technologies and new media products and uncertainty of changing technical standards. The problem is that the two arguments are fundamentally incompatible and at the very least should lead the authors to temper their final judgement as to radical changes in the media landscape. Which view one takes may depend as much on temperament as on rational analysis and data. In my view it is important to resist the hype associated with supposed technological and economic restructuring. It is, on the contrary, difficult to exaggerate the slowness with which the communication landscape changes. So many of the lords of the global media village have already fallen by the wayside. This does not mean that we should not pay attention to the potential regulatory dangers, but at the same time we should not be hypnotised into incapacity by an exaggerated fear of them.

Finally and thirdly it argues on the one hand, again following Irwin, that we are witnessing a technologically driven Schumpeterian wave of destruction and intensifying competition in the media industry worldwide. On the other it argues that there is decline in competition in all sectors, except possibly film production. In my view, once again, these positions cannot be reconciled or if they can be the paper does not succeed in doing so. But which position one takes is crucial. The Irwin position broadly supports a noninterventionist, deregulatory position. As with Ithiel de Sola Pool in *Technologies of Freedom*, it supports arguments that see the cost and control of technology as the main problem and technological development as a deus ex machina expanding freedom of expression by breaking up concentrations of communication power and democratizing such power through cheap technology. Those who focus on increased concentration on the other hand, such for instance as Ben Bagdikian or Herbert Schiller, see the problem as one of market power and dynamics with technological development as endogenous and regulation as the only means of democratizing communication power.

10 APPLICATION OF NEOCLASSICAL ECONOMICS TO AFRICAN DEVELOPMENT: A CURSE IN DISGUISE

Bernard Z. Dasah

Since the early 1980s a number of Sub-Saharan African countries have undertaken structural adjustment programs (SAP) aimed at reducing economic distortions and financial imbalances. The programs have sought to achieve, within the medium term, a sustainable rate of economic growth consonant with relative price stability and a viable external sector. The International Monetary Fund (IMF), in close colloboration with the World Bank, usually requires the countries to meet certain conditionalities before it provides advice, technical and financial assistance, and acts as a catalyst for international resource flows.

This paper argues that the IMF, the World Bank, and the General Agreement on Tariffs and Trade (GATT), since they are controlled by Western countries, view development through the prism of neoclassical theory, which considers human relations as commodity exchange relations only. It is also argued that the neoclassical model does not fit the economic culture of Africa. Consequently, forcing the neoclassical model on Africa through structural adjustment programmes may do more harm than good in the long run. The chapter concludes that an information-communicatory-cultural view of economic development is an appropriate alternative for Africa.

1. Foundations of Neoclassicalism

1.1. Radical Individualism

Traditional economics is concerned primarily with the efficient, least-cost allocation of scarce productive resources and with the optimal growth of these resources over time to produce an ever expanding range of goods and services. The foundation of neoclassical economics is simply the aggregation of individualistic desires and wants, indeed the whole theoretical explanation of production, distribution and prices is based on the single assumption of radical individual self-interest. Adam Smith, whose *An Inquiry Into the Nature and Causes of the Wealth of Nations* (1776) is the germinal book of both classical and neoclassical economics, explained the relation in this way: "It is not from the benevolence of the butcher, the brewer, or the baker, that we expect our dinner but from their regard to their own interest." The ultimate rationale for the theory or model of economic activity is his famous notion of the invisible hand of capitalism. Accordingly, if each individual consumer, producer, or supplier of resources pursues self-interest, he or she will, as if led by an invisible hand, promote the overall interests of society. This is to say that the invisible hand transforms private vice into public virtue.

1.2. Price Directed System

In the main body of neoclassical literature, the economy is assumed to be constrained by its limited capacity for obtaining and processing materials, not by any limitation on its ability to process the information required to organize and co-ordinate these activities. As a result, neoclassical economics historically has had a very limited conception of information, so much so that in 1961 George Stigler, Nobel laureate in economics, remarked that information occupied "a slum dwelling in the town of economics" (Stigler, 1961). Indeed neoclassical economists traditionally view the price system itself as the sufficient information mechanism. For neoclassicists, prices are "guides" and "disciplinarians" (Sametz, 1970, p. 3) of the way resources are used and outputs distributed. The overall economic results are simply a summation of the effects of billions of decisions made by millions of producers and consumers. Basic questions of what and how much to produce are assumed to be determined by the aggregate preferences of all consumers as revealed by their market curves for different goods and services. Producers are assumed simply to respond to sovereign consumer preferences, and to be motivated by the desire to maximize profits. They are assumed to compete with each other on equal terms in the purchase of resources and the sale of products.

The market system is seen then as an elaborate mechanism for unconscious co-ordination through prices of the knowledge, desires, abilities, and actions of millions of individuals. Buyers and sellers come together in markets where there results a circular flow of commodities and labor power from sellers to buyers in exchange for money. The operation of the free-market system, so argues the theory, maximizes individual welfare given the initial conditions (endowments) and the Pareto criterion. Since consumers are assumed to maximize their utility and since production responds to consumer wants, it follows that the result is welfare maximizing. If allowed to operate without certain types of constraints (e.g., legal or monopolistic constraints), the entire economy becomes a pleasure-maximizing machine in which the differences between consumer benefits and production costs are increased to the highest level possible.

1.3. Exchange Relations

Human relations in the free market model are not personal or communitarian but merely exchange relations based on individual greed, mediated by commodities and by money. Human interactions in the market model, therefore, are means to end—the disposal and acquisition of products or services to gain higher "utility." Information facilitates such exchanges by assisting economic agents to locate each other, and to make them more aware of the attributes of the commodities bought and sold.

The neoclassical economist's notion of perfect competition is central to this whole process. It assumes that all prices, wages, and interest rates are determined by the free play of the forces of supply and demand and that each of the millions of consumers and thousands of producers is so small in relation to total demand and supply that no one can individually influence to any extent the market prices and quantities of goods, services, and resources bought and sold.

However, the neoclassical view raises a number of issues. First, information appears differently when perceived by the individual, the class, and the whole. Second, commoditized social relations in production and consumption underplay or exclude interpersonal and communicational relations. Finally, "property" is not a tangible thing but is a socially defined bundle of rights based on human relations; to say the least, these relations vary from culture to culture. Nevertheless, the neoclassical paradigm underplays the importance of cultural differences in economic development.

2. Extension to Africa

The neoclassical paradigm has been extended to Africa through the General Agreement on Tariffs and Trade (GATT), and by the structural adjustment programmes (SAP) of the International Monetary Fund (IMF) and the Bank for Reconstruction and Development (otherwise known as the World Bank).

Both the IMF and the World Bank believe that external disequilbria are usually a consequence of excess aggregate domestic demand, caused by excessive credit expansion. Consequently, the standard IMF stabilization programme prescribes demand management and price adjustments by requiring the country to meet certain conditionalities. These include removing all subsidies, increasing taxation, cutting public expenditure, reducing the money supply, sizeable currency devaluation, and liberalizing trade. According to its proponents then, SAP encompasses interrelated policies for stabilizing economies through orderly reduction of domestic demand for external resources, and for engineering sustainable long-term growth through changes in relative prices designed to make the economy more efficient, more flexible and better able to use resources (World Bank, 1988, p. 1). In short, SAP attempts to streamline developing economies in accordance with policies implicit in neoclassical price theory.

The basic premise behind SAP is that the development of African economies requires only the enhancement and exploitation of resource endowments, the application of technology to the resources, and the development of market oriented institutions. It is futher assumed that this approach promotes harmonious interplay of these elements for all concerned, generating sustained economic growth. This is because to repeat, neoclassical economists see human relations as mere commodity exchange relations, with value confined to exchange value. Consequently, culture is regarded as an exogenous factor.

The treatment of culture by economists as exogenous should be a major concern to many social scientists in other disciplines. For example, technological knowledge is never culturally independent. It may exist as pure platonic form, but if it is to be expressed as a tactile, functional artifact, it must be mixed with both base matter and other varieties of culturally based technological knowledge no matter the primitive nature of this knowledge. Nevertheless, culture remains a subvariable to the economist and to policy makers at the World Bank and the IMF. Therefore, there is little consideration for the impact of the host culture on the usual structural adjustment programmes nor the repercussions of structural adjustment upon the social fabric. The typical macroeconomic country analyses on which major development initiatives are predicated lack sophisticated understanding of the local context. The initiatives are mainly based on what is regarded as universal principles that generate Pareto optimality. As a result, implementation is difficult and there is only limited sustained flow of benefits to the intended beneficiaries. Even when resouces—money, technology, technical assistance, etc.—are made available, they are not fully and gainfully used, and their contribution to human development is limited because they are not effectively anchored in the local operating context. For example, a study by Harrigan and Mosley (1991) indicates that the rate of return on World Bank program aid measured in terms of the impact of GDP growth rate has been disappointing. In addition, the study established a negative correlation between structural adjustment loans and investments.

The application of neoclassical economics through SAP in Africa is nothing less than replicating Western cultural traits in African countries. For example, the major economic policy objective of African countries in the postwar years has been to maximize output of goods and services and the principal measure of development progress has been gross national product (GNP) per capita. African countries found such a policy attractive because of both the historical experience of the industrial countries, and colonial patterns of development. They assumed that they could replicate the historical experience of the developed countries if they embarked on a period of rapid and self-sustaining growth after achieving a critical threshold of economic maturity (Rostow, 1960). Social and economic disparities would then decline, as they did in the industrial nations. However, evidence indicates that the most outstanding facts in this regard are the worsening distribution of income (Weissman, 1990) and the declining real income of the rural poor of these countries. Also, per capita food production and infant mortality rates of many African countries have been deteriorating since the introduction of SAP. Furthermore, though in absolute terms African external debt is much smaller than that of Latin America, the debt servicing ratio or the debt-burden of African countries is much higher. Consequently, forcing the neoclassical model on Africa through SAP may do more harm than good in the long run.

SAP, in my view, issues from the colonial policy of "the center-periphery doctrine." According to this doctrine, countries on the periphery (the colonies) are to supply the center (the metropole) with its needs of raw materials; hence economic development is limited to the export enclave of each colony where Western cultural traits are promoted (Sowell, 1983).

The center-periphery doctrine, as well as SAP, is often cloaked under the guise of the benefits of international trade based on comparative advantage in a free market setting. Adam Smith (1776), the proponent of foreign trade, argued that it "overcomes the narrowness of the home market and provides an outlet for the surplus product above domestic requirements." This means, international trade acts as a vent for any surplus. Smith further argued that international trade improves the level of productivity of the participants. To this end, as maintained by David Ricardo (1951) and his intellectual progeny, countries that have comparative advantage in the production of certain commodities should specialize in their production because by doing so, the total welfare of the world in general will be enhanced. By this logic African countries are "encouraged" through the IMF and the World Bank to engage in mechanized agriculture, uprooting existing and self-sufficient villages in order to produce for export.

However, the commodity composition of world trade favors manufactured goods more than food and raw materials. Furthermore, the production of raw materials exhibits diminishing returns on the supply side and an inelastic demand with respect to price. This means there is less total revenue for agricultural exporting nations when relative agricultural prices fall. Also, the per capita income elasticities of demand for agricultural foodstuffs and raw materials are relatively low compared with those for fuel and minerals. For example, the income elasticities of demand for cocoa, sugar, coffee, tea, and bananas have all been estimated at less than one, with most in the range of 0.3 to 0.5 (Maizel, 1968). Thus, only a sustained high rate of per capita income growth in the developed countries can lead to an even modest expansion of these particular commodities (Todaro, 1985). Even more fundamentally, the theory of comparative advantage assumes both external immobility of capital (Daly and Cobb, 1989) and the prevalence of a "free market," that is, unfettered competition and bargaining between equals, with prices being the result of the combined actions and wishes of sellers and buyers. In practice, however, international exchange does not operate in such a free manner. Transnational corporations administer flows of both capital and commodities among countries as they seek their own absolute advantage.

In addition, the Heckscher-Ohlin theorem, an offshoot of the neoclassical theory of trade, postulates that export of any country will embody relatively large amounts of the resources in which it has the highest relative abundance. By this then, underdeveloped countries, which contain two-thirds of the inhabitants of the world, should engage in labor intensive exports and the developed countries in capital intensive exports. For the United States, for instance, one would therefore expect its exports to embody large quantities of capital; and one would anticipate that the U.S. products most subject to import competition would contain large inputs of labor. A celebrated group of studies by Wassily Leontief (Vernon, 1972, p. 96), the "éminence grise" of industry analysis and input-output techniques in the United States, however, generated puzzling results. The studies revealed that U.S. exports as a whole are slightly more labor intensive than are the U.S. products that are most subject to competition from abroad. Where then is the principle of comparative advantage? One has but to agree with Daly and Cobb, Jr. that "given the great importance of trade to the nations involved and the rapidly changing global situation, economists would have done well to check the assumptions underlying the principle of comparative advantage against the facts" (Daly and Cobb, Jr., 1989, p. 218).

3. Inappropriate Assumptions

3.1. Thriving Microenterprises

The neoclassical model does not suit the African context. While the economic picture of Africa is one of stagnation and hardship, in part at least due to SAP, family businesses are thriving. This is best explained by their ability to reconcile African social and cultural values and traditions with the need for economic efficiency (Dia, 1992). Mammondu Dia has rightly pointed out that this indigenous system has enabled family firms to navigate through and survive major economic difficulties. Management, largely a family affair, relies greatly on informal and personal types of business relationships. This is so because the African social system, as Lewis Hyde puts it, is governed by "the erotic nature of the giving of gifts in contrast to the selling of commodities" (Hyde, 1979, p. 60). To African entrepreneurs, a commodity is often afforded the characteristics of a gift. A product is seen to have a unique "worth" different from its exchange value, depending on the context in which it is purchased. Thus, the circumstances surrounding economic dealings are more important than the impersonal forces of supply and demand. Commercial transactions, prices, and terms of payment depend, for example, on the relations between the operators and their clients. There is one price for friends, another for family members, and yet another for foreigners; therefore, prices are not exclusively market determined. These microenterprises maintain family and ethnic ties, reinforce the group's solidarity, and facilitate the redistribution of income which, in the context of the extended family, constitutes the essence of the group's stability and moral equilibrium. This is in direct contrast with the economist's ethnocentric approach to culture (Hunt, 1989) that assumes that the basic goal of any society is to achieve the same values characterizing Western countries (i.e., spirit of enterprise, profit motive, material security, individual autonomy, and self-interest). Countries not exhibiting such values are viewed as primitive and underdeveloped.

Thus the neoclassical or mainstream economic treatment of human relations as merely interactions for commodity exchange ignores the importance of culture and of community, and so misrepresents African economy, society and culture. The need to understand and take into account idiosyncracies of African sociocultural structure is of paramount importance for economic development in Africa. This requires economic models that pay particular attention to information and patterns of communication peculiar to African countries.

3.2. Hidden Cultural Traits

There is a number of African cultural traits that the developed countries have failed to observe properly (Wiredu, 1980, pp. 37–50). As noted by Mamadou Dia, African economic psychology is generally characterized by power connections between objects, humans, and the supernatural (Dia, 1992), and I draw freely upon his work in this section. Although the emphasis put on each of these elements and the interrelationships among them can vary from one ethnic group to another, the quest for equilibrium with other human beings and with the supernatural is generally the dominant guiding principle (Abraham, 1969, p. 51). The frontiers separating collective preferences from individual ones are often nonexistent or quite vague.

Ethnicity and group loyalty inherently take precedence over individualistic self-reliance, self-interest and national goals. Interpersonal relations and timely execution of certain social and religious or mystic activities are valued more than individual achievements. The circumstances and sometimes the rituals surrounding the economic transactions are often more important than strictly financial principles concerned. The value of economic acts is measured in terms of their capacity to reinforce the bonds of the group.

The African's sense of accumulation is quite different from that of the Westerner. There is a social and mystical need for what neoclassical economists may call "wastefulness." Mamadou Dia reports that among the Diola of Senegal it is common to massacre heads of cattle (750 in one instance) to celebrate circumcision ceremonies, and it is not uncommon for poor, malnourished farmers to give away vast quantities of foods on the occasion of marriages, circumcisions, or burials (Dia, 1992). Exacerbating matters further is the fact that the extended family is always present and always likely to be "imposing" itself in time of need. From early childhood one is taught to be responsible for the welfare of blood relatives. Often this produces a feeling of being compulsively responsible, which necessitates rendering every possible assistance to all relations, no matter how remote. Excess income is distributed first to close members of the extended family, then to the neighbors, and then to the ethnic group. Excess income, therefore, simply leads to more lavish consumption and a widening of the circle of those benefiting from the income redistribution as a form of investment against future uncertainties. Economic success achieved outside the group may lead to social ostracism. This is definitely contrary to the radical individualism notion of the orthodox economic model. A desire for clan prestige frequently provides a justification for these behavioral traits. For example, Mammondu Dia reports that Baoule funerals in the Ivory Coast are famous for their extravagant expenditure of family treasure (such as jewels, gold dust, etc.). This practice occurs in other African countries too and a higher level of education may not matter in such cases. Mammondu Dia has rightly argued that from the development perspective, the problem is that this tendency (attaching little value to the self-control needed for saving) runs counter to the prerequisites for promoting private investment and African entrepreneurship.

African society is generally hierarchical, yet very consensual. Little prone to individualism, it tends to be egalitarian within the same age group, but hierarchical in group-to-group relations, with marked subordination of the younger members. Within each group, individuals possess equal legal status and the capacity to perform specific actions, but a person wishing to go beyond his or her own circle can do so only with the permission of the father or some other authority (i.e., a chief). These hierarchical structures have often been regarded by Westerners—who highly value assertiveness, individual freedom, and responsibility—as running counter to productivity and creativity. But this is not always borne out by fact or history. First, in most rural areas, the type of aggregation (lineage kingship) and the size of the unit (large extended family or small nuclear one) will determine how land and labor are allocated. Also, if there is considerable pressure within the community or group to adhere strictly to traditional and socially acceptable behavior, it may be difficult to induce isolated individuals to adopt innovations that tend to alienate them from the society. For instance, work on certain days or at certain times may be forbidden in deference to bush spirits. In part of Burkina Faso, the "chief de terre" has an absolute mystical power on all matters relating to land allocation and introduction of new farming techniques (Maurier). In this setting, it may be necessary to adopt extension methods that use the group as the focal contact point instead of individual farmers. A society founded on dependence and hierarchy may thus prove just as creative as any other. Indeed, the impulse to bring oneself to the attention of the "prince" may be a more powerful incentive than self-achievement. Even if paternalism and dependency ultimately slow the pace at which an entire population changes and evolves, they need not prevent progress, research, and economic development.

A promise or commitment, which is the manifestation of intention in legal actions, is no simple thing in the African context. The presence of several witnesses is a frequent requirement, and their role generally goes well beyond those of neutral bystanders. In some instances, they may be expected to remember the facts should one of the parties renege on the deal. In other instances, their presence and acquiescence (particularly if they are heads of family or village chiefs) are necessary to legitimize the act. Loans obtained by pawning or pledging an object are also symbolic acts. But here the symbolic value of the pledge is more important than its mercantile value. These pledges are accepted as evidence against debtors when disputes arise, but they primarily personify the debtor, who in a sense offers a part of himself as pledge, and having done so, can no longer go back on his word. This generates a higher rate of loan repayment in the traditional and informal financial system then the formal banking sector in Sub-Saharan Africa.

The tendency to value group solidarity and socializing has generally led Africans to attach a high value to leisure and the attendant ability to engage in rituals, ceremonies, and social activities. Indeed, an inadequate recognition of the social benefits attached to leisure, as well as the impact of traditional leadership and organizational patterns on labor availability, may lead to an overestimation of labor supply. The high value Africans attach to leisure has often been misconstrued by foreigners as "laziness."

Economists have explained this tendency in terms of a backward bending supply curve of labor. However, these activities serve as a means of reinforcing social bonds, which are the foundation of society. Thus, the marginal return of so-called unproductive labor (i.e., leisure) is generally very high in social terms if not in market or commodity terms. As a result, farmers tend to adopt innovations only when the expected return, measured in both social and economic terms, is likely to be substantially higher than what they are already receiving from the prevailing combination of leisure and productive activities.

4. Conclusion

The reconciliation of these traditional values with the imperatives of economic efficiency and accumulation is, therefore, crucial to economic development. The communicologist's thesis that economic processes should be viewed as but special instances of more general communicatory processes (see Babe, chapter 2 above) is better suited for African economic development than is the traditional neoclassical approach. Economic activities after all are exchange activities and all exchange activities are social behaviors, defining spheres of influence and power. Consequently, certain activities that appear irrational according to the economist's individualistic model may be quite rational and beneficial from the community's point of view and to appreciate and understand the differences requires broad-based information, its context, and comprehension of its relativistic nature.

References

Abraham, W. E. (1969). *The Mind of Africa*. Chicago: The University of Chicago Press.
Babe, R. E. (1993). "The Place of Information on Economics." *Information and Communication in Economics*, R. E. Babe, ed. Boston: Kluwer Academic Publishers, pp. 41–65.
Bryant, C. (1992). "Culture, Management, and Institutional Assessment." Africa Technical Department Institutional Development and Management, Washington, D.C.: The World Bank, March.
Dia, M. (1992). "Indigenous Management Practices: Lessons for Africa's Management in the 1990s." Africa Technical Department: Institutional Development and Management, Washington, D.C.: The World Bank, April.
Daly, H. E., and J. B. Cobb, Jr. (1989). *For the Common Good: Redirecting the*

Economy Toward Community, the Environment, and a Sustainable Future. Boston: Beacon Press.

Harrigan, P., and P. Mosley. (1991). "Evaluating the Impact of World Bank Structural Adjustment Lending: 1980–87." *Journal of Development Studies* 27(3):63–94.

Hunt, D. (1989). *Economic Theories of Development: An Analysis of Competing Paradigms.* Savage, Maryland: Barnes and Noble.

Hyde, L. (1979). *The Gift: Imagination and the Erotic Life of Property.* New York: Vintage.

Maizels, A. (1968). *Exports and Economic Growth of Developing Countries.* London: Cambridge University Press.

Maurier, H. (1976). *Philosophie de l'Afrique Noire.* Verlag des Antropos-Instituts, St. Augustin Bei, Bonn.

McCall, J. J. (1965). "The Economics of Information and Optimal Stopping Rules." *Journal of Business* 38(3):300–317.

Ricardo, D. (1951). *Principles of Political Economy and Taxation.* Sraffa edition. London: Cambridge University Press.

Rostow, W. W. (1960). *The Stages of Economic Growth.* London: Cambridge University Press.

Sametz, A. W. (1970). "The Free-Enterprise Economy: A Price-Directed Economic System." In R. Kaminsky, *Introduction to Economic Issues.* Garden City, New York: Anchor Books. 2–12.

Smith, A. (1979). *An Inquiry into the Nature and Causes of the Wealth of Nations*, Vol. 1. Indianapolis: Liberty Press.

Stigler, G. J. (1961). "The Economics of Information, A Perspective." *Economic Journal Supplement* 95:21–41.

Sowell, T. (1983). "Second Thoughts About the Third World." *Harper's* (November):34–42.

Todaro, M. P. (1985). *Economic Development in the Third World*, Third Edition. New York: Longman.

Vernon, R. (1972). *Manager In the International Economy.* Englewood Cliffs, New Jersey: Prentice-Hall.

Weissman, S. R. (1990). "Structural Adjustment in Africa: Insights from the Experiences of Ghana and Senegal." *World Development* 18(12):1621–1634.

Wiredu, K. (1980). *Philosophy and an African Culture* [especial Chapter 3, "How not to Compare African Traditional Thought with Western Thought"] London: Cambridge University Press.

World Bank. (1988). "Report on Adjustment Lending." Washington, D.C.: The World Bank, August 1.

11 COMMUNICATION, INFORMATION, AND TRANSNATIONAL ENTERPRISE

Jill Hills

Introduction

International communications have always been the subject of government intervention. Technology, economics, and politics have been interwoven in the competition between the major industrial powers to control both the physical means of communication and the information flows through those physical links. The value of information in reducing the unpredictable is enhanced by speed, which in turn allows greater centralization and control. Each new technology, which allows information to be passed at greater speeds from one part of the country to another or from one country to another, enhances the power of those who collect and control that information. As one American government official said in 1977, "Trade doesn't follow the flag any more it follows the communication system" (US Foreign Relations Subcommittee, 1977, p. 12). And almost ten years later another such official stated "We know that the manipulation and control of information is among the greatest weapons of conquest in the modern world. We know above all that information is power, more valuable than oil and more precious than gold" (Dougan, 1985, p. 55). For these reasons, traditionally, governments have been among the major users, providers, and controllers of information as well as controllers of the networks on which information transfer rests.

But in the past twenty years private companies have made massive capital investments to ensure such information transfer in secure conditions. And new service industries, particularly in finance, have grown up around global information transfers. Private electronic networks ensure speed, flexibility, and control of the information transferred. They also contribute to a global, rather than domestic, division of labor. Information networks allow the utilization of cheap labor in developing countries, not only in the manufacturing of products in subsidiaries brought under central control and direction, but also in the processing of the data relating to that production. Hence, for instance, in 1992 the British government hired an American company employing workers in the Philippines in order to transfer citizens' tax files into computer readable form (*The Guardian*, 1992, 26 June). For developing countries such employment is similar to that of a manufacturing screwdriver assembly plant, with the value added centered in the industrialized country and little, if any, technology transfer. The difference rests in the lack of transfer of a physical product, and the virtually simultaneous processing of the raw material in the industrialized country, which online international communications allows.

New communications technologies produce new cost parameters, which in turn provide the possibilities of new products, new services, and the opportunities for new entrants to a market. As capital costs fall so entry costs are lessened. In communications technology declining costs of information transfer have come with the introduction of digital switching, coupled with the wide bandwidth of satellite and fiber optic transmission. New micromillimeter radio technology can provide cheap line of sight transmission, while mobile technology of cellular radio and satellite tracking allows information transfer with employees on the move. So, for instance, via Inmarsat and Eutelsat satellites truckers delivering to the European Continent can be monitored en route by their headquarters (*Public Network*, 1991, pp. 42–74). The new information and communications technologies allow either greater control from the center or a dispersal of information and responsibility.

Lower costs and new technology can produce more choice for the user and a greater variety of products and customised service offerings. Communications over the past ten years has been no different from other industries in seeing greater product and service differentiation. As a result new companies have entered the market to provide new information services at national and international level. Among specialist data bases financial, patent, publication, and legal data can be accessed worldwide. In common with other service industries some communications-based information services have transferred into products. So, for instance much of the previous telephone white and yellow pages service in Britain is now met by the sale of the information on laser discs. There is no easy dividing line therefore between information services and products. Each may grow out of the other. On-line communications links increase as the number of personal computers and work-stations increase.

Improvements in communications technology and declining costs of provision have also contributed to the process of the globalization of manufacturing and services, both by allowing easier and faster information transmission and by facilitating control from the centre. Where once subsidiaries might be semiindependent entities catering to the local market, communications technology has allowed not only a reduction in that autonomy, but aso integrated manufacturing on a regional or global basis. In the financial market, banks, such as Chase Manhattan, and financial service companies, such as Visa, handle all transactions from a region, such as Europe, in one center (Horton, 1991).

Other company strategies are dependent on communications. As product differentiation increases so companies seek partners to cover areas of the market in which they are weak. As research and development costs increase so they spread the risk by forming national and global alliances and seek to market products on a global basis to offset research costs against economies of scale. Or in an alternative but often parallel strategy, they form alliances to buy in the use of a particular technology. As the time to market of a new product can make up to 30 percent difference in its profitability, so time-based competition becomes of strategic importance and communications networks needed on an intra- and inter-firm level (Purton, 1991).

Within the international political economy transnational companies have become preeminent in their demands for information networks. But their success in achieving their demands cannot be attributed to market competition alone, nor to technology alone. In focussing on markets neoclassical economics disregards the notion that markets are political artifacts structured by governments, thereby divorcing economics from state and societal power. Technologists tend to see technology itself as the driving force of economic activity, again downplaying the role of hidden or transparent intervention and how technology contributes to power. In practice, governments restructure markets and retard or advance technological innovation in the interests of certain sectors of the economy (Hills with Papathanassopoulos, 1991).

Although the globalization of production and distribution with its concomitant demand for information, and technological advances in communications have contributed to the preeminence of large business in communications, it is not possible to ignore changes in the regulatory environment brought about by state action. Transnational companies have pressured governments to relax regulation of communications networks. Hence information, networks and regulation are all interlinked in the current realignment of the international political economy. The major actors in this realignment are transnational business users, national network operators, and the nation states of the industrialised West.

Industrialized country governments, and in particular those of the USA and Britain, are pressing for a new definition of international communications networks in the interests of their transnational companies. Whereas throughout the nineteenth century and most of the twentieth the pattern of telecommunications provision was on a national basis, with governments responsible for standards, equipment, network provision, and regulation under monopoly provision, in the 1990s the very concept of a telecommunications network is changing. From an international system seen as provided on a national basis joined by international gateways, the concept is changing to an international network seen as from company A in country A to company A in country B, without any reference to geographical or national boundaries. The emphasis in the industrialized West has switched away from domestic considerations to the provision of international telecommunication services and to global alliances between network operators to undertake that provision. The previous nationally based network operators (PTTs) are themselves becoming transnational companies.[1]

Increasingly the needs of large users of telecommunications have come to dominate the technological and regulatory agenda of the industrialized West. Such domination comes partly from the skewed nature of telecommunications traffic. More than 60 percent of traffic in any one country comes from about 10 percent of users. The more skewed the traffic pattern, the less the development of the network beyond urban areas and business users, the greater their impact on policy. The more any one country depends on multinationals for its exports or on financial services, the keener the consideration of their needs. So, for instance, in Britain, which saw the product of financial services grow from 14 billion pounds in 1980 to 30 billion in 1990 and where the attraction of foreign investment has been a prime strategy of government, the communications needs of these companies were a prime consideration in introducing a second carrier into the telecommunications network (Hills, 1986, p. 123).

Then, because of the skewed traffic pattern, the more competition is allowed into domestic network operation the more the primacy given to the largest customers' demands by the major network operator. Network operators in Britain and Australia are among those which have undertaken internal reorganization focussing on the satisfaction of large users (*BT Management News*, 1991, p. 7). The skewed traffic pattern combines with the mercantilist aspirations of governments, and their restructuring of markets to provide a communications and information environment favorable to large business.

Increasingly therefore the driving force behind changes in the international organization and regulation of telecommunications and information are transnational private companies. These include those who wish to operate such networks in competition with the nationally based operators, those who wish to use such networks for internal purposes, and those who wish to supply information through them via databases or broadcasting of programs or advertising. And, in turn as national PTTs from the industrialized countries invest overseas, so they become major international users as well as suppliers of transmission capacity.

Statistics on services, although notoriously suspect, indicate nontraded services—intracompany communications—to be the largest part of information communication activities on an international level. Nevertheless within the United States it is information service providers who have been the major force in pressing for worldwide liberalization of networks (Sauvant, 1986, pp. 90–91; Hills, 1989, pp. 14–19). In particular they have sought "an enforceable liberal international regime for data-service transactions." In the words of Karl Sauvant:

> "Obstacles" are defined broadly and include the introduction of taxes or tariffs on the value of data-service flows, certain conditions placed on the operation of leased lines, certain data-protection provisions, local content requirements, lack of software protection, market access barriers, certain equipment policies and telephone monopolies (Sauvant, 1986, p. 14).

In turn national governments, and particularly the United States, line up behind their transnationals in international institutions, promoting their interests. International institutions themselves are moving towards a form of privatisation which allows such companies a greater say in international regulations previously the province of national governments (Tarjanne, 1991, pp. 19–21).

These current trends are rooted in history within the industrialised West, and particularly within the USA and Britain, where since the 1980s cost allocation within communications networks has favored large business. Nevertheless in both countries (although more so in the USA) poorer consumers have been protected by regulation from bearing the total costs of capital investment in the public network. In both countries liberalization of the network has been followed by both fragmentation and domestic political settlements on the distribution of costs and benefits. In seeking replication of its market structure throughout the world, without any compensating political settlement in favor of smaller nations and in seeking advantage for its transnational companies the United States government has sought to use not only international agencies such as Intelsat, and the ITU, but also financial institutions such as the World Bank and GATT. And outside these multilateral agencies bilateral arm-twisting utilizing the Super 301 clause of the 1974 Trade Act has been used against specific countries.

This article will trace the various mechanisms by which the British and then the American governments have acted to alter physical infrastructure, information flows, and regulation in favor of their transnational companies. The article takes as its starting point a structural view of the world economy, one where the rich, be they states or companies, wield power and where the poor are subject to control. In the information sector, to be rich in information resources is to gain power.

Economic and political theories all represent the interests of one section of a community against another and can be used by government to gain political legitimacy. The hegemony of classical neoliberal economics propounded in the international arena of ideas by such multilateral offspring of the industrialised countries as the OECD, the World Bank and International Monetary Fund, the General Agreement on Trade and Tariffs (GATT), and the European Community, as well as by industrialized country governments of Left and Right, coupled with the financial deregulation of the 1980s, have culminated in a recession within the industrialized world in the 1990s, and created conditions of starvation in the poorest countries. It is against this background not only of a collapse of communism (of command control economies) but of a threatened collapse of capitalism that the current neomercantilist actions of the three industrialized regional blocs—the Americas, Europe, and Japan—has to be seen. Such a neomercantilist framework for the analysis of international economic relations is presented by writers, such as Gilpin, who have foreseen the future as a potential disaggregation into regional blocs (Gilpin, 1987).

However, there is no one economic or political theoretical grail which can explain the workings of the international economy or the behavior of states or companies. The conjuncture of market structure, institutional competence, political structure, historical conditions, and state interests will differ over time and issue. So, for instance, the increasing competition between regional blocs in communications products, technology, and services, has to be seen against fragmentation within the EC, where the neoliberalism of Britain and the Netherlands and their concern for multinationals is lined up against the dirigism of France and the poorer Southern European states. One can argue also that the industrialized powers in conjunction with middle income industrialized countries, such as New Zealand and Australia, combine in the 1990s in a mercantilist attitude to developing countries, increasingly seen as the place where new profits can be made from privatization.

There are certain themes which recur in the study of the impact of transnational companies on the global economy, evident also in the study of the international political economy of information and communications. One such theme is the advantage of free trade to the largest companies and thereby the threat which nonprotectionism raises for infant industries and poorer countries. This disadvantage to free trade has been formally recognised within the General Agreement for Tariffs and Trade (GATT) and by the World Bank which in a recent study acknowledged that proposals for free trade between Latin American countries and the USA would benefit the USA to a much greater extent than the smaller countries (World Bank, 1991). A second theme is the fear of loss of sovereignty by developing countries, and recently, in relation to information and communications by industrialized Europe (Commission of European Communities, 1989). This fear is also linked to concerns regarding cultural imperialism—that is the swamping of indigenous cultures by Western media, or in Europe by American media.

A third theme revolves around the potential for control which transnationals may give to their home country through the extension of domestic legislation to the international arena. These fears of American control of their transnational companies for political ends was exacerbated by U.S. government action in preventing American technology being used to build the Soviet pipeline, and has been raised more recently in its proposal to enforce its anti-trust provisions overseas (Woolcock, 1982, pp. 611–624). These moves stand in stark contrast to statements in multilateral fora that the American government cannot control the behavior of its companies overseas, despite developing country requests that it should do so. A fourth theme is the increasing importance of international institutions in imposing American inspired neoliberal market structures both on the international economy and on individual country economies and in transferring power to private companies through enforced privatisation.

And finally, a fifth theme, specific to the information and communications sector, is what appears to be a drive by the United States government with allies in Britain to remove policy considerations regarding equitable access and universality of service from international telecommunications. Their attempts to privatize Intelsat and Inmarsat and to undermine international accounting rates, are designed to limit transfers of funds to public communication networks in poorer countries. These moves follow those designed to protect the free flow of information in UNESCO, and via the OECD's Transborder Data Flow guidelines (Roach, 1990, pp. 283–307; OECD, 1981). They presage an era where private communications networks and private information flows on a global basis take precedence over those giving access to the general public. In this passing of control of information and communications to private entities, for the purpose of national economic advantage, the communications and information sector reflects the realpolitique of the New World Order.

The Gulf war, with its imposition of American military command over US allies together with the break-up of the Soviet Union have left the USA as the undisputed military hegemon. However the recession in the USA has produced a perception of falling living standards and of failure by the American government to profit by its international leadership role. A hardening of mercantilist attitudes has taken place with developing countries claiming they are ignored within the UN and other international institutions. The New World Order set out by President Bush took shape as a regime unprepared to compromise on American economic interests, and the indications in January 1993 are that the Clinton regime will take a tougher stand on trade policies (Tisdall and Walker, 1992). At the same time developing countries find themselves with no alternative hegemon to turn to for advancement of their interests. In information and communications the advancement of U.S. interests is the advancement of the interests of its transnationals, which, in turn, encompasses their ability to provide and use international networks without regulation by nation states and to have the unprecedented right to inwardly invest in any country they so wish. Such proposed imposition of private rights over sovereign nations, backed up by the threat of trade sanctions, is predominantly about political control through economic power. It is a strategy of micropolitics—the application of economic incentives to political institutions through liberalisation and privatization

(Pirie, 1988). Its aim is to regain the perceived loss of American hegemonic status through the rolling back of the power of other states in the international system via the imposition of a free market and the dominance of its transnationals.

Transnational Enterprises and Communications

Oswald and Gladys Ganley suggest that we should distinguish between the conduit of information, its content, its format, its hardware, and its function. The conduit or transmission medium may be via cable, satellite, microwave, or a newer radio-based transmission technology. The content may be data or different types of broadcasting program or advertising or on-line video. The format or the "physical form of the display of the content," ranges from simple voice reception of the telephone to facsimile, to display on a computer terminal, to images on a television. And the hardware describes the machinery involved in transmission and reception—telephones, computers, TVs, and radios (Ganley and Ganley, 1982, p. 245).

Helpful as it is, this method of breaking down the information and communications sector tends to overstate the technological convergence of the traditional sectors of broadcasting (point to multipoint communications) and telecommunications (point to point). Each tends to be regulated separately at a national level with broadcasting controlled for content. Nor does it differentiate between different types of data communications. These may be in the form of person to person communications, information services utilising data bases and data processing. Telecommunications traffic is still overwhelmingly voice traffic although public data networks have been in operation since the 1970s (Purton, 1991). It is through the use of private data networks and primarily amongst the largest companies that the major changes in information usage have taken place.

It is sometimes alleged that information has replaced capital as the strategic resource of transnational companies. However information and communication networks require massive capital investment together with perpetual maintenance and upgrading. For instance in 1992 the Hongkong Shanghai Bank is spending almost $2 million simply on a service contract to maintain its packet switched data network in 35 countries (*BT Today*, 1992, p. 14).

For manufacturers communication networks now provide essential tools to link subsidiaries to company headquarters, to link component suppliers to factories, to link retailers to the company. Such networks allow central control over costs, over design, over production processes, over stocks, and over cashflow. Communications links expand the span of control both over a range of activities within companies and across geographical boundaries.

When data processing of information was first introduced into companies it was based on large mainframe computers requiring cards to be punched and fed in a central department. But as the costs of computing fell with a commensurate increase in power and decline in the size of computers, many companies introduced Local Area Networks, linking up numbers of personal computers. The strategy of investment in information collection and analysis through advanced technology, although expensive, was thought to provide a necessary competitive edge over other companies. The reality has not been so successful. Many large companies seem unable to specify how much their networks cost and the problems of incompatibility of equipment has resulted in companies installing several networks. Integration of these networks is then expensive. In the current recessionary climate, major companies, such as Nomura Securities, are cutting back on investment in computer systems by up to 40 percent (Terazano, 1992; Manchester, 1991).

Companies such as General Electric, which had early experience of management information systems, sold that experience to others through their own information service companies, but, in general, companies specializing in information systems have tended to come out of computer and software companies, such as IBM (International Business Machines) in the U.S.A. or ICL (International Computers Limited) in Britain. Banks have also capitalized on their early experience with information transmission by setting up system suppliers. But today both these types of information service companies are competed against by the telecommunications network operators themselves. These PTTs compete for individual company accounts and collaborate in global network offerings. For instance, in 1990, AT&T, BT, Sprint, Cable and Wireless, Transpac, Infonet, and GE Information Services all competed for a contract for Unilever's European network. In 1991 British Telecom, DBP Telekom of Germany, and NTT of Japan set up Pathfinder with participation from IBM, to provide end-to-end communications networks for global companies.

The banking sector and the airline sector were the first to establish sectorwide international electronic networks in the 1970s. By 1986 more than 1,400 banks were members of SWIFT, the Society for Worldwide Interbank Financial Telecommunications. The electronic network could handle more than one million messages per day, yet this was not enough and the network had to be upgraded in 1987. Financial services followed manufacturers in its global distribution. Then financial deregulation in the American market had a worldwide impact with American banks taking the lead in setting up subsidiaries worldwide (Moran, 1991).

Coupled with the growth of off-shore markets, such as the Eurobond market, an increase in the securitization of debt, and increased competition for safe borrowers, banks were encouraged into investment in private international networks. The recession of the early 1980s forced both banks and companies into controlling costs and into making their cash work for them. Banks increasingly looked to low-risk Fortune 500 customers while these large customers demanded fingertip control of their financial information, and electronic payment systems to reduce the time in which cash was nonutilized. At the same time these companies were able to use the securities market, rather than the banks to raise cash, driving bank margins lower, and increasing bank incentives both to create new financial products as a means of making money and to automate further to cut costs of paper transactions and staffing levels. In the domestic market automated tellers reduced staff, then were joined up in international private networks to serve tourists and businessmen.

Floating exchange rates allowed transnational companies to develop their own foreign exchange departments to earn profits for the company, and commensurately required both up to the minute information and the means by which to effect transfers. Transnational companies, whether in manufacturing or services, have themselves increasingly taken on the characteristics of financial service companies (Lascelles, 1985).

The Big Bang in London in 1987, which effectively removed many of the barriers which previously divided securities dealing from the banking sector, added new impetus both to electronic trading systems and to electronic information provision. With easier finance available for mergers and takeovers these burgeoned on an international scale, thereby fuelling further demands for up to the minute information of share prices. The market in securities became global with trading on a 24-hour basis in New York, Tokyo, and London as well as smaller financial centers. When Tokyo closes London opens and when London closes it is morning in New York. And as a corollary when security holdings become internationalized, so companies utilize electronic information systems to put the corporate image across to international stockholders, holding annual meetings with video links via satellite.

Electronic communications may substitute for physical transport. Following the Gulf War for instance the decline in transatlantic air traffic parallelled a massive increase in the demand for international video conference links in Britain. As well as minimizing physical risk to their executives companies also found such communications saved on costs. Similarly electronic communications can obviate time differences as well as making for easier physical access to a market or bypassing inefficient postal systems. Newspapers have begun to print in several locations via satellite. Among others utilizing this technology, the Japanese newspaper Yomiuri Shimbun prints editions in the United States, Bangkok, and London via satellite. Telecommunications obviates the time difference as well as transport costs. Information reaches London and New York at the same time as Tokyo. Fax machines spread particularly quickly in Japan, because the written language is clearer than the spoken, but also in Australia where large distances are made more difficult by poor internal transport and postal infrastructure. Fax has also obviated time differences.

Communications links also act to increase market transparency, thereby shortening the response time to changing market conditions and lowering barriers to entry (Rada, 1987, p. 156). Caught in the conflict between global marketing to achieve economies of scale and small batch runs to meet demands for product diffentiation and customer specification some companies, such as Apple computers, have taken to siting the manufacture of core products in one country within a region. These core products are then "flavourized" for particular customers or distributors as orders come in from the international market. The system obviates the need for large stocks, while capitalizing on the lower labor costs and investment incentives of the lesser industrialized countries.

In tandem with this globalization of production and financial services, has come demand for information provision, customized for particular applications. Reuters has moved from being a news agency to a provider of financial information on a 24-hour per day basis, servicing stock markets throughout the world. However, online databases consist of data geared to users in developed countries and are accessible at reasonable cost only through data networks. For potential users in developing countries the expense of access via the public telephone network limits availability (UN Centre on Transnational Corporations, 1983).

The packaging of information into data bases is an industry demanding large-scale initial investment and still dominated by the United States. In turn American domination of the industry has created incentives for protectionism within Europe. In an attempt to foster its infant database industry, worth about $3 billion per year, the EC proposed in 1992 that both the selection and arrangement of the database and the raw facts themselves should be protected by copyright, thereby not only preventing pirating but also competition. A reciprocity clause was evidently designed to place pressure on the American industry, where similar unfair extraction legislation had been rejected by the Supreme Court (Cane, 1992). Such legislation would make it impossible for other countries to develop their own database industries, thereby perpetuating the current market structure.

The economics of information provision are such that the costs of provision lie in the original creation, whether it is a database or a software package or a broadcasting program. Its replication and distribution are almost costless. Hence economies of scale demand the widest possible distribution, preferably to a global market.

In the broadcast programming market economies of scope demand the use of that information in numerous technological formats for separate markets—cinema, video, television, laser disk, audiotape, books, magazines, newspapers. Hence multinational companies with interests in a number of information media and communication distribution systems have grown up to take advantage of market segmentation and economies of scope and scale (Locksley, 1988). Advertising in one segment reinforces sales in another while satellite technology allows cross-border television transmission and reception.[2]

As companies have globalized production, processing, and distribution, so in the 1990s the demand is for more efficient, secure, and fast communications and for large business users to have more choice in how they configure their communications networks. Demands made on the telecommunication network operators in the industralised West for fast, flexible, secure communications have therefore been extended to include all telecommunications networks throughout the world. As the competitive edge of one global company against another increasingly depends on the methods by which it can transfer and utilise information, so the pressure on governments to provide telecommunications infrastructure for their benefit increases. As a result poorer countries with old telecommunications systems find themselves handicapped in the competition for inward foreign investment, and upgrade international communications for business links before investing in their domestic infrastructure.

At the same time network operators in the industrialized countries are seeking to upgrade their service offerings to transnationals, through arrangements with other operators which allow one-stop shopping for those companies wishing to establish global networks. This option provides the transnational with billing in one currency, and allows it to evade the problems of dealing with numbers of national PTTs. Transnational companies currently have the choice of leasing a variety of international and national lines from PTTs and operating the network themselves, of buying in the services of a company to set up and operate the network, or of utilizing software designed networks from the PTT. The cost parameters of each are changing. Whereas previously companies would establish private networks via leased lines and would run them in-house, the problems of connecting equipment with incompatible standards and of maintaining the network requires expensive expertise. In the current recession outsourcing—that is, contracting with a third party to set up and run a network—is increasing as companies cut back to their core business. But, as PTTs invest heavily in software and provide "intelligent network" services that allow large users flexibility, the ability to decide on the routing of a message and increased cost control, so users may move from leased lines back onto the public network (*Public Network,* 1991a, p. 238).

Increasingly the architecture of a network depends on software, and on the manipulation of database information lodged within the network. PTTs will regain advantage over large users because they continue to control the information within the network. From a decade of hostility between national PTTs and large business users, it seems that, as in other sectors, the supplier/retailer/customer relationships in communications networks have become increasingly interdependent (Darmaros, 1989).

Yet, from the transnational's perspective unless a whole new regime of international regulation can be imposed to supercede national regulation, state owned PTTs and state based regulation will continue to provide barriers to the cross-national communications of global companies. The failure of BT's Syncordia venture, set up in 1991 to provide voice, data, and video links to multinational companies has been widely attributed to the restrictions by governments on the range of services that can be offered by any foreign company (Dixon, 1991). It is to that political control and to attempts to alter the international regulation of communications networks that we now turn.

Governments and Control of Communications

Communications have always been linked to industrial competitiveness, to political control, and to national security. In the nineteenth century the telegraph was linked to the expansion and consolidation of British colonial power. Its international routes reflected the requirements of the British government and of the trading companies whose interests coincided with those of the government. Starting with the telegraph and with submarine cables whose technology was subsidized by the British government, the Imperial system of telegraph communication created efficient communications between the British government and its colonial possessions. The telegraph had the effect of not only shortening communication times between the countries of the Empire but also of centralizing control in Whitehall, reducing the autonomy of colonial administrations (Kieve, 1973).

The control of physical links went hand in hand with the centralization of information gathering and information distribution. Until the 1920s the British Post Office, the monopoly provider of both telegraph and telephone ran an "information department" with a similar function to that of a news agency. It is no coincidence that the British news agency, Reuters, the electric telegraph and the financial markets of the City of London grew hand in hand. Information and its speed of transmission to those markets created profits for its insurers and traders.

Through the patent system British manufacturers controlled the core submarine cable technology. British companies laid the cables, operated them, and took the profits available from information transmission. The high prices which they charged reflected both the risk of the ventures (many cables were lost) to their shareholders and the value of the information to those sending and receiving it.

When radio became a reliable means of communication and its cheaper up-front costs promised the potential of large numbers of new entrants into communication carriage, it threatened the established interests of the cable companies. It was the British government that convened a conference that decided that because communications by cable were more secure than those by radio, cable company interests were of paramount importance to national security. And because wireless allowed the colonial countries to consider the provision of their own international communications at a cost cheaper than that charged by the cable companies, it was the British government that intervened to attempt to prevent such autonomy. As a result of this decision the international communications of British colonies were handled by the British company Cable and Wireless until after the Second World War, and in the case of Hong Kong still provide the financial and geographical base for that company's expansion into a global network operator (Barty King, 1979). In similar fashion, ITT (which took over AT&T's foreign interests in 1934) was closely linked to the American government, and was involved in the 1970s in that government's adventures in Latin America.

Just as the British emphasized the establishment of cable as the basis for secure communications and supported the activities of Reuters, so in the 1930s, the American government and companies railed against British communications and information hegemony and fostered radio as its means of international penetration (Ganley and Ganley, 1982, p. 79). After the Second World War, American objections to the British Imperial preference in trade were parallelled by concerted efforts to rectify the imbalance in control of international communications, both in terms of infrastructure and in terms of information gathering. With cable technology still firmly under British hegemony, American attention was directed to satellite communications. Intelsat, established in the 1960s, became the focus of American efforts to create an American controlled monopoly of long distance radio communications. The rest of the world contributed to the research and development of space communications by American companies. In addition the American newsagencies Associated Press and United Press International dislodged Reuters, and the increased export of American movies spread the message of American individualistic values worldwide (Terrell and Korner, 1987, p. 257).

As the American government increasingly took over from the British government as the world's policeman, its interests were served by the overseas expansion of American companies. American companies invested heavily in overseas subsidiaries, first in Canada and Europe and then in Asia. International telecommunications across the Atlantic became widespread after the introduction of TAT 8 in 1956, a submarine cable which linked Britain and the USA, thereby ensuring that traffic from the rest of Europe crossed Britain. American monitoring stations in Britain retained control of those communications. Only in 1992 will a submarine cable, TAT 10, link the USA directly with the European continent (*Public Network*, 1991b, p. 10).

During the Cold War of the 1950s and 1960s American domination of satellite technology allowed new forms of information gathering. Satellite surveillance of military installations were crucial in the Cuban missile crisis. In addition the process by which raw materials was extracted from developing countries, processed and sold back to them was extended into the area of information. Landsat surveyed the geographical resources of the developing world and sold the ensuing pictures to potential investors and back to the governments of those countries. Developing countries objected to what they perceived as further exploitation of their natural resources by the transfer of information without their prior consent to transnationals and breaches of their sovereignty (Sauvant, 1986, p. 94). Perhaps because of the problems of information ownership, which the U.S. government insisted accrued to the satellite operator, although the business itself was privatised in the 1980s the satellite itself remains American government owned.

During the immediate postwar years developing countries gradually gained independence from their colonial powers and joined the United Nations. Through the UN and its specialized agencies they began to press their case for a less inequitable international order. For newly independent nations sovereignty was a predominant concern. But also as the gap between rich and poor continued those in developing countries began to question the predominant views of the North in relation to modernization and the trickle-down thesis of economic growth by which the poor would benefit as the rich grew richer.

Industrial modernization was seen by American academics as the precursor to political modernisation. And in turn political modernization would be aided by media penetration. Hence the mass media were viewed both as an indicator and as a tool for economic development and political stability (Lerner, 1958; Pye, 1963; Schramm, 1964; Rogers, 1976; Schramm and Lerner, 1976). Their potential for the creation of instability, through the part they played in the downgrading of indigenous knowledge and goods in favor of Western commodities and knowledge, was unforeseen. Nor were the penetration of Western ideas and the information gathering and distribution of Western news agencies seen as detrimental to the sovereignty of developing countries.

Yet for developing countries these were major areas of concern. Just as they challenged the industrialized consensus on free trade as evidenced by GATT, and sought both exemptions and the establishment of UNCTAD, so these same ideas of sovereignty and protection fed through into debates within UNESCO on the New World Information Order. Just as they challenged the inward investment of multinationals as a threat to their sovereignty so newly independent countries challenged the penetration of Western culture. Whereas once the colonial dominions of the British had challenged the centralised gathering of information and control of channels of communications so the newly independent nations challenged the ideas of the free flow of information which favored the West (Osolnik, 1991, p. 479).

But even while the United States was suffering the aftermath of withdrawal from Vietnam and the cartelization of oil producers in OPEC together with the oil shocks of the 1970s seeming to alter the balance of power towards developing countries, the political Right was gathering force within the USA. Increasingly irritated at the lack of gratitude of developing countries and the failure of U.S. hegemony within international institutions American politicians began to press for increased protectionism. In 1984 the United States withdrew from UNESCO and contemplated withdrawal from the ITU.

The debate in UNESCO was primarily about the control of information and not about the control of the means of communications. A similar debate took place during the 1970s in the OECD and in the UN on Transborder Data Flows. Once again a concern for sovereignty was paramount, but not only confined to the developing countries. Among the industrialized countries privacy and data protection legislation sought to control the passage of personal information outside geographical borders. For some developing countries, such as Brazil, data flows were controlled by physical gateways in order to ensure that data processing took place within the country (UN Centre on Transnational Corporations, 1983; Marques and Oliviera, 1991, p. 402). Brazil became targetted for American retaliation.

Developing countries were not united on the issue, some seeing privacy legislation as a means by which the industrialized were preventing data processing being done in low cost countries. The issue gradually departed from the international agenda as the industrialised country recession of the early 1980s forced countries to vie for multinational investment and as communications themselves became increasingly important to those companies. In 1987, under new leadership, in tune with the predominant neoliberalist ideology, and bowing to the realities of a debt crisis which had stripped power from developing countries, UNESCO itself came down in favor of free flow of information. Nevertheless the data protection legislation of the industrialised countries used to prevent files on personnel from crossing borders provides a barrier to that free flow and a means for states to exercise some control over international data communications (Bradshaw, 1990).

During the 1970s the Americans were handicapped in developing international communications by the existing domestic system, then under the monopoly of AT&T. Gradual liberalization favoured large business users. And the open skies policy of the 1970s can be seen as a means for U.S. industry and the U.S. government to benefit from U.S. predominance in satellite communications. When it allowed international carriers to transmit both data and voice communications the FCC required AT&T to utilized both cable and satellite for its international communications—to protect Intelsat.

But as its hegemony over satellite technology was challenged by the Europeans, and it lost influence within Intelsat to the developing nations which joined the co-operative, so within a decade the U.S. government mounted pressure on Intelsat to allow private satellites to operate internationally. Such satellites could boost its flagging satellite industry and provide a cheaper leased line service to international business. In turn, the threat of competition turned Intelsat's attention to satisfying the needs of its largest users, rather than the majority of its poorer signatories. Vsats—small aperture reception dishes—were developed specifically for their benefit, together with spot beams for heavy traffic routes and alterations to planned satellites to give higher Ku band service for large business (Intelsat, 1991, p. 14).

In addition in 1990 the American and British together with the Australians succeeded in gaining an alteration to the Intelsat constitution which opened the door to private regional satellites to compete head to head with Intelsat. With private- and country-owned satellites competing for large business customers in the growth area of the Pacific Basin, and the prospect of competition on its Atlantic route from which revenues have cross-subsidized tariffs to poorer countries and thin routes, the stage is set for transnationals to have cheaper international communications and poorer countries to bear the costs.

At the same time as its government first moved against Intelsat the FCC allowed privately owned submarine cables to be laid across the Atlantic and Pacific, taking leased line traffic and competing with the cables of the national telecommunications operators. The impact of increased capacity has been to lower tariffs for large business users (and the American government) and to place pressure on Intelsat, which for the first time in 1990 reported a drop in profits.[3] In turn this drop in revenue provoked an attempt by the British and American governments to privatize Intelsat, thereby attempting to turn de facto control by transnational business into de jure control and to further marginalize the public access needs of developing countries (Hayes, 1991, p. 1).

Just as in the domestic systems of both Britain and the United States, these moves have been legitimated by economic theory—in particular the concept of cost-based tariffs. This theory legitimates the deaveraging of tariffs so that the large user and heavily used route pay less per unit than the small user or thin route. The theory also encompasses usage versus capital costs. Since the definition and distribution of common costs is contestable, the theory has come under attack as a theoretical vehicle for the political interests of large business. In the United States, where AT&T still must average tariffs, the theory is not practiced, and even in Britain it has lost its evangelical force (Oettinger, 1988; Carsberg, 1990; Hills, 1993). Nevertheless it remains the accepted economic truth in such organizations as the OECD and EC and under a privatized Intelsat could be imposed on developing countries.

As the quotations at the beginning of this article demonstrate, the geopolitics of information and communication are no less important in the 1990s than they were in the 1890s. Just as in the nineteenth century the British concern with secure communications led to the laying of cable in the Caribbean which avoided Spanish held Cuba, so in the twentieth century Pacific cables go through Guam where U.S. interests are protected. It was American companies, which in the nineteenth century attempted to lay landlines across the then Russian territory of Alaska to join up with cable laid across Russia to take traffic from Europe to the United States. But a century later, despite the fall of communism, a fiber optic landline across Russia to Japan has been vetoed by COCOM on security grounds (Dixon, 1990). Since fiber optic networks are being laid by American companies in the previous satellite states of the Soviet bloc, the fact that European traffic would thereby bypass the United States may well have been the prime consideration. There is little doubt that the ownership and control of international infrastructure remains central to American security interests.

Regulation of International Communications

Throughout the nineteenth century and on into the 1970s telecommunications was controlled by governments. The international agreements that allowed national systems to interconnect through international gateways reflected the primacy accorded to national communications. States held sovereignty over their communications networks. They decided standards, they set tariffs, and they invested in the growth of networks and penetration. It was they who were signatories to the International Telecommunications Union treaties, and they who signed the postwar agreement on Intelsat. In general the political settlements reached within the industrialized countries prioritized the diffusion of the telephone, and up to the 1980s benefitted residential and rural users. A form of economic transfer took place from large business users and urban areas. But as the recession of the 1980s took hold, this transfer was increasingly questioned by large business seeking to reduce its costs. Liberalization of the network in America, Britain, and Japan was followed later (but retaining monopolies over voice service) by other EC countries, thereby advantaging large users (Hills, 1986, p. 203).

Just as in domestic telecommunications systems so in the international network a similar system had evolved through the mechanism of international accounting rates. These rates, determined on a bilateral basis, split the cost of transmission of an international message between sender and recipient PTT (sometimes with a transit PTT as well) on a 50/50 basis. The sender payed the recipient. Hence those countries with subscribers who initiated telephone calls tended to make payment to those who received. In general high accounting rates benefitted the recipient country and low accounting rates the sender.

In the post-war years, until the 1990s, the system went unremarked. The United States paid out billions of dollars to other countries for transmission of its subscribers' messages (Schenker and Lynch, 1991, p. 8). Because European countries benefitted the issue was not raised by them within the ITU. Also benefitting were developing countries who relied on international traffic and the high charges they levied for profits to expand their network.

Although the ITU recommended that accounting rates should be in line with costs, as the costs of transmission decreased similar decreases in accounting rates did not occur. Just as in the domestic system a form of welfare transfer had arisen between different sets of users, so in the international system hidden payments occurred between the United States and other countries. The issue was drawn attention to by the ITU's Maitland Commission on the global development of telecommunications. The Commission saw accounting rates as a means by which the industrialised West could contribute to the expansion of the network in developing countries, by the contribution of more than 50 percent of the costs of transmission (Independent Commission for Worldwide Telecommunications, 1984). This proposal was subsequently taken up by the developing countries themselves, who argued that their costs of line provision were far in excess of those in the industrialized world. However, the politicization of the issue within the ITU then drew a backlash from the United States, which during the 1990s has sought to undermine the existing regime and to establish one which allows its companies to evade the cost of accounting rates on international transmission. In 1992 after years of American pressure an international agreement has been reached that accounting rates should be decreased over the next five years. However the American demand that international tariffs should take account of the costs of providing only international transmission, which would have deprived developing countries of including the capital costs of their national networks, was unsuccessful (Schenker and Lynch, 1991, p. 8).

Crucially debate has centered around the D series recommendations of the ITU's CCITT. Historically an international organization to serve the coordination needs of government controlled monopoly PTTs, these D series recommendations prevented other than those entities or Recognized Private Operating Companies (such as AT&T) from providing international communications. For most countries high international tariffs paid for lower domestic rates, for capital investment, and the high equipment prices of national suppliers, and sometimes for subsidies to national treasuries or postal services. High tariffs relied on the PTT monopolies of international communications.

The inauguration of the world banking electronic network SWIFT in 1977 and slightly later that of the world airline network SITA were presented to the ITU as fait accomplis, to which it had to accommodate its previous protection of PTT interests. Through Recommendations D1 and D2 of the ITU's Consultative Committee on International Telegraph and Telecommunications (CCITT) for the first time in 1980 privately operated international networks were given legitimacy (ITU, 1985, pp. 915, 267). But while transnationals could lease international lines from public operators, they could not lease that capacity and resell it to others.

This was the regulatory situation which the FCC set out to change in the early 1980s by another fait accompli. It ruled that private companies could lease lines both domestically and internationally and could resell that capacity to third parties. It was forced to leave this proposal on the table for international lines, such was the outcry by European governments on behalf of their PTTs and such the fear of a backlash by the potential beneficiaries (Hills, 1986, p. 163).

In late 1988 the ITU held another plenary meeting termed WATTC88 to update the international regulations governing telecommunications. Backed by Britain, the United States pressed once more for the maximum freedom possible for its transnational companies, calling for a wording which would have allowed them to establish networks for international telecommunications in other countries subject only to national law (ITU, 1988).

For many developing countries the prospect of transnational companies enabled at will to bypass their national networks would have spelt financial disaster. The final compromise allowed the establishment of private value added networks where both countries agreed, but avoiding harm to third countries. An Opinion attached to the Article took into account the fears of developing countries concerning national sovereignty. The United States alone voted against it.

Under these regulations bilateral agreements could be reached between countries to introduce simple resale of capacity on leased lines. Subsequently simple resale agreements have been reached between the United States and Canada, and between the United States, Britain, and Japan, thereby lowering the costs of international telecommunications for transnational corporations who no longer contribute to national network infrastructures via the accounting rate system. Finally in 1991 the United

States and Britain achieved their aim in relation to the D series recommendations. Under the new series resale was allowed where both ends of the connection was agreed as was sharing of resources and the interconnection of private into public networks. In addition tariffs for leased lines were to be flat-rate based, rather than based on volume of data passed—an agreement obviously in favour of transnationals (Schenker, 1991, p. 5).

As increasing numbers of companies bypass the international public network we are witnessing the gradual transfer of the international network into one which resembles that of the United States—fragmented public and private provision in which the private pays nothing towards the public. In this new world order the possibility is raised that national network operators may not be able to retain their commitment to domestic universal service (McLelland, 1992, p. 258).

This move towards private control of infrastructure has been further exacerbated by the debt crisis and American demands within the World Bank for a greater role for private enterprise in developing countries. The World Bank's International Finance Corporation has pressed privatisation and liberalisation of networks onto developing countries (Ambrose, Hennemeyer, Chapon, 1991). With multilateral funding more difficult to find against increasing competition, many of the newly democratic countries in the East European bloc, together with those in Latin America and Asia have succumbed to the concerted pressure of the IMF and World Bank. Without effective regulation, both privatization and liberalization as mechanisms of gaining international investment hold the concomitant political costs of loss of sovereignty over internal communications. Also, in often agriculturally based communities, privatization promises the development of long-distance and urban, not rural, networks. Large business is the beneficiary—both transnational users and those PTTs which have bought into these networks.

Finally, within the Uruguay round of GATT, U.S. pressure for the inclusion of services overrode developing country opposition. In 1992 in the telecommunications sector negotiations it is following through on the demands of large information service suppliers for a replication of its domestic market worldwide (Hills, 1989, p. 1419). It is also demanding the right of foreign investment for its transnationals—in other words, that the rights of private companies should override the sovereignty of states (*Transnational Data Report*, 1992, p. 5). If agreed then the resulting international communications system will be drawn up to benefit the very largest companies, with the losers being sovereign nations, the rural population in the developing countries and the citizen everywhere.

Conclusion

This article set out to show how the information needs of the transnational companies, themselves a product of recession, costcutting, globalization, and specialization, coupled with the potential of fast data transmission offered by the falling costs and wide bandwidth of optic fiber, are producing a realignment within the international political economy of communications. This realignment cannot be attributed to free market economics alone, nor to technology alone. Although the technology itself has contributed to the growing preeminence of transnational companies, the changes could not have taken place without political backing from the major industrialised countries and particularly the United States. Free trade is an economic theory which benefits the largest companies. Under this legitimating economic ideology transnationals may penetrate and oligopolize increasing numbers of industrial and service sectors over a wider geographical spectrum. When those companies and governments form coalitions that ideology of free trade is also a political mechanism of mercantilism.

We can characterize each national market as one which contains the oligopolistic competition of transnational companies together with a traditional market economy of the industrialised nations and an informal economy in the developing (Sunkel, 1985, p. 48). As transnational companies move into sectors previously within the traditional national market economy, so large proportions of national markets become both oligopolistic and interdependent with those of other countries. In particular the transnationalization of telecommunications is important to the further globalization and integration of transnational companies. Following a restructuring of the American domestic telecommunications market to benefit this very process of wider geographical corporate distribution and enlarged span of functional control, we are witnessing in the 1990s a similar restructuring of the international market. In the words of Osvaldo Sunkel:

> The United States economy constitutes... a hegemonic and predominant segment of a highly transnationalized and interdependent capitalist system. The interests of transnational capitalism require the restructuring of both the world economy and of its core, the United States economy, so that they can become mutually compatible and functional to the further progress of the transnationalization process.... If the restructuring of the transnational system could achieve high levels of dynamism, particularly in the core of the system, the transfer of resources from the rest of the world to the United States could continue for some time to come (Sunkel, 1985, p. 50).

As the world's communications infrastructure is increasingly configured and run to meet the information needs and the profits of transnationals, so it moves away from the previous consensus that access to communications are crucial to democracy. Whereas marginalist economics ignored the political, the new neoliberal economics equates market competition with political democracy. The assumption is that free trade and liberalised markets will shore up, rather than undermine, democratic political institutions. In so doing it ignores the market and political power of international oligopolies within domestic markets and political systems. It ignores the power which information and communications bring to transnational companies, it ignores the trends towards privatisation of information, and the trends towards centralization of control over that information. And in the New World Order it ignores the extent of the measures the United States government is prepared to take in altering the rules governing the international political economy of information and communications in order to regain its previous economic primacy.

When a government insists that private domestic law is applicable to its transnationals stationed in other countries, then the communication networks of those companies become the conduit for potential political control. When a government attempts to impose the rights of those companies over the rights of sovereign states, then it is attempting no less than a reversal of the rules of the post-war international political system. In attempting this reversal to the equivalent of the British imperialist system of the nineteenth century, communications and information is as crucial now as it was then.

Notes

1. Investment in running networks overseas by telecommunications operators includes Bell Atlantic & Ameritech in New Zealand Telecom; France Telecom STET (Italy), Telefonica (Spain) in Argentina; Telefonica in Chile; U.S. West and Bell Atlantic in Czechoslovakia; Cable and Wireless in Russia; AT&T in Poland; Bell South and C&W in Australia; Pacific Telesis in Germany and UK; Nynex and SouthWestern Bell in UK; Nynex in Gibraltar.

2. Media giants include Time Warner (U.S.), Bertelsmann (Ger.), News Corporation (U.S.), Hachette (Fr.), Sony (Japan), Dun & Bradsheet (U.S.), Paramount (U.S.), Times Mirror (U.S.), International Thomson (Canada), Capital Cities/ABC (U.S.). Between 1985 and 1991 they spent over. $150bn on takeovers.

3. Intelsat's revenue dropped from $614m in 1989 to $499m in 1990.

References

Ambrose, W., P. R. Hennemeyer, J. P. Chapon. (1991). *Privatizing Telecommunications Systems, Business Opportunities in Developing Countries*. International Finance Corporation, Discussion Paper No. 10, Washington D.C.: World Bank.

Barty King, Hugh. (1979). *Girdle Round the Earth: The Story of Cable and Wireless*. London: Heinemann.

Bradshaw, Della. (1990). "Privacy Laws Hamper the Cross-border Flow of Data." *Financial Times*, 19 January.

BT Management News. (1991). February.

BT Today. (1992). 14 July.

Cane, Alan. (1992). "One Step Forward and Two Back." *Financial Times*, 16 June.

Carlsberg, Sir Bryan. (1990). "The Integration of Telecommunications and Broadcasting." Paper to Economist Intelligence Unit Conference, London, 17 September.

Commission of the European Communities. (1989). Com (88) 154 Final; *Official Journal of the European Communities*, 24 November.

Darmaros, Theodore. (1989). *Beyond the Sales Pitch: Realising ISDN in the US, Japan and Europe*. Working paper No. 5, Science Policy Research Unit, University of Sussex.

Dixon, Hugo. (1991). "Deutsche Telecom set to Take Stake in BT Venture." *Financial Times*, 7 October.

Dixon, Hugo. (1990). "U.S. Blocks $500m Soviet Fibre Optic Cable." *Financial Times*, 6 June.

Dougan, Lady Diana. (1985). "Keynote address." In OECD *Transborder Data Flows*, Amsterdam: North Holland.

Ganley, Oswald H., and Gladys D. Ganley. (1982). *To Inform or to Control? The New Communications Networks*. New York: McGraw Hill.

Gilpin, Robert. (1987). *The Political Economy of International Relations*. Princeton: Princeton University Press.

Hayes, Dawn Hayes. (1991). "Intelsat Goes into a Spin." *Communications Week International*, 27 May.

Hills, Jill. (1986). *Deregulating Telecoms: Competition and Control in the USA, Japan, and Britain*. London: Pinter.

Hills, Jill. (1989). "Dynamics of US International Telecom Policy." *Transnational Data Report*, February.

Hills, Jill. (1993). "Universal Service: Connnectivity and Content." In Mads Christofferson (ed.), *EuroCPRS '92*. Holland: IOS.

Hills, Jill, and Stelianos Papathanassopoulos. (1991). *The Democracy Gap: The Politics of Information and Communications Technologies in the United States and Europe*. Greenwood: Westport.

Horton, Monica. (1991). "Private Networks: Backbone of the Worldwide Corporate Structure." *Financial Times*, 7 October.

Independent Commission for Worldwide Telecommunications (Maitland Report). (1984). *The Missing Link*. Geneva: ITU.
Intelsat. (1991). *Annual Report 1990–91*. Washington D.C.: Intelsat.
ITU. (1985). "General Accounting Principles: Charging and Accounting." *CCITT, Red Book, Vol II Fascicle 11.1*. Geneva: ITU, pp. 915, 267.
ITU. (1988). "WATTC 88, 'Butler Draft'" Article 9, Geneva: ITU.
Kieve, J. L. (1973). *Electric Telegraph: A Social and Economic History*. Newton Abbott, David and Charles.
Lascelles, David. (1985). "When a Company Turns into a Bank as Well." *Financial Times*, 11 June.
Lerner, Daniel. (1958). *The Passing of Traditional Society*. Glencoe: Free Press.
Locksley, Gareth. (1988). *TV Broadcasting in Europe and the New Technologies*. Brussels: CEC.
Manchester, Philip. (1991). "Multiple Technologies, Big Costs." *Financial Times*, 17 September.
Marques, Maria Elizabeth, and Omar Souki Oliveira. (1991). "Information Processing in Brazil: An Alternative to Transnationalisation." *Media Development*, XXVII(1).
McLelland, Stephen. (1992). "The International Dimension: PTTs." *Telecommunications*, International edition, 26(6).
Moran, Michael. (1991). *The Politics of the Financial Services Revolution: The USA, UK, and Japan*. London: Macmillan.
Oettinger, A. (1988). *The Formula Is Everything: Costing and Pricing in the Telecommunications Industry*. Programme on Information Resource Policy. Cambridge, MA: Harvard University Press.
OECD. (1981). *Guidelines on the Protection of Privacy and Transborder Data Flows*. Paris: OECD.
Osolnik, Bogdan. (1991). "The MacBride Report Ten Years After." *Media Development* XXVII(1).
Pirie, Madsen. (1988). *Micropolitics*. London: Wildwood House.
Public Network. (1991). "Heavens Open for Earthly Callers." March.
Public Network. (1991a). "Intelligent Networks in Europe," March.
Public Network. (1991b). "Cable Confusion Resolved in Shakeup," June.
Purton, Peter. (1991). "Belated Explosion Imminent." *Financial Times*, 7 October.
Pye, L. W. (ed.) (1963). *Communications and Political Development*. Princeton: Princeton University Press.
Rada, Juan F. (1987). "Information Technology and Services." In Orio Giarini (ed.), *The Emerging Service Economy*. London: Pergamon.
Roach, Colleen. (1990). "The Movement for a New World Information and Communication Order: A Second Wave?" *Media, Culture and Society* 12.
Rogers, Everett M. (ed.) (1976). *Communications and Development: Critical Perspectives*. Beverly Hills, Calif.: Sage Publications.
Sauvant, Karl P. (1986). *International Transactions in Services: The Politics of Transborder Data Flows*. Boulder: Westview Press.

Schenker, Jennifer, L. (1991). "CCITT Reaches Leased-line Accord." *Communications Week International*, 1 April, p. 5.

Schenker, Jennifer L., and Karen Lynch. (1991). "Resale: A Means to Drive Down Prices." *Communications Week International*, 16 December.

Schramm, Wilbur. (1964). *Mass Media and National Development: The Role of Information in the Developing Countries.* Stanford University Press.

Schramm, Wilbur, and Daniel Lerner (eds.) (1976). *Communication and Development: The Last Ten Years—and the Next.* Honolulu, Hawaii: The University of Hawaii Press.

Sunkel, Osvaldo. (1985). "Towards an Understanding of the Emerging Transnational System." *The CTC Reporter* No. 20, (Autumn) p. 4850.

Tarjanne, Pekke. (1991). Interviewed in *Public Network*, March.

Terazono, Emriko. (1992). "Nomura Vacates Floor of Tokyo Headquarters." *Financial Times*, 7 July.

Terrell, Robert L., and Regina Korner. (1987). "NWICO: A Framework for Policy Makers." *Media Development*, January, pp. 25–27.

Transnational Data Report. (1992). "Offical US Text Submitted to GATT Secretariat." May/June, p. 5.

UN Centre on Transnational Corporations. (1983). *TDF: Access to the International On-line Data Base Market.* New York: United Nations.

United Nations Centre on Transnational Corporations. (1983). *Transborder Data Flows and Brazil.* New York: United Nations.

United States Foreign Relations Subcommittee. (1977). *New World Information Order*, p. 12. Quoted in Cruise O'Brien, Rita, and G. K. Helleiner. (1980). "The Political Economy of Information in a Changing International Economic Order." *International Organisation.* 34(4).

Woolcock, Stephen. (1982). "US-European Trade Relations." *International Affairs.* 58(4).

World Bank. (1991). *Free Trade Agreements with the US: What's in It for Latin America?* Washington D.C.: World Bank.

12 COMMUNICATIONS AND ECONOMICS
James W. Carey

I

The heroic efforts, underway for at least four decades now, to create a rapprochement between communications and economics, to create an economics of communications (or, for the more committed, a political economy of communications), to find one frame of reference within which to contain these two social practices and disciplines, has yielded substantial results but not as yet general satisfaction. That is the paradox I want to explore in this brief essay.

There is no mystery concerning the renewed urgency of the inquiry into the economics of communications. Jill Hills essay in this volume describes a new phase in the political economy of the world in which both national governments and private firms recognize that trade no longer follows the flag but the communications system, in which knowledge, always a source of power, is bleached into information, adapted to a new technology of digital encoding and modelling, made still lighter and more transportable, for the primary end of manipulation and control. The radiant arc of a communications satellite 22,300 miles above the earth synchronizes time and ingests the globe into homogenized space. The computer abstracts geography into the galaxy and miniaturizes the clock of awareness to the pico second. The conquest of time and space, the dream of nineteenth-century romantics, explorers, and imperialists (they were sometimes the same person), has now been realized. While Professor Hills explores this from the producer good side of the equation, Time-Warner, with an eye on consumer markets, announces "The World Is Our Audience." The aggressive transformation of publics into audiences, which in the late nineteenth century created the "imaginary community of the nation," is now a global process.

Sometime in the 1970s, to chose a point of arrest in a continuous social process, a stable—though not an altogether satisfactory—structure of economics, politics and communications broke up and new forces were set loose in the world. The symptoms and symbols of the break-up were two technologies and commodities, computers and satellites, simultaneously producer goods and consumer goods, which reconfigured the map of social relations. Economic activity, political sovereignty, and cultural production changed shape and consequence within a new scalar dynamic: not the city, the nation, or even the empire but the globe became the habitus of these processes (Appadurai, 1990). Cultural fragmentation and postmodernist homogenization became two constitutive trends of a single global reality: a splitting in which social life simultaneously expanded and contracted, the stage of human activity enlarged to the globe and collapsed to the village making the nation state itself appear increasingly problematic.

The only concepts and ideas that have emerged to contain these developments are the desiccated symbols of information and the information society. However, information and the information society are products of the theory and technology driving these developments rather than critical reflections on the practices they represent. As symbols they suggest that the new conquest of time and space is orderly, systematic, and benign. The information society is announced as fact and globalization declared a reality when both are in the planning stage. The future is colonized such that neat geometric lines run into the horizon imploring us to lift our eyes from the chaotic present to apprehend a global utopia.

Meanwhile, out on the streets, where we actually live, all is chaos. There the convergent order of the information society dissolves into ceaseless and disorderly flows: new people and new things flowing to new places along new routes: flows of migrants, guest workers, tourists, entrepreneurs and itinerants; new flows of capital, factories, messages, products, ideas, images, and currencies. Capitalism, though not capitalism alone, keeps the pot boiling: new things flowing from new places to new places, upsetting established patterns of geography, trade and communications, imploding and exploding at the same time. The information society turns out to be an unstable and in many ways an unfriendly place in which ethnic nationalisms again occupy the center of the stage. Everywhere state and nation are pitted against one another; primordia have been globalized and identity politics practiced on a world scale. A new information class, along with the new technology, has brought us to, in the words of the former chairman of Citicorp, Walter Wriston (1992), "a twilight of sovereignty" for that class has the skills to write a complex software program that produces a billion dollars of revenue and still walk past any customs officer in the world with nothing of "value" to declare. But what are we to make of this class, one now bred in the universities, and whose sovereignty is being ended and what is the pretender to the sovereign throne?

Privatization is yet another, and perhaps more useful, term by which these processes are currently understood and that notion fits well with Walter Wriston's image of products slipping by customs agents because they are lodged in the head. However, the process of privatization is a more general and rigorous one than is commonly understood. The first, and most general, focus is the privatization of broadcasting in the wake of satellite communication. Once satellites were available and satellite parking spaces over Europe allocated, it was a foregone conclusion that some firms, most likely American, were going to invade the television space of European countries and siphon off mass markets. To prevent this, or, alternatively, to preserve a European "high culture" tradition, country after country has either given up state run television or permitted the growth of private networks.

Consequently, broadcasting was transformed from a phenomenon of collective public provision to more uniformly a matter of private market transactions, though given the quasi-public good character of cultural production, it was rationalized through an advertising based distribution system. In turn, the costs of television production, even for state systems faced with reduced revenues, forced increasing amounts of co-production across national and linguistic boundaries. Depending on which side of the coin one examines, this looks like either the Americanization or Canadianization of the world: Americanization if one emphasizes the dominance of the strongest exporter and co-production partner; Canadianization if one emphasizes the deracination of production and the resulting "cultural soup" that spreads on a world wide basis. Pastiche cultures, assembled from a cross-national production process, further displace indigenous cultural forms.

In one sense, then, privatization refers to the displacement of indigenous cultures by pastiche or postmodern cultures and the elimination or decline of public or state run broadcasting. In another, perhaps stronger, sense, privatization refers to the world wide transformation of political and cultural publics into political and cultural audiences. In multi-channel environments, broadcasting connects more firmly to individual preference structures. The connection of a fragmented structure of private production to a fragmented structure of home reception results in a secondary and more problematic diremption of a public sphere, one in which the entire notion of public communication and a common culture of politics and pleasure evaporates. Balkanization, whether of groups or individuals, displaces a common arena of discourse and communication. Culture is not not only privately manufactured and privately distributed but its audience is conceived as statistically concatenated individuals or members of segmented transnational groups rather than as citizens of a common polity or participants in a common tradition.

How are we to contain and explicate these developments? As I said earlier, the only framework widely available is the theory of information and the information society. However, the conclusions from that framework are foreordained by, on one side, the conception of communication embodied in information theory which generates and rationalizes the technology at the heart of the problem and, on the other, by the system of neoclassical economics which generates the commodity view of information, which reduces communication to the warming metaphors of conquest and weaponry, a mere process of the transmission in space for purposes of manipulation and control.

In fact, the attempt to integrate communications and economics into a consistent framework is at the heart of the problem. Communications and economics constitute contradictory frameworks. That was I think the great insight of Harold Innis even as he tacked back and forth between them, borrowing from both in order that they might check off one another's biases. I agree, then, though in a very special sense, with Bernard Dasah's conclusion (this volume) that the "communicologist's thesis that economic processes, should be viewed as but special instances of more general communicatory processes is better suited for African economic development than is the traditional neoclassical approach." However, we must understand, first, that everyone's development, not just Africa's and not economic development alone, is better served by placing economic processes within a communications framework. Second, the reasons for doing so is not to produce a uniform or consistent theoretical framework. That is impossible and when it has been tried it ultimately converts the phenomena of communications into the variables of economics.

The framework one should seek is the framework of difference, the framework of countervailing power in which the phenomena of communications contain and control economics in the name of public life and discourse, and, on the contrary, economics permits a sphere of private life and action. Public in this sense must refer to something other than the state or state broadcasting. (Similarly, though it is here beyond my point of reference, private must refer to something other than commerce.) Public must refer to a domain outside both the state and the economy. If the public sphere has been dirempted by the creation of an international private sphere, the answer is not to internationalize the public sphere, which can only be accomplished with state power, but to create public life as a countervailing force at the local level. It is not a matter of thinking globally and acting locally; it is a matter of thinking locally and acting globally.

II

In the following commentary I want to make a case for the incommensurable relation between economics and communications. That is the heart of the legacy left of us by Harold Innis and, as with Innis, it comes down to making a plea for time. I will make it through some well known but not always well understood propositions.

Communications and economics are, in the first instances, human practices. However, they are practices that stand in a contradictory relation to one another; they are, historically though not ontologically, mutually exclusive activities. Economics is the practice of allocating scare resources. Communication is the process of producing meaning, a resource which is anything but scare, indeed is a superabundant, free good. It is hard to apprehend and take full account of this contradiction because the practice of communications, like all other human practices (religion comes to mind) has itself been so transformed by the theory and practice of economics that the former (communications as a practice, meaning as a resource) can hardly be recognized given the dominance of the latter.

The contradictions at the level of practice means that reflections on these practices also contradict one another. The disciplines that emerge to reflect back on the practice and aim to make the bases of the practices explicit, to codify everyday knowledge in theoretic terms, similarly stand in a contradictory relation to one another. Communications and economics as disciplines, therefore, cannot be reconciled with one another;

they confront one another blankly because they proceed from incommensurable premises. There is no way of integrating the propositions of each into a consistent framework or of making these disciplines simple complements to one another wherein each borrows from the other the resources necessary for its respective completion.

I go too far. In our time communications and economics can only be reconciled by an evacuation of the resources of meaning in the service of profit and power. Therefore, the only useful relation between communications and economics is a countervailing one both at the level of theory and practice. Communications and economics derive from different motivational structures and produce incommensurably alternative pictures of human action and social life. They can cancel or neutralize one another; they can check off each others biases but otherwise they will be fiercely resistant to any form of integration. They constitute a contradictory order of things: their root meanings and consequences are opposed both in theory and practice.

It will be difficult to sustain this argument in a few pages and much will have to be left to the imagination of the reader. Moreover, a series of strategic retreats will have to be made at certain critical junctures. For example, because economics as practice and discipline relies upon the resources of communication—it is rather difficult to organize work or enunciate a theory without recourse to language—a strong case can be made for making economics a special case of communications, a case made with unusual force by the economist Donald McCloskey (1985). However, I want to by-pass the more delicate and refined parts of the argument to make a bald but I think necessary case for the analytical independence of communications and economics as revealed within modern history. That independence is necessary to salvage a domain of politics and culture that can resist the insidious imperialism of the economic and give us the possibility, though not the assurance, of a public life.

There is only one form of economic theory and practice these days, the neoclassical form, the form which reflects and explains modern capitalism. As theory and practice, it is one of the great achievements of the human mind, but it exacts a terrible price in the domain of politics and culture. Let me repeat and restate what is now a very old story.

Economic theory, or at least its neoclassical mainstream, though these days the mainstream has no tributaries, has as its basic assumption that individual behavior is motivated entirely by self-regarding preferences. This assumption which Steven Jones has called "calculating avarice" has proven to be a very powerful one for organizing human activity through the institution of the market. Neoclassical economics starts from the assumption, and its institutions manifest the fact, that the desires that motivate human action are individual and subjective and therefore unknowable to an observer, unsharable via conscious acts, or purely exogenous. These subjective desires, these given and individual preferences are expressed in human action as an attempt to maximize utility or the pleasure and happiness that the satisfaction of desire brings. Of happiness and despair we may have no measure, but we do have a theory.

To paraphrase and extend Mary Douglas (1992) economic theory has its impenetrable cohesiveness—that is, its resistance to all disciplines beyond economics and to all social practices other than the economic—because of the professional intensity of its discourse and because Western thought is impregnated with the Western experience of the market. As Albert Hirschman (1977) has pointed out, the idea that greed is the dominant human motive only came to be gradually accepted after the sixteenth century when the market itself became dominant and was expected to be a motive force that would curb the passion for power. The economic mode of thought and the economic as a differentiated sphere of activity enjoys, in the words of Louis Dumont, "an ideological supremacy over the political in the liberal and capitalist worlds thanks to its embodying a purer or more perfect form of individualism" (1985, pp. 259–260). In the market the focus is upon individuals exchanging privately owned goods; the individual and the rights that accrue to him from ownership are the given of the economic mode of thought, the rarely questioned starting point of the analysis. This is true, paradoxically enough, even with the most extreme critiques of capitalism, for those on the Left, who because they are no less worshipful of the market, technology, individualism and individual rights, continuously fall into the assumptions of the objects of their contempt. As a result, socialist economics rarely becomes more than neoclassical economics at the extreme: monopoly, the technocratic state, and the self-regarding individual.

We may understand the limits or margins of economics from our own experience—we, after all, do encounter, in ourselves and others, actions and motives that are selfless and other-regarding; we need not resort to sociobiology to explain altruism—still economics has no room for moral feelings. Gary Becker was rewarded with the Nobel prize for economics by imperializing three central economic assumptions—maximizing behavior, stable preferences, and equilibrium—to illuminate all types of decisions, including politics and family. And, of course, he was correct, though in the way self-fulfilling prophecies are correct and not, as economists often pretend, the way natural laws are correct. The assumptions of the market have so invaded and transformed all human activity and relations that little remains outside the imaginative orbit of the market. Interest group politics, about all that is left to politics, crime and deviancy, incantations of individual rights, charity and virtue, alternative families—all are now plausibility explained by such assumptions. At the morbid margins of the social, economists can do little more than wring their hands and lament cultural lag or insist that moral progress somehow does not keep up with material progress.

Neoclassical economics presumes a society of people with preferences but is silent on the question of how society can exist at all. In analyzing the market for private goods, classical economics jumps from individual self-interest to community interest, the interest of society, the common interest, by invoking the magic of an invisible hand. Behind it lies the community engaged in its normative debate and the laws, conventions and social values to which the normative debate give rise. It is this normative framework of the social, and the debate and the discourse which sustains and expresses it, which economics must either ignore or transform into an economic activity, a mere pursuit of self-regarding preferences. And that is historically exactly what has been pursued and achieved, though in two rather different ways. In this sense, economics as practice and discipline is devoted to the suppression of communication; the conceptual device through which the suppression is pursued is information.

Economics has no sense of the social beyond that provided by the market. The social is the mere derivative of the self-regarding pursuit of utility by atomized selves. Because, the maximizing assumption leads to neither a theory or practice of the social, noneconomic social theory has generally been unhappy with the claim of economics to explain the operation of modern societies. Unfortunately, the formulation of a response to economics is either in terms laid down by economics or in the spaces left uncovered by economic theory. The social sciences, again in their mainstream form, simply transferred the assumptions of utility theory from the individual to the social. Utility, no longer in our heads, is relocated in our genes or the environment. Sociobiology is an example of the first strategy; behaviorism and sociological functionalism are examples of the second.

Behaviorism and functionalism in turn provided the underpinning for our understanding of communication at large, but these positions, as I have attempted to suggest, are derivations of the limitations of economics rather than independent views of communications. Certain assumptions about communication eventually underwrite neoclassical theory (the theory of representation, the self-righting process in the free market of ideas) and have undergirded the belief that the quest for utility can produce a progressive social order—economically, morally and politically progressive. The "invisible hand" works in both the marketplace of ideas and products. The utilitarian conception of human conduct and society, then, was twisted out of its originally subjective framework and resituated in the objective world of environment, biology or social structure. It is a form of utilitarianism nonetheless: the objective utilities of natural ecology, the utilities that promote the survival of the human population or the given social order.

III

Ayn Rand somewhere wrote that "Civilization is the progress toward privacy. The savage's whole existence is public." Thus, speaks an authentic voice of the economic spirit, one that rules out communications from the outset. For nothing is more primitive, in the sense of primordial, savage, in the sense of at the root of our humanity, and public, in the sense of the common and shared, than communications. In this sense communications establishes the challenge to the self-regarding preferences that undergird economic thinking. Communication is nothing if not a collective activity; indeed, it is the process by which the real is created, maintained, celebrated, transformed and repaired. The product of that activity, meaning, establishes a common and shared world.

Words are the names of, the other side of, practices. And, despite its vagrant history in this century, communication has never shed the trace of its origins in the common, communal and community, any more than politics, despite the depradations of our time, has lost its trace of origin in the polis. Both are the names of certain forms of human practice grounded in a shared intersubjective world of common action. As the quote from Ayn Rand suggests, this century is one that has turned against the common, the public, and the political in the name of the private, the subjective and the economic. One aspect of our being prevents us from complete success in this enterprise. There can be private property, private selves, and perhaps even private thought but there cannot be private languages, as Wittgenstein, among others, taught us most successfully. Language is the one collective and sharable phenomenon we have: not something created and then shared but only created in the act of sharing. While intellectually, this century has devoted itself to finding some way by and around language, to a state of pure vision and epiphany, language, the irreducible bedrock of human tools and talents, keeps reminding us of a shared and associated life. There is no removal of communication from its ancient associations with sharing, participation, association, fellowship, and the possession of a common faith. Communication, is the process, in the happy words of Stanley Cavell, of wording the world together: not some mere transmission of language, an extension of messages in space, but the maintenance of society in time; not the act of imparting information but the representation of shared beliefs.

The archetypal case of communication, once saturated by the economic world view, is the extension of messages across geography for the purpose of control. However, primordially and politically, the origin of communication is at one with the origins of ritual and religion: not the transmission of intelligent information but the construction and maintenance of an ordered, meaningful cultural world that can serve as a control and container for human action: a world of time rather than space. In this sense, communications can at best act as a control and check upon the economic motive, the motive of self-interest, from taking over the entire household of the social.

Mary Douglas (1992), in an essay that has powerfully influenced the views outlined here, though it is not an essay concerned with communications in a direct way, has summarized an aspect of this outlook:

> Humans speak, they use rhetoric and scrutinize one another's speech. Their individual conflicts surface and are overruled as they try to persuade one another to compromise or stand firm. Faced with conflict, contestants have to resort to the rhetoric of the common good to support their private claims. DeTocqueville, writing of public associations, identified the basic mechanism of the normative debate that sets the ground rules for any form of social structure, whether that of a market the state, or the voluntary associations with which he was primarily concerned. Citizens he argued, "converse, they listen to one another and they are mutually stimulated to all sorts of undertakings. As a result, they may even "learn to surrender their own will to that of all the rest and to make their exertions subordinate to the common impulse" (pp. 127–128).

The classical tradition of sociology, for which Durkheim can serve as an exemplar, showed an intense interest in religion even though it is a highly secular tradition, one skeptical about the history and claims of religion. (Here it bears a certain similarity to the religiously ironizing spirit of Harold Innis.) Because language, religion, and ritual preceeded the world of practical action, it was in such forms that the search for the integrative mechanisms of the social were sought. Inspired by the complexity of anthropological studies of social reproduction, Durkheim invented notions of "collective representations" and "collective conscience" to explain how societies were held intact in the midst of conflict and strain. When he applied his analysis to modern societies, though my chronology is off here, he tried to show capitalist societies depended for their very existence and stability on an inherited, precapitalist society—the so-called precontractual elements of contract. Gesellschaft society, the society regulated by utility and contract, could not work without the integrative mechanisms of Gemeinschaft society: nonutilitarian values, beliefs, traditions, and so on. To the old slogan that money is to the West what kinship is to the rest, he added that kinship performs a continuing integrative function in advanced societies. (The fact that all such mechanism are now, in a Foucaldian phase, seen as derivatives of the market and the power implicit in market relations, is a measure of our impoverishment.) In a sense, Durkheim inverted the relations of base and superstructure: the capitalist economy thrives on the root system of traditional society. Therefore, to destroy that root system is to destroy the very possibility of a stable social order. In many ways, this is precisely what capitalism does. It is implicit in Joseph Schumpter's (1987) mournful requiem to the creative destruction unleashed by capitalism; it was more directly faced by the sociologist Charles Cooley's (1927) assertion, that capitalism promoted lawlessness as the condition of its own rule.

We live in a world where the imagination of the market, what Harold Innis called the penetrative powers of the price system, have transformed all social relations. And in this sense we, particularly in the United States, are testing the proposition whether the market can be used as regulative mechanism for all these relations, subordinating politics, religion, culture, family, and community life to its rule. It would require far more time and space than is available to show how interest group politics and the intrumentalization of language that comes in its wake, the rights revolution, the penetration of the law into family life and the state into the community is but an extension of the market mentality. It is an attempt to transform communication into an instrument of manipulation or the pursuit of rights, that is, a weapon in the competition for scarce social goods. These activities do not extend communication but destroy it and that was prescient truth in Harold Innis's notion that improvements in communication make communication not only more difficult but more problematic.

Economists recognize that market transactions do not include all rational transactions. Measuring the spillover to the community from individual market transactions is one approach to the nonmarket used by economists. Externalities are a powerful tool for analyzing certain problems in a market society. But externalities are fundamentally a theory of market failure and market failure is, as Mary Douglas notes (1992,

p. 128), "an elaborately backhanded way of studying the collective interest." The approach to communication and politics through market failure, oddly enough, was attempted by the greatest American student of communications, John Dewey, early in this century. *The Public and Its Problems* (1927) is an analysis of the eclipse of the public by the forces of industry and the market and a plea for the restoration of the public as a real force in the political realm. In that sense, it was squarely in the tradition of Jefferson and the Federalist Papers: an attempt to recreate a republican tradition of politics and social life adequate to the modern era. The public in eclipse was the face to face public of direct interaction. In trying to restore this public Dewey argued against individualism and pointed to a shared domain of cooperative experience and identity formation. Individualism, as noted earlier, assumes that transactions occur between discrete individual persons, bound only by contract, and, properly speaking, such transactions concern only the individuals directly involved. Dewey argued that a public interest arises whenever there are indirect consequences of individual private transactions. Therefore, the public and a public interest came into existence whenever externalities were created. But while externalities had steadily expanded, the domain and competence of the public had steadily shrunk. The interdependencies created by industry and commerce were nowhere matched by the interdependencies of public life. It was Dewey's hope, forlorn as it turns out, that the new instruments of mass communication could transform the great society into a great community, bring externalities into conscious awareness and create or restore public life on a scale matching that of industry.

Dewey created an unusually abstract and regressive definition of the public, one defined by the function of dealing with externalities. Because the public interest became a mere externality of private markets, the domain of the public and the community was a pure derivative of private action. The public sphere, rather than possessing a prior and integral identity as a constraint on private life, was a mere residual to the ever widening private sphere, continuously involved in a self-defeating chase to catch up. Dewey was well intentioned enough. He was trying to counter elitist notions of democracy put forth by Walter Lippmann (1922) and a subsequent army of social scientists who reduced communication to the transmission of information from those who monopolized knowledge to those who needed to be controlled in its name. But Dewey's necessary response gave away the essential tension that must exist between markets and publics, between the self-regarding actions of individuals and the other-regarding actions of communities. Economists have been willing to grant that communities are secondary and derivative, formed by contract to deal with externalities. However, the goal of economics is to reduce externalities by viewing them as examples of market failure and, therefore, to cut away the community in the name of the individual and his or her self-regarding preferences. Economists are even at times willing to admit to the existence of public goods as defined by Paul Samuelson as goods which are freely available and from the enjoyment of which no one can be excluded. But what counts as a public good and a private good ultimately rests on a collective decision. As Mary Douglas puts it, public availability is conferred by the collectivity itself, but:

> From the point of view of a community based on market relations, public goods can only be envisaged as a residual class, a set of goods which inherently escape from market conditions, products which cannot be appropriated or costs which cannot be reclaimed. From the standpoint of such a society the fact that transactions in these goods have to be external to the market will appear as the crucial characteristic. Being without bounds or centre the market type of society is not well placed to think of collective goods except as residual to all the private goods (1992, p. 146).

The entire history of modern communications is the turning of the resources not only of information but of meaning itself into a phenomenon of the market. This is true not only with those forms of meaning which are mass produced and marketed and therefore subject to the explicit controls of the price system, but extends as well to all other aspects of culture and meaning down to the most ordinary transactions of daily living. That is what Harold Innis meant by the penetrative powers of the price system.

IV

In summary, the practices of communications and economics and the disciplines which rationalize them contain two opposing conceptions of the self, politics and community life. The communications side of this divide asserts that we are not bearers of selves wholly detached from our aims and attachments; our preferences are not simply exogenous. Certain of our roles are constitutive of the persons we are—as citizens of a country or members of a movement or partisans of a cause. If we are partly defined by the communities we inhabit, then we must also be implicated in the purposes and ends of those communities. The story of my life is always embedded in the story of those communities from which I derive my identity—whether family or city, tribe or nation, party or cause. On a communications view, the narratives and stories, and the purposes they embrace, which emerge out of these communities make a moral difference not merely a psychological one. They situate us in the world and give our lives their moral particularity.

What are the practical differences between communication understood through the prism of the market and communication understood through the prism of the community? What are the practical difference between a politics of rights and interests and a politics of the common good? If the party of communication is correct, our most pressing project is a moral and political one, one that cannot be contained within the concept of information or the information society, within the theory of markets or a politics and morality derived from the market. The project is, to put it too simply, to revitalize our understanding of communications independent of economics and to revitalize, as a consequence, those civic republican possibilities implicit in our tradition but fading in our time.

Economists are willing to grant a conception of community based on conventional individualist assumptions which take for granted the self-interested motivations of persons. This account conceives community and communication in wholly instrumental terms and evokes the image of a private society where individuals regard social arrangements as a necessary burden and cooperate only for the sake of pursuing their private ends. They may even be willing to imagine a community where individual interests are not uniformly antagonistic but in some cases complementary and overlapping, where some may take account of the welfare of others and seek to promote it, where interests overlap the way indifference surfaces overlap. Individuals may have motives which are self regarding but benevolent but in any case the social is a derivative of the individual. What economists cannot admit is a strong sense of the social, the communal and the public, the strong view that Michael Sandel (1982, 1984) whose words I am paraphrasing lightly and resituating, outlines:

> On this strong view, to say that the members of a society are bound by a sense of community is not simply to say that a great many of them profess communitarian sentiments and pursue communitarian aims but rather that they conceive their identity—the subject and not just the object of their feelings and aspirations—as defined to some extent by the community of which they are a part. For them, community describes not just what they have as fellow citizens but what they are, not a relationship they choose (as in a voluntary association) but an attachment they discover, not merely an attribute but a constituent of their identity (1982, p. 150).

It was this sense of community that John Dewey rediscovered and which Harold Innis never abandoned. Innis analysis of the relations of time and space was precisely an analysis of the difference between instrumental communities formed through markets and the extension of the market into politics and social life and constituent communities in which the right was prior to the good, identity prior to self interest, language and meaning prior to markets and information. His conception of monopolies of knowledge was designed, though this would take much elaboration, to describe the consequences for politics and culture when economics overtakes the public sphere. In an Innis like statement Dewey returns at the conclusion of *The Public and Its Problems* to a view which remains as much of a challenge to us in the age of globalization and the information society as it did in 1927 at the moment broadcasting entered society:

> The generation of democratic communities and an articulate democratic public can be solved only in the degree in which local communal life becomes a reality. Signs and symbols, language, are the means by which a fraternally shared experience is ushered in and sustained. Conversation has a vital import lacking in the fixed and frozen words of written speech. Ideas which are not communicated, shared, and reborn in expression are but broken and imperfect thought. Expansion of personal understanding and judgment can be fulfilled only in the relations of personal intercourse in the local community. We lie, as Emerson said, in the lap of an immense intelligence. But that intelligence is dormant and its communications are broken until its possesses the local community as its medium (1927, pp. 217–219).

References

Appadurai, Aran. (1990). "Disjuncture and Difference in the Global Cultural Economy." In Mike Featherstone (ed.), *Global Culture: Nationalism, Globalization and Modernity*. Newbury Park, CA: Sage Publications, pp. 295–310.

Becker, Gary. (1976). *The Economic Approach to Human Behavior*. Chicago: University of Chicago Press.

Carey, James W. (1989). *Communication as Culture*. New York: Routledge.

Cooley, Charles. (1927). *Life and the Student Roadside Notes on Human Nature, Society and Letters*. New York: Knopf.

Dewey, John. (1927). *The Public and Its Problems*. New York: Henry Holt.

Douglas, Mary. (1992). "The Normative Debate and the Origins of Culture." in *Risk and Blame: Essays in Cultural Theory*. London: Routledge.

Hirschman, Albert O. (1977). *The Passions and the Interests*. Princeton: Princeton University Press.

Innis, Harold A. (1950). *Empire and Communications*. Oxford: Oxford University Press.

Innis, Harold A. (1951). *The Bias of Communication*. Toronto: University of Toronto Press.
Jones, Steven. (1984). *The Economics of Conformism*. Oxford: Blackwell.
Lippmann, Walter. (1922). *Public Opinion*. New York: Macmillan.
McCloskey, Donald N. (1985). *The Rhetoric of Economics*. Madison: University of Wisconsin Press.
Sandel, Michael. (1982). *Liberalism and the Limits of Justice*. Cambridge: Cambridge University Press.
Sandel, Michael. (1984). *Liberalism and Its Critics*. New York: New York University Press.
Schumpeter, Joseph. (1987). *Capitalism, Socialism and Democracy*. Boston: Unwin Paperbacks.
Wriston, Walter B. (1992). *The Twilight of Sovereignty*. New York: Charles Scribner's Sons.

Index

Adams, Walter, and James W. Brock, x. xiv, 59, 138–44
Administrative research, 151, 204
Adorno, T., 200
Adverse selection, 51
Advertising, x, 3, 44, 55, 75, 80, 114, 116, 178, 297, 305
Agca, Mehmet Ali, 183
Air Cal, 132
Airlines, 132ff, 140, 302
Akerlof, George, 51
Aksoy, A., and Robins, K., 113
Allen, Beth, 44
Alma Ata, 216
Althusser, Louis, 200–1, 203
American Airlines, 132
American Association for Adult Education, 154
American Institute of Public Opinion, 164
American Library Association, 116, 118
Ameritech, 111
Anaya, Herbert, 188–9, 193
Anthropology, 142
Anthropocentrism, 60
Anti-trust, 111, 128, 134
Antonelli, Cristiano, 94, 96–7, 99–101
Apologetics, xiv, 128
Appropriability, 16–7
Argentina, 185, 186
Armour, 132
Arrow, Kenneth, ix, 5, 13, 17, 27, 35, 36, 47, 48, 51, 52, 71
Associated Press, 111, 193, 308
Asymmetry, 4, 17–21, 37
AT&T, 113, 117, 212, 215–6, 218, 302, 307, 310, 311, 313

Atlanta Journal and Constitution, 118
ATN-Bosch-Telekom, 216
Australia, 7, 11, 297, 299, 311
Automation, 94
Avarice, 61, 85, 283

Babbage, C., 3
Babe, Robert E., xiii, 92–101
Bacon, Francis, 3
Bakhtin, Mikhail, 58
Bangkok, 217, 218, 304
Banking, 44, 112, 225, 302–3
Baran, Paul, and Sweezy, Paul, 106
Barcelona, 213
Barriers Down, (Cooper), 111
Bateson, Gregory, 58
Baxter, William, 128
Beatles, The, 85
Beck, Ulrich, 96
Becker, Gary, 41, 42, 144, 327
Beholdenness, 85
Behaviorism, 328–9
Bell, Alexander Graham, 2
Benavides, Colonel, 194
Benelux, 227
Berry, Chuck, 85
Bertelsman, 112, 140, 237, 258, 259, 261
Best, S., and Kellner, D., 88
Bias, 177
Bias of Communication (Innis), x
Bikhchandani, S.D., 29
Billboard, 258
Birmingham School, 201
Bit, 36, 53
Book-of-the-Month Club, 257
Bork, Robert, 128, 130–1

Boulding, Kenneth E., x–xii, 5, 18, 41, 47, 55, 59, 127
Brain, 38
Braman, Sandra, x, xv
Brazil, 93, 142, 192, 310
Breed, Warren, 177
Bristol, 218
British Telecom, 216, 218, 302
Broadcasting media, 54–5
Brussels, 215
Brzezinski, Zbigniew, 184
BTM (Belgium), 217
Budapest, 212
Bulgaria, 183–4
Bundepost Telecom, 216
Bureau of Applied Social; Research (Columbia University), 147, 148
Burns, Ken, 257
Bush, George, 138, 202, 300
Bushnell, John, 185
Buxton, William, xii, xiv, 200–6

Cable and Wireless, 218, 302, 307
Cable television, 111, 114, 117, 131–3, 140, 246, 255–6
Cambridge, 218
Canada, 111, 308, 314
Canal Plus, 263
Cannan, Edwin, 3
Cantril, Hadley, 161ff, 205–6
Capital, 74, 93, 142, 229, 276, 287, 301
Capital Cities/ABC, 237
Capital intensity, 9
Carey, James W., xi, xv, 58–9
Carnegie Corporation, 154
Cartel, 111, 132
Castro, Fidel, 188, 192
Cavell, Stanley, 330
CBS, 154, 157, 160, 162, 205, 237, 245
Center/periphery, 286
Centralization, 75, 307
Chandler, A.D., 22, 94
Chase Manhatten, 295
Chavez, Bishop Rosa, 194
Chicago, 255
China, 212, 217, 218
Cineplex Odeon, 235
Chomsky, Noam, 178, 202
Chrysler Corp, 134, 257
CIA, 180
Citibank, 112
Citicorp, 118
Clarke, Arthur C., 2
Clarke, C., and Brennan, K., 259

Clinton, Bill, 202, 300
CNN, 117
Coase, Ronald, 48, 49
Cobb, John, 60, 287
Code, 57–8
Cognition, 18, 37–9
Cognitive dissonance, 38
Cognitive economics, 38–40
Cohen, S. and Zysman, J., 28
Columbia Entertainment, 233–5, 257, 262–3
Columbia University, 206
Commodity, x, xii, xiii, 3, 9, 25, 36, 42, 43, 49, 51–3, 55, 56, 59–61, 70, 71–3, 78–89, 98, 107, 114, 283, 286–7
Commodity fetishism, 72, 229
Commoditization, 46, 50, 52, 55, 61, 74, 77, 93
Communications Act (1934), 152–3, 168
Communication, and knowledge, 38
 neoclassical treatment of, 36–7
 as relation, 36–7, 58, 321–35
 as process, 37
Communication studies, xii, xiv, 142–3, 147–70, 321–35
Communication system model, 56
Community, 58, 328
Comparative advantage, 2, 25, 42, 59
Comprehension, 45
Compuserve, 240
Computer, 112, 211
ConAgra, 132
Concentration, 111–2, 116, 130–2, 233–64, 274
Conglomerates, xiv, 113, 114, 140, 235ff, 270–1, 278
Congress, 119, 154, 185
Congressional Budget Office, 116
Consciousness, xii, 126
Consumer Federation of America, 117
Consumer goods, x
Consumers, 112, 113
Consumption, 80, 82
Content, 45–6
Continental Airlines, 132
Continental Illinois, 134
Control, 3, 17, 77, 294, 302, 321
Convergence, 23, 111–2, 234, 241, 275–6
Cooley, Charles, 331
Cooper, Kent, 111
Cooper, William, 154
Co-ordination, 21, 27, 45, 99, 283
Copenhagen, 216
Copyright, 59, 75, 78

Corporate Control, Corporate Power (Herman), 209
Corporate information flows, xiv
Costs, 4, 16–7, 36, 37, 48, 52, 76, 234, 294, 304, 305
Cost-benefit, 98
Countervailing power, 325
Cremer, J. and Khalil, F., 4
Cristiani, President Alfredo, 185, 188
Crompton, R., 259
Cross ownership, 111, 235ff, 252, 254–6
Cross subsidization, 113, 243
Croydon, 224–6, 227
Cruz, Arturo, 182–3
C-SPAN, 117
Cuba, xiv, 178, 187ff, 308, 312
Cuban Update, 192,
Cultural studies, 201, 203, 205, 321–35
Culture, xi, xiv, 29, 45, 58, 108, 140, 200, 284, 288
Culture, Society and the Media (Gurevitch), 209
Cybernetics, 99, 114

Daly, Herman, 60, 287
Damas, Archbishop, 194
Darwinism, 128–35
Dasah, Bernard, xi, xiv, 324
David, Paul, 222
DBP, 302
DC Comics, 256
Debreau, G., 36, 51, 69, 81
Decentralization, 4
Deciding (Marshak, 7, 17)
Decision theory, 5, 6
Decode, 56
Deconstruction, 88
Deindustrialization, 23, 26, 27, 218ff
Deleuze, G., 88
Delia, Jesse, 150–1
Delta Airlines, 132
de Onis, Juan, 185
Deregulation, xiv, 42, 111, 116, 117, 119, 241, 296, 303
Derrida, J., 88
Descartes, R., 82
de Sola Pool, Ithiel, 279
Deutsche Aerospace, 216
Development, xi, 2, 3, 20, 26, 39, 142
Devlin, K., 18, 19, 37
Dewey, John, 332, 335–6
Dezalay, Tyves, 97
Dia, Mamadou, 287–91
Dialogue, 56, 59, 60
Diebold, John, 220

Dimmick, John, and Wallschlaeger, Mikel, 244–5
Disney, 112, 140, 237, 264
Distribution, xii, 78–80, 112, 139, 211, 296, 305
Dominican Republic, 218
Doubleday, 258
Douglas, Mary, 77, 330–3
Dow Jones, 140
Dretske, F., 18, 19, 29, 37
Drucker, Peter, 224
Duarte, President, 188
Ducatel, Ken, 220
Duesenberry, J., 84
Dumont, Louis, 327
Dunn, D.A., 22
Durkheim, E., 330–1
Dyer, Alan W., 61

Ecological interaction, 39, 56, 60–1
E. A. Miller, 132
Eastern Airlines, 132
Eastern Europe, 212, 216, 217, 315
Economic geography, 211–28, 229–31
Economics of internal organization, 16
Economics of management, 16
Economist, 8
Ecosystem, 60–1, 220
Ecuador, 193
Edinburgh, 215
Education, 6, 27, 44, 82, 116, 153, 154, 204–6, 220
Efficiency, 8, 42
Electronic colonies, 218–9
El Globo, 140
El Rescate Chronology, 191
El Salvador, xiv, 178, 183, 185, 186, 187ff
Emotions, 55
Empire and Communications (Innis), x
Energy, 57
Engelbrecht, H.J., 11
England, 215, 218, 294–5
Enos, J.L., 20
Entertainment, 75
Entropy, xii
Environment, 60–1, 220
Equilibrium, 42
Equity, 2, 9, 29, 45–6, 75, 105, 117–8, 121, 142
European Central Bank, 213
European Community, 211, 213, 221, 226–7, 298, 299, 311, 312
European Commission, 216, 221
Eutelsat, 294
Everly Brothers, 85

Evolutionary economics, 38–40, 55, 71
Evolutionary theory, xii
Exchange, 56, 70, 78–80, 84, 112
Exhibition, 112
Exploratory Activity, 14
Externalities, 22, 60–1, 76, 331–3

Factors of production, xi, 19, 37, 78
Federal Communications Commission (FCC), 55, 117, 119, 155–9, 168, 252, 310–1
Federal Radio Commission (FRC), 154, 157, 158
Federal Radio Education Committee, 159
Feedback, 56
Fess, Simeon, 154, 159
Fiat, 217
Fibre optics, 140, 294, 312
Fintelcom, 216
Fiji, 7
Financial Times, 218
Firm, 36–7, 48
First Amendment, 274
Flexibility, 112, 113, 114
Forbearance, 243
Ford, 217
Forester, T., 26–7
Form, 57, 58
Fortune, 500, 245
Foucault, Michel, 119, 121
Fox, 113, 256, 258
FMLN, 193
Frames of reference, 38
France, 7, 299
Frankfurt, 213
Frankfurt School, 200, 209
Free goods, 2
Freedom of expression, 274
Freedom of Information Act, 186
Friedman, Benjamin, 105
Fujiisankei, 263
Functionalism, 328

Galbraith, John Kenneth, xii, 84, 115
Gallup, George, 164
Ganley, Oswald and Gladys, 301
Gannett, 237
Gans, Herbert J., 177, 179
Garnham, Nicholas, xv
GATT (General Agreement on Tariffs and Trade), 43, 59, 75, 94, 97, 281, 284, 298, 299, 309, 315
General Electric, 236, 237, 302
General equilibrium, 51, 71, 78, 81–3
General Motors, 257

Germany, 75, 93, 111, 138, 227
Ghorbanifar, Manucher, 187
Gift, 61, 81, 84, 96, 99, 287–91
Gitlin, Todd, 149–51
Glasgow, 215
Globalization, xi, xiv, 9, 23, 25, 29, 74, 110–2, 140–2, 211ff, 233ff, 270, 275–9, 294–6, 304, 321–2
Golding, Peter, and Murdoch, Graham, 105
Gort, Michael, and Swanson, Eric, 243–4
Gramsci, Antonio, 200, 203
Gray, Horace, xii
Greed (see avarice)
Greene, Judge, 111
Griliches, Zvi, 18
Growth, 8
Gruson, Lindsey, 185
Guam, 312
Guatemala, 182–3, 186

Habits, 85
Hachette, 140
Hahn, F., 71
Halifax, 225
Hall, Stuart, 201, 209
Hamilton, Lee, 186
Harrigan, P., and Mosley, P., 285
Hartman, Carl, 193
Harvard University, 276
Harvey, David, 112
Hatfield, Henry, 155, 159
Havas, 111
Hayek, F.A., ix, 5, 47
HDTV, 234
Health, 220, 230
Heckscher-Ohlin Theorem, 286–7
Hegel, Georg, 72
Hegemony, 200, 203
Henderson, Jefferey, 217
Herman, Edward S., xii, xiv, 200–6
Hepworth, Mark, xi, xiv, 229–31, 269–73
HBO, 257
Hierarchy, 19, 36, 37
Hills, Jill, xi, xiv, 321–2
Hirschmar, Albert, 327
Historiography, 150, 204
Hogarty, Thomas, 242
Holland, J.H., 23
Holly, Buddy, 85
Hollywood, 111, 113, 233ff, 276–7
Homeostatic change, 39
Hong Kong, 217, 307
Hong Kong Shanghai Bank, 301
Horizontal integration, 112

Horkheimer, Max, 200
House Committee on Energy and Commerece, 132
Huber, Peter, 97
Hungary, 216
Hyde, Lewis, 287

Ideology, 178, 179–80, 187ff, 200–1, 208–9, 298, 316
Ideological criticism, 200
Improbable structures, xi
Independent producers, 113
India, 142, 225
Individualism, 27, 56, 61, 282, 288, 308, 326–7
Indivisibilities, 52, 54, 76
Indonesia, 217
Industrial Institute for Economic and Social Research (Stockholm), 10–1
Industrial organization, 42, 45–6
Infon, 18
Infonet, 302
Information, 322
  asymmetric, 4
  characteristics of, 9, 16, 24–5, 52–3, 57, 305
  costs of, 4–6, 36
  defined, 57
  free flow of, 21, 59, 75, 98, 300
  free and balanced flow, 60
  hierarchic conceptions of, x
  investment in, 4
  neoclassical conception of, xii, 43–56, 79, 95
  transmission, 56–7
  and culture, 55
  and consumer goods, x, xiii, 69ff
  and coordination, ix, 45, 99
  and consciousness, xii, 37–40, 45, 55, 87–8, 125–35, 142–3
  and development, xi, 2
  and economic geography, 211–28
  and entropy, xii
  and equity, 2, 29, 45–6
  and free goods 3
  and market failure, x, 22, 25, 51, 52–3
  and measurement, 7, 44–6, 49, 50, 52–3, 57
  and organizations, ix, xiv, 12–5, 48
  and persuasion, x
  and policy, xii, 22
  and power, xii, 55, 87–8, 98, 293
  and pure competition, 46
  and public goods x
  and uncertainty, ix, x, 48–9 55
  as commodity, x, xii, xiii, 9, 25, 36, 42, 43–56, 59–61, 98
  as macro sector, ix, 6–12, 42, 43–5, 47
  as factor of production, xi, 2, 19
Information and Investment, (Richardson), 4
Information city, 211ff
Information economy, 1–29, 34–40, 43–5, 91–4, 211ff
Information economics, 5, 39–40, 42, 48, 53, 59
Information industries, x, 3, 45–6, 59
Information occupations, 11
Information society, 26, 107, 122, 321–2
Inquiring (Marshak), 6, 17
Inmarsat, 300
Innis, Harold, x–xi, 86, 324, 330, 331, 334–5
Innovation, 4
Institutions, x
Institutional economics, x, xii
Insurance companies, 112, 225
Intellectual property, 25
Intelligent electronics, 26
Intelsat, 298, 300, 310–1, 312
International Business Machines (IBM), 111, 218, 240, 302
International Computers Limited (ICL), 302
Internationalization, See Globalization
International Monetary Fund (IMF), xiv, 281, 285, 286, 315
International Telecommunications Union (ITU), 2, 29, 309, 312, 313, 314
International Telephone and Telegraph (ITT), 307
Interpress, 191, 193
Interpretation, 58
Interpretative skills, 21–2, 29, 75
Irwin, Manley, 238–40, 275, 278–9
Italy, 183

Jackson, Michael, 256
Jamaica, 218
Janik, Allan, 205
Jansen, Sue Curry, 121
Jantsch, E., 96
Japan, 7, 75, 92–3, 112, 113, 138, 140, 211, 212, 216, 217, 218, 221, 222, 235, 263, 312
Jones, Alex, 118
Jones, Quincy, 257
Jones, Robert, 204
Jones, Steven, 326
Jonscher, Charles, 13, 48, 50

Journal of Economic Literature, 4
Joyce, James, 82
Justice (see equity)

Kaplan, Abraham, 44
Katz, Elihu, 148
Kazakhstan, 216
KDKA, 153
Keynes, J.M., 84, 86, 138, 222, 230
KGB, 183–4
Kiev, 212, 216, 217
Koon, Cline, 158
Knight, Charles, 3
Knight, Frank, 3, 4, 5, 36, 41, 48, 49
Knight Ridder, 140
"Know-how", xi
Knowledge, 3, 19, 38, 48, 83
Knowledge industry (Machlup), 6, 8, 43
Korea, 181, 217
Kornai, J., 17
Kuhn, Thomas, 149

LA Law, 258
La Prensa, 182–3
Labor, 4, 10–15, 26, 44, 47, 51, 75, 112, 113, 118–9, 211–2, 217, 218, 224–5, 229, 275, 294, 304
Lacan, J., 88
Lamberton, D.M., ix, xiii, 34–40
Landsat, 308
Language, 57, 58, 111, 329–31
Lazarsfeld, Paul, 147–53, 204–6
Learning, 16–7, 36–7
Ledeen, Michael, 184
Lee, Wilson, and Cooperman, Elizabeth, 242
Leontief, W., 17, 287
Levi-Strauss, Claude, 77
Libya, 181, 184
Liebenstein, H., 84
Licensing, 153–4
Lifeline, 119
Link-up, 119
Lippmann, Walter, 194, 203
Literary Guild, 258
Litman, Barry, xi, xiv, 46, 244, 269–79
Little, Brown, 257
Lockheed, 134
London, 212, 215, 217, 218, 219, 220, 222, 226, 227, 303, 304, 307
London Evening Standard, 212
Lorimar, 257
Los Angeles, 255
Lotus Marketplace, 118

Lowery, Shearon, and De Fleur, Melvin, 55
Lux, Kenneth, 109

M'Bow, Amadou, 181
Mainstream economics, *See* neoclassical economics
Machlup, Fritz, ix, 5, 6, 8, 23, 43, 47, 59, 74
Madonna, 141, 257
Madrid, 213
Maitland Commission, 313
Malaysia, 7, 142, 217
Malthus, Thomas, xiii, 106, 109, 140
Management, 17, 37, 94
Manchester, 213, 215, 218
Manilla, 218
Manufacturing, 23, 27, 43, 94, 212
Marginal productivity theory, 78–80
Marshak, Jacob, ix, 5–6, 12, 17, 35, 36
Markets, 6, 9, 36, 42, 44, 48, 51, 54, 107, 114
Market model, 56, 283, 327–9
Marshall, Alfred, 45, 46–7
Marshall, John, 156–7, 159, 161ff, 205–6
Martella, Ilario, 183
Maruyama, M., 96
Marx, Karl, xiii, 70, 72–3, 86, 106, 109, 200, 202, 208–9, 229
Mass media, 44, 74, 75, 233ff
Matsushita, 112, 140, 233–5, 263
Matter, 57
MCA, 233–5, 262–3
McCarty, H.B., 160
McCulloch, John, 3
McGraw Hill, 140
McLoskey, Donald, 106, 326
McLuhan, Marshall, 84, 93, 94
McNeil Lehrer News Hour, 184
Mead Data, 140
Meaning, 38, 45, 50, 57, 58, 82
Measurement, 7, 44–6, 49, 50, 52–3, 57, 79, 97, 99, 114, 118–9
Meatpacking, 132, 140
Melerba, F., 16–7
Mello, Fernando de, 192
Mergers, 131–2, 140, 233ff
Merton, Robert K., 206
Merz, Charles, 194
Methodoligical collectivism, 29, 58
Methodological individualism, 29, 56, 58, 59, 83
Metropolitan dominance, 211ff, 269
Mexico, 142, 193
MGM/UA, 233–4, 262

INDEX

Mind, 38,
Mill, John Stuart, 107, 140
Mills, C. Wright, 149, 204
Miranda, Jorge
Mishan, E.S., 60–1
Misui, 113
Mitsubishi, 113, 217
Modernization, 8
Modelling, 1, 2
Money, 44, 48, 56, 59, 70, 72, 283, 303
Monfort, 132
Monitoring, 16
Monopoly, 48, 75, 76, 77, 116, 132–3, 283, 296, 307, 310, 314
Moral hazard, 51
Moral philosophy, xiii, 105–122
Morrison, David, 150
Mosco, V., xi, xiii, 93
Moscow, 212, 216, 218
Motion Picture Association of America, 255
Motion picture industry, 233ff
Motion Picture Export Association, 111
Motorola, 217
Mueller, Willard, 236–8, 242–3
Murray, Charles, 115
Myth, 85

Naming, 61, 329
Nation, The, 143
National Advisory Council on Radio in Education (NACRE), 154ff
National Association of Broadcasters, 162, 167
National Cable Television Association, 255
National Committee on Education by Radio (NCER), 154ff
Natural selection, 39, 82, 128, 130, 135
NBC, 114, 154, 160, 162, 237
NEC, (Japan), 113, 217
Neoclassical economics, 42, 55, 60, 70, 72, 78–9, 86, 106–7, 125–35, 282, 288, 295, 326–7
  and communication, 36–7, 325–9
  and internal validity, 42
  and external validity, 42
  and information, ix, x, xii, xiii, 6, 36, 42, 72, 76, 79, 95, 101
  as ideological system, x, xiv, 59–60, 87–8, 125–35, 139, 298, 316
  extensions of, 41, 126, 284ff, 327–8
Netherlands, 299
Neurons, 38
Network economics (Antonelli), 94

Networks, 16, 25, 39, 112, 113, 142, 211, 296
New International Information and Communications Order (NIICO), 59–60, 187, 309
New Statesman, 187
New World Order, 300, 317
New York, 212, 219, 255, 303
New York Times, 1, 114, 117, 178, 181–2, 184, 185, 186, 187ff, 202
New Zealand, 7, 111, 299
News, and maket factors, 178; and structural factors, 178
News agencies, 111, 308
News Corp, 112, 140, 237, 258, 259, 261
News coverage, xiv, 143, 177
News International, 276–7
News owners, 177–8, 180
Newspapers, 111, 118, 304
News values, 177ff, 202
Newsweek, 143
Nicaragua, 182–3, 184–5, 190
Nobel prize, 144, 327
Noise, 38
Northern Telecom, 111
Northern States Beef, 132
Northwest Airlines, 132, 134
NTT (Japan), 302
Nuclear industry, 134
Nussbaum, M., 18

Objectivity, 178, 202
Occupations, 10–1
OECD, 34, 74, 298, 300, 310, 311
Oettinger, Anthony, 116
Office of the Management and Budget, 98
Office of Radio Research, Princeton University, 55
Office of Technology Assessment, 117
Ohio Institute for Education and Radio, 158
Oldham, 225
Olivetti, 115
Oniki, H., 18
Oregon, 119
Organization, 57, 212, 222–3, 269
Organizations, 9, 12–5, 19, 27, 36, 37, 39, 48, 94, 111–6
Orwell, George, 9, 183, 195
Ownership regulations, 252–3
Out-sourcing, 24
Ozanich, G., and Wirth, M., 261–2, 264
Ozark Airlines, 132

Pacific Telesis, 240

Paquet, Gilles, xv
Papua, New Guinea, 7
Paradigm, 58
Paramount, 237
Pareto, V. 83128–30, 135, 283, 285
Parker, Ian, x, xiii, 54, 92–101
Paris, 219
Partial analysis, 45
Patents, 2, 6, 18, 75, 78
Pathe Communications, 233–4
Pattern, 57
Pattern recognition, 38
Pay-per-view, 113, 114
Payne Foundation, 154
Peking, 217
Pelton, Joseph, 45
Penetrative powers of price system, 72, 331, 333
Penta Entertainment, 263
Pentagon, 180
People Express, 132
Percept, 38
Perception, xiv, 18, 37–9, 55
Perceptual systems, 38, 55
Perfect knowledge, 48, 76
Perry, Armstromg, 157
Persian Gulf War, 141, 300, 303
Persuasion, x,
Personal Influence (Lazarsfeld), 149
Petersmann, Ernst-Ulrich, 97
Phenomenology of Mind (Hegel), 72
Philanthropy, 85, 152ff
Philippines, 142, 217, 218, 225, 294
Philips, 113, 217
Piedmont, 132
Poland, 186
Policy, 22, 25, 97–101, 147–70, 178, 179–80, 187ff, 202
Political economy, xii, xiii–xiv, 42–43, 55, 59–61, 89, 95, 97, 105–22, 125–35, 138–44, 147–70, 212, 295, 321
Polygram, 237, 263
Pope, The, 183–4
Popieluszko, Jerzy, 186
Population change, 39
Porat, Marc U., ix, 43–4, 59, 92, 226
Positivism, 106, 135, 140
Posner, Richard, 41, 42
Post industrial society, 1
Post office, 44, 307
Potlach, 77
Power, xii, xiv, 55, 59, 75, 77, 98, 111, 112, 121, 127, 131–5, 139, 179, 200, 246, 293, 321
Prediction, 3

Preferences 85
Prices, as information, ix, 45, 46, 47, 49, 50–1, 61, 80–1, 282
Pricing (telecommunications), 117–9, 311
Primary information sector, 6–7, 23, 44
Princeton Research Project, 147, 151–3, 204–6
Privacy, 118–9, 310, 329
Private networks, 112, 216, 294, 300, 301
Privatization, xiv, 42, 93, 116, 118, 294, 299, 300–1, 308, 310–1, 315, 323–4
Probability theory, 5, 49
Prodigy, 240
Producer, 112, 282–3
Production, 78–82, 112, 296, 305
Production and Distribution of Knowledge in the United States (Machlup), 6, 43
Production function, 37, 82
Productivity, 23
Professional news values, 177
Profit, 48
Program on Information Policy (Harvard), 116
Propaganda, x, xiv, 75, 141–2, 178–95
Property 52, 56, 75, 78, 94, 139, 283
Public, The, 324–5
Public Communication, xv, 321ff
Public good, 105
Public goods, ix, 52, 76, 220
Public Opinion Quarterly, 165
Public sector, 42
Public Relations, x
Pure competition, 46

Qadaffi, President, 187

Radio, 150–70
Radio and the Printed Page (Lazarsfeld), 205
Radner, Roy, 51
Rand, Ayn, 329
Rational choice, 39, 126, 135, 139, 144
Rational expectations theory, 4
Ravenscraft, David and Scherer, F.M., 242
RCA Records, 258
R&D, 8, 14, 25, 211, 223
Reagan, Ronald, 115, 128, 138, 182, 184, 222
Reciprocity, 243, 305
Recreation, 220
Reductionism, 36
Reich, Robert, 111, 115, 218
Religion, 330
Republic Airlines, 132

INDEX 345

Resources, 2, 37
Restructuring, 110–6, 140, 224–5, 236ff, 271–2, 278
Reuters, 111, 113, 191, 304, 307, 308
Rhetoric, xiv, 59, 97–8, 125–35
Rhetoric of Economics, (McLoskey), 106
Ricardo, David, xiii, 86, 106, 107, 140, 286
Richardson, G.B., 4
Riding, Alan, 185
Rio Group, 193
Risk, 48, 71, 96–7, 113, 234
Ritual, 77, 85, 330
Roach, S.S., 13
Robbins, Lionel, 2, 3, 21
Robinson, Gertrude, xv, 208–9
Robinson, Joan, 78
Rockefeller Archive Center (Pocantico Hills, NY), 152
Rockefeller Foundation, xiv, 150, 152ff, 203–6
Rockefeller, John Jr., 154
Rolling Stones, The, 85
Romer, P.M.
Rosegger, G., 1, 16–7
Rothchild, Kurt, 127
Rothchild, Michael, 51
Rowland, Willard D., 151
Royal, John, 162
Russia, 312

Sachs, Jeffrey, 105
Samuels, Warren J., xv
Samuelson, Paul, 333
Sandel, Michael, 334
Satellites, 75, 114, 132, 140, 213, 294, 304, 323
Sauvant, Karl, 297
Scale economies, 8, 9, 74, 76, 140, 241, 294, 304–5
Schelling, Thomas, 86
Schiller, Herbert I. x, xiv, xv, 59, 93
School of Public and International Affairs (Princeton University), 167
Scotland, 218
Schumpeter, Joseph, 4, 107, 279, 331
Secondary information sector, 9, 23
Sectoral analysis, ix, 5–11, 43–5, 47, 74–6, 111
Seligman, Ben, 48
Semiosis, 56
Semiotics, 58, 72–3, 79–89, 96, 99
Senegal, 289
Senior, Nassau William, 3
Sensory input, 37–9

Seriability, 17
Shackle, G., 5, 17
Shadow prices, 81
Shakespeare, William, 70, 72–3
Shannon, Claude, and Weaver, Warren, 53
Sheffield, 218
Shepherd, William, 45–6
Shevardnadze, Eduard, 192
Shin, H.S., 4
Signs, 57
Silicon Valley, 218
Simon, Herbert, 5
Singapore, 7, 142, 217, 218
SISMI, 182–3
Sismondi, Jean Charles Leonard, 125, 127, 135
SITA, 314
Sky Cable, 258
Smith, Adam, xiii, 3, 25, 34, 78, 106, 107, 108, 120, 140, 282, 286
Smith, Anthony, 110, 112, 115, 244
Sochay, Scott, xi, xiv, 269–79
Social marginal cost, 60–1
Social relations, 109, 283, 331
Socialization, 139
Sociobiology, 328
Sony, 112, 140, 233–5, 237, 240, 256, 263
South Carolina, 119
South Korea, 22
Soviet Union, 181–2, 186, 187, 190, 192–3, 216, 299, 300, 312
Space bias, x–xi
Spence, A.M., 51, 52–3, 54
Sports Illustrated, 257
Sprint, 302
St. Lucia, 218
St. Petersburg, 216
Stanton, Frank, 147, 148, 205–6
Star Trek, 256
State Department, 180, 185
Steel industry, 133
Stephens, David, 156
Stigler, George, ix, 41, 42, 49, 50, 51, 282
Stiglitz, Joseph, 51, 52, 54
Stocking, George, 148
Structural Adjustment Program (SAP), xiv, 281–91
Studebaker, John, 159, 162
Sub-Saharan Africa, 281–91
Subjectivity, 58, 106
Sustainable development, 61
Sunkel, Osvaldo, 316
Swedish Telecom, 216
SWIFT (Society for Worldwide Interbank

Financial Telecommunications), 302, 314
Symbols, 6, 57
Symbolization, 61, 101
Synergy, 235ff
Sweden, 7, 13

Taiwan, 217
Tastes, 85
TAT, 308
TCI (Tele-Communications Inc.), 113, 131, 237
Technologies, xi, 20, 22, 23, 26, 28, 74, 77, 107, 108, 114, 140, 211, 238, 269, 275, 293, 295
Technologies of Freedom (Pool), 279
Technology push, 8–9, 24
Technology transfer, 25
Telecommunications, xiii, 113, 142, 296, 301, 304
Telegraph, 57, 307
Telephone, 1, 2, 112, 114, 116, 117, 119, 254, 307
Teleports, 215, 218
Television, 114, 116, 140
Texas Air, 132
Thailand, 7, 217
Thatcherism, 222
Thayer, Lee, 57–8
The Public and Its Problems (Dewey), 332, 335
Theory of the Leisure Class (Veblen), x
Theory of the Moral Sentiments (Smith), 109
Third World, 77, 142, 181
Thoreau, Henry David, 135
Time, 143
Time Inc., 233–4, 257
Time, 55, 112, 304, 321, 335
Time bias, x–xi
Time-Warner, 112, 131, 140, 236, 237, 240, 257, 259, 261, 262–3, 322
Titmuss, R.M., 81
Toffler, Alvin, 229
Tokyo, 212, 216, 217, 219, 303
Toronto, 218
Toshiba, 263
Totalitarianism, 9
Toulmin, S., 38, 206
Trade, 25, 28, 29, 42, 43, 59, 60, 78, 298
Traditions, 77
Transformation, 39, 72, 73, 82, 94
Transmission, 56, 140, 154, 295, 301
Transnational business, xiv, 60, 74, 94, 111, 142, 217, 241ff, 286–7, 293–316

Transpac, 302
Transportation, 220–1, 230, 304
Trucking industry, 134
Turkey, 183
Turner, V., 77, 245
TV Guide, 258
TV Marti, 190, 193
TWA, 119, 132
Twentieth Century Fox, 258, 262
Two-step flow model, 148
Tyson, Dr L., 154–6, 159, 161

Ukraine, 216
Ulysses (Joyce), 82
UNCTAD, 309
Uncertainty, ix, x, 2, 3, 9, 12, 48–50, 51, 54, 55, 71, 78
Unemployment, 4, 23, 26, 27, 117, 218ff, 270
UNESCO, 59, 97, 181, 187, 300, 309, 310
United Airlines, 134
United Kingdom, 7, 116, 215, 216, 219, 220, 270, 277, 296, 297, 308, 311, 314–5
United Nations, 20, 188, 309
United Press International (UPI)
United States, 7, 59, 75, 111, 116, 142, 153, 181–4, 188ff, 211, 216, 221, 235, 275, 287, 296, 297, 298, 299, 300, 304, 308, 311, 312, 313, 314–5, 316
University of Chicago, 144
US Postal Service, 115
US Air, 132
US West, 113
Utility theory, 5, 70, 83–4, 126

Validity, 54–6, 59
Valladares, Armando, 188–9
Value, 45, 49, 54, 60–1, 70, 107
Veblen, Thorstein, x, 55, 69, 71–2, 84
Veja, 192
Venezuela, 7
Vertical integration, 112
Videla, General Jorge, 185
Vietnam, 309
Virtual corporation, 272
Visible Hand (Chandler), 94
Visnews, 113
Voice of America, 98

Walker, E.R., 1 Wagner, Robert, 155
War of the Worlds (Welles), 54–5
Warner Communications, 233–4, 256, 258, 264
Warsaw, 216

INDEX

Wealth, 97
Wealth of Nations, (Smith), 107, 108, 282
Weapons industry, 134
Weaver, Warren, 53
Weber, Max, 110
Webster, Bethuel, 157
Weizsacker, Carl Friedrich von, 57
Wellenius, B., 7, 8
Welles, Orson, 54–5
Western Airlines, 132
Westphal, L.E., 22
Wheels and Wires (Hepworth), 220
Willis, Frederic, 157, 162
Wittgenstein, L., 329

Wolff
World Bank (Bank for Reconstruction and Development), xiv, 216, 281, 284, 285, 286, 298, 299, 315
World Wide Broadcasting Foundation, 160, 204
WTN, 113
W1XAL, 160

Yerevan, 216
Yomiuri Shimbun (JapanP), 304

Zuboff, Shoshana, 118